BORN IN FLAMES

HOWARD HAMPTON

Termite

Dreams,

Dialectical

Fairy

Tales,

and

Pop

Apocalypses

BORN
IN
FLAMES

HARVARD UNIVERSITY PRESS

Cambridge, Massachusetts
London, England

2007

Library of Congress Cataloging-in-Publication Data

Hampton, Howard, 1958–
    Born in flames : termite dreams, dialectical fairy tales, and pop apocalypses /
Howard Hampton.
        p.   cm.
    Includes bibliographical references and index.
    ISBN-13: 978-0-674-02317-8 (alk. paper)
    ISBN-10: 0-674-02317-X (alk. paper)
    1. Motion pictures—Philosophy.   2. Motion pictures and music.   I. Title.
PN1995.H238   2006
791.43'611—dc22   2006043680

For Mom

CONTENTS

II. Shoot the Guitar Player

III. Waterloo Sunset Boulevard

BORN IN FLAMES

Introduction

Meet *The Furies* /

Pop Goes the Apocalypse

THE ALLURE OF EXTREMITY: it's a self-evident yet enigmatic proposition. Pressed into axiomatic black-and-white form in Anthony Mann's flamboyantly stark, visceral western *The Furies* (1950), it is personified the moment Barbara Stanwyck's willful anti-heroine hurls a pair of scissors into the face of her father's smug mistress. No portrait of disgust and loathing has surpassed her enraged/horrified look as the scissors find their target and her disfigured rival's screams fill the bedroom. A shuddering, mirror-image chain of catastrophe is put in motion, reaching its apotheosis when the domineering father has her Mexican friend/ex-lover lynched. In a startling desert-expressionist sequence, Mann sets hard, statuesque faces (the about-to-be-dead man's mother looms like the bust of a peasant Sphinx) against a steep Delphic hillside: Stanwyck leaves the condemned man in the foreground to make a circuitous trek through silhouetted henchmen and giant cacti, up a rocky trail and out of the shot, moving brusquely from John Ford–type scenic nobility into primitive-modernist Welles / Georgia O'Keefe terrain.

"It's me you should have hung," she shouts to the old man, before taking her horse and fleeing into the horizon. "You won't see me again until the day I take your world away from you." The film generates unrelenting scorched earth vivacity, pioneering a whole once-upon-a-time-in-the-West epoch that will turn moral and cinematic conventions on their shiny heads. Everything is linked by terrible, malignant fate, with the mother's screams at the hanging echoing the scissor victim's cries: there is no justice, frontier or otherwise, only ageless furies that have been unleashed and won't be appeased until revenge has had its way. A restless, piercing dynamic is at work in these improvised rites, with salvation and damnation smeared together like blood and paint on a canvas.

"Underworld beauty" (in the spirit of Suzuki's gangland poetics) is another term for this knifing, angular-to-anguished, gut-level quality. In extremis, things are thrown into the sharpest relief: a dynamic of attraction and attrition, a roll of existential dice signaling the aesthetic gambler's intuitive cubism: modernity's extremist tendencies colliding with pop culture's seductive primal instincts. This oblique, surreal glamour isn't measured in heavy-duty celebrity or intellectual status seeking but in kilowatts of magnetic energy and glimmering provocation. It has a constant ability to surprise, to make fabulist sparks fly by breaking down the limitations of the material or finding a cache of untapped possibilities locked away inside too-familiar premises. It's an ominously ticking heirloom that will cross from noir into punk: "She's your own flesh and blood." "She's a cancer to be cut out." Here pulp action-romance transcends its thin, subsistence-level origins, or high art lives down its pretensions and loses its cerebral inhibitions. All it requires is a Stanwyck glare, an aura-laden Jane Greer entrance, Sheryl Lee or Naomi Watts as a walking exit wound, a self-fulfilling Belmondo death wish, the Melville-Cobain fever pitch reached by *Pola X* or the band X's motto in *The Unheard Music*: "The world's a mess / It's in my kiss." Then everything comes poetically unglued, turns black, goes boom.

A few other not-quite-random landmarks along this primrose path would include the gleefully futile getaway spree *Gun Crazy* (preferably on a stir-crazy, pent-up double bill with *The Exterminating Angel*—society paralyzed from the mind down), the military-baiting, world-as-brothel *Story of a Prostitute* (likewise paired with the world-as-madhouse *Shock Corridor*), and maybe the ballsy, unexpurgated *Baby Face* of 1933 (with the original snub-nosed 1932 *Scarface*). Along this road of ecstatic tears and bad intentions, there is a whole string of disheveled motel rooms and cheap apartments stretching from *Touch of Evil*'s bugged-and-drugged bitter-suites, *Psycho*'s taxidermist floor plans, and *Peeping Tom*'s roving bedsit eye to Mr. Lynch's phantasmagoric *Eraserhead–Blue Velvet–Lost Highway–Mulholland Dr.* neighborhood. The interplay of convoluted vices and abstract patterns will be charted; feral memories will be unearthed by fits and starts; unsublimated urges will be paid for in forbidden currencies. This simultaneously claustrophobic and wide-open black market is extremity's stamping ground: the haunts, habitats, and destinations of what D. H. Lawrence called "the pitch of extreme consciousness."

The extreme isn't cruel blatancy or cutely excruciating shock tactics—it is a volatile, uneasy rapprochement between the ancient and the contemporary, a take-no-prisoners zone of emotional chaos and tightly latticed excess where lucidity and unreason face off. Stanwyck's way of throwing her arms around the sordid, impossible facts of life epitomizes *The Furies*, which sports other expansive-compulsive, Leone-scale performances: Walter Huston's robustly monstrous last hurrah as the "old rogue bull" cattle king to end them all; Gilbert Roland as the proud romantic who becomes rope fodder in the father-daughter battle; Judith Anderson's maimed matron; Wendell Corey's archcynic, rough trade gambler; and Thomas Gomez as ranch overseer "El Tigre." They're abetted by the script's savory, overripe argot (weakling brother to big sis: "No one but you would have bone enough to come into her room"; this Mae Western exchange between a B-girl and Stanwyck: "I'm new in town, honey." "Honey, you wouldn't be new anyplace."), which is used to deliver enough crosshatched exposition and high melodrama to fill three *Godfathers*. The movie straddles short-order Greek tragedy and the Freudian banks of *Red River*, the purple side of O'Neill and *Duel in the Sun*, but rushes past these stumbling blocks with the momentum of a beautifully orchestrated riot. Mann zeros in on incestuous power plays, thwarted desires, manic outbursts, jaggedly symbolic acts, and baroque vengeance, cramming sex/hate/love/guilt into the same durable box with coffin-nail gusto.

Stanwyck's androgynously named Vance Jeffords is a mix of exacting calculation and girlish avidity ("You'd like to hit me right now, wouldn't you? Go ahead"), a woman with a crazed Ayn Rand glint around the eyes and more "bone" than all the men put together. Ebullient, ruthless, intermittently buffoonish and/or vulnerable, Walter Huston's leering patriarch T.C. ("Scratch my sixth lumbar, daughter") is a nimble precursor of son John's wizened land baron in *Chinatown*. By the end of the story, the movie shifts gears, and the daughter gets to view him in a peculiarly forgiving light, as if molestation (certainly psychological and probably physical) and murder were just the character-building lessons to make a worthy heir of her. *The Furies* imagines a junglelike West won by amoral giants who lived and died by their own twisted laws—swindled out of everything by his daughter, T.C. is proud of her for proving she really is daddy's girl, after all. They reconcile, bygones are bygones, except for the sharpshooting old Mexican "witch" who gets the last laugh by plugging the randy, unrepentant bastard.

If *The Furies* lays the groundwork for hyperbolic fem-dom horse operas *Johnny Guitar* and *Forty Guns*, it proceeds with barreling, absolutist conviction that sidesteps the camp pitfalls those films flirted with. The picture deploys Stanwyck's centrifugal intensity to blast ahead with the same irresistible mix of forward motion and lateral vision as Lee Marvin's dark-suited hammerhead navigating the tricky, obstacle-strewn aquariums of *Point Blank* and *The Killers*. (By contrast, Lili Taylor's student wraith wending her lost way through the grotto-like learning curve of *The Addiction* and ice station Deneuve's pale blueblood *Belle de Jour* move counterclockwise and counterintuitively, backing themselves into frightening realms of sadism, horror, and devastation.) Stanwyck makes her own field of gravity as she goes, neither moving with the flow or against the grain but carving out a black-hole presence around which the entire movie is then organized. It becomes a testimonial to thicker-than-dark-matter love, blood ties that are so strong they bring the world crashing down around them. From that chaos, the movie tries to palm off a dose of homespun order and regeneration at the finish, a doomed marriage of narrative convenience to wipe the scar tissue away and try to fill the psychic hole up with hopeful potting soil.

As a virtually identical figure in *Forty Guns*, Sam Fuller gives her much less leeway; she is kept off to the side of the movie, swooping in and out to raise some dust with her miniature army in tow or presiding amusingly over a Xanadu Drop Inn dining table like a middle-aged Citizen Kitten with a whip. Fuller uses her strictly as a tart copycat foil for stolid, dependable he-man Barry Sullivan. The director dispenses flare-ups of intensity like Tabasco sauce, to liven up what would otherwise be a gun-of-the-mill oater, a hit-and-miss dispersal of white heat to compensate for the faux-folksiness of the "Woman with a Whip" ballad, irritatingly variable acting (Gene Barry just warming up for his steel-jawed *China Gate* turn), comic-strip hokum (the buxom lil Al Capp gunsmith), and the pervasive, indicative absence of physical chemistry. The power of *The Furies* is tied to casually ambiguous details of the intimacy between the Jeffords, with the harsh sexual byplay between the daughter and the partner she enlists against her father having the earmarks of an audition to see if a new stud can measure up to the one who boasts he's spoiled her for other men. Fuller's signature *Forty Guns* effect is to break Sullivan's gunfighter into sharp piecemeal segments, striding legs and narrowed eyes plastered across a widescreen frame like a poster come to life. But when the director goes to put the angles back together, Stanwyck's svelte objectification never threatens to mesh with Sullivan's stalwart beef-iness—Fuller's thrilling inventions and formal eccentricities don't extend to the characterizations, where an underutilized Stanwyck is made to ride herd on a stampede of bum steers.

By then, there are already signs of a creeping irony that allows a hip audience to view extremity from a safe aesthetic distance, unimplicated by anything that transpires on the screen. Next stop, the art-splattered spaghetti western, with its exaggerated, overlaid patterns of stubble and sweat, tomato-paste eruptions, silk-screened toughness, distance-enhancing dubbing, kitsch-genius music, and Warhol-mythological overtones. Another line of descent from *The Furies* can be traced through *Forty Guns* and on down to *Faster Pussycat, Kill! Kill!* and eventually *Kill Bill*. Where Anthony Mann condensed a plot-heavy panorama into ninety-odd minutes (while still managing to find time for strange interludes and digressions), Quentin Tarantino's massive, two-part über-B-movie is a celluloid python that lovingly devours tons of lumpish reference points without ever establishing a persuasive reason for being.

In "Underground Films," Manny Farber talks about landscaping activity having "the feeling of a clever human tunneling just under the surface of the terrain. It is as though the film has a life of its own that goes on beneath the story action." *Kill Bill* reverses the process, shuffling a series of discrete, incredibly elongated, modular genre facades where the acting, backdrops, and pictorial stylization all resemble in-jokes told with a monumentally straight face. There's no sign of any life going on six inches beyond the focal point of a given routine or shtick. Tarantino achieves this anti-autonomy by imposing a devout connoisseur's attitude on long, sticky strings of cult and exploitation film platitudes. Personal interaction never stands a chance when every interminable scene is geared to making baggage-laden actors into beasts of burden lugging iconic wares across parched terrain. The interior of cluttered trailer becomes a miniature Death Valley, while a wedding chapel picturesquely yawns like a black-and-white Grand Canyon. No *Kill Bill* habitué can move without scrambling for a place on Q.T.'s list of Top Hundred Coolest Poses. Cultivating the nonexistent mystique of David Carradine or molding Uma Thurman into a Monica Vitti Action Madonna is like erecting a Home Depot Superstore to hawk Indian relics and underground trinkets. There's a wide emotional disconnect between *KB*'s cavernous, fluorescent-mayhem display aisles loaded with hyperchoreographed tête-à-tête brutality and later attempts to build human interest in the long-deferred hit-mother and child reunion. Tarantino plugs in random-access sentiment like memory upgrades when the narrative lags or requires an extra dimension to alleviate the emotion-starved monotony. But passion isn't the same as a bottomless enthusiasm for white-haired kung fu masters, samurai Morse codes, Nancy Sinatra B-sides, or Sonny Chiba's greatest smacks.

Extremity in a vacuum winds up either cartoonish or narcissistic: Darryl Hannah at least had the sensual grit and experience to make something halfway alive out of the wispy nicotine eye-patch snake fetishes that constitute *KB*'s poor Elle Driver. To truly experience aestheticized cartoon narcissism, though, *Sin City* is the place to be. A graphic novel brought to pristine half-life through the wonders of digital tinting, process shots, and rear projection, *Frank Miller's Sin City* (as it is officially titled, though *Sim City* would be more like it) travesties hardboiled mannerisms with lurid, unswerving resolve. This illustrative, postmodern/postliterate approach to cliché aims for a vertically integrated density of caricature — male dinosaurs and humanoid apes battling over a parade of strippers and streetwalkers who might have stepped out of a Kentucky Fried Hooters commercial. (Your choice of juicy breasts, thighs, and stumps.) *Sin City* has all the marks of deconstruction but pays obstinate lip service to ludicrous paternalistic fantasies of "honor" and "innocence." Caught up in a frenzy of the obligatory (every painstaking gratuitous act arrives via Calvinist predestination), its stilted idiom evokes the soundstage-bound *Dogville* without the fake iconoclasm, combined with the thick-as-a-Kubrick rigor mortis of *Eyes Wide Shut*. Paralleling horror movies, there's a great investment in frazzle-dazzle impersonality, junk formalism, outmoded conventions, Cheez-Whiz violence, and arrested sexuality, with purpose-driven imagery used as insulation to irony-over any cracks in the grim-reaping cannibal mask. This is the extreme at its terminal oversaturation point—where artists and audiences alike cease to differentiate between parody and homage, travesty and luminosity. Meanwhile, back at the raunch, labeling Noé-Breillat-Dumont-etc. exercises as "the New French Extremity" merely evokes the appetite-suppressant qualities of New Coke: more "carbonated dyspepsia" for lactose-intolerant intellectuals, the usual lineup of morbid sacrifants and chic victims. Even a film as good as the pop-Kafka, cat-and-mouse *Oldboy* becomes trapped by its own paranoid game-playing bravado and ultimately can't make the leap from stylishly mapped fragmentation to tragic awareness. The descent into schematic masochism and atonement uses hellishness as a high-low concept, a Marquis de Palma gimmick. Laboriously tricked into committing incest, the tormented Everyman hero is persecuted by a demented, omnipotent practical joker: instead of the desired *Vertigo* headiness, the lachrymose ending falls somewhere between a Korean *Punk'd* and what Don Siegel might have done with *Elvira Madigan*.

The push to exceed limits often dead-ends in a mountain climber's because-it's-there syndrome, where oxygen deprivation can be taken for a peak experience epiphany. Instead of aiming simply for wicked, can-you-top-this jolts (after cutting off your own tongue, what do you amputate for an encore?), the painterly approach Seijun Suzuki adopted in *Pistol Opera* is more provocative. Taking dexterously art-directed action to its natural conclusion in pulsating abstraction, using a multitude of theatrical devices together with a fantastic geometric range of movement, color, sound, and design, *Pistol Opera*'s spatial harmonics and absurd lyricism suggest a cinematic equivalent to the songs of Laurie Anderson and Brian Eno, or "This Must Be the Place" in *Stop Making Sense*.

Mischievously setting actors in geometric relief against real and artificial backdrops, Suzuki opens up fresh areas of melancholic irony and bullet-riddled repose, expertly framing pop-movie forms as a clean-lined, cryptically ceremonial new wave Kabuki experience.

Suzuki employs deadpan visual cues the way Anderson uses verbal ones, and it's as easy to imagine her adapting *Pistol Opera* into futuristic D'Oyle Carte Sprechstimme as it is to see him making a Dadaist thriller from Eno's "The Fat Lady of Limbourg." There is an enchanting serpentine progression from *Branded to Kill* and *Tokyo Drifter*, Suzuki's post-Godard adventures in style and displacement, to *Pistol Opera:* a very loose quasi-sequel to the former, it revisits and rearranges the candy-wrapper look of the latter, using the studio as a gestural laboratory for some of the most individualized brushstrokes ever put to film. He creates a cool, jazzy, nonlinear tangent universe of sensation and texture, where *Kill Bill* and *Oldboy* get bogged down trying to reconcile cartoon-epic aspirations (Anime squared) with processed, thirdhand vestiges of realism. And while *A History of Violence* delivers a sterilized, precision-retooled Public Service allegory of aggression-as-addiction (America as haunted crack house), Suzuki realizes a deep, pensive ambivalence about guns, fetishization, violence, and senselessness through formal means — pointed indirection and rhythmical compositions rather than narrative or character, to say nothing of the inspired use of Japanese ska music for spaghetti western effect.

Going too far is the hallmark of extremity, but there is a special art to disorientation: a way of undermining expectations, disrupting conventions, with emotional intensity and plasticity instead of clobbering the viewer with programmatic-didactic excess. In its unyielding, creation-through-self-destruction method, it requires a singular focus that is actually tougher to nail than social realism or ideological climate control in the *Notre Muzak* vein. A director such as Takashi Miike will dish out dozens of viciously outrageous cult flicks at a vending machine clip, but while a high school girl shooting poison darts from her vagina is a good sideshow act, it seems instantly dated and film-geekish next to the circa 1950 tough-mindedness of *Nightmare Alley, Gun Crazy, In a Lonely Place, Les Enfants terribles, Night and the City, Los Olvidados, Diary of a Country Priest,* or *The Furies.*

The Mann-Stanwyck film was predicated on the notion that "furies" made as apt a metaphor as any for the daemons of unreason, folly, lust, mania, despair, humiliation, covert knowledge, and romantic nihilism underpinning our world. Taking humanity to extremes, operating less beyond good and evil than below them, *The Furies* is a field where the unsatisfied demands on life are acted out. "It's all been wonderfully arranged," the father's mistress explains to the daughter, a systematic dispossession that will leave the younger woman with nothing. Except, that is, for a pair of scissors and the concerted burst of rage, dread, and frustration with which she retaliates against a "wonderfully arranged" life. The movie's ruthless personalities and fluxed-up passions are draped on a cantilevered edifice where orthodoxy is eternally plagued by the unkempt human nature: the glamorous medium of Dietrich and von Sternberg is reconciled with the pariah-shaped monstrosities, washed-up fortune-tellers, and border-crossing time bombs that will compose *Touch of Evil.* Like refugees from vagrant antiquity, these furies have no ultimate message, goal, or program beyond making the indelible mark Stanwyck does here. With its zest for disintegration, multiplicity, flat refusal, found objects, and fetish outfits, *The Furies* should have inspired that el misterioso punk chestnut by the Pixies: "Gouge Away."

*   *   *

A PIXIES NUMBER—"Where Is My Mind?"—serendipitously plays over the glamorized mini-Armageddon at the finish of the slaphappy terrorist comedy *Fight Club:* all those financial towers falling like beautiful dominoes, as the music becomes the ideal objective correlative to the unreliable narrator's "Trust me. Everything will be fine." The pixilated air of fantasy and metamorphosis is redolent of those slow-motion cheerleaders in Nirvana's "Smells Like Teen Spirit" video, wearing the A-for-Anarchy symbol on their uniforms like a scarlet letter of courage: a rapture of the unaccommodated. The Nirvana video's dreamlike images of intensity-perversity-humor will in time migrate into the pop apocalyptics of *Buffy the Vampire Slayer,* where they'll underwrite years of invigorating trauma, fervor, and absurdism, from narrowly averted pre-Columbine massacres to death-and-resurrection self-annihilation.

"Smells Like Teen Spirit" begins in a gym where some school assembly is taking place: the kind where you dream you're naked in front of the whole class. The camera pans across the tapping of scruffy feet in the bleachers, cheerleaders doing their routine, a nondescript band performing on the basketball court. Machine-made fog and mine-shaft spotlights making artificial sunbeams, as the video cuts to an antique janitor who looks like he wandered in from a Bresson casting call by mistake. The song is picking up steam, building tension, piling on layers of implication. The singer, who isn't naked but now might as well be, steps forward into the light: he speaks as one of them, as the crowd's secretly elected representative. They're rocking harder now—the cheerleaders are moving in tighter unison; even the janitor has started to bob in sync with the song. The old man's face is impassive and shining;

all of the faces are. The cheerleaders look beguilingly sinister (where did those rough trade tattoos come from?), junior oracles using pompoms for entrails; the place is hellishly alive, while the singer grins either satanically or cherubically. Audience members are doing somersaults, pouring out of the stands, churning the court into a mosh pit, merging with the band. Slow motion gives the entire scene an aura of ecstatic, unnamable purpose: as if the gym had turned into the last-stand church in John Woo's *The Killer* or the final courtyard showdown in *The Wild Bunch*, with voluptuous chaos breaking out everywhere.

Yet the orgiastic, go-go dervish cheerleaders, the head-banging throng, and the wraithlike singer all seem so perfectly of a piece, so typical and ordinary. Or at least what ordinary would look like if the line between waking and dream life collapsed without warning. In the song, the corpse of the epithet / sick joke / plague "Teen Spirit" is torn limb from limb, only to be reborn in the motley free-for-all of the video's sound and images. It comes back from the dead as a sense of human agency. The song doesn't confer this from above in some artist-to-audience mouth-to-mouth resuscitation; it just triggers the agency that is dormant—waiting for the right time and signal—in every member of the sleeper cell crowd. Below the riptide surface, a more mysterious agency's at play: the cheerleaders and freaks and wallflowers are transformed into a roiling little army of the night. They seem prepared and able to go to any extremes—to stage-dive into the search for a new world or happily embrace the end of this one.

Years later, after that convulsive moment has faded from view if not collective memory, a new blond transfers to a high school that happens to be built on the mouth of hell. An erstwhile cheerleader, the good bad girl's extracurricular activities now involve weekly field trips into the heart of proverbial darkness. For her, sex and homework and death and proms and nihilism and salvation will all be rolled into one darkly comic romance. Episode by episode, the ambiance of "Smells Like Teen Spirit" seeps into the corners of the *Buffy* universe, into the show's snappy repartee and deceptively normalized David Lynch–meets–*Heathers* mise-en-scène. (The arrival of tattooed alter ego Faith will raise the bad cheerleader ante considerably: "God, I could eat a whore.") As Buffy, Sarah Michelle Gellar wears an expression of incrementally deepening bitterness under the mask of Southern California hedonism—someone growing more apart from the world the more she is in it. Like Lynch's heroines, Corin Tucker of Sleater-Kinney screaming "Dig Me Out," or Cobain himself, she fights her version of the good fight but still finds herself sinking into the undertow, pursued by the furies of her own nature, where inside every victory waits a greater loss, some unappeasable or irredeemable gravity, a gaping aperture in the midst of blond life.

Seven years of Armageddon as rite of passage go by, countless poignant and hilarious scenes of young, weirded-out America trapped inside a pop-cult gold mine of perversity and twisted innocence, until their last Apocalypse arrives. So once more unto the Hellmouth, with a few inspirational words from your cool new black principal: "Welcome to Sunnydale High. There's no running in the halls, no yelling, no gum chewing. Apart from that, there's only one rule: if they move, kill them." The perfect *Wild Bunch* allusion, waiting inside the show all those years like a tiny time capsule, it was an explosive joke pointing to a frame of reference that encompassed everything from poetic-melancholic Peckinpah bloodbaths to gnostic MTV residue. Opening up the underground even as it drove the mainstream into uncharted topography, this sensibility occupied and fleshed out an intrepid new hybrid-stripped-bare space between the unlikely likes of *Apocalypse Now* and post-Nirvana female fun in extremis (including PJ Harvey, *All*

Hands on the Bad One, and *Ghost World*). In the process, *Buffy* confirmed your suspicions that the smell of napalm in the morning and the scent of teen spirit were identical.

Inside "Smells Like Teen Spirit," you can imagine a private battle of the bands taking shape: between confrontational Peckinpah–Kurtz–*Shock Corridor* mordancy and alternative-independent teen sensitivity. (Sam Fuller's asylum might have made the perfect setting for a Nirvana video; Cobain would fit right in among the demented idealists and autistic prophets.) Or if you prefer, a hand-to-mouth struggle between the epistemologies of the Beatles' impassioned, tenaciously fortune-grubbing "Money" and Robert Bresson's bleak, recessive, stiffly measured *L'Argent*. Such internal dialectics have the potential to break down artificial barriers of taste and virtuousness in any given direction (high/low, smart/"Dumb"), as the coursing, unbalanced, multifold perspective of Nirvana's video "takes on a life of its own." You could have eavesdropped on a similarly teeming life in 1975 if you'd tracked down a copy of the Cleveland art-punk band Pere Ubu's homemade single "Heart of Darkness": carefully positioned guitar shards strung out over an ominous bass/drum line, leaving lots of claustrophobic room for sung-spoken narration poised halfway between Iggy Pop and Orson Welles. No mention is made of Conrad's Kurtz, but instead we meet H. G. Wells's (or Charles Laughton's) archetypal mad scientist Dr. Moreau. A prescient substitution, for though *Apocalypse Now* and Marlon Brando's corpulent totem/golem Kurtz are still years away, the song leapfrogs right over them to conjure up the haywire 1996 remake of *The Island of Dr. Moreau*. That hypnotic debacle will feature Brando as Moreau, doing a hilarious, appalling parody of Kurtz, of himself, even of Welles in his final beached-whale days, covered in pancake makeup, murmuring sly nothings while padding about in a diaphanous muumuu.

In "Heart of Darkness," singer David Thomas (former stage

name: Crocus Behemoth) peers into an absurdist crystal ball and glimpses "the horror" of pop reification to come: "I don't see anything that I want." He might also be gazing into pop culture's fairytale past, where Welles prepared but never filmed his own *Heart of Darkness*, in which he would have played both Kurtz and Marlow as well as directing. His mirror-manic screenplay was the purest self-conscious, convoluted madness, the kind of thing you'd imagine film student Jim Morrison wanting to try thirty years later if some desperate-enough studio mogul handed him $10 million to make the youth-cinema equivalent of the Doors' *Strange Days* ("KURTZ'S VOICE: 'Look! Is that the moon down there below us?' Over the reflection of the moon we SUPERIMPOSE Kurtz's face and—"). Fortunately, Welles made *Citizen Kane* instead—that glamorously expressionist comedy of American manners and extreme ambition (the subject's and the auteur's), ceaselessly entertaining in its cynically ingenious visualization of success and dissolution, playing at seriousness with such puppyish ardor, rendering tragedy a necessary charade to disguise the thrill of make-believe self-destruction. In short, the story of an American Ubu, a prince of unreason who would resurface upriver in 'Nam humming "The End," the Doors' Oedipal anthem whose undisclosed password could only be . . . "Rosebud."

What's appealing about this kind of keenly festering, omnidirectional activity is how it cuts across emotional boundaries, spatial compartmentalization, whole forms, eras, genres, modes, and hierarchies of significance. Pere Ubu termed this shadow play "The Modern Dance": a jittery marathon where society's enchantments jostle cheek to cheek (and eyeball to sliced eyeball) with the misfit's abiding disenchantment. It mostly keeps to those shadows, usually operating off to the side of the cultural limelight where solemn, heavy-duty vacuum cleaners like Sean Penn, Trent Reznor, Todd Haynes and Björk suck up praise and awards with fluent anteater efficiency. In the stylized passion of certain Hong Kong actors—Maggie Cheung, Chow Yun-Fat, Brigitte Lin—you can see a screen presence, and presence of mind, that has largely been lost to the Western imagination: a risky balance between the mythic and the quotidian, the unconscious and the self-aware. Our massive, clogged-artery blockbusters and anorexic art-housings aim instead at tightly policed demographics—movies and music as little more than secure gated communities, suburbias, exurbias, ghettos, and bohemias of the complacent.

Looking for a passage out of those confining districts, you might follow Harry Lime's trail into the Velvet Underground (where he'd hew to John Cale's classicist side of the tunnels: "Fear is a man's best friend"), double back through "Nebraska," make a left at *Cloudland,* and follow the *Ashes of Time* to *La Jetté.* From there, it's a short leap to *Peking Opera Blues, London Calling, Videodrome,* or "Doppelgangland," exhilarating landscapes where art's outward show of unity collides with the world's boundless capacity for productive disintegration. For good company, I'd take Alyson Hannigan's supporting work as *Buffy*'s Willow Rosenberg in a heartbeat over legions of important, highly decorated artistes: developing the character step by incremental step, she deftly maneuvers nice-girl sidekick normalcy to the outer limits of the territory Steve Erickson surveys in *Our Ecstatic Days.* Out there in "the Age of Chaos," For mood music I'd put on "Mohammad's Radio," Warren Zevon's live excavation of the Los Angeles highway blues, along with a few of his running Peckinpah-cum-Lester Bangs let-it-splatter commentaries: "Splendid Isolation," "Ain't That Pretty at All," "The Indifference of Heaven," the ever-heartwarming "I Was in the House When the House Burned Down."

These travels through parallel dimensions of music and film (movies as rock 'n' roll, rock as imaginary cinema) mean to dig up the visceral logics connecting iconic forms. They're also talismans of underground continuums — often-unrecognized co-conspirators carrying on surreptitious conversations with each other, and within themselves, part and parcel of the inescapable spectacle we're immersed in. All of the figures assembled here — Asian painting-with-action directors, punk visionaries, critical thinkers/dreamers, charming or clueless frauds, teenage riot grrrls, and Hollywood's lunatic fringe — are mere bit players in a bigger picture. Within a context where life is constantly being remade as a lousy sequel to itself, what's at stake in any creative situation is the ability to seize an opening and inject a note of danger, ardor, obsession, or black humor into the proceedings. What informs this aesthetic, whether in the febrile language of *Beat Rhythm News* or Manny Farber, the dialect-dialectics of *The Big Sleep* or *The Last Bolshevik*, is a tactile, sensual, timeless modernity: a force field that establishes its own present tense, just as fashion-based idioms forge an instant passé-tense for themselves.

Therefore, these pieces are not in chronological order but are organized instead by affinities, intensities — call it chthonic order. (Dates of original publication and any significant revisions/modifications are given at the end of each chapter.) No attempt has been made to divide them along pre- and post-9/11 lines: the more "everything changed" and apocalyptic events escaped the confines of pulp fantasy, the more human behavior has remained the same. (Paraphrasing *Casablanca*, another wartime reverie: The Fundamentalist things apply / As time goes by.) So in the aftermath of the apocalypse du jour, we send out search parties, looking for missing persons, missing realities, and an intact underground to call one's own.

PART ONE

The Glamour of Extremity

Fairy Tales from Strangers

Cat Power—*Ghost World*—

Lora Logic—Phoebe Gloeckner

LATE SHOW

HALF PAST MIDNIGHT and a strange, ectoplasmic gust is coming from the TV: an out-of-nowhere, out-of-body sound, a hum of self-effacing displacement. Its source is a stoic, private-worldly vocalist accompanying herself on piano, who looks and sounds like nothing so much as the long-lost daughter of Neil Young and Nico—hello, cowgirl in the sandbox. Playing slow, seesaw chords, she feels her way through the music like a nursery-rhyme torch singer, with every careful syllable weighing whether she wants to be found or stay on the lam forever. Each hovering, halting note makes the hour grow much later—as though the singer came from a place where it is always four in the morning, a land of the permanent full moon.

This flannel-swaddled insomniac performs under the name Cat Power, a sobriquet fit for both a cult figure and an occult one, your neighborhood oracle reading life's intestines as though they were the earliest known form of Braille. Not the sort of act you expect to see on television these or any other days, especially not following Bob Dole on the David Letterman show less than a week into the invasion of Iraq—a moment of unreconstructed culture shock. This is too quiet, too opaque, too intimate, too abstract: something recessive and contrary in her voice draws you in and pushes you away in the same breath. "There's a dream that I see," she softly insists, and now the TV studio is gone, its place taken by the shadow of an undiscovered country, a new world or a buried one. Words hang in the air like fog over a marsh: "Shake this land." ". . . nothing to *lose*." "We could all be free / Maybe not. . . ."

The song turns in, doubles back, on itself—not as some navel-directed gaze but a vision shaped like a question mark. Equally striking/intimidating, there's the sheer concentration of the performance, all of Power's ageless, free-floating gravity, as though the song's ellipses harbored great undigested tracts of dark matter. What you hear then is not the sound of a singer singing, addressing an audience, conveying a particular set of meanings or some kind of message, projecting a version of herself outward. Rather, it is her listening hard to some inner murmur, leaning forward, trying to make out what that archaic, unaccountable voice is saying ("The turn of the tide is weathering thee"), patiently waiting for it to answer her.

PHANTOM EMPIRICIST

THE STILLNESS IN Cat Power's voice recalls another moment of listening, an absolute attentiveness to the call of the unknown: the scene in *Ghost World* where Thora Birch's Enid puts a blues lp on her tiny record player and encounters Skip James's "Devil Got My Woman" for the first time. In the span of less than a minute and a half, the movie measures the seismic impact of the 1931 recording in seven briskly economical shots, a one-way passage from genesis to revelation. Fade-in from black on the phonograph needle as the record spins beneath it. Cut to Enid, fidgeting with her wet hair in front of her medicine cabinet mirror as the first crepuscular guitar notes register; briskly turning off the water, she turns round as James's voice materializes. Medium shot of the bathroom doorway as she walks toward the sound, the camera dollying back as she takes over the frame, mesmerized. Then a short reverse angle over her towel-draped shoulder, looking at the now-totemic record player. Cut back to shoulder-high, slow-motion pan over her features as she absorbs the music fully, the image returning to real time but her breathing, her heartbeat, remains in suspension. It's as though the song has taken possession of her, but subtly, almost playfully, a hint of a smile passing her lips, her body entered not by some Holy (or Unholy) Spirit but more along the lines of a Gnostic poltergeist. A tighter close-up of the stylus as James moans, "Nothing but the devil changed my baby's mind." Dissolve to the time-standing-for-still-life portrait of Enid lounging in front of the player in a thrift-shop print dress, only moving to pick up the needle when the record ends, putting it back in the groove to play it over again as she recrosses her legs and sinks back into her reverie: the vacuum of the world around made solid and palpable, evidence of another, more interesting universe somewhere out there in the great beyond.

So the expression on the face of this smart, sardonic-cherubic, subsuburban teenager is as inscrutable as cadences of James's measured, doom-scarred seventy-year-old blues. What form of identification is seeping under her skin or into her bones? The song is made of estrangement, a kind so deep and inescapable that it assumes the form of a pitch-bleak serenity. "I'd rather be the devil" — well, what teenager worth her pillar of salt wouldn't? But there's something more: the shadow play of the incorporeal and corporeal, the spectral hex cast by James's voice and the way it seems to turn his fatality into venereal flesh. "Devil Got My Woman" is metaphysical poetry as a visceral disease (or unease). Unless the condition is already present there, lying dormant inside your genes or your reality, just waiting to be triggered by a certain chord, a weird shift in rhythm, microtone scraping eardrum like a match on a barn door. Call "Devil Got My Woman" the embodiment of negative pantheism or a love letter from hell, but either way it proffers the lure of the open void. Make a wish: for an infinitely more alive existence or everlasting damnation, merely two sides of the same Janus-Judas coin tossed into the fountain of oblivion. James's song evokes a world made of loss, doubt, and despondency, which seems to give Enid hope even as it crystallizes her incipient sense of amputation. The music is like the memory of a limb she never realized was missing, an absence that haunts her every dismayed step as she stubbornly trudges the streets, a stalker searching for signs of a life that has so far eluded her.

Enid is on the prowl but hasn't figured out what she wants (except that it's the opposite of everything she's grown up with). She returns to Seymour, the middle-aged record collector, garden-variety misanthrope, and "clueless dork" who sold her the album with the James track: "Do you have any other records like that?" Steve Buscemi's Seymour responds to her naïveté with nervous, affectionate incredulity: "There are no other records like that." And a beautiful, slightly insane friendship is born, the wary love of terminal misfits, a mutual recognition society tenderly blinded by its own desperation. (Both are drawn to eccentric artifacts, dispossessed curios, found anti-art, and a mirror-mirror nostalgia for that which can't be assimilated by commerciality: "This is like my dream room," Enid gushes when she's admitted into his lovingly archived and assembled inner sanctum.) Enid's an artist who doesn't know it yet: filling a notebook with a teenage diary in obsessive pictures, drawings both tossed off and elaborate, hers is a shadow worldview in the making. Staving off boredom amid a landscape of anonymous strip malls, adult bookstores, convenience marts, chain diners, multiplexes, coffee dispensaries, roach motels, and penal colony apartments, she keeps trying on and discarding various masks and costumes: junior miss, green-haired punk vintage '77 (cued to the Buzzcocks' mewling Pap smear "What Do I Get?"), mock vixen (the leather batgirl-catwoman-dominatrix eyewear she wheedles Seymour into buying for her at the porno store).

Ghost World imparts its exquisitely disquieting sense of place in the way it details the impersonal, in bleakly layered textures of sterility and protodecay (31 flavors of cul-de-sac), in the looming walls that turn the people in front of them into forlorn billboards, desolate pop compositions that feel like photorealist redrawings of sixties Godard and seventies Bresson—feminine/masculine dynamics and stiffly slouching, plaster-cast postures redolent of "The Devil Got My Woman, Probably." Enid's quest for something that will help liberate her from her surroundings is set off against vacant slabs of concrete and indifference. When we first glimpse her alone in her Dead-End Street room, she is wearing her graduation gown the night before the ceremony, dancing in front of her portable TV to a wild Indian rock number in a Bollywood musical video she has discovered. The song "Jaan Pehechaan Ho" suggests a mad scientist's distillation of every Elvis movie crossed with the impetuous garage mania of, oh, "Wooly Bully." It's a spellbound riot of surf guitar, dapper horns, suavely panting vocalist, zany choreography, and frenzied drums. This, too, is a sign of the difference Enid is after, the soundtrack to a fractured fairy tale, a there-are-no-others-like-that record. She's this bundle of inchoate impulses and contradictions in search of a grail that will show her the way to become her own author. Indian rock-a-hula and Skip James and Seymour are puzzle pieces in the crazy quilt of associations and affinities she's putting together, arduously processing knowledge in order to work out her own logic of what it would mean to be free.

POPCORN VOID

DIG OUT A now-old record, a 12-inch 45 with a label sporting a cheerful, vaguely ominous picture of a person wearing a huge plastic March Hare head. The needle kisses vinyl, a good, insinuating modern-circa-1979 guitar hook appears, and then a young woman's voice abruptly plunges into the middle of a lecture or a seduction or a gaping wabbit hole: "But basi-cal-*auhhh*, we are a-lo-ne / But you better pay attention to detail / Life ain't gonna show at a retail pri-iiiii-ice." Who, what, where is this coming from? This sounds like an urban cosmonaut, purposefully moving through the confined spaces of bedsit England with all the pent-up angularity of a Constructivist poster child. "Wake Up" is the nonnegotiable number's title, but what kind of comrades is this call to arms hoping to find? Lurkers of the world, unite; you have nothing to lose but your chain stores? Maybe (or maybe not), but in any case that doesn't account for the attraction of opposites running through the song's blisteringly compressed two and a half minutes like a light brigade charge of ions. Drums and saxophones join the fray; the music keeps shapeshifting, instruments rise up and drop out, bass lockstep gives way to Tinkertoy soprano sax bleats, the singer's voice serving as both moving target and surface-to-hare missile, a furious center that won't hold still.

The song married a beside-itself delight straight out of "Jaan Pehechaan Ho" with a sense of unrelenting foreboding—foreclosure—worthy of Skip James, all in the person of an eighteen-year-old postpunk singer and saxophonist whose presence was as cryptic as it was emotionally lucid. Hers was the voice of the Chesire cat that swallowed the canary-in-a-mine-shaft. "Warbling" was the term she used for her vocals, and it fit perfectly the sound of someone practicing in front of her mirror the night before her big day, making ready to storm the Winter Palace, single-handedly if necessary.

"I'm a cutoff sort of girl," went "Quality Crayon Wax O.K." the lead track on the other side of *Essential Logic*, the brief, eponymous four-tune EP that promptly vanished into the ranks of quasi-collectable obscurities. (Disney threatened to sue over the March Hare, whom it seems they'd manage to trademark, and the record was pulled out of circulation faster than you can say, "Mister Mike's Least-Loved Bedtime Tales.") But the cutoff girl, who had rechristened herself Lora Logic a couple years earlier as the original sax player for the epochal punk band X-Ray Spex, was hardly daunted. Essential Logic next made a full-length album for Rough Trade, complete with rerecorded versions of "Wake Up" and "Quality Crayon Wax O.K.," descriptively enough called *Beat Rhythm News*.

Not as deliriously raw as its predecessor, it more than made up for it in the way Logic sustained, elaborated, and repositioned her ideas over the course of nine brazenly convoluted and mysteriously transparent songs. Though in actuality, they came across less like verse-chorus-verse per se than brain-flexing word-and-sound canvases, hieroglyphic allegories spun out in glottal falsetto and sotto chirp, beautifully irregular collages of timbre pressure drops, alternating currents/tempos, register quick-changes, and instant tonal mood swings.

"We're in a room," Lora Logic keened. "It doesn't matter where." Everywhere and nowhere, this was the modern world in its all-enveloping, willy-nilly emptiness and glory. In that room, sensations, apprehensions, and aspirations were crushed together like a run-on life sentence in the prison of the social. But inside, the girl cosmonaut took off her helmet and picked up a shovel: she became the archeologist of her own reality, tunneling into its recesses, excavating a playground beneath the floorboards.

No one in pop music had ever quite used language the way Lora did on *Beat Rhythm News* — every phrase an adventure in syntax, each drawn or spat-out syllable a tactile tactic, block-letter abstractions deployed like battalions engaged in serpentine flanking maneuvers, a churning mix of precocious flair and brilliantly ad hoc poetic technique. An ordinary expression ("Collecting Dust") might be spun off into a series of topical variations ("Selecting rust . . . Molesting trust . . .") on entropy until alchemizing into a looping, phantasmagorical epiphany: "I was just in the bath when I started to laugh / I was cut half in half when I started to laugh." Something like "Alkaline Loaf in the Area" is on the face of it a straightforward feminist anticonsumer tract ("Small girls must play with dolls," etc.), but there's a fundamental oddity to it that resists advancing a formulaic agenda, instead taking pleasure in tiny lyric-sheet homophones ("Will they marry Davis / Or live alone with peat?") and the bluntly enigmatic way Lora declares, "We don't have time for love at the moment." (Triumphal annunciation or defiant regret, take your pick, though as with any Essential Logic number, either/or may not apply, and there is no money-back guarantee.) Consider her fastidious asymmetries and word-playfulness as the invisible handwriting on *Ghost World*'s pointedly blank walls: "World Friction." "Cheap, strange disorder rules." "I'm not a thoroughbred puppet." "His total end in society." "Wow!! You're such a lucky boy." "And he's only a joke you know."

Most of *Beat Rhythm News* has finally made it to CD on the Kill Rock Stars compilation *Fanfare in the Garden*, along with assorted Essential Logic singles, B-sides, Lora Logic's luxuriously squiggly discoid album *Pedigree Charm*, and a number of intriguing, unheard recent tracks. Missing for decades, Lora's heroic teenage incarnation arrives in the Age of Irony and Information not a moment too soon, where she is just as happily not at home as ever—the universe is still crumbling, and her music is still a better noise. Eternally probing authority, she's Dispossessed Girl, puckishly cutting through the cant of "Shabby Abbott" religion whilst trilling "Diesel injection of light / Medieval rejection of life." But was the former line meant to indicate force-fed uplift or industrialized magic, the latter crabby hatred of the flesh or the coolest possible negation? (Was she baiting a Papal Bull or the church of Pope John Rotten?) There's such a persistently swarming quality to her Essential Logic music, attacking a question from all cubist angles, limning the streaming consciousness of every "Popcorn Boy" and girl with casual rigor; her point of view always seems to be morphing into some new perspective, changing direction in mid-sentence, reversing the shot. (What does it say about her hermetically hermeneutic, made-up-from-scratch aesthetic that the radically piecemeal "Popcorn Boy" is also a sing-along, and its deconstructive pedigree isn't out of Beefheart / Roxy Music but childhood faves à la T. Rex and Paul McCartney's "Uncle Albert / Admiral Halsey"?) In "The Order Form," a resolute human-animal parable worthy of Kafka, our dear little Lora fills out a coupon to buy a pelican, so she can stare at him. She gets a self-freeing model instead of an albatross for a necklace, but before the zoo story's happy-ever-ending, there's a moment where she gazes into her crystal ball and sees the bottomless pit. "To the packer, to the dealer," she warbles innocently, as though tasting blood for the very first time: "Make sure this one's a squealer."

Girl from a Different World

"SOME PEOPLE THINK little girls should be seen and not heard." Thus spake Poly Styrene in the 1977 intro to X-Ray Spex's greatest record, and it might provide the preface (or the epilogue) to Phoebe Gloeckner's impossibly harrowing and tender illustrated novel *The Diary of a Teenage Girl*: "But I think, *Oh bondage, up yours.*" Gloeckner's meticulously autobiographical book encompasses a year in the life of Minnie Goetz, who is roughly the age of Poly and Lora when they recorded that song. With entries beginning in March 1976 and concluding in March 1977, it occupies a parallel universe to X-Ray Spex's quest for I-den-tity, though punk is still a couple of years away from Minnie's San Francisco: there's no definitive alternative to Peter Frampton concerts, just glitter-soul Bowie and transvestite runaways living for midnight showings of *The Rocky Horror Picture Show*. There's no sign yet of the scene people like Penelope Houston of the Avengers and Debora Iyall of Romeo Void will make, but Minnie is an avatar of their intelligent, acerbic depth perceptions—where desperation and appetite served as home schooling for young ladies with independent miens.

In *The Diary of a Teenage Girl*, Gloeckner pays incredible attention to detail: it is the same attention that keeps "Little Minnie" alive and in one piece as she passes through a tilted world like an upside-down Victorian lass caught up in a progressively sleazier anti-Wonderland of bad sex, unrequited love, depression, alcohol, and crystal meth. "My introduction to love" sets the downward spiral in disastrous motion:

> In all matter-of-factuality, it happened like this:
> One night, my mother's boyfriend, Monroe, let
> me drink some of his wine. We were sitting on the
> living room couch. My mother and my sister Gretel
> had gone to sleep. I got drunk and he kept putting
> his arm around me. "Look at that silly flannel night-
> gown," he said. . . . "It makes you look like a little
> girl. But you're fifteen right now Jesus Christ I can't
> believe it it seems like just yesterday that I met you
> how old were you then? Eleven or twelve, right.
> Jesus Christ." He sort of rubbed my breast through
> my nightgown but I was so surprised by what he was
> doing that even though I half-felt that it was rude
> and presumptuous of me to think he was doing this
> intentionally, I backed away because I didn't want
> him to feel how small my breasts were.

"Rude and presumptuous of me" is the heartbreaker, because the moral seriousness behind its mixture of literary formality and adolescent self-doubt seems so true to an embryonic voice trying to find itself, an in-way-over-her-head girl who out of sheer necessity is forced to become more mature than all the pathetic arrested development cases — partying mother, creepish pseudostepfathers, the old shrink who helpfully gives her a vibrator to work off her sexual frustrations — posing as adults around her.

"A succession of jerks, assholes, criminals, creeps'n'slobs" is how R. Crumb characterized a goodly portion of them in his adoring introduction to Gloeckner's *A Child's Life*, a 1998 collection of her comics and artwork, many of whose drawn-from-life stories served as a rough punk draft for her *Diary*. An accomplished medical illustrator by trade, Gloeckner poetically dissects emotional states by combining disparate forms in a dense, overlapping manner — documentary-novel, diagrammatic comic-book panels, exquisitely crafted drawings ("*The left side of my room*"; "*She's strong but I know I beat the fucking shit out of her*"), floor plans, lists (Little Minnie's favorite movie: *The Virgin Spring*), doodles, scraps, all planted like so many sleeper cells in her conspiracy of the evocative. There's no division of things into melodrama and the mundane, horror or longing, intensity and ennui, shame or euphoria: it all coexists in *The Diary of a Teenage Girl*'s "hipknifing whirl" as it does in damaged life, which is to say life that hasn't been socially or artistically sanitized for your sensibilities' protection.

There are dual impulses at work in Gloeckner: to put you in the most immediate proximity to Minnie's world but also to see it in calm, philosophical perspective — seeing it from inside and outside at every juncture. But *Diary* neither seems fictionalized nor confessional as such, instead possessed of an unstinting devotion to simply getting things right, to doing justice to the meta-incongruities that crop up in the most unlikely and unjust places. (In the midst of a nightmarishly abused lost weekend on quaaludes, she reports having a grilled cheese sandwich that is the best melt-in-mouth thing she has ever tasted.) In contrast to a snapshot memoir like A. J. Albany's *Low Down: Junk, Jazz, and Other Fairy*

Tales from Childhood, the picturesque squalor is seen through less of a self-conscious "Tunnel Rat" perspective. As steely-lovely as Albany's book is, there is a whiff of hardboiled romanticism—the sentimentality of the would-be unsentimental—to its short, sharp shock effects. You believe nearly every word of *Low Down*, yet it seems to weigh what the audience might be thinking, composing part of itself for the tourist trade, guiding the straight reader through the convincingly waxy museum of Hollywood lowlife. *Diary* doesn't feel like it's picking at old wounds or anesthetizing them, either, attempting some therapeutic catharsis to get all that trauma out of her system. (Signing the 1993 comic "Fun Things to Do with Little Girls" as "Phoebe 'Never gets over anything' Gloeckner," she used her earlier works to binge and purge all that well-earned rage.) It's presented and framed with only its own terms in mind, using the languages of comix and coming of age as a springboard into an emancipation from the constraints of those preset languages, a head-down dive as far into pure experience as she can go.

"Disarmament, I give my arm to you," Lora Logic sang from her own city of lost-and-found children; "Disenchantment, I made this chant for you." Just as Gloeckner's book is a gift to Minnie from her future self, Essential Logic's music was a letter to the person Lora would become, perhaps the reflective woman "Under the Great City," the sensible exile who will not be found out. On Cat Power's *You Are Free*, "Maybe Not" is followed by "Names," recalling missing-in-action casualties from the war zone of growing up. The song is suffused with regret, yet also with wonder and awe at the things we endure and sometimes prevail over in the course of trauma: some are destroyed or just disappear, but Power lived to tell. At the end of *Ghost World*, Enid Coleslaw gets on an out-of-service bus and disappears into the unknowable. In each of these misfit-girl works, the cost and worth of listening for that implacable

inner voice is revealed; the immense difficulties of finding, cultivating, and holding on to it are made manifest. They are aimed at
their own private constituencies, all the few or the many Minnies
and Enids and those maladjusted fellow travelers Enid ruefully refers to as "our people." The tables are thus turned on the world at
large, which is consigned to its very own "popcorn machine," to
borrow announcer Chick Hearn's pet phrase for oblivion (Enid:
"smothered in delicious yellow chemical sludge"). Escaping assorted fates worse than death, our heroines pursue a dream of
freedom, the sound of their own voices. Out of the popcorn machine and into the line of fire, exceptional girls will heed the call
of Lora Logic from long ago and once upon a time: "We are born
in flames."

[2003]

2

Chinese

Radiation

Tiananmen Square—

Liberation Music Orchestra—

Cloudland

MUSIC IS MEMORY MADE audible. Mapping loss, it gives it a name, a geography, and a fated permanence. But it may also promise what's lost can be retrieved, relived on different term's—*one's own.* I'm sitting in an empty room, listening to sounds that elegize a world that never came to pass. I want this music to jar my memory, to disclose the ideas, images, emotions—the unmade world—that have been sucked into the black hole of current events. Waves of propaganda and doublethink put meaning under siege: these are the shock troops of a generalized public silence, dissent driven so deep into privacy (and consequently, privation) it registers only as disembodied grief.

Silence is forgetting institutionalized. And while I am thinking here of the clampdown that quietly, efficiently proceeds in China, I am also thinking some of my own country. The fallout from China has reached us as a nightmare — if an inadmissible one — of the implacability of power and the cravenness of the discourse it generates. Hearing America's leadership in unison mouth platitudes about "freedom" as the dismantling of abortion rights prefigures an entire revanchist crusade against civil rights and social choices; watching the rabid opportunism of the hysteria over flag burning and the pettiness of the arts-funding debate is to be reminded of how ambivalent this country is about free speech, personal autonomy, the works. Except, that is, as symbolic constructs: ideology as a drug, a means of producing a more formidable unreality.

It's symbolism as inoculation against surplus freedom — as though freedom can only be conceived of as something external to ourselves, a sign placed in protective custody or under house arrest, a struggle thousands of miles away colonized by the stoic gaze of TV surrogates. Tiananmen squared: a site of projection and longing, subsuming real lives and history in an ecstasy of appropriation. *That couldn't happen here* go the reassuring passwords: the massacre or the uprising?

In any event, that's a lot to ask a piece of music to cut through. One twenty-year-old album I know manages to; it might have been made with these times in mind. In a way, Charlie Haden's *Liberation Music Orchestra* was. A deliberate, radical anachronism in 1969, it was made as both the New Left and Free Jazz were collapsing under the weight of their own rhetoric. Reaching beyond the freneticism of its own moment, *Liberation Music Orchestra* achieves a serene historicity. Using the Spanish Civil War as reference point and almost Homeric talisman, Haden and arranger Carla Bley meticulously crafted a bricolage of mnemonic associations, where plaintive old recordings are interwoven with stark reharmonizations of folk laments and marches. With the nuanced, vocal grain of Haden's upright bass driving it, and the horns of Roswell Rudd, Don Cherry, Dewey Redman, Gato Barbieri, et al. bristling with ardor and mournful wit, the music constitutes a hymn to the indominability of the revolutionary spirit.

It's an exceedingly sentimental idea brought to life by its linkage to the Marquezian vicissitudes of historical process. "Song for Che," the record's most celebrated number, is emblematic of courage in the face of defeat: a muted, voluptuous plea that erases the distinction between past, present, and future. A cry of pain diffused by infinite hope, it also erases the distance between the world-historical and the private. This is the pure poetry of liberation, where the discontinuity of modern experience and official impoverishment of life is effaced by a collective consciousness that gives its participants the means to rejoin the history that has disowned them.

Such is the story—or part of it—of the Chinese student movement. It is, at least, why the authorities had to crush it. A few months back, I caught a news special on the uprising and its suppression. A tape was shown—a political as well as personal last will and testament—of Chai Ling, one of the student leaders. Softly, with certainty, she said a bloodbath was inevitable in the square. The government would then reveal its true ruthlessness, but it would take perhaps sixty or seventy years for the realization of what this meant to sink in, for this to be avenged by a full-scale revolt of the people. That revolutionary impulse would have to build over an almost unbearably long time, out of sacrifice and martyrdom.

But I do not want to die, she went on to say with a sadness suggesting those who would be spared would live out another kind of death. As the Tiananmen Square occupation had raised the most unreasonable, insatiable hopes, it had activated a sense of the possible that, once smashed, would scar any touched by it. This was the deepest object of the government's campaign of terror and disinformation: the countless people who slipped between the cracks in the roundups and purges would be delivered into a normalcy that denied all they had seen and felt. Life goes on as if nothing happened. Life thus becomes a mockery of the survivors, their living a betrayal of the dead. The most profound events and emotions are returned to the oblivion from whence they came, and indifference is elevated to the currency through which survival is transacted.

The sinister underside of a notion like "life goes on" is alien to Americans. We take it for granted that indifference is the cornerstone of liberty: the right not to care about anything is an inextricable component of the pursuit of happiness. In practical terms, democracy by apathy means the apparent stakes of life are by definition lower here than in more repressive societies. Freedom's a more vivid, potent idea inside a police state, just as it is more alive in our country to those who would roll it back, who would ration it ever more strictly, until it only existed on the black market. So it is we strain to hear poignant, heroic music of liberation, but it keeps drifting out of earshot. We find life goes on with or without our consent, watching as hope is atomized, made available on some installment plan whose terms we feel cheapened just by considering. Or it is displaced onto brave, remote faces we lonesomely scan for signs of ourselves.

I can hear Haden's music now as a gloss on Chai Ling's demure premonitions. His skewed agit-jazz pocket orchestra crisscrosses through Ornette Coleman's "War Orphans" as though they were carrying the song's subjects — even the children Chai spoke one day having — through a minefield. The drama is overwhelming but carefully framed as a revolutionary memento mori — a race memory bequeathed by thousands of years of struggle, numberless victims. Charlie Haden's ballads of human impulses that refuse to be forgotten help place a Chai Ling in a historical continuum, but as this makes sense of her context, it also diminishes what's unknowable, irreducible, in her actions and desires. "We Shall Overcome," played obliquely but without irony, comprises the last notes of Haden's album. It's a moving, worthy conclusion, but Chai's hushed tones in the back of my mind insist neither life nor revolution is ever half so simple.

Music is memory made selective. It purifies and universalizes what is recalled, but the impurities — the specificity — it omits have their own power: that of circumstances beyond the control of art or theory to put in order. *Liberation Music Orchestra* is a plea for solidarity, but the Chinese situation reveals the limits of identification. It is very easy now — almost unavoidable, even — to feel like an exile in the America we encounter. But the dissidents who disappear in China do so by force. We merely disappear, more or less of our own volition, into private holes in the social fabric. ("People hiding, people like bees," sang those honorary Americans the Mekons, "Talking of unity, crippled by fate / Divided and lonely, too weak and too late.") The numbness of exclusion is not the horror of persecution, no matter what we tell ourselves when we're tanked up on rum and bitterness. Our dissent is personified by its dispersal. We pretty much come and go as we like, finding just how easy it would be to lose ourselves — who would be looking for us, after all?—amid foreclosures forgotten in the sheer volume of real estate stretching into infinity.

*   *   *

> I'll tell you a story about the golden age:
> 30 cents a gallon, the Superhighway!
> You could fly like the wind through the hollow of the day.
>
> —PERE UBU, 1989

IN ANOTHER TIME, Pere Ubu cut a song called "Chinese Radiation"—an incandescent, drunken-noted meditation of the Cultural Revolution as embodied by its propaganda posters of impossibly zealous, beaming Red Guard youth. "He'll be the Red God, she'll be the new world, he'll wear his gray cap, she'll wave her red book," warbled singer David Thomas. From the postindustrial dreamscape Cleveland the band resided in and celebrated ("The city's like a magic beach," they sang in "Heaven": street waves to ride, dark ages to ride public transportation through, adventures down every blind alley), such a future looked as probable as any.

Here and now, the song has taken on the burden of disillusion—ironies, the song's mix of the pensive and the chaotic reveals, it was ready for all along. But early Ubu was already about existence in the shadow of some great, unspecified aftermath. "My baby said," Thomas declared on the same debut album with "Chinese Radiation," " 'we can live in the empty spaces of this life.' "

There's an American ethos for you. It is in those spaces—in the images of freedom they seem to hold out—that we divest ourselves of the energies we might channel into collectivity. Trying to conjure meaning out of the blank check of the open road, trying to connect with some sustaining passion on the run, we're left to sublimate the desire for community in obsession—with any luck, shared obsession. The pseudocommunity of religion and authority absorbs the detritus and roadkill: Jesus—or Jim Jones—promising to make everything all right by making everything stand still, enforcing unity of thought, purity of deed, dissolving questions in impassive edicts, when all else fails falling back on preordination. Yet those who don't flee privacy and free will but take flight after them turn those qualities into another kind of quest for redemption. Romantic love becomes the obsessive repository of all kinds of wishes for transformation, grace, justice. Passion goes forth as a means of redeeming society and our powerlessness within it—a protest against isolation and a secret form of it.

Pere Ubu's album *Cloudland* happens to be a fantastic, deeply reflexive anatomization of this condition. Especially in pop music, the ideology of love takes on the stature of a full-blown episteme—a whole shorted-out circuitry of assumptions and elisions by which people understand their world and era. What *Cloudland* does is traverse the language of love as though it were a crooked road; metaphors rise from strained relations like mirages off desert asphalt. "The things that we had," David Thomas sings patiently, "The good and the bad / Now it's parking lots!" The loss is real, palpable, but undercut by sense of giddy discovery. Confronted with the likes of "Lost Nation Road," a true lost highway that carries him over a terrain of self-generating signifiers, the singer can only smile. The visible is charged with its own reasons, reality outstripping its metaphors as fast as those metaphors can take on a squirrelly life of their own.

"In the early part of the 20th century," Thomas intones, as though reading a news bulletin, "deep inside the American wilderness, in the state of Kansas, 82,000 miles of flat, there were two automobile cars. On July 5, 1904, they ran into each other." After the song's chorus interrupts him, he continues: "For some reason, I thought of you. And me. And I remember the day as if my life were flat. I looked up and there you were. I said to myself, *Look out, honey, here I come.*" In the present, that American wilderness is more social than geographic—it's been converted into a psychic space where lovers try to find some breathing room, only to have that externalized emptiness come seeping back into their union against it. Maybe it was an idea whose time had come, he muses; or maybe, he answers himself with a question mark, it had just seemed like a good idea at the time . . .

The music on *Cloudland* is melodious, assured, with the pop clarity of the sound—Allen Ravenstine's customary synthesizer scrawls are pushed into the margins, where they repeat like playful smoke alarms—keeping the focus on Thomas and on the narrative he's making out of love gone missing in action. The lucidity doesn't feel like a departure for Ubu but a refinement: it heightens the affect of Thomas's rambunctious hurdy-gurdy delivery, conspiratorially drawing you into his musings about elusive happiness, elusive everything. *Cloudland* is pop recast as native magic realism: deadpan and mercurial, an enigma waiting for a place to happen, a fire at your house viewed from a distant ridge.

As the utopia of love implodes here, all embers and picturesque little detonations, a semblance of life proceeds. Hope fails, but its failure is treated with tender good humor. The sorrow that becomes evident, as though built into the landscape all along but only now noticed, is taken in stride—turned into a ghost waltz, a runaway mystery train or ice cream truck, a load of memories dwarfed by the indifferent land they came out of. "Them good days are gone!"

Thomas shouts aboard a bumpy reworking of "Sloop John B." (perhaps 'cause its been moved to landlocked "Nevada!"). What persists is the incommunicable: some idea of happiness that can escape a vast country of loss, some mutual liberation that cannot be imagined, let alone articulated.

Cloudland's structured as a monologue addressed to the narrator's absent wife, an endless entreaty that circles back on itself like a snake dining on its own tail. At the end of the album, still talking to himself, he promises to make everything right if she'll stay. We'll go to Paris, he pleads. We'll see the Eiffel Tower; he'll even learn how to dance. We'll go out West, he insists, drive and drive, see all the sights (in the confinement of the car, he sweetly reasons, "We'll have to talk!"). Finally, blissful and forlorn, he chants, "Every day will be a holiday!"

The record ends; the world moves on. One is left with a handful of debris from an explosion that has yet to happen. Seventy-odd years ago, René Magritte painted this anticipatory moment as *On the Threshold of Liberty*, and that is where we remain. The cannon hasn't fired, the panels haven't fallen, what is on the other side is either our collective mystery or our collective amnesia. If it at last goes off, then the world as we know it will cease. Then every day really will be a holiday. Or the world will cease, period.

But now we wonder if it will ever be fired, or if instead we'll be left to live with those accursed panels watching over us, never seeing the other side of them—and by extension, the other side of ourselves. Maybe we are going to be stranded on this threshold forever, our hopes receding from it like a tide that isn't coming back. "The Great Sorrow is on your track," David Thomas sings; maybe that's an old Chinese proverb. Or a new one. Either way, we're left with the burden of trying to outlive that truth, to be at hand — and of assistance — at the birth of a fresh truth. Because when, or if, Magritte's cannon does fire, our fierce and helpless daydreams tell us, we'll hear the music we have spent lifetimes preparing for.

In memory of Mark Moses, 1956–1989.

[1989]

3

Venus,
Armed

Brigitte Lin

*T*HERE COMES A MOMENT
of truth in so many Brigitte Lin
movies — the good *(The Bride with
White Hair)*, the great *(Swordsman II,
Ashes of Time)*, and the indifferent
(Deadful Melody, Fiery Dragon Kid) —
when she whirls and unleashes The
Look. Suddenly she will return the
camera's mesmerized gaze with a blinding, eye-for-an-eye intensity — a blast of
Dreyerian silence before the poetry of
doom will be writ in blood and severed
limbs. Playing a kind of anti–Jeanne d'Arc in
The East Is Red (1993), Lin flies through the air
like an exterminating angel, a negationist
Pandora: "I come to bury everything." If there is
a heaven for heretics, then Luis and Louise

must be smiling at that line and the absolute believability of Lin's delivery. The most striking and idiomatic representative of Hong Kong cinema, and just possibly the most uncanny presence in film today, Brigitte Lin is the late twentieth century's last, strangest movie goddess.

In the West, outside of true Hong Kong (HK) aficionados, Lin (full name Lin Ching-Hsia; in Cantonese, Lam Ching Ha; in Mandarin, Lin Qing Xia) is best known by way of Wong Kar-wai's films: as the split-personality/gender Murong Yin/Yang character(s) in *Ashes of Time* (1994) and the drugdealer in *Chungking Express* (1994). In the latter, she is presented as an almost purely iconic abstraction, an assemblage of evocative scraps: blond wig, sunglasses, cigarettes, trenchcoat, loaded gun, alcohol, and low, frayed voice. (Lin seems to be having a good time beneath those film noir accoutrements; answering the remark, "You look terrible" with a bleary, "I'm not sleeping," her English is "broken" only in the Marianne Faithfull sense of the term.)

"Are you a man or are you a woman?" someone belligerently asks in *Ashes of Time*. Straddling the lapidary interiors of von Sternberg and the primeval landscapes of *The Searchers*, Lin's Defeat-Seeking Loner—as her character is irresistibly nicknamed—alternately imagines herself both. Evoking images of Dietrich and *The Shanghai Gesture*'s pansexual Mother Gin Sling, she's equally indebted to the umbilical blood-knot that binds Ethan Edwards to his hated Scar. Lin embodies "the other half" that *Shanghai Gesture*'s Dr. Omar dreamily and bitterly spoke of being "lost in the dust of time": incestuously attracted to herself, a walking mirage of shame, fear, and desire. In this woman passing as a man, becoming in turn the Man (or Woman) With No Gender, disguise exists to unravel itself—and the world the nomad has turned away from. Lin drifts through *Ashes of Time* like a specter of movie passion, a beatific wraith whose calligraphic gestures etch themselves in memory the way a sword delivers its coup de grâce.

We do well to keep in mind that her Defeat-Seeking Loner is a knowing variation on the romantic swordswoman she essayed in *Dragon Inn* (1992), together with the mythic sex-changeling called Asia the Invincible in *Swordsman II* (1991) and *The East Is Red*. (To say nothing of several lesser forays into mayhem and myth — Lin's persona has done the work of both Leone-era Eastwood and his imitators/parodists.) As this poetic archetype of the irrational, Lin has presided over the martial arts fantasy film, emblematic of the form's most extreme and seductive qualities. *Ashes of Time* traces Lin's anguished nobility, her emotional displacement, with the precision of a caress; it defers her rage indefinitely, turns her violence in on itself.

There is a glimpse of that anarchic capacity in the flashback (or is it flash-forward?) where she gores Tony Leung Kar-fai and exits laughing. And another when we leave her, walking on a lake, unleashing the mystical "sword energy" that sends slow-motion explosions erupting at her feet as though she were a ballerina strewing depth charges instead of rose petals. Yet the potential for havoc on the (dis)order of 1993's *The Bride with White Hair* (in which she and Leslie Cheung are apocalyptically star-crossed lovers) or *The East Is Red* (in which questions of identity are more problematic — and apocalyptic — still) is never far from Yin and/or Yang. The collision of those severed personalities never happens, but part of the held-breath quality Lin sustains amid the languorous *Ashes* is that at any moment she might (à la her bullwhip-wielding Bride) reduce the unwary to a mound of chopped liver and soup bones. Or command (as Asia the Invincible does in *East*), "Give me your hearts" and see the obliging organs burst from the backs of a row of men in perfect Peckinpah-cum–Busby Berkeley unison.

This is not the suffocating realm of cinematic civility, where the Id is either banished or domesticated and social roles are reproduced with alarming fidelity. Instead, a creation like Asia the Invincible unites the sublimely ritualized sexual confusion of Ichikawa's *An Actor's Revenge* with the deranged pop bravado of Sam Raimi and *Carrie*. ("Transsexual martial artist" is an entry we'll never see on Meryl Streep's resume — more's the pity.) Conventional film wisdom may be able to account for Wong Kar-wai (though what's most recognizably "serious" and "important" about him is also what's least interesting), but it's short-circuited by a baroque visionary like Ching Siu-tung. As the action-director on Tsui Hark's epochal 1986 *Peking Opera Blues* and later the director of *Swordsman II* and codirector of *The East Is Red*, Ching devised the nocturnal, erotic terrain Lin commands: a stage where color, emotion, and action converge as pure visual opera, the tumultuous music of the unconscious.

The best description of the radical imagination at work in these movies — a sense that the impossible might break out at any time, a world where nothing is as it appears — comes in a passage that predates them by three decades. It is from a communiqué of the tiny post-Dadaist French collective that called itself the Lettrist International — a motley band of defeat-seeking loners including Michèle Bernstein (whose dictum "No useless leniency" neatly sums up Lin's screen persona) and Guy Debord (future author of *La Société du Spectacle* and director of its 1973 film version). The Lettrists were the children of Marx and Marcel Carné, daydreaming of the Arthurian quest and its secret meaning, conjuring up the Round Table that will find its way to Dragon Inn. "These knights of a mythic Western were out for pleasure: a brilliant talent for losing themselves in play; a voyage into amazement; a love of speed; a terrain of relativity."

* * *

BRIGITTE LIN MADE her feature debut in the 1971 Taiwanese feature *Outside the Window* while still in high school. Appearing in more than a hundred films since then, she married in 1994, moved to San Francisco with her husband, and gave birth to a daughter. Lin remains in de facto retirement, but then, by Hong Kong standards, anyone making fewer than four films a year—simultaneously, for that matter—is "retired." Even in the event she doesn't return to the screen, Lin has cut probably the broadest swath of any actor in the Hong Kong "new wave." Besides *Peking Opera Blues*—which did more than any film before *The Killer* to put Hong Kong back on the cinematic map—she earlier played a supporting role in Tsui's landmark (albeit overrated) *Zu: Warrior from the Magic Mountain* (1983), which reinvented the "legend" mode in modern terms. (With *Ashes of Time*, Lin is present for the birth of postmodern legend—less the deconstruction of romance than the romance of deconstruction.) Thanks to the wildly successful *Swordsman II* and its many offshoots and ripoffs, she has become almost a one-woman genre.

Beyond the considerable feat of bringing a new archetype into the world, Lin has also run the gamut from high seriousness to slapstick comedy with unwavering aplomb. She won Taiwan's 1990 Golden Horse as best actress for Yim Ho's aching, elliptical romantic tragedy *Red Dust* and acquitted herself well in Ann Hui's simultaneously underdramatized and overwrought exercise in innocence lost, *Starry Is the Night* (1988). But she also made a good foil for Andy Lau's shaggy-dog antics in the amiably preposterous *Handsome Siblings* in 1992 (Hong Kong's idea of a family comedy: cannibalism, quasi-incest, and random violence abounding) and has shown a consistent, relaxed flair for self-satire. It isn't merely that she passed unscathed through hyperactive gibberish like Jeff Lau's 1993 *The Eagle Shooting Heroes*—the infamous, cartoonish *Ashes* spoof that made it into the theaters before its target—or Wong Jing's *Royal Tramp II* (1992) but that she emerged somehow more radiant than ever.

This gift for transcending schlock is especially evident in another Wong Jing smirkfest, playing a lesbian Dirty Harry type in *Boys Are Easy* (1993). The movie is stupefying (apocryphal rumor has it Wong will soon helm *Ace Ventura: Enema Bandit* for kindred soul Jim Carrey), but as the violent cop who goes "straight" thanks to the ministrations of effete gigolo Tony Leung Kar-fai (you don't want to know), Lin's an oasis of cinematic cool. With her smart white suit, slicked-back hair, and lethal impatience, she's delicious even as the gags pile up like a stampede of mad cows. After all, she did apprentice in the crackpot films of Chu Yen Ping, whose Ed Wood–meets–Sam Fuller approach to narrative by non sequitur has ensured that nothing fazes her. Aptly billed as Venus Lin in the likes of 1984's back-to-back *Golden Queen Commando* and *Pink Force Commando*—bizarre, mock–spaghetti western fare with a healthy dose of women's prison and *Dirty Dozen* elements on the side—she early on mastered an unflappable composure in the face of the most outlandish circumstances. (*Pink* is the lesser of the two but features the quintessential Chu Yen Ping moment: in penance for violating the female outlaw "code," Lin cuts off her left arm samurai style, then replaces it with a prosthetic rifle.)

Given her implacable aura of female machismo, it's surprising Lin has never done a major contemporary action picture. Not that one imagines her being accepted into the bloody boys' club world of Woo or Lam, but considering the massive number of "girls with guns" sagas Hong Kong has churned out since the mid-1980s *Angel* craze, it would seem inevitable she try her hand at modern gunplay. (True, Lin isn't athletic like Michelle Yeoh, but the lack of gym-

nastic skill didn't impede Chow Yun-Fat in A *Better Tomorrow*, or
the ravishing Anita Mui in A *Better Tomorrow III*.) One of her few
brushes with the genre — apart from serving as the distress-interest
in the 1986 *Police Story* — is in Clarence Ford's, a.k.a. Fok Yiu
Leung's, giddy-dopey *Black Panther Warriors* (1992), which is actually a parody of a parody (namely, *Once a Thief*). Incoherent
junk that it is (self-consciously so, in fact), *Black Panther Warriors*
still has swoon-inducing bursts of flamboyant, mannerist chic — the
credits ought to read, "Miss Lin's wardrobe by Edith Headroom" —
and offers a taste of both the swagger and glamour she may yet
bring to the hardboiled form.

Lin's overwhelming screen presence recedes into blandness
when forced to play maudlin (the gruesome 1986 tearjerk-thriller
Lady in Black), dumb (as a conniving careerwoman in Tsui Hark's
faux-Hitchcock *Deception* (1989), or the stalker-bait in Patrick
Tam's 1985 Antonioni-run-amok *Love Massacre*). She has no feel —
or maybe stomach — for portraying "feminine wiles," that stock-in-
trade of the Mainland's Gong Li that has so endeared her to
Western viewers. Indeed, while Lin and Gong are each force-of-
nature film goddesses, they're polar opposites. Lin epitomizes an-
tinaturalism, relentlessly stylized and fiercely enigmatic, driven by
currents of irony and unreason. Gong Li sprinkles the good earth
of socialist realism with stardust, be it as forlorn peasant girl or
duplicitous vamp (respectable even when luxuriating in decadence), always single-minded, profoundly unthreatening.

Though the two symbolize separate aesthetic universes, they have
actually performed together in the wonderfully titled but otherwise
atrocious HK costume fantasy *Semi-Gods and Semi-Devils* (1994).
There a moonlighting Gong Li serves as Lin's stern, fireball-hurling
Superego, looking for all the world like a Kabuki Mary Poppins.
(This one is strictly for diva buffs and camp-followers.) More interesting, though, Gong Li's most engaging foray into HK film is

the 1990 A *Terracotta Warrior* for none other than Ching Siu-tung, which in turn suggests a wry comic-strip send-up of Lin's gloomy, unnerving reincarnation tale *Dream Lovers* (1986). It is telling that Gong really comes to life here not as the tragic heroine of antiquity but as the dizzy, petulant thirties movie queen she returns as: the temporal looks fetching on Gong Li even as the metaphysical eludes her.

Dream Lovers itself is drenched in the metaphysical—a fable of unsuspected history invading and disrupting comfortable modern lives. Less accessible than Stanley Kwan's vaguely similar ghost-of-love-past story *Rouge*, it offers no such bittersweet warmth: the two successful urbanites (a very boyish Lin and an unformed, intriguingly feminine Chow Yun-Fat) drawn together by visions of themselves as lovers in a previous life are inexorably led to reexperience the anguish of their prior tragic ending. The fatalism is truly cosmic—the universe conspires to bring them back together, only to tear them apart anew and forever. At the film's end, the two have traversed sexual abandon and are almost physical as well as spiritual twins, dead ringers. Yet side by side, they are desolate, inconsolable. "The past was like a bad dream," Lin cries, unable to escape its curse. "But now the present is like another nightmare."

That sentiment describes the feeling of *Red Dust*, a tone poem of history as that nightmare from which there is no waking. As narrative, the movie encompasses oblique modernity, soap opera, folktale, and sweeping historical panorama; it gives the impression of a movie conceived on a grander, more complex scale than director Yim Ho had the resources to make. Lin plays a willful author and intellectual (we see bits of her allegorical stories juxtaposed with the events of her life) who becomes involved with a collaborator during the Japanese Occupation. The story spans the wrenching, bitter end of the affair and that of the Occupation, followed by the outbreak or civil war; finally on the brink of being

reunited, they are separated in the chaos of refugees scrambling for the last boat out of China before the Communists arrive. In the bleakly ironic coda, her aged lover returns decades later to find out what became of her and learns she was a famous propaganda symbol, saved from drowning by People's Army soldiers.

But the real heart of *Red Dust* isn't in this exploration of romance and betrayal, of romance as betrayal; it's in the miraculous currents of empathy—very nearly osmosis—between Lin and Maggie Cheung, who plays a lifelong friend who belongs to the Resistance. The pair suggest all that was elegiac and inchoate about 1900 distilled into the poetry of their bond: Lin's attentive tenderness, Cheung's fatalistic smile. The trappings of realism dissolve the way Cheung's image does as she exits a room never to return (it's as though she were taking a final bow), becoming a ghost before our eyes. She will be killed in a government massacre of students, echoing Tiananmen Square as surely *Peking Opera Blues* prefigured the student movement's spirit of ebullient revolt. The sense of loss is shockingly palpable: Lin at the deserted scene, only bloodstains on concrete remaining, the rain turning them into a red flood that engulfs the country's soul.

At the end of *Dream Lovers*, memories of 2,000 years ago overwhelm the present, and in them a distraught Lin straddles the terracotta statue that holds her executed husband's remains. With ritualistic care, she slits her own throat, the blood turning her white jade necklace into a horrifyingly organic piece of viscera, dripping on the terracotta like an ancient form of action painting.

That image contains the paradigmatic essence of Brigitte Lin, but not the only one. "Myths are made up of actions that include their opposites within themselves," Roberto Calasso has written. I think of Lin and Maggie Cheung (again) in *Dragon Inn*, the enchantment and mischief of the private duel where each tries to strip the other naked, two errant knights of a midsummer's dream by way of *Johnny Guitar*. And *Ashes of Time*, set in the same imaginary desert after sandstorms have driven all but the hermits away — just the play of shadows on her gaunt, lovely face. From *The Bride with White Hair*, there's the painterly fairy-tale setting and how within it she goes from Pre-Raphaelite innocence to one-woman *Guernica* in the blink of an eye. There are the sumptuous sexual ambiguities of *Swordsman II*, gravity-and-gender-defying leaps into places both Cocteau and Boorman feared to tread. Then the sheer erotic delirium of *The East Is Red*: Asia the Invincible's return to destroy the cults that have sprung up in her name, carrying her concubine (and imposter) off into the clouds. And not to forget her glorified cameo in *Chungking Express* — viewed from a certain angle, and mixed with *Dream Lovers*, we have *Leaving Las Vegas* in utero, only with 2,000 years of despair behind it (as opposed to glossy, concerted amnesia).

Last and best of all, there's the peerlessly exhilarating *Peking Opera Blues*: another dream movie, a reverie of rebellion and desire, androgyny and heroism. Are there a more purely, deeply pleasurable final twenty minutes in any film than these, jumping from Lin's harrowing torture scene to the inspired bedroom farce with the dead General (a slapstick Mapache), culminating in the astounding, full-costumed gun battle and rooftop escape from the opera house? Life and art, revolt and opera, become one — the images of Lin hurtling through the air at her father's killer and the whole chain reaction of split-second events unfolding as sheer rapture compose the most emotionally charged action sequence I've ever come across. Perhaps no other living actor could make the last line of the movie ring so stirringly true: "After the revolution, meet you in Peking."

[1996]

4

American
Maniacs

Natural Born Killers

versus *Forrest Gump*

IT'S THE QUIET ONES you have to watch out for: that polite young Norman: so helpful, so good to his mother, living proof of the axiom "Shit happens." Or his sweet cousin Forrest, whose own ma ran a boardinghouse instead of a motel (the corpse of southern hospitality being harder to dispose of than Janet Leigh). That Gump boy made it out into the world, though, unlike homebody Norman, and got to meet all kinds of important folk: he made his mark. But truth be told, our Forrest is no serial killer himself. His aptitude isn't for homicide but cinemacide. He's a computer-generated cannibal eating the celluloid hearts of his precursors. Swallowing everything from *Awakenings* to *Zelig*—you'd need Dustin Hoffman's *Rain Man* to count the titles in between—*Forrest Gump* indiscriminately turns the tanned flesh of movie pathos into the sweet compost of "the human spirit."

Gump is a historian as well, or rather a counterhistorian: dogging Oliver Stone's footsteps like a shadow self, patiently erasing Stone's every revision, whitewashing his every laborious desecration of Flag and Country. There's Forrest next to both JFK and LBJ, dispelling all echoes of dread and suspicion with that "What me worry?" grin—as though the travails of the nation were just a cosmic bad-luck streak. He infiltrates Stone's Vietnam and makes it into a Hallmark sympathy card; stateside, Forrest reunites Ron Kovic and his MIA penis, while throwing in a pair of prosthetic legs as a bonus. Gump relegates the Dionysian sixties to mere aberration (reversing "Break on Through," he leads us back from the "other side" to safety). He even becomes a shrimp tycoon, revalidating Gordon Gekko's "Greed is good"—by the hand of God, no less, which wipes out the seagoing black sharecropper competition: supply-side economics as divine providence, just as the *Wall Street Journal* always insisted.

But perhaps we, like Stone himself, might dream of a double-Gump: a twin who moves through these plague years not as a source of moral immunization but as a carrier. Here is the identity of the second gunman in Dallas—shucks, it was that crack shot and natural-born pawn Forrest G. And why not Private First Class Gump as a member of Lieutenant Calley's platoon at My Lai, carrying out orders even as he puts them in folk-wisdom perspective ("Stupid is as stupid does," he says amid the slaughter)? Later, goodfella Forrest could be there to utter the last words Jimmy Hoffa ever hears: "My momma always said, life is like a box of chocolates, you never know what you're gonna git." Finally, to go with that copy of *Curious George* under his arm, he could bring the AIDS virus back from Africa: the dunce ex machina of our time. *Forrest Gump* and *Natural Born Killers* are movies that converge as they assume diametrically opposed positions. Secret sharers, they constitute the magnetic poles of America's mania for order: on one hand, the hunger to impose it at all costs, in the form of a fanatically policed "innocence"; and on the other—like "love" and "hate" tattooed on a televangelist's knuckles—the insatiable appetite for the carnival of violation. In *Gump*, we have a back-to-the-future attempt to perform the cosmetic, reconstructive surgery of "reillusionment." As a virtual Born Again on the Fourth of July pageant, *Gump* (rhymes with "stump") grafts severed American verities back onto maimed scar tissue and presents the result as wholeness, to say nothing of wholesomeness: the war as family entertainment.

With *Natural Born Killers'* sitcom-of-the-damned "I Love Mallory" as its paradigm of domesticity, family entertainment is just the happy face society puts on its sadism. (A laughtrack for the torture chamber, the executioner's song sponsored by Nike: "Just do it.") At the very least, the audience desperate to prostrate themselves upon *Gump's* spongy field of dreams is proof that *NBK's* walking dead are among us—zing go the strings of their zombie hearts, but BATONGA! BATONGA! BATONGA! go the tribal drums of zombieland. Implicit in *NBK* is the sense that these sentimental consumers, nostalgic for a past where a lie was something you really lived, not merely went along with, are the same folks who tune in Wayne Gale's "American Maniacs," indignantly bemoaning decadence and permissiveness as they wallow in every sensational reenactment and heavy-breathing sermonette. (Brilliant as Robert Downey Jr.'s maggot-ridden Gale is, he actually falls short of *A Current Affair*'s virulent Aussie Steve Dunleavey, who fuses the paternal moralism — and politics — of Pat Robertson with the delicate sensitivities of a snuff cineaste.)

The real fantasy at *Gump*'s core is of an America where everyone's IQ is 75: the bliss of the mentally challenged but emotionally pure. Intelligence is treated as affliction or, worse, corruption — a moral failing to be overcome by faith and diligence. *NBK* meanwhile says this pipe dream has not only arrived; it has come armed: drunk on love, puerile longing, and revenge, Mickey & Mallory are innocents with itchy fingers on their triggers. They've got a lot of livin' — and killin' — to do. Like Forrest, they have a destiny to fulfill. "We're fate," drawls Mickey, set to enact the secret wishes of a nation in other people's blood.

Perhaps the line between dueling saviors Gump and "the King" (Manson) is thinner than we think. Doesn't Forrest assemble a "family" of sixties casualties, devoted misfits and outcasts? Certainly abused, feckless waif Jennie fits the Manson-chick profile to perfection: a willow in the wind, one who might perform ritual murder as mindlessly as going to an antiwar demonstration. Forrest and Chuckie both operate as fantasy figures, invitations to projection, two sides of the coin of the realm. After all, there's no Christ without an Antichrist; *NBK* tries to raise the anti- and break the bank. Goodness may be a useful tool, but evil is really necessary to the siege-mentality-as-thrill-ride that holds the status quo in place.

Thus, in the blessed dialectics of order, Forrest winds up playing good cop to *NBK*'s lethal vaudeville act of bestselling detective-author Scagnetti and Warden McClusky. He personifies the promise that if we play by the rules like good boys and girls, we won't be made examples of like Mickey & Mallory — we'll get to live in Mister Gump's Neighborhood instead of landing on Death

Row next to all those scary, angry black faces waiting to turn white America into so much shrimp food.

As metamovies, the two films must negotiate an endless plain of sources. The difference is, *Gump* invokes the movie past for a doubly secondhand frisson of pathos: the most inadvertently funny scene is the 'Nam voiceover where Forrest tells they're always "lookin' for some guy named Charlie," because the only *Charly* on the film's mind is the one that landed Cliff Robertson a Best Actor Oscar. (Hanks might already be mentally rehearsing his next acceptance speech on behalf of humankind; there's so little going on in his one-note performance that he makes Hoffman's tic-tock savant look like Glenn Gould.) *NBK* calls up at least as many influences, from *Bonnie and Clyde* and *Wild at Heart* through *A Clockwork Orange* and *Weekend*. But Oliver Stone's kamikaze intent is to fuse all of *NBK*'s antecedents in one big bang that wipes the slate clean and then supersedes them, pushing every moment and gesture past its referents and finally itself, diving into the void like the Wild Bunch falling down a bullet-riddled rabbit hole.

To say this movie is *Badlands* as Bruce Conner might have kinetically spliced it together isn't to take anything away from Stone: the shotgun wedding is performed with such élan and true passion (even if its passion is nihilism) that it brings forth something new, resonant. *Badlands* was a still life about dead souls, kept at a safe artistic remove. We're thrown right into the charnel midst of Mickey & Mallory, with no signposts to get our bearings, as if they were everywhere around us (and inside us), so near we can't really separate their videogenic charisma from their murderous lunacy. As media creatures, they permeate the landscape of *NBK*, like the images that bombard us in order to become us. Moving through this terrain of the unconscious, experiencing scenes play out via multiple ways of seeing, we are sucked into a vortex of the unreal.

Here simulacra invade the present, and the populace welcomes them with open arms: they come to bring history to a halt and usher in the dictatorship of the rerun. In the world according to Gump (Gomer Pyle as puppet ruler), this effacement of events and ambiguity is positive, a public service. In the funhouse national atrocity exhibition Stone sends up so rapturously, it's the worst crime of all — and the highest rated.

One reason *NBK* is dismissed by many is that it forges a true pop style of its own: avant-pulp. Stone has cut it to rock rhythms, veering from the jarring to the almost subliminal, as if Godard had brought the Rolling Stones on board for *Weekend* and found a way to integrate their sensibility into the action. Stone uses layers of association to comment back and forth on each other, but they aren't literary-theoretical; they're pop-mythic. (Mickey & Mallory aren't the children of Marx and Coca-Cola but of Gary Gilmore and MTV — yet there is also a suggestion of Flannery O'Conner's Misfit as well, escaping the Bible Belt and becoming a postmodern Jerry Lee Lewis, the Killer complete with helpmate child bride.) *NBK* and Gump both mine their rock soundtracks for defining motifs: the latter reducing the dread and rage of "Fortunate Son" to a chopper-commuter jingle ("Fly the unfriendly skies") or revealing "Turn! Turn! Turn!" for the crummy prophecy of appeasement it always was. Stone, thanks to the sonic collage assembled by Trent Reznor, uses music more integrally and evocatively (for counterpoint, displacement, and affect) than anyone has since *Pennies from Heaven*. When the jukebox needle drops on "Shitlist," and Juliette Lewis translates the song into action, the scene draws a line and crosses a threshold: whatever you're prepared for, what will follow is going to obliterate it.

The setting may be dubbed "Route 666," but that's just an alias for Bob Dylan's site where all branches of American spectacle meet: "Abe said where you want this killin' done / God said out on Highway 61." This is the same highway where Chuck Jones's Roadrunner loses himself in a reverie of speed and mayhem (vouchsafed by Tommy Lee Jones's turn as penology's Wile E. Coyote). A place of pitiless metamorphosis, just as soundtrack pundit Leonard Cohen functions as the debonair bad conscience of this dream-West, Rodney Dangerfield will materialize as his evil, desublimated alter ego (make that id). Like Dylan's roving gamblers, everybody here is having too much fun with their anomie to stop. The laconic, deadpan Mickey is so utterly affable and matter-of-factly vicious, he demonstrates he really is born to his calling. And Mallory, from her lithe ultraviolence to the sensuality of her unshaven armpits (which caused men to actually gasp in the theater—talk about totem and taboo), might have sprung straight from the riot grrrl subculture as well as godmother Patti Smith. She's as confused and undeniable as "Rock'n'Roll Nigger" is on the soundtrack, a jumble of romantic gestures and nightmarish contradictions.

"The whole world's comin' to an end, Mal," muses the fugitive Mickey. Their holiday may be a continuation of Godard's, but with a quarter century more decay behind it and society more entrenched than ever. In 1968, *Weekend*'s apocalypse seemed already under way—a revolution at everyone's door. Nowadays revolt, a spirit Forrest Gump casts out as yesterday's news, can exist in *Natural Born Killers* only as tabloid performance art—gratuitous acts in a media-saturated wasteland. Mickey & Mallory's tourism suggests nothing so much as the Sex Pistols' "Holidays in the Sun," right down to Leonard Cohen imploring, "Gimme back my Berlin Wall," all the better for our lovers to go over it the same as Johnny Rotten did at the song's end. An unfinished story slipping through the cracks of its own noise and uncertainty ("I don't understand this bit at all," Rotten/Stone chortle. "Cheap dialogue, cheap essential scenery"), it rises from the shallow grave of what Rotten would term "hiss-torr-ee" — shit list as engraved invitation to a world without end.

[1994]

5

Jungle

Boogie

Apocalypse Now Redux

Maybe I'm nothing but a
shadow on the wall.

—PERE UBU,
"Heart of Darkness"

SOMEWHERE FAR UPRIVER, two
or three clicks past the last outpost of
progress, the last figment of civilized
imagination, they're still out there. Still
riding the backwash of the war as deep
into the jungle as their recon boat will take
them, still set on completing their mission.
Or simply trying to remember what the hell
they were looking for in the first place (maybe
in the back of their blown minds some recall
"Nirvana Now!": the peace-and-love slogan this

war turned upside down on them). Whatever it was, Willard had dragged Lance and the rest of them (shades now, ghosts of some American Experiment, as if they were anything more in life) all this way to find it; if he was going down, they were going with him. So the crew drifted toward the mouth of the whirlpool, the undead and the dead floating where the current takes them now, slowly circling the black hole at the heart of the world. . . .

Of the 10,001 things that can said of—or read into—*Apocalypse Now Redux*, Francis Ford Coppola's reedited, gorgeously restored three-hours-and-nineteen-minutes "Director's Cut" of his most insanely audacious and problematic film, the first and last has to be that Coppola's Doors-and-"Valkyries"-and-'copters Vietnam fantasia remains just as wild and crazy and unresolved after all these years as it was when it was first shown at Cannes in 1979 as "a work in progress." If anything, the *Redux* version that premiered all over again in 2001 at Cannes is that but even more so: a methodically luxuriant jungle-fever dream—a *stately*, processional Acid Trip through a tropical Inferno—from which its inhabitants (and perhaps its audience) can never really awaken, where no real ending is possible. At least none that can satisfactorily square the conflicting debts (of history and poetic license, hubris and ambivalence, sensuality and intellect, vision and blindness) the movie so recklessly incurs. In its new shape, burrowing further inward even as it spills into new terrain, *Apocalypse Now Redux* (a dud title no one seems to have been able to talk Coppola out of) hasn't untangled the original's meanings and deceits and cross-purposes but instead has lovingly elaborated the strangeness inherent in the journey to begin with. Everything here feels both dispersed and intensified, making those darkness-visible contradictions feel more viscerally and poignantly irreconcilable: the bitterness, the giddiness, the savagery, the mockery, the California surfers, the Playboy

Bunnies, the crackpot mythopoeia, the white man's angst, the banality, the absurdity, and the overriding romance of Otherness. And all of it in a mesmerizing, open-ended form that manages to combine your classic tragical-history Odyssey with your basic let's-fuck-Gidget-and-kill-anything-that-moves Beach Party, so even if you happen to feel some gnawing unease about something Francis left out (or in) this time around, there are other potential versions waiting their eventual turn, other footage that has yet to be resurrected, the eternally dubious Willard-and-Lance-sail-away wrap-up that might still be jettisoned in favor of "the other one" he described to *Rolling Stone* in 1979: "Ending with Willard up on the steps, after killing Kurtz. He's in front of the people; the people all bow. He looks, he looks back, he looks again—then it goes to the green face and 'the horror, the horror.'"

After all, he said at the same time of all the things that were cut in the first place: "We don't have another hour of real stuff. What we have is there." So who is to say if by 2021 he may not have a change of heart and mind again, reenlisting ace editor and sound designer Walter Murch to go on another "fishing expedition" (just like Willard) back into the vaults, getting Canal Plus to again put up seed money and releasing the whole shebang as an interactive digital Super-Hi-Def holographic DVD: *Apocalypse Now Deluxe,* fourteen hours long, including all of the stunning, desperately naked (and funny) behind-the-scenes footage Eleanor Coppola shot that was included in the documentary *Hearts of Darkness,* the destruction of the Kurtz compound (omitted from the rerelease because it can't be integrated into the story, yet the one passage where Francis Coppola truly found the beautiful and terrifying visual correlative to "the horror" he was after), the virtual reality option where you can see the action unfold through Captain Willard's or Colonel Kurtz's or even Coppola's own bloodshot 1970s eyes. (When

Orson Welles prepared his adaptation of Joseph Conrad's *Heart of Darkness*, he planned not only to play both Kurtz and Marlow—renamed Willard in *Apocalypse*—but to shoot the entire movie from Marlow's point of view: if it had been greenlighted instead of *Kane*, it likely would have gone down as the grandest folly in film history, and the Conrad source material seems to have had much the same effect on Coppola, goading him to try out a new form of "method directing" by attempting to turn himself into Willard and Kurtz, too.)

For now, though, we'll have to settle for *Apocalypse Now Redux* to hold us over for the next couple decades, and it will more than suffice in the meantime, thank you. "I began to think in terms of the kind of movie that is impossible," Coppola said after completing the original version, and it is those latent traces of impossibility that has always given *Apocalypse Now* its spectral allure, the enduring hold on the imagination that no other Vietnam film—indeed, few other movies, period—can claim. The bare bones of the plot itself is nothing special—Martin Sheen's burned-out Willard sent to find and assassinate Marlon Brando's renegade Colonel Kurtz—and even in *Redux*, with more room to breathe and less emphasis on steadily advancing the putative story, it never escapes from the script's origin in John Milius's flaky, zap-pow comic-book sensibility. Willard, Kurtz, Robert Duvall's pitch-perfect caricature of the Air Calvary cowboy Colonel Kilgore (think John Wayne in *The Surfers*), the old-new Hollywood PBR boat crew (Sam Bottom's surfing stoner Lance, Albert Hall's by-the-book black skipper Chief, Fredric Forrest's "wrapped too tight," zoned-out Chef, and Larry Fishburne's baby-faced kid Mr. Clean), the Bunnies, the French colonial holdouts—they're all ciphers and stereotypes, and you can still see the remnants of dialogue balloons coming out of their mouths. They're figures in an AWOL passion play, draped in the progressive layers of irrationalist allegory and allusion Coppola kept churning into Milius's psychedelic-warrior mulch, then bathed in cinematographer Vittorio Storaro's ravished, otherworldly auras of light and darkness. (*Apocalypse Now Redux*'s new Technicolor dye-transfer print has an almost overabundant richness of painterly detail: Brando's shaved head looming out of the pitch-blackest shadows like some primeval lunar talisman or the play of sunlight off the water and the lens making the river itself into a silent, watchful character amid the floating carnage and desolation.) What keeps the movie from either coming unglued altogether or imploding under the weight of its solipsist tendencies is the presence of another dimension behind the main action, the uncanny penumbra of things unseen but suggested, intuited—a fitful trance where the madness and unreason of war intersects with the madness and unreason of moviemaking.

"My film is not a movie," you can watch Coppola tell the assembled press corps at Cannes in *Hearts of Darkness*, facing down a thousand-odd reporters in 1979 to refute the years of rumors, half-truths, and innuendo that both dogged the film's immensely difficult production and elevated it to legendary status before even a frame had been seen by the public. "My film is not about Vietnam. It *is* Vietnam." That's Kurtz talk, or maybe Francis speaking in the guise of Orson Welles playing Citizen Kurtz. (Peter Cowie's *The Apocalypse Now Book* reports Coppola sent former Godard collaborator Jean-Pierre Gorin the following telegram: "Come to the Philippines and teach me two or three things about Godard, and I'll teach you two or three things about big-time filmmaking!" You supply the dialectics—I'll supply the war.) But watching the movie, you have to take him at his word. Not because "it's what it was really like" in any remotely literal, realistic way—looking to *Apocalypse Now* for historical perspective is like reading the Book of Revelations for stock tips — but that it captures a highly infectious strain of balls-out, full-tilt viral craziness: "the way we made it was very much like the way the Americans were in Vietnam. We were in the jungle, we had access to too much money, too much equipment, and little by little we went insane." That visionary megalomania comes straight from the heart: he's built a bridge between the ambitions of Welles and the counter-cultural hangover represented by Dennis Hopper (whose gibbering acid-casualty sidekick routine in the film tortures the audience more thoroughly than Kurtz does Willard), the idea of an at once larger-than-life metamovie and a "terminate with extreme prejudice," end-of-cinema *Last Movie*. (As in the phantasmic Do Lung Bridge sequence, Coppola blows the film up and rebuilds it in an endlessly spasmodic loop that begins with "The End.")

Apocalypse Now aspires to be more than a mere film, more than even a "masterpiece," but instead a total work of art that absorbs reality (the fusion of opera and documentary) and transforms it into an all-encompassing experience: the dream that feels more real than life. It isn't a picture of the real war or the real people there but a peerless evocation of the war as filtered through technology, the mass media, and the ruins of dead mythologies. In Coppola's 'Nam, what's inescapable isn't the VC so much as TV (that wonderful cameo of Coppola's as the television news producer yelling at Willard and his men to pretend like they're in combat: "Don't look at the camera"), old movies (the supposedly "authentic" voice-overs Michael Herr wrote for Willard sound to me like standard hardboiled dick talk, as if Conrad's Marlow had metastasized into Raymond Chandler's Marlowe), show business (let's hear it for those fabulous USO-touring centerfolds, minus only Bob "What's a senile bastard like me doing in the middle of this crazy war?" Hope) and the buzzing feedback of rock 'n' roll. *Apocalypse Now* isn't about how we invaded Vietnam so much as how the war invaded our psyches, how it permeated pop culture (Jim Morrison serving as the PBR's unofficial tour guide), and came to be the sight and soundtrack to a new, bad American dream. In that idyll of apocalypse, defeat takes on a perfect, preordained inevitability — *when you've got nothing left to lose, on some level the war really does become Disneyland with live ammunition, at least until your ticket's punched* — and it develops its own downward-spiral momentum and exhilaration. Kafka would have understood the somnambulist journey undertaken here; he would recognize Willard and Kurtz as brothers-in-mutilated-arms (though he might have given them less mumbo jumbo to mutter); he would smile at the conceit of this fairy-tale Amerika fighting so zealously on behalf of its Playmates' innocence and for the inalienable right of every redblooded soldier-boy to take his turn defiling that innocence.

* * *

I'm a nation's long, golden dream.

— KURTZ in ORSON WELLES'S
Heart of Darkness screenplay

SOME OF THE fleshed-out sections in *Apocalypse Now Redux* (particularly involving the more irreverent, adversarial relationship between Willard's PBR crew and that murderously "goofy fuck" Colonel Kilgore) heighten the feeling that the movie at least periodically has one foot situated in an actual time and place. There's even a new moment where Brando gives Kurtz a shot of lucid intelligence, and for the only time in the movie you glimpse the authority and force of personality that could have made him a threat and a real leader: calmly reading *Time* magazine's deluded war reporting to his just-about-broken captive Willard, quoting a supposedly well-versed expert who says, "Things felt much better, they smelled much better over there." And then in an aside to poor Willard, Kurtz savoring the witch-doctor irony of that assessment: "How do they smell to you, soldier?" The previously unused Medevac scenes and the fabled, fog-enshrouded French Plantation sequence (the *Apocalypse* faithful have waited for it as if it were footage of the Last Supper) have the opposite effect, expanding the film into an interior landscape of hallucination and breakdown. The boat stops at a medical evacuation post that is almost submerged in rain and mud (the exteriors shot during a real monsoon) where the Playmates who fled the riot at the USO stage are now stranded, which proceeds into an evocatively deranged vaudeville (mudville?) sketch where soldiers wrestle each other in the slop, a plaster water buffalo and weirdo personnel look on ("I'm just a working girl," an enlisted man tells Willard), and the blithely prostituted Playmates are so much sexual cannon fodder. "They made me do things I didn't want do," sighs Cyndi Woods's malleable Playmate of the Year, paralleling the dehumanization of the war just a tad too neatly, but the way Walter Murch intercuts between her scene with equally doe-eyed Sam Bottoms and Colleen Camp's with Fred Forrest (Miss December rattling on about birds while Chef gets her into the wig and pose he remembers from the magazine layout) manages to build to a suitably creepy punch line. After a corpse of "someone's son" falls out of a coffin, a semihysterical Woods is comforted by Lance, only to see Clean's eager face in the window. "Who're you?" she snaps. "I'm next, ma'am."

The French Plantation is something else again—a trip back in (or out of) time where the viewer travels to meet the ghosts of Colonialism Past. The tough, romantic fatalists Willard's crew encounters are also ghosts of the movie past, a band of hearty French resistance fighters who settled at Fort Apache. (The Vietnamese Communists are their Indians: resourceful, cunning, invisible adversaries.) As gallant military men, they assist in Clean's funeral; the ceremony's stirring displacement is straight from an imaginary Jean-Luc Ford Far Eastern. That feeling carries over to the dinner — shot in autumnal tones verging on sepia — where as natural aristocrats the French serve their visitors an elegant dinner and talk history, albeit the phantasmagorical kind where a cranky old uncle appears with an accordion and blurts, "We are dead — I believe in nothing." The discussion veers from B-movie poli-sci to outright travesty; then Sheen and Aurore Clément sneak off for a little ludicrous romantic interlude, very 1950s soap opera with a dash of nudity and opium and perfumed howlers like, "There are two of you — one that kills and one that loves."

There remains a degree of conventionality in even the film's most brutally harrowing sequence, when Clean mistakenly opens fire on a sampan carrying Vietnamese refugees: Willard's ruthless execution of the female survivor makes for a too-facile contrast — both ironic and sentimental — with the unscathed puppy Lance adopts. The same goes for the much-too-beloved Kilgore helicopter attack, with its blaring Wagner and thrilling action spectacle, brilliantly staged, edited, and mixed, but whose satiric qualities pale in the wake of its war-machine exhilaration. You get a sense of the limits of Coppola and Co.'s imagination when you realize the VC girl who wordlessly throws a grenade into one of the choppers and is then instantly hunted down from the air is the closest thing to a Vietnamese presence in the whole three-plus hours. *Apocalypse Now Redux* is still very much about the white man's blindness, but it's also afflicted by it (as with the newly added story Clean tells about an American GI's revenge on a South Vietnamese officer who messed with his copy of *Playboy:* "Blew his ass clean off the dock." To which Chef philosophically replies, "Bummer for the gook, though").

But the deepest paradox of *Apocalypse Now* (*Redux* or otherwise) is that none of this really diminishes its weird power: in some perversely appropriate way, its hopeless blind spots and unrealized possibilities embody the doomed, chaotic essence of the Vietnam Trip just as much as its fully realized set pieces. The private war going on in Coppola's head is whether to try and impose some kind of moral order on all this abject irrationality or jump ship and join Kurtz and Willard in deserting reality and enlisting in their cause of controlled madness. However, the arrival and confrontation at the Kurtz compound is still paralyzed by a fatal indecisiveness, a loss of nerve or inspiration or willingness to pursue the ghosts and demons he shared with Willard and Kurtz to the end of the line. At that point, he falls back on gimmicks ranging from spooky synthesizer music and ominous lightning flashes to Werner Herzog-ish images of tribalism conquering the conquerors (*Aguirre the Wrath of God* obviously made quite an impression on Coppola; Chief's earlier, ignominious death-by-spear derives from the same source) and ritual human sacrifice. Instead of Kurtz as the shell of a once-great man, we see Brando, the impetuous, bored shell of a once-great actor: a fearsome mask with nobody inside it. (Perhaps if the last three reels had fallen silent, Coppola might have discovered the danger and enigma he was after, instead of drowning his images in all those hollow, posturing explanations.) "Can you imagine," Coppola rhapsodized to his wife Eleanor in postproduction, "improvising the whole ending and it all being there, and being great." *Apocalypse Now Redux* hasn't salvaged the ending, or even attempted to; it's just made it more superfluous.

On the DVD of the original version, Coppola gives a brief account of how the phosphorescent, abstract footage of the Kurtz compound going up in strobe-light flames came to be shot, why it was excluded from the final film, and the mistake he made using it for the credits of the 35mm version. He explains why it doesn't fit and why it only gave people the wrong impression of how the movie really ends. Then he goes on to interpret the ending he settled on, saying, "I wanted Willard to throw away his weapons and have the Montagnard followers throw them away as well, and have him take young Lance by the hand and maybe lead him to a new age." In light of everything that transpires before that moment in *Apocalypse Now*, it is hard to accept such an unambiguous, untroubled resolution, and reading what Coppola said in *Rolling Stone* in 1979, he doesn't sound so convinced by it himself. He saw in Kurtz "the idea that you could go so far that you couldn't get back, even if you wanted to get back." And he described the alternate ending that was never released, with Willard on the steps, "oscillat[ing] back and forth between [staying or going back down the river], caught in that dilemma of choice. . . . I thought that was what the movie was about." I'm sure it's that intense aura of contingency and the provisional that keeps *Apocalypse Now* alive, a work in progress to this day, its meanings far from exhausted, a Pandora's Box worth of choices, still in doubt and open to revision. The journey isn't complete, and there's no going back in the movie to the safety of civilization and closure: the myth and mise-en-scène have assumed an independent, unpredictable life of their own. There's no telling when *Apocalypse Now Redux* itself might be subject to some future change as small as substituting the funky

Otis Redding version of "Satisfaction" heard in the rough cut—a minuscule detail that might open up a whole set of considerations (racial and otherwise) and begin to turn it into a new movie all over again.

[2001]

6

Metal-liad

Metallica—

Guns N' Roses—

Nirvana

IN THE WANING MONTHS of 1991, as America passed from recession to "economic free fall," a struggle for the hearts and minds of the white teen proletariat took shape. Reaching the top of the charts, heavy metal's established meanings and ingrained signifiers — the boundaries of what can and can't be said, of what constitutes the genre itself — were suddenly in a free fall of their own. A civil war began within the borders of a semiotics that time forgot.

Representing fanatical sonic fundamentalism, raising disillusionment to a fiercely mystical pitch, Metallica mounted a jihad against everything craven, impure, compromised. Instead of sex or Satanism, they speak bitterly of power as a plague and the entire world and its denizens mere carriers. *Metallica*, their latest slab, jettisons the mindless instrumental ballast of the group's earlier music, extracting organic matter from pure mass with surgical deliberation. The collective roar is dense almost beyond reckoning: darkness visible as the risen body of the unconscious, now resurrected in fable, in parables of noise. The album is a Trojan horse that lays waste to the mainstream from within, entering the charts at number one even as it rebukes everything else on them.

As debauched apostle of phallic aggression, preprogrammed insanity, and tongue-in-chic chaos, Guns N' Roses are strictly from Planet Hollywood. From the outset, the band's release of their dual *Use Your Illusion* albums is structured as a meta-event: each the equivalent of a two-record set, two and a half hours of music between them, an epic gambit aimed at securing rock 'n' roll immortality and the financial redemption of the music business in one fell swoop. History initially seems to oblige, falling in line with the script like a row of State Department dominoes: the twin blockbusters leapfrog over Metallica and the rest of the *Billboard* pack, moving as preordained into the first and second sales slots. (Thus, the reasoning goes, returning lost fans to the record store fold: Axl Rose anointed as blessed savior, only driving the money changers back into the temple.)

Yet the campaign falters; the fantasy machine stalls. All too soon, *Illusion I* and *II* are slip-sliding gently down the charts, overtaken not only by the predictable likes of Michael Jackson and that unstoppable zombie Garth Brooks but also by a resurgent Metallica and a trio of skanky punk insurgents calling themselves Nirvana.

Nevermind, Nirvana's major label debut (one they share with Guns N' Roses at that), happily heaps insult on injury. Having no comparable publicity or hype behind it, *Nevermind* gets across on the basis of the single and video "Smells Like Teen Spirit" — corrosive and insinuating, a great, derisive snort in the wilderness of mall culture. The song's particulars hang seductively out of reach — cryptic phrases swallowed in midsentence, plaintive melody playing hide-and-seek with thrashing chords — but the meaning couldn't be clearer. A stench is haunting young America, and it's coming from the decomposing corpse of "youth rebellion" itself, the same moldering dead parrot that glib salesmen like Guns N' Roses keep trying to pass off as the living article. ("Beautiful plumage," chimes an anxious Axl to calm the corpse's newly dissatisfied owners.)

If Kurt Cobain's keening voice recalls R.E.M.'s Michael Stipe, it is only to reinstate the desperation Stipe has made a nice career out of equivocating. Cobain sings as a faceless member of a vital demographic — "Here we are now, entertain us" — baiting the infinitely self-assured stars that push remote-control buttons marked *fear* or *hope, hate* or *love.* We feel "stupid and contagious": cattle in a pen at feeding time. "It's fun to lose and to pretend," we want to believe. "I'm a Beatle," he shouts, or perhaps "beetle," a shell, a receptacle — a beetle/Beatle-shaped ashtray. There's rage at being used and at the neediness that makes any of us susceptible in the first place. Behind that, the realization that faked emotion may be better than nothing, even as better-than-nothing is staged as the apotheosis of everything. There's a shrug in the groping fury of "Smells Like Teen Spirit" and a wistful dirty grin: "Yet I guess it makes me smile / I've found it hard, it's hard to find." Looking for that elusive smile propels the song, which only makes its denunciation of stasis-as-pleasure more cutting: "a denial" made into a mantra.

Denial is the thin white lie running through the two *Use Your Illusions*, invoking the real in order to suppress that much more systematically. Rose's paroxysms are emaciated, antiseptic tantrums that spell sociopath M-I-C K-E-Y M-O-U-S-E, guiding you through the "sordid underside" of L.A.: the sleaze, madness, ultraviolence, and awesome price celebrity exacts from its victims. Which is the central conceit here—Axl Rose as the victim of fame, of the media, of the soul-stealing bitch armies of the night, of his urges and the voices in his head. This persecution complex is the engine of his charisma—every curse really a cry for help, every taunt a secret plea for understanding and unconditional love.

Hard as it is to find under Rose's omnivorous persona, there is music as well here—blustery, derivative, impressively well played, conspicuously consumable, with the expensive finish of designer barbed wire. *Illusion I* and *II* turn energy into artifact, extremity into a conversation piece. The result is coffee-table heavy metal, an instant version of those boxed-set retrospectives now flooding the market. The band seems to grow in stature as the albums unfold, so that by the conclusion of *I* and through most of *II*, they make everything they steal their own. (Merging Led Zeppelin with the Osmonds in "Bad Apple" may be a dubious feat, but it's a feat all the same.) Still, there's a pervasive remoteness to these wrought-iron gesticulations, like they were on loan from a hard-rock museum/morgue. That's what people mean when they call Guns N' Roses "postmodern," as Elizabeth Wurzel described the band in a dizzy seven-page *New Yorker* rave. There, with the barest nod to irony, she praised the group as "the most harmless experience of subversiveness there is right now." (Sounds like postmodernism, all right.) The subtitle of *Use Your Illusion* ought to be "Bask in the Disease"—reification as communicable virus (swine flu?).

This has always been the lingua franca of heavy-metal alienation, so Metallica's thrust is all the more jarring. It's almost a pop-cult restaging of Simone Weil's commentary on *The Iliad*: "Might is that which makes a thing of anybody who comes under its sway. When exercised in full, it makes a thing of man in the most literal sense, for it makes him a corpse." On *Metallica*, the coercive logic of force is dissected from under its thumb. There's nothing to bask in, just a terrifying sense of helplessness before the fact that, as Weil put it, "nothing is sheltered from fate." Everyone is as a child before social powers that have assumed the guise of natural destiny: "stripped of all but pride," the unaccommodated man or woman roams the world in exile from it, even in dreams. Hence the child's nightmare of "Enter Sandman" is father to the adult's in "The God That Failed." Despite the token saber rattling of "Don't Tread on Me," this sound exists to make the void beneath it more real — a sculpture in the crumbling image of the godhead of your choice (religion, communism, free enterprise, rock 'n' roll). It's the sound of the human condition approaching the close of the twentieth century, with nothing better on the horizon. "Sad But True," proclaims Metallica, doing rough justice to the aching desperation of a disenfranchised audience but refusing to pander to the audience's illusions. That's what makes this music hard to shake off. "I'm your life," James Hetfield roars. "And I no longer care." There isn't malice or contempt in his voice: the pitilessness contains a germ of hope, at least that the truth will set you free. *Nevermind*, by wasted virtue of its casually slapstick-punk-pop idiom, is an overt debunking of the whole truth-seeking process. "He's the one who likes all our pretty songs," Cobain croons. "But he don't buy what it means." Flux and ambivalence have entered the truth-freedom equation.

Kids and the Jung-at-heart are drawn to the recognizable strains of Guns N' Roses, who (as a spin doctor recently said of his public relations work) "help people resolve their cognitive dissonance." But these uprooted fans also feel the grave pull of Metallica's unforgiving battleground and the glee in Nirvana's demolition of youth-culture piety. Nirvana's canny primitive-populism may feel a little shopworn/overcalculated to followers of Dinosaur Jr. or the Pixies, but to millions of bushy-tailed initiates for whom punk was never much more than an ugly rumor, its music hits home like a Smart Bomb payload. What new consensus may emerge from all this is unclear, but for now a door is open, and someone's in there pissing on a pair of sneakers that cost a fortune.

[1992]

7

Smells

Like . . .

Sonic Youth—

Kurt Cobain

THE DISHEVELED PRESENCE of Kurt Cobain materializes throughout *Experimental Jet Set, Trash and No Star*, dripping between every other line, seeping through the cracks like leftover stigmata. With the disappearance of Sonic Youth's most famous compatriot into that ultimate heart o'darkness ("Mistah Kurt, he dead"), his phantom can now join Karen Carpenter in the candy-rock heaven of *Goo*'s "Tunic" ("Hello Janis, hello Dennis, Elvis . . . / I finally made it"). Cobain's there in less metaphorical form—not by much—in the Sonic Youth tour movie 1991. *The Year Punk*

Broke. We see Nirvana opening for them in Europe, mere moments before the release of *Nevermind* made Cobain the superstar he detested, so pale and out of it he already seemed to be auditioning for a remake of Lech Kowalski's *D.O.A.* Most vividly of all, he's finally revealed the buried context of Sonic Youth's 1992 "Chapel Hill," made its pop-goes-the-Videodrome lines into real prophecy: "A hair in the hole in my head / Too bad the scene is dead."

With the new Sonic Youth album chock full of titles like "Winner's Blues," "Androgynous Mind," "Self-Obsessed and Sexxee," "Doctor's Order's," and "Waist" (a song about—take your pick—anorexia, AIDS, or shooting up), it's easy to hear *Experimental Jet Set* as an obituary before the fact. The album means to flesh out bad fate and perhaps bad faith, somehow force them beyond the vicarious-thrill confines of media voyeurism and hip piety alike. But it mostly can't touch that cryptic-mocking epitaph from "Chapel Hill." Instead, there's a blurry freeze-frame quality of furtive gestures arrested (or abandoned) in midair—it's Sonic Youth's first album since *Evol* that some segment of the band's audience won't label a sellout, and it's the band's most insular one since, in the bargain. From "Skink" (Kim Gordon cooing, "Down to the bottom / And oh what a bottom it is" as though rehearsing for the next *Buttwoman* video) to "Self-Obsessed and Sexxee" (Thurston Moore snickering, "I remember your bloody trail to the top"), noise keeps mutating into static, insistence fading into acquiescence.

Experimental Jet Set leads off with the acoustic "Winner's Blues," a decent stab at throwing the listener off balance (latent Neil Young tendencies surfacing against a backdrop of the Stones' dazed and euphoric "Moonlight Mile"). But the number's done before the sting of "Burn out your eyes, burn out surprise" can register; it recedes into strummed fog, and the album scurries back to familiar ground. Song by song, piece by piece, the album lowers your expectations for disruptive surprise/pleasure and proceeds to meet every diminished one. While the title *Experimental Jet Set, Trash and No Star* sounds like an anagram of New York Dolls conceits, its coyly ironic disengagement fits together as snugly as a Warhol jigsaw puzzle (a Marilyn soup can in an electric chair, say). A tone of in-jokey self-parody pervades the music, though it's hard to tell who this bunch is putting on, themselves or us.

The alternative-rock litany of "Screaming Skull" ("Society / Hüsker Dü" or should that be "Society = Hüsker Dü"?) comes off as no more than a half-baked novelty: "Surfin' Bird" reduced to stiffly thrashing Japanese wind-up toy. "Waist" may refer to a fashion victim's slow death but could just as easily be a commercial for Kim Gordon's X-Girl line of apparel—active wear for the riot gal on the go, the social casualty who doesn't want to be late for a date with X-tinction. (The line for the tar pit forms on the right.)

Where in the past Sonic Youth has sought to supersede art, this is simply art for art's sake: a nice medium-cool take on a sign system, not some insidious affront to it. Only with "Sweet Shine," the last and most conventional track here, does a song really take on a life of its own. Gordon sings it as a star-struck nonentity— someone who could be fifteen or forty, as oblivious to the world as it is to her, only knowing that when the object of her obsession performs, he's whispering secrets meant for her ears alone. "I dreamt you were my vacation," she whispers back to her idol-lover on the radio. "Went to find desire and dislocation." But it finds her first—Gordon's voice goes hoarse, unintelligible, straining against boundaries it can't name, slipping back into the womb of a child's stoned singsong. "Sweet Shine" invokes an imaginary re-lationship that's more real than anything else in a person's life is or could be: a wish for deliverance from a hole in yourself into the image you want (or are) in dreams.

That doomed need to feel something in the face of nothing can't

help but summon Cobain's spirit — the harsh, all-consuming awareness he had of the void. A sense of nothingness as social force — a
kind of subterranean social contract — is what Sonic Youth and Nirvana had in common. "Smells Like Teen Spirit" and "Scentless
Apprentice" shared likeminded radar for cultural betrayal with
"Kool Thing" and "Teenage Riot" — a nose for pop rot and grooving
decay. But in the stampede to enshrine Cobain in the wax mausoleum of youth-cult myth — lovingly stuff him into a heart-shaped
box and file him away in his own little corner of Lennon's Tomb —
that loathing has been conspicuously glossed over. Obit upon obit
quoted the "Teen Spirit" chant of "A denial," then proceeded to
carry it out: gamely working to turn "Fuck you" into "Have a nice
day" or "We shall overcome" or "I believe the children are the
future."

"There is no resistance to . . ." a raw, flailing Gordon screams on
an old bootleg of "Making the Nature Scene," retitled "Blood on
Brighton Beach" for the occasion and sounding it. With only her
rough bass for accompaniment, she makes the idea of no resistance
into a talisman of betrayal, the cultural equivalent of Citizen Tricky
Dick's credo of "plausible deniability." It's the America Sonic
Youth designated *Daydream Nation*, public spaces and individual
personalities dissolving into a landscape of myth: "Schizophrenia"
as the national anthem of a populace guided by reassuring voices.
Making an adventure out of contesting the irresistible, both losing
and discovering themselves in a maze of two-way mirrors, Sonic
Youth have mapped the nature scene of domination as pop culture.
Their disconcerting blend of cerebral detachment and passionate
explosion doesn't speak of rebellion as immutable fact of subcul-
tural identity but, rather (as per noise economist Jacques Attali),
speaks of revolution as a lack ("Teach us how to fail" are the by-
words on "the riot trail"). Their gnomic-gnostic politics are rarely

overt, but even the blatant "Youth Against Fascism" (potshots at straw dogs Bush and Jesse Helms) addresses a subtler fascism as well. "It's the song I hate," Moore sings like a scratchy broken record.

The broken record is the low-level oppression perpetrated by a fraudulent song, a lie repeated over and over until it sounds like the truth, or a truth hammered into your head so relentlessly it becomes a lie. For me, it's the generational song-sung-blue the coverage of Cobain's death became, summed up by this ever-so-thoughtful line in Ann Powers's *Village Voice* report: "Whatever the particulars of his anger, if [Courtney Love's] career is stalled, that will also be a significant loss." Too bad Kurt isn't here to roll that sentiment around his tongue — or what's left of it — and come up with the scream of disgust that nugget deserves. Let's look on the bright side of death: he's pushing up the daisies, but Nirvana's flagging sales sure got a shot in the arm. Don't we all feel a whole lot better knowing those cathartic extra units are being shifted? The business of youth cult must go on, even bearing the "artistic tragedy" of not having Kurt and Courtney to play Sid / Tom 'n' Nancy / Roseanne for our edification. We'll have to wait for the movie, which we can then put on permanent auto-repeat in the VCR of our pure pagan hearts: A *Star Is Reborn*.

The punk song that foretold Kurt's fate beyond anyone's wildest dreams was Magazine's "Shot by Both Sides": "They must have come to a secret understanding." Yet the comforting fiction of Us versus Them persists in the face of every indication to the contrary, as though punk's only legacy had been to bless the very public void Cobain indicted so often. For all that spokesmodel-of-a-generation talk, the most striking thing is how unheard his voice remains — the disbelief, even now, that his hate and shame were real. Behind the sad, resigned good-byes, there is a secret sigh of relief. Nirvana's meanings are fixed once and for all, Cobain's scornful dark humors explained away by the pathos of pathology. Maybe he was giving the people what they wanted at last, the dutiful product of years of sociogenetic engineering. Ladies and gentlemen, presenting for the first time anywhere the self-assassinating rock star, John Lennon and Mark David Chapman as a one-man band, doing a command performance of that old Sonic Youth favorite: "Kill Yr Idols."

[1994]

8

Vamp

Irma Vep—

Olivier Assayas

FROM THE OUTSET, Olivier Assayas's breakneck behind-the-camera satire *Irma Vep* immerses the viewer in the heady desperation of movie-making. The first shot slowly pans over fresh-faced production assistants blithely hustling investors and creditors with phone solicitations worthy of seasoned bunco artists. Enter cheerfully self-effacing Hong Kong superstar Maggie Cheung as herself; she has arrived to play the title role of a latex-encased femme fatale in a projected remake of Louis Feuillade's legendary proto-Surrealist 1916 serial *Les Vampires*. This is ironic inasmuch as virtually everyone involved in the ill-fated undertaking descends on her in a frenzy of need, ego, and desire.

Although handheld camera work gives *Irma Vep* the look of cinema verité, the film flows with the seamless speed and panache of Hong Kong fantasy flicks. Maggie Cheung is someone at home in both worlds: her work has spanned Stanley Kwan's exquisitely nuanced *Centre Stage* (a 1992 biography of a thirties Chinese film legend that mixes tragedy and documentary) and Johnny To / Ching Siu-tung's sublimely demented 1993 adventure *The Heroic Trio*. Indeed, one of the most electrifying moments in *Irma Vep* is when Assayas abruptly cuts away from Cheung getting into a car to a *Heroic Trio* clip — replete with flying bullets being sliced in half by ninja daggers. Blending the mundane with the ever-so-slightly hallucinatory, Assayas's meditation on cinema as cabin fever is both a send-up of and homage to the romantic mythology of auteurism. The smitten film director who shows Cheung this video snippet of herself (even as she protests that a stunt double was used) is played by Jean-Pierre Léaud, whose status as nouvelle vague icon lends yet another layer of association to a picture full of echoes from new waves gone by.

Because Assayas began as a critic for *Cahiers du Cinéma* (like Truffaut and Godard more than two decades before him), and because *Irma Vep* (his sixth and best film) is so steeped in allusions, it's easy to make too much of all this. As tempting as it is to compare *Irma Vep* to Truffaut's *Day for Night*, the latter is at best a point of departure — a set of chords on which to improvise a series of polyrhythmic riffs. In *Irma Vep*, Assayas distills a whole panoply of reference points into an entirely personal sensibility: the shifts from one tone to another, from one reality to another, touchingly incongruous. Léaud's querulous, burned-out René Vidal — a director working himself up to a nervous breakdown — tries explaining to Maggie the poetic affinity he sees between Feuillade's film and *The Heroic Trio*. "Very, very beautiful," he stammers about her duel there, "like floating in the air." But Assayas's style brings that other worldly quality down to earth without sacrificing its supernal allure. His technique is as lithe and taut as the moves Muhammad Ali favored: "Float like a butterfly, sting like a bee." (*Irma Vep* also ought to prompt attention to Cheung's neglected HK oeuvre, not only for *Centre Stage* and the atmospheric *Days of Being Wild* but for such inspired pop-cult fare as the nuttily erotic *Green Snake* and the gloriously satisfying East-meets-Western *Dragon Inn*.)

Though none of Assayas's previous films have been released here, they constitute a fascinating body of work (or considering their provisional, exploratory nature, perhaps work in progress). Assayas's 1986 debut *Désordre* (Disorder) was a doomed but somehow engaging marriage of Dostoyevsky and the postpunk scene (band members kill a music shop owner while stealing equipment and suffer the metaphysical fallout in a veritable "Crime and Joy Division"). *L'Enfant de l'hiver* (Winter's Child, 1989) made the chilly best of a masochistic scenario, but *Paris s'éveille* (Paris at Dawn, 1991) was a leap forward, displaying a sense of life in all its mercurial, unforeseen contingency. Though 1993's *Une nouvelle vie* (A New Life) has been called "the purest expression of his aesthetic," it seems to me, despite its visual brilliance and formal daring, the most unconvincing thing Assayas has done—a relentlessly minimalist exercise that renders Bergmanesque alienation as ambient imagery. (It must be noted that the figures in Assayas's *Une nouvelle vie* are no less one-dimensional than those of the average Jackie Chan flick; they just inhabit a more esoteric dimension, that arthouse never-never land where you can always rely on characters taking the most self-defeating path.)

The 1994 made-for-television *L'Eau froide* (Cold Water) is the antithesis of all that: at once a beautifully observed study of teenage frustration and an allegory of blocked revolt, it contains a magnificently sustained twenty-minute reverie that both dissolves and apotheosizes its narrative. A teenager recites Allen Ginsberg's "Wichita Vortex Sutra" as he sets out through the forest to a party at an abandoned house; unbeknownst to him, his girl (who has escaped from a mental institution) is already there, coming unglued. He finds her, and the camera tracks their wary reconciliation as record after record plays, from Leonard Cohen to Alice Cooper, waves of indelibly charged yearning rolling across the nocturnal landscapes. There's never been a better use of rock as both history and mythology: Creedence Clearwater's "Up Around the Bend" plays as kids dance around a bonfire; then, without warning, the needle is yanked off the record—the silence is gut-wrenching, a black hole devouring the light. It's an intensely realistic moment and yet utterly phantasmagorical, as if John Fogerty's guitar had single-handedly transported the youthful rebellion of Jean Vigo's *Zéro de Conduite* to the Halloween revels of *Meet Me in St. Louis*.

In *Irma Vep*, there's a scene where a Neanderthal interviewer tries to browbeat Maggie Cheung into saying that the art cinema of people like René Vidal is finished, kaput; he crows over the master race of action heroes (Arnold Schwarzenegger, Jean-Claude Van Damme) that takes movies back to the Stone Age. But I don't know that cineastes should take too much comfort in Assayas's satire. While he regards Léaud's Vidal with rueful tenderness, Vidal's replacement is a nightmare. Played by Lou Castel, the project's new director suggests a couch-potato hybrid of two Marcos: Ferreri and Bellocchio. His boorishness reminds us of the gap between cinema's lofty rhetoric and often venal motives (the medium's line between artist and bullshit artist is a fine one indeed). And the presence of Maggie Cheung points up the error too many serious film enthusiasts make: dividing art and entertainment into the same hopelessly neat either/or compartments as the imbecile journalist who badgers her.

As Assayas's movie progresses, the production disintegrates, events and emotions spiraling out of control. Cheung alone retains a sense of distance and proportion; those orbiting her lose themselves in individual fantasies of "Irma" (when Maggie is fitted for her catwoman costume in the back of an S&M lingerie shop, the fetishized nature of the character's mystique couldn't be more hilariously evident). An alchemy of cultural collision is at work here: Cheung—speaking English in a charming, vaguely working-class British accent—is a lonely voice of pragmatism and compassion amid a deluge of French absolutism, intransigence, and self-absorption, a flood of projection that inexorably casts her as the phantom of backstage soap opera and cinephile longing alike. (Nathalie Richard as the lovesick costume designer gigglingly refers to Maggie/Irma as "a plastic toy.")

At one point in *Irma Vep*, the film crew half nostalgically, half derisively, watches a video of some post-1968 Marxist agitprop they once made: "Cinema is not magic" goes a slogan there. But in linking Feuillade and Maggie Cheung, Assayas reactivates all the abandoned possibilities of film, magical and theoretical alike. In an extraordinary passage, Cheung listens to Sonic Youth in her hotel room in full cat-suit regalia. Soon she's prowling the hallway and sneaking into another woman's room; she has fallen into the dream of Irma. Stealing some jewels, she makes her escape onto the rain-drenched rooftop (which for good measure is lit like the climax of *The Heroic Trio*): in an ineffably perfect gesture, she tosses the jewels over the side of the building like so much stardust. The beauty of *Irma Vep* is that, in the same breath, it shows the impasse cinema has reached and points the way out.

[1997]

9

Screaming

Target

Seijun Suzuki

URINE PICTURESQUELY running down a hit man's socks into his wing-tip shoes; a systematic pillow girl servicing an army battalion on the Manchurian frontier; a cold-blooded killer getting aroused sniffing at a pot of rice; a frustrated student pounding a piano's keys with his erect penis.

There's no business like Japanese show business, at least as practiced by sixties B-movie genius Seijun Suzuki. Favoring violent non sequiturs and theatrical artifice over narrative continuity and genre boundaries, he hit audiences with hot and cold blasts of displacement, playfully tactile uses of image and sound, mind games masquerading as handjobs. In a dizzy succession of heedless low-budget vehicles, Suzuki transformed cheap thrills into outbursts of unaccommodated emotion. Staging banal exploitation as hallucinogenic threepenny opera, he deployed imagery and editing for sensual alienation effects, modifying cinematic syntax as casually as a rock modifies stained glass. They're the work of a middle-aged rug rat feverishly tunneling from the whorehouse to the art house—shades of John Zorn's *Spillane*, a work whose dada's-got-a-gun ambiance itself paid aural tribute to Suzuki. (The album cover even featured a cool rearview shot of Suzuki favorite Jo Shishido.)

In America, we're only now getting a chance to catch up with Suzuki's lost-in-baroque-spaces oeuvre—movies that seem even farther out today than when they were first made. Never granted a theatrical release in the United States, Suzuki's campy, somewhat atypical *Tokyo Drifter* (1966) and his electrifying 1967 jigsaw massacre *Branded to Kill* were officially released on video in 1998 for the first time. *Branded to Kill* is the film that got Suzuki fired from Nikkatsu studio on the grounds of being "incomprehensible," no small feat in a film culture where the weird, the perverse, and the obscure have always been staples. With its black-and-silver-nitrate landscape of identity crisis and incipient nervous breakdown— gangland interpreted via dating-game theory: kinky assassin with ego crisis seeks like-minded sphinx fatale—the film suggests a delicately barbarous hybrid of two contemporaneous opposites, a *Point Blank* makeover of *Persona*.

With *Branded to Kill* as the apotheosis of the Suzuki-Shishido collaboration (visionary auteur and his right-hand ham), it converges with other dream teams belonging to the sixties' art equivalent to the Gemini Project, a consciousness-distending inner-space program. Besides such zeitgeist couplings as Marvin-Boorman, Leone-Eastwood, Ullman-Bergman, and Godard-Karina, Suzuki and Shishido also kept pace with fantastic voyagers like Cecil Taylor and Jimmy Lyons (*Nefertiti, the Beautiful One Has Come; Unit Structures*), Lou Reed and John Cale *(White Light / White Heat)*, John Coltrane and Rashied Ali *(Interstellar Space)*: all launching themselves outside conventional precincts into unsuspected new regions of modernity.

Recently four more Suzuki titles have reached America: *Youth of the Beast* (1963), *Gate of Flesh* (1964), *Story of a Prostitute* (1965), and *Fighting Elegy* (1966). All emerge from culture's "undermind," where bad dreams fondle gothic forms and hysteria softly oozes through cracks in the hard imperial shell of manhood, militaristic sadism, and sublimation. Combining the off-key lilt of Sam Fuller's two-fisted hyperbole with Jean-Luc Godard's cartoon nihilism, penchant for enigmas, and delight in entropy for its own sake, these pictures are saturated in the squalid and the ridiculous. Alongside Papa Sam's and Uncle Jean-Luc's more excessive incursions into stylized brutality, they join a fetish-movie roll call marked by irony and obsession: *Johnny Guitar, Kiss Me Deadly, Touch of Evil, Videodrome*, and *Naked Killer*, to name a few.

Not to omit David Lynch: *Eraserhead* and *Lost Highway* could each pass for a divergent variation on the erotic-paranoid themes of *Branded to Kill* (which gives you an indea of what a far-reaching, far-fetched endeavor it is). Lynch's lovingly specific methodology is closer to Suzuki's fastidious grab bag of poetic dissociation than the intellectualized sleaze of even Nagisa Oshima's celebrated *Cruel Story of Youth* (1960). It is possible to argue that Suzuki represents the last word in Japanese schizo-aesthetics, that idiomatic confusion of high and low, sleazeball content and contemplative form. But at the same time, the sticky tendrils of his work reach across territorial confines, or beneath them: the mad intersexuality of *Branded to Kill* feels less like homage than a makeshift cinematheque where clips from German expressionism, French new wave, Monogram shoot-outs, and softcore porn are scrambled and superimposed. It's a cinemaniac's fantasy version of film history—celluloid as a ravenous organism that knows no borders.

* * *

"JUST SHUT UP and watch."

So snarls a frenzied gangster-pimp to baby-faced tough Jo Shishido as the creep whips a prostrate prostitute. There's plenty for the naked eye to absorb: the delicate calligraphic detail of the bloody lash marks, set off by her tasteful black cocktail dress and the even redder carpet where she's sprawled like a Jackie O rag doll. The psycho's horned-rimmed glasses are a nice conservative touch—he fumes like an accountant gone nuts. Outside the mansion's sliding-glass doors, a freakish *Forbidden Planet* sandstorm is raging, an ill wind blowing straight from the id. If this were a Goya etching, it could be titled *The Sleep of Reason Breeds Mobsters.* Now the hysterical woman tries to flee into the orange-yellow desert, but Whip Boy leaps the railing and catches her, resuming his attack as the camera captures the whole sequence in one virtually static shot from inside the yawning house. (In its *sang*-Freud stoicism, this eloquently framed doorway-to-hell view suggests Ozu if an action imp spiked his green tea with acid.) The assailant falls on her, then a jagged cut to him as he fervently kisses his half-nude victim, her limp fingers tracing unconscious lines in the dunes.

With *Youth of the Beast* from 1963, after eight years and an astonishing thirty features gestating in the nether reaches of the Japanese B-movie circuit, Seijun Suzuki's axiomatic world comes into sudden focus. It's a visceral universe of brutal non sequiters and coolly theatrical artifice, one whose limpid irrationality seems to look back toward silent cinema even as it basks in wild crypto-pop stylization. *Beast* is not so big on youth but tilts toward thugs and slatterns who look as if they were born middle-aged. Featuring Suzuki's patented *danse macabre* of rough trade sadists and murderous masochists, it positions Shishido as the scowling centrifuge around which all these random particles revolve. This was the second film Suzuki made with his favorite lead torpedo, following on the heels of *Detective Bureau 2–3: Go to Hell Bastards*. Two qualities stand out: the sense of a director hitting his stride, full of devil-may-care assurance and try-anything imagination, coupled with an uneasy, palpable boredom at the stale trappings (in the most literal sense of the term) of the cops 'n' *yakuzas* form. *Youth of the Beast* rapidly escalates into an exercise in making diametrically opposed impulses complementary—Suzuki discovers a special comic-melodramatic gift for turning ennui into excitement, simultaneously outflanking the brusque rawness of Fuller and the blank-teller alienation of Michelangelo Antonioni.

At first, the film looks to be a standard film noir setup: good cop and bad girl lie dead, the pair photographed with blunt detachment, while cynical dim bulb investigators read the note at the scene and declare it an open-and-shut double suicide. But over in the corner of the semidocumentary frame, a startling object beside the black-and-white crime scene: a single radiant red rose. Thrusting us straight into Unpleasantville, there's a shocking cutaway from the corpse cop's upside-down slab of a face to a garish pack of teenage girls dancing in the full-color street (is that a jukebox next to them? On the *sidewalk?*). Some swaggering Manciniesque jazz kicks in as Your Hit-Man Parade introduces Shishido, who in short order proceeds to senselessly stomp some street punks, manhandle a waiter, and get drunk with a beehive of bar girls. In what will become typical Suzuki fashion, the hearty-sullen antihero is soon displaced within the cheap environs, made a forlorn figure isolated from the noise of the crowded bar as the camera observes him from behind a two-way mirror in a soundproof room, an aquarium effect conveying a barracuda's fishbowl existence. Later, in the rival gang's headquarters in the balcony of a movie theater, instead of a back wall we see a hallucinatory jumble of moving pictures (back to black-and-white again), American and Japanese flicks projected behind the "real" gangsters, asynchronous clichés mocking the hard-boiled puppet theater of the main action. (In *Branded to Kill*, the film-within-a-film projections have an even more surreal, he–Man Ray quality.)

On one level, *Youth of the Beast* operates as a nasty, pachinko-machine burlesque of contorted triple-cross plotting: it plays like a serial we've arrived in the middle of, impatiently bypassing the nuances of narrative except for periodic bursts of catch-up exposition that are sprung on the viewer, then unceremoniously mislaid in the shuffle. Shishido is a disgraced ex-cop called Jo Mizuno, trying to atone by avenging the death of the fellow officer who stood by him. Mizuno hooks up first with the nightclub outfit and then cuts a deal with the screening-room bunch, both sets of gangsters arrayed to suggest your basic studio boss-execs-flunkies hierarchy: they "produce" crime with a ruthless bottom-line mentality, with pink flamingo strippers and matinee double features as window dressing to cover extortion, narcotics, hookers, etc. These goons carry a *Big Knife* (at one point, Mizuno's forced to suck on one while being interrogated) and wield a mean razor to boot, so they're easy to pit against each other. Then there's a third party girl (the trenchcoated junkie-prostitute) enlisting Jo to find the "Sixth Woman" — the real brains behind the central racket. Because *Beast* was adapted from a Haruhiko Oyabu novel (as was *Detective Bureau 2–3*), and bits of clumsy motivational-psychology residue turn up like latent fingerprints, I suspect there was an elaborate, carefully worked out plot here that Suzuki didn't so much abandon as fast-forward through: saving what plays well, ditching the interstices that connect the A-to-B-to-C dots.

On another plane, the film uses the incongruous beauty of that glimpsed rose as a spore gradually infecting the rest of the picture with irrational feeling. Not necessarily human feeling, though. Using an aerosol can to set fire to a man's hair during a shakedown is the kind of loving detail Suzuki can be counted on to deliver, a rapturous counter-sentimentality. Lean, hungry aestheticism is used strictly to circumvent threadbare conventions, making this in some ways Suzuki's most self-contained movie, a conglomeration of somersaulting details delivered in quick brushstrokes, a closed-circuit transmitting impractical visual information (how to gun down a couple men while tied upside down to a chandelier; how to crawl across a floor to tear the stuffing out from a chair while being whipped and going through writhing, screaming heroin withdrawal).

The emotion is much more disembodied than it would be in the later, much greater *Branded to Kill* or *Story of a Prostitute* (possibly his finest film). It doesn't tie into characters or cruel plot twists but to the geometrical forms and fractured compositions, abstraction situated in a histrionically commercial context, the poignant spaces Suzuki carves out of laughing displacement and the shadow of meaninglessness. When the avenger finally slumps along a remote hallway, having succeeded in his quest ("Hirokawa? I've cracked that case at last.") and lost everything in the bargain (a real suicide this time), he's engulfed by desolation, inertia. Mizuno's haunted, stricken look is replaced by an end title, an ashen painting with bright blossoms superimposed on it: everything's coming up roses in the graveyard of honor and humanity.

Sense is made and unmade experimentally, one camera movement, outrageous jump cut, or scenic flourish at a time: what counts in a film like *Tokyo Drifter* is the insipid flaneur's powder-blue jacket set in slim relief against the snow, a canary-yellow cabaret and the matching plumage of the canary who sings there, the loopy refrain of the title song. *Fighting Elegy* is as close as Suzuki comes to nominally coherent, seminaturalistic storytelling, a potent if rather pat demonstration of sexual repression feeding fascist idealism. Though it contains some of his most amazing images (the penis-pianist tickling the ivories; a call-and-response sequence that splits the screen in two), *Fighting Elegy* is also a film that a more reputable figure like Kon Ichikawa might have directed. Its relative austerity stands in subdued contrast to *Tokyo Drifter*'s rampant quirks, and while each movie has been trumpeted as definitive Suzuki, his best work grows out of more unstable motives, less-fixed meanings.

Something like *Gate of Flesh* is by nature suspect: a nudie film as critique of the American Occupation, with a group of sex-pistol streetwalkers banding together against the straight world. Going both Godard and Zorn one better, the movie assumes the veneer of a neo-sadomasochistic musical. After the girl gang tortures a betrayer, they break into a cappella song as if auditioning for the first Doo-Whip group. But that spectacular dissociation only intensifies the gloating survivalist glare these women shoot back at the camera. Especially Yumiko Nogawa, an erstwhile innocent who is raped by GIs and grows so hard-bitten she sexually assaults a well-meaning American priest: her performance exudes a plaintive loathing that fits well with the black-market comedy of a postwar fire sale, humanity 50 percent off. Nogawa returns in *Story of a Prostitute* as another feral working girl, a film whose voluptuous negativity goes much further. It brilliantly equates the invading soldiers—this time Japanese—with the prostitutes who serve them, as both Nogawa and the kneeling orderly she falls for are treated like dogs by the same tyrannical officer. There's a priceless moment when she hatefully regards the commandant, and he is held in freeze frame; then his image is torn in pieces as if being shredded by her gaze—if looks could indeed kill.

Framing anguish and ever-growing mounds of absurdity within the most eloquent of compositions (figures posed against voidlike doors, halls, and archways; Nogawa frantically running through a battlefield where tracer bullets suggest shooting stars), the director achieves a blend of tragic grandeur and rhapsodic farce. Like the inadvertent death that closes *Branded to Kill* on a spastic grace note, *Story of a Prostitute*'s randomness masks great passion. Insignificance here contains its own naked, crazy profundity: surely the real world is just as disorderly as the one Suzuki builds out of pulp and lust and discarded archetypes, just not so insanely beautiful.

[1999/2004]

Blood

Bring Me the Head

Poet

of Alfredo Garcia

RATTLING ALONG THE BACK
roads of Mexico in a scrap-heap con-
vertible, Warren Oates is taunting his
passenger. Sodden and borderline incoherent, he's full of bile and paranoia and
woozy sentiment: a drunk on a lethal
bender, spewing out the poisoned remains
of an undigested life. Strangely, the top is
up and the car permeated with flies and
stench. This may have to do with his silent
companion, who impassively receives this
string of verbal abuse. However, when the
second party is a severed head in a bloody
burlap bag, the conversation is an easy one to
dominate.

We're in Sam Peckinpah's *Bring Me the Head of Alfredo Garcia* (1974), probably the most disreputable and unnerving autobiographical film ever made by a Hollywood director. This is a fever dream of hard-boiled manhood, a massive sick joke on the tough-guy genre, as well as on Peckinpah's entire chaotic career, life, and obsessions. A nakedly coked-out, convulsive send-up of the cult of machismo that the director had come to personify, it's a declaration of spiritual bankruptcy. Yet Peckinpah overloads the parody with such intimate, revelatory shades of regret, shame, and futility that the picture glows with the dying light by which failure sees its true reflection.

If there's a cinema of guilty pleasures—or anyway morbid ones—this film takes it to a wanton, unrepentant new dimension. *Alfredo Garcia* is a tactile ode to the erotics of folly, but without the safety net of aesthetic distancing devices. The rich, mythic compositions of *The Wild Bunch* and *Ride the High Country* are here dissolved by rancor and spite. The sadistic professionalism of *The Getaway* and *Straw Dogs* has been turned into lurching slapstick: *Bring Me the Head of Alfredo Garcia* rubs the viewer's out-of-joint nose in the despair film violence so often elides. Having previously pushed violence to its most cathartic and ambivalent extremes, Peckinpah has nowhere left to go but down into the pit where the bloodbath's spent bodies repose.

Our unwitting guide is Bennie, Sam's miserable alter ego, a washed-up piano player doing "Guantanamera" for the tourists in a Mexican dive. It's a self-projection worthy of Peckinpah's oft-repeated motto: "I'm a good whore, I go where I'm kicked." Played with peerlessly dissolute concentration by Oates, Bennie's sunken face is a roadmap to that Joycean region "where dwell the vast hosts of the dead." They've taken up housekeeping behind the cheap sunglasses he wears like a beaten hipster clown; the aftermath to every senseless act to come is already etched in the lines around his thirsty mouth.

The movie begins, as it will end, at the ranch of a brutish patriarch, a Mexican godfather (the indelible Emilio Fernández) who rules his domain like a feudal lord. As his assembled clan and serfs look on, he has his unwed pregnant daughter's arm broken to extract the name of the baby's father. (He presides over this torture as though performing high mass.) Lamenting that Garcia "was like a son to me," the Don offers a million dollars for his head: an act of symbolic castration that picks up twisted implications with each new turn of the search. Soon a couple of gringo henchmen walk into the bar where Bennie's working. Passing a photo of Garcia around, they flash money. Bennie smells a score, which leads right to his own backyard: he discovers the man was last seen with his girlfriend Elita (Isela Vega).

Mortified and enraged, Bennie confronts her, learning his rival died in a car accident. So he gets Elita to lead him to the rural grave of her lover. He intends to avenge his sexual horror and in the process make a tidy dowry with which to marry his beloved—appeasing his own acute sense of psychic mutilation through crazed, profitable ritual. "Loser," one of the hoods sneers when a sweating Bennie tries to cut himself in on a piece of the action that's been out of reach all his life. "Nobody loses all the time," he spits back, the venom more real for the transparency of his bluff.

Moment to moment, the tone of Peckinpah's self-mockery shifts without preparation, as it passes from benevolence to laceration and beyond. The loving details of lowlife excess—like Bennie dousing his privates with whiskey to treat a case of crabs—give way to a grimmer vaudeville rictus. (Tired of waiting, the tramps locate Godot and decapitate him.) The hit men he deals with are faceless moneymen, stand-ins for every producer and studio flunky who ever treated Peckinpah like a hired hand. But there's no satisfaction when Bennie eventually guns down the lot of them. The unsmiling cackle behind the parody says that while these bastards were expendable, once they've gotten their hooks in you, you're fish bait for life.

In *Alfredo Garcia*, Peckinpah pushes the masculine mystique to the outer Bogie-Bukowski limits of confusion, ignominy, and pain. It's a vision bound up in layers of dipsomaniacal allusion, with injokes and semiautomatic, disinterested violence thrown up against a phantom subtext of literary and cinematic touchstones, modes of identification drawn not only from Peckinpah's voluptuously messy oeuvre but also from Hemingway and Bogart's prospector in *The Treasure of the Sierra Madre*. "I didn't catch your name, mister," Oates will say to Gig Young's bleary-eyed hood. "Dobbs," he answers like a man who can taste his own liver. "Fred C. Dobbs." The contempt and resignation in that almost subliminal exchange loads a simple movie reference with irrational intensity, as though the process of memory and association itself had become a curse. *Alfredo Garcia* plows into the fractious impulses and affinities underpinning Peckinpah's work: both homage and negation, it is a fleshy actualization of the unmade movies concealed in the ones we see.

This is most apparent in the vivid, halting scenes between Oates and Vega. The long interlude as they drive to Alfredo's grave takes over the movie and slows it to a crawl—the rhythms have a half-paralyzed quality, as if the pair's tongues were swollen with their own unrecognized feelings and needs. It's a beautifully natural digression that deliberately forces the movie out of whack. Peckinpah's tarnished compassion and sadness go beyond what the action/adventure framework can support. When the actors are returned to the plot, the story seems to cave in on itself. Reaching their goal, the couple are ambushed, Bennie left for dead in the grave with the beheaded Garcia. The shot of Oates's forlorn arm rising out of the earth is extraordinary: emblematic, uncanny, suspended in the gap between resurrection and madness.

The movie keeps going, but next to nothing registers when he finds and shoots the two hit men and kills his way up the chain of command. Yet this lack of conviction is brazenly effective at conveying Peckinpah's revulsion. The bits with Oates haranguing his formerly human cargo (the head needs ice—lots of ice) are closely observed riffs on suicidal tendencies (including the artistic kind). Oates's relentless absorption in the role—pitched between Peckinpah impersonation and autopsy—holds the movie in a grip of scorn as it staggers to the final gundown. Presenting Garcia's head to the grateful patriarch, Bennie decides the only way he can salvage his honor is to shoot it out, in an antiseptic, pocket-Armageddon restaging of the all-consuming *Wild Bunch* finale. "Come on, Al, we're going home," he mutters as he totes him off into the sunset, or rather a hail of bullets. The last shot, in every sense, is of a machine gun firing in slow motion straight into the camera. "Directed by Sam Peckinpah," says the superimposed credit, underlining the loathing and despondent bravado in that image and the long, strange dance of suffering and expiation that precedes it.

[1992]

Sympathy for the Devils

Assassination Movies

Well, I mean, why not
shoot the President?

—ENGLISH BOB in
Unforgiven

THIRTY YEARS AFTER John F.
Kennedy's assassination, the movie is
still showing in the mind's eye—the last
reel missing, all the most vital scenes left
on the cutting-room floor. *In the Line of
Fire*, directed by Wolfgang Petersen, is
only the latest attempt to stanch the bleeding, somehow assimilate the shock through
soothing tropes of genre and stardom, and
exorcise that event's terrible spirit. Kennedy's
shooting was, and remains, the primal trauma

of postwar American life, a breach in the consensus of well-being that opened onto a new world of dread. As much elegy as thriller, *In the Line of Fire* takes on the burden of compensating for that violation of history as orderly procession by containing a firestorm of irrationality within the sleek confines of well-tooled entertainment.

The displacement here of movie history into real history is given its most literal—and spectral—visualization in a flashback to Dallas that permits us to glimpse a young Clint Eastwood in the background between JFK and Jackie. Not just any image of him, either, but one lifted from *Dirty Harry* has been computer processed, digitally groomed, and patched into a blown-up film snippet. Which in turn cues the inevitable Zapruder footage, placing Eastwood's Secret Service agent just out of frame as the president is hit— rewiring the fatal moment, folding celluloid legend into real violence and chaos. Lee Harvey Oswald and Harry Callahan, together at last: this unbalanced (yet on some level preordained) symbolic marriage is the core of *In the Line of Fire*.

Eastwood's withdrawn, haunted Frank Horrigan lives in the perpetual aftermath of the Dealy Plaza motorcade's 5.6 seconds of film in which the entire structure of reality seemed to shatter along with the president's head. Sleepwalking through the wreckage of the nation's self-evident truths, Horrigan is marking time until he can awaken from his nightmare. That possibility materializes in the person—if "person" is the right word for an all-knowing Nietzschean superassassin—of John Malkovich's Mitch Leary, who affords Horrigan a second chance. Stopping Leary is Horrigan's means of imposing an honorable, just resolution on the horror that has permeated the culture since November 22, 1963. *In the Line of Fire* employs the specter of assassination and its fallout to invoke notions of disorder and redemption, national rupture and personal closure.

The operative mode of the central characters is playback: Leary pushing Horrigan's buttons the same way *Dirty Harry*'s Scorpio Killer pushed Harry's (and the audience's)—only with more élan and psychological sophistication. (Malkovich has much better buttons at his disposal, in terms of both script and acting technique, than poor drooling Andy Robinson did.) The mind games Leary plays with Horrigan recapitulate *Dirty Harry* as they undermine the pitiless righteousness Harry wore like armor: the positions of Horrigan and Leary are more ambiguous and unresolved, their complicity less repressed.

So as *In the Line of Fire* teasingly builds up to the big death-date tryst of Horrigan and Leary—the intimate late-night phone calls, the hide-and-seek courtship rites—the two refract the assassination subgenre, a floating crap game of messianic psychos, dumdum valentines, paranoiac conspiracy scenarios, and malaise-Americana that comprises the cinema of sniperdom. Malkovich's embittered ex-CIA "wet boy" joins a succession of misfits with a gun and a chip-on-shoulder compulsion, perched in a high window and taking deliberate aim. Besides Gary Oldman's "patsy" Oswald in *JFK* (where's a young Jerry Lewis when we really need him?), there's Laurence Harvey's brainwashed, ready-to-wear proto-Oswald, Raymond Shaw (asking balefully, "They can make me do anything, can't they?"), in *The Manchurian Candidate.* John Lithgow's baby-faced G. Gordon Liddy–E. Howard Hunt composite in *Blow Out* and Christopher Walken's otherworldly martyr in *The Dead Zone* qualify but not Warren Beatty's investigative reporter posing as a potential recruit for the corporate assassination bureau in *The Parallax View.* (Beatty's inescapable star aura violates the sniper's essential condition, which is anonymity.) And hovering above all the rest there is the patron saint of John Hinckley and disaffected loners everywhere, Robert De Niro's superloser Travis Bickle in *Taxi Driver.*

At the other end of the shooting gallery, Eastwood's agent is a virtual synthesis of Frank Sinatra's I-wake-up-screaming Army Intelligence officer from *The Manchurian Candidate* and John Travolta's desperate soundman in *Blow Out*. He also carries a lot of baggage over from *Dirty Harry* and *Tightrope* — the cop stalking, and stalked by, his psychosexual surrogate. More obliquely, there's a trace of Oliver Stone's obsessed Jim Garrison, who as *JFK*'s judicial Dirty Harry performs a frontal assault on the Warren Commission findings as Harry once did on the decisions of the Warren Court. This is the mien of allegory as magic bullet: as if by restaging the past, turning it into ritual and liturgy and passion play, its sins — of omission and Warren Commission — could be atoned for.

Part of what makes *In the Line of Fire* work is how it succinctly frames that quest for absolution in movie terms: thriller conventions acting as a buffer for the guilty consciousness the film tweaks and toys with. This watchful patina of distance gives the action a strangely contemplative feel, but cosmic-chess-game remoteness of the proceedings throws Eastwood and Malkovich into blissful relief. They fairly jump off the screen, because Horrigan and Leary are themselves performers, caught up in the self-referential irony of their roles — tortured hero and driven villain each fulfilling his respective function in the theater of assassination. Extracted from pure pop-mythic lore, wearing their archetypal status on their professional sleeves, the two can entertain the audience's worst doubts and fears because the ending is never in question.

As a walking repository of movie mythos, Eastwood's presence alone guarantees a host of overtones, his persona now consumed with ringing echoes of a Hollywood the Man with No Name came to bury. Once the most recessive of screen heroes — scowling pioneer of the Rorschach method — here he peels back the weathered layers of implacability. It could be that impersonating John Huston in *White Hunter, Black Heart* dislodged some obstruction in him, for there's a mournful grandeur (and puckish delight) to his old Secret Service warhorse. Salvaging the dead souls of Dirty Harry and Harry's wasted-loner brethren, Eastwood clearly savors this role, and the pleasure is infectious (though the winks that signal how good a time he's having are a minor annoyance — a tic that seems endemic to every last action hero). It's an unspoken joke that Eastwood has so much more stature than the nonentity president he's supposed to be projecting now. A self-proclaimed "dinosaur," Horrigan's linked to JFK (and to Lincoln, whose Memorial presides over the wooing of fellow agent Rene Russo) by the mystic umbilical cords of memory. Well, nostalgia, really: a haze of lost virtue and doomed ideals, the phrase "What might have been" etched in too-human flesh like a tattoo.

Opposing him, Malkovich is the ultimate unwanted blood brother: hanging over the action like a biblical curse, he makes a wonderfully solicitous monster. Leary wants to resurrect Horrigan in order to give him a fate worthy of his stature — worthy of the two of them. Malkovich distills the essence of the audience's divided *response* (revulsion and excitement; revulsion *as* excitement) to the screen's killer elite. Leary's an aesthete of mayhem who bristles at the comparison to a boob, an *amateur*, like Oswald. He sees himself as a man of taste and "panache" (he could have stepped right out of "Sympathy for the Devil" — "Who killed the Kennedys?" indeed), proper heir to John Wilkes Booth: master thespian turned romantic prophet of history.

Pricking more than just campaign rally balloons, Leary will level the entire JFK cult with one perfect, emphatic crackpot shot: "His favorite poem was 'I Have a Rendezvous with Death,' which is not a good poem." The tyranny Leary sees himself overthrowing is not political but existential — boredom as an agency of the social order.

Oswald and Kennedy are pegged as partners in banality, a man with zero style fulfilling the schoolboy death wish of one who personifies empty style. Leary casts himself as the Oswald-who-should-have-been, giving the audience what it secretly yearns for: a gesture of sabotage to turn the world inside out, *intensify* experience, redeem vacant lives the way he does Frank Horrigan's. In smashing a symbol of freedom (the president) that conceals total obedience, the assassin holds out a blood-curdling, chiliastic deliverance to his assembled witnesses — the promise of tragedy and high drama, exaltation and license. Through a cloud of splattered blood and tissue, there may be a mad glimpse of liberation in the sudden void. *Just like in the movies.*

* * *

IN THE 1968 DOCUMENTARY *The Doors Are Open*, Jim Morrison, already sounding like an Oliver Stone mouthpiece, mumbles to a Brit interviewer: "I think, uh, these days, especially in the States, you have to be a politician or assassin . . . to really be a superstar." There were plenty to go around, direct from Central Casting — RFK and Sirhan Sirhan, Martin Luther King and James Earl Ray. To say nothing of Nixon running on all the attendant fear and paranoia, Chicago under police siege, radicals in the streets, the war sucking everything into its top-o'-the-world maw. "No one here gets out alive," Morrison chanted, as fellow future Stone poster boy Jim Garrison was chasing phantoms of his own down the same blind alleys.

JFK was still a long way off, while the backlash is much nearer at hand: *Dirty Harry* (1971) will offer us a cool synthesis of assassin and politician, the superstar cop who uses his .44 Magnum to express the will of Nixon's "Silent Majority." This is the role Eastwood will forever be most identified with — a definition he has spent the last two decades both resisting (*In the Line of Fire* is only the latest attempt to critique the Callahan legacy) and surrendering to (a whole string of limping, law-of-diminishing-returns sequels — maybe Harry's a closet masochist, after all). Harry's one-man death squad is the purifying avatar of Travis Bickle's trembling wet dreams, angelic pistol-packing herald of a bloodbath that will "wash all the scum off the streets."

Harry's opposite number is the Scorpio Killer, counterculture evil incarnate. Has there ever been a more programmatically depraved fiend than this? Scorpio leaves no scummy rock unturned: a hippie deviant sniveling about his civil rights, in truth a cold-blooded sniper (his first victim is a swimsuited chick on a rooftop: centerfold bait as instant dead meat) who branches out into kidnapping, rape, torture, and all-purpose perversion. *Dirty Harry* reaches a crank apotheosis when the sicko has himself beaten up by a hulking black so he can accuse blameless Harry Callahan of police brutality. (This is the timeless rationalization of the Rush Limbaugh crowd: some no-good rotten troublemaker gets his face split open or takes ten to fifteen rounds in the back just to make the police look bad to the bleeding-heart media.) Because Harry is on "our" side, he can afford to be as dirty and inhuman as he wants — as he *needs* — to be: it takes an assassin to catch an assassin. Unburdened by our naive, weak-hearted illusions (the Bill of Rights and all that liberal hogwash), he instinctively knows the only language maggots understand is that of the exterminator.

Beyond its political elaboration on the old RAID commercials ("Kills bugs dead"), *DH* is an S&M porno-vigilante fantasy, a stroker's paradise where the viewer's invited to revel in the killer's kinky games while licking his chops at the overdetermined punishment Harry will mete out when he saves the day. Seen on VHS video, for all the formidable reputation of Don Siegel's as-thethumbscrews-turn direction, it has come to inhabit the same furtive, tawdry city-of-sin San Francisco as the Mitchell Brothers' X-rated fare of that period. The sadistic-erotic trance that sustains Harry and his quarry could have been transferred directly from the shabby 16mm mise-en-scène of *Behind the Green Door* and *Femmes de Sade*. So, too, the themes: the kidnapped and violated innocent essayed by Marilyn Chambers (the erstwhile Ivory Snow model, no less) in the former, the brute sex-psycho on a rampage in the latter. The legendary ending of the long-suppressed *Femmes de Sade* only makes explicit the inevitable culmination *Dirty Harry* couldn't show: the victims get their revenge by pissing and shitting on the crawling, groveling creep. That's Harry's dirty job, to make the monster-deviant crawl before us, make him beg, and give full cathartic expression to the bumper-sticker phrase "Eat shit and die."

The rooftop scene in *Line of Fire* invokes the violence-as-sex metaphor to ironically devalue it, as if to mark the distance Eastwood (and the audience) has traveled to arrive there. Horrigan dangles from a ledge (a momentary case of *Vertigo*), held by Leary's outstretched arm. He pulls his pistol on the killer, who impulsively deep-throats the gun barrel. It's a bravura bit of business (improvised by Malkovich, like the crack about "I Have a Rendezvous with Death"), a Dadaesque gag on Clint's persona as Public Phallus Number One. But that's all: it would make a great précis of *Reservoir Dogs*, but here it's a sign of absence—psychic abstinence. Horrigan can't bring himself to pull the trigger and kill them both (nihilist Harry lived for such an orgasmic moment). He lets Leary save him and shoot his partner. The sequence isn't indicative of Horrigan's impotence (which in thriller terms must be cured by offing the villain) but rather that we are in a different moral universe from *Dirty Harry*'s. The rules of this game are more convoluted.

The old myths have been undone by JFK's killing: there's no going back, no escaping the fatal moment. The Fall will be looped and rewound constantly, with new actors dubbing old lines and old actors rerecording new ones. But the symbols have been dispersed, the signs shuffled like an unmarked deck. Leary can't represent the forces of evil any more than Horrigan can stand for those of good: they pass through one another like dual projections on a single screen, allusions floating in the dark. But the existence they allude to is already gone, having perished before their eyes, the remains tucked away in archives and newsreels.

This sense of loss gnaws at them, as it does the audience—a source of irony and mutual desperation. In *Tightrope* (1984), Eastwood's most blatant (to say nothing of schematic) attempt to dissect the Dirty Harry myth, the jumpy moral ambivalence of his sexually compulsive new Orleans cop, walking on the wild side of Jim Garrison's home turf, is merely the precondition to a tidy resolution. He slays the creature of the id and purges his own inner black lagoon in a single stroke. Nominally, in chaste terms, that's what happens in *Line of Fire*: hero saves the president, kills the assailant, reclaims his courage and honor, gets the girl, walks off into the sun.

But it doesn't play exactly that way. The acting—Eastwood's characteristic detachment giving gradual way to the emotion he has denied for decades, Malkovich's sardonically modulated intensity turning an abstraction into something ever more visceral and suggestive—overrides the movie's pat, commercial circuitry. The redemptive violence of the protracted shootout and the smiling, happy afterglow hardly register except as window dressing. They're a reward for the dogged expectations the performers have already undermined. The real resolution, or the refusal of one, can be seen in the jagged, abrupt shot of Leary's corpse staring up into space—

even in death, the look seems to say, I'm more alive than you'll ever be—and in the moment when Horrigan returns to his apartment to find Leary's soft, familiar tones on his answering machine, the voice of memory, communion, oblivion.

This is close to the metaphysical country of *Blow Out* (1981), where disembodied sounds on tape (a tire being shot out, a woman's death cries) are the last link to a reality that has receded into the vanishing point of a seamless, all-encompassing cover-up. In Brian De Palma's virtuoso tour of distance and engagement, John Travolta's shell of a sound-effects specialist gets an opportunity to atone for a terrible he blames himself for (a short in his wiring of an undercover informant led to the man's discovery and execution). But unlike *In the Line of Fire*'s hero, Travolta's eager-to-be-saved lost soul is hopelessly in over his head: he nails John Lithgow's renegade political operative (spun from rumors that Nixon's not-so-wet boys were behind Ted Kennedy's disastrous accident), but at the cost of the witness he uses as bait. History repeats itself; another person who trusted him dies. And as *Blow Out* avidly fuses fevered bits of actual events and movie fetishism (Chappaquiddick meets *Blow-Up*, Dallas does *The Conversation*, Watergate seen through *Rear Window*), it short-circuits to a degree itself. But it details a vital element of the assassination mystique. The more evidence you collect on the event and the more connections you make, the more elusive it becomes. Solutions solve nothing.

*   *   *

OF COURSE OLIVER Stone's *JFK* purports to solve everything, blow the lid off the case, uncover a conspiracy that reaches to the highest levels of yadda yadda yadda. It's a True Believer epic after the eternal Hollywood manner: Stone's such a brave idealist he can afford to use the most cynically manipulative devices and distortions in the service of a higher goop — er, good. Very accomplished on an almost obscenely abstract plane — as a dream-logic assembly of stirring images and hypnotic apprehensions, a shotgun wedding of Leni Riefenstahl and Frank Capra — *JFK* is a reactionary morality play dolled up in a muckraking crusader cape. Stone wants to discredit official myths with his own gonzo-populist "countermythology": replace one set of lies with a set of more viscerally compelling, politically satisfying mystifications. It turns conspiracy theory into sacrament: swallow it, and you'll attain a state of half-baked grace.

The assassination of President Kennedy introduced more ambiguity into American life than it had ever known. (And more than its power structure could readily accommodate.) Yet *JFK* not only attempts to surgically excise every shred of doubt from the murder; it attacks the notion of ambiguity itself. The movie's premise is ecstatic, unadulterated propaganda: a political savior is murdered by the Establishment when he proves to be incorruptible (present here as the belief Saint Jack — his reckless, contradictory tendencies magically dissolved — would have bucked the military and withdrawn from Vietnam). To avenge this act of political Deicide, another all-American knight must take up the fallen idol's shield and confront the military-industrial dragon. Kevin Costner's Jim Garrison is too pure of heart for this world: his weapon is superhuman integrity, untarnished zeal. But then, he doesn't really inhabit any place so mundane as New Orleans. His true home is shining, ruined, starstruck Camelot. He might as well be Shane staring down vicious Jack Palance (LBJ) as wife Grace Kelly wrings her delicate hands at High Noon in the courthouse while the buckskinned lawyer tries treasonous, epicene Clay Shaw (Angela Landsbury, this time both reprising Raymond Shaw's agent-provocateur mother and weakling-pawn Ray himself).

We are delivered back to *Dirty Harry*'s realm of absolute moral certainty, lonely virtue against the massed armies of night, Us versus Them in spades. Folks who might blanch at *DH*'s crudely authoritarian polemic (while of course admiring its brutal *effectiveness*) are more disposed perhaps to accept Stone's propaganda at face value. (Same as the viewers of *America's Most Wanted* accept the show's "dramatic re-creations" — whose vocabulary of ominous slow-mo, pseudo–cinema verité shots Stone borrowed to indicate guilt in *JFK* — as footage of the actual crimes themselves.) For many, Lyndon Johnson has always been a bogeyman, anyway: a Scorpio killer in redneck-politico drag. So *JFK*, using sophisticated artistic gimmicks to put over a very primitive, iconic sentimentality, makes it easy to go with the ideological flow — to experience history as a head trip, with Jim Garrison opening the doors of perception and murmuring, "This is the End, beautiful friend."

The problem with this sort of "enlightenment" is how easily the poles of conspiracy could be reversed, left to right, without altering the movie's fundamental assumptions. Imagine the scenario this way: Kennedy is killed by a diabolical homosexual-Communist-civil-rights-movement cabal inside the government, which feels he's moving too slowly on integration. Johnson, a Negro Sympathizer and front man for Zionist bankers, escalates the war in Vietnam while "tying the military's hands." The war rages on as a smokescreen for Johnson's subversive "Great Society" programs (designed, you know, to destroy America's moral fiber and moral purity). Now if one were to play off the absurdity of such paranoia against the reality of assured, evasive domination — the kind that seems to come from *within* instead of some Pentagon Black Mass — then perhaps we might see what lies beyond the JFK myth. We could call it *The Manchurian Candidate II*.

Surely *The Manchurian Candidate*, the most politically evocative film of 1962, gives us more sense of the deranged climate that produced Oswald and the death of JFK than Stone's magnum opus. John Frankenheimer's film of the Richard Condon novel not only anticipated the assassination but provided a stunning premonition of Oswald via Laurence Harvey's brainwashed mole, making the spooky satire all the more stinging. Here we get the true realization of Costner's big line, "We're through the looking glass, people": Joe McCarthy as a Red puppet, while a war hero is groomed for a rendezvous with the sniper's nest by his upstanding patrician mother. *The Manchurian Candidate* pictures the Cold War as a delirious, corrupt Wonderland; even assassination is scripted like a commercial, the shot to come on cue for the maximum consumer impact.

The movie has none of Stone's insistent innocence to lose (his losing-my-illusions sagas are really about recovering them on a more exalted plane: Garrison not as Ahab but instead Billy Budd). It's wise to the machinations at all loose ends of the political spectrum — that ideology finally isn't the name of the game; power is.

There's no Kennedy figure in *The Manchurian Candidate* (though William Richert's *Winter Kills*, a fitfully engaging conspiracy send-up based on a later Condon novel, does try to drive the same outrageous nails into the coffin of the Kennedy dream), but the presence of Sinatra compensates for that. As offscreen liaison between Hollywood and Camelot — not to mention his long-standing mob ties — he summons a crucial aspect of Jack Kennedy's hold on the imagination, namely, the cult of celebrity. The first president who was not only a leader but a leading man, JFK moved in an aura of pop fantasy and action — going thermonuclear "eyeball to eyeball" with the Soviets, Jackie by his side and Marilyn stashed in Palm Springs. (Can you really picture Bill Clinton banging Madonna? Loni Anderson, maybe.) Though Stone won't

sully his hands with such considerations, they infuse how he ro-
manticizes Kennedy. *JFK* filters the past through the same gauzy
lens Ronald Reagan did. Not out of any ideological affinity, but
because Stone shares the same Hollywood values, subscribes to the
same rugged, sappy Man-of-the-People clichés. Stone gives us a
persecuted, saintly Jim Garrison because the audience couldn't be
expected to identify with someone driven mad by American craziness—as though paranoids couldn't really have enemies after all.
In such terms, Oswald has to have been framed, because someone
so puny is unthinkable as the giant killer. (Though from *The Manchurian Candidate* to *Taxi Driver* to Hinckley, we see just how
thinkable he can be.) To have a vast, all-purpose conspiracy behind
the deed is comforting compared to the horrific alternative: that an
extra would shoot the leading man right in the middle of the picture.

Oswald as pure product of America—a defective version of mass
culture, the nobody who would be king for a day—creates a nameless unease. When *In the Line of Fire*'s Leary starts raving about
the things the CIA made him do, made him fucking *be*, echoes of
The Manchurian Candidate abound. He's part of a system that's
disowned him—and to paraphrase Sam Peckinpah's greatest line,
he wants to be able to enter his own charnel house justified. In
this, he yearns for the air of duty and sacrifice that drives Christopher Walken's broken, freakish Johnny Smith in David Cronenberg's *The Dead Zone* (1983). Smith is the assassin turned savior:
he has visions that reveal to him that the next president will start
a nuclear war. But the dead zone Leary sees into isn't the future:
it's the present that stretches into an eternity of boredom. Leary's
a twisted looking-glass reflection of every remorseless action film
hero who has ever pulled a trigger: making life interesting by redeeming it through death.

If there's one man who personifies that dead zone, lugging it around in his head like a scrapbook, it is *Taxi Driver*'s Travis Bickle. Dear Travis is the most emblematic of alienated, time-bomb loners: a warped national icon, an Oswald who ends up anointed as Dirty Harry—an amateur exterminator. Totally disconnected, he's a void in search of anything to fill it: Boy Scout fantasies and Times Square porn have blurred into the same grainy movie for him. He wants to act out his imploded dreams, even if he can't remember them anymore. There's a ubiquity about him, as though he might pass from the screen to the outside world without a blink. Which in a sense he did, with John Hinckley using the movie as a how-to-pick-up-girls blueprint to get a date with Jodie Foster. But Hinckley also inadvertently gave us something else. He supplied the ending Stone must have wanted for *JFK*, the one where the president shrugs off his bullet wounds with a smile: "Honey, I forgot to duck."

Taxi Driver remains the most armor-piercing look at an American dreamscape that converts both assassins and their targets into the loose currency of myth. The line of fire dividing order from disorder in this society is as thin as a strip of celluloid, as the audience grapples with that division within themselves. There's a sigh of relief when *In the Line of Fire*'s Horrigan walks away from his doubts and losses at the end and moves on. But Leary's voice hangs in the air, a wisp of smoke from a public burning no one has been able to put out yet.

[1993]

"Nebraska"

Someday, I'd like to see some of
this country we've been travelin'
through.

> —*They Live by Night,* 1949

But I ride by night and I travel in fear
That in this darkness I will disappear.

> —BRUCE SPRINGSTEEN,
> "Stolen Car," 1980

Ever'where that you look
    in the day or night
That's where I'm a-gonna be.

> —WOODY GUTHRIE, "Tom Joad," 1940

I want this picture to be a commentary on
modern conditions, stark realism.

—*Sullivan's Travels*, 1941

DOUGLAS, WYO., JAN. 29 (AP)—CHARLES
STARKWEATHER, 19, RUNTY NEBRASKA
GUNMAN SOUGHT IN NINE SLAYINGS,
WAS CAPTURED TODAY IN THE BADLANDS
NEAR THIS WYOMING COWTOWN.
   A TENTH MURDER VICTIM WAS
FOUND NOT FAR FROM WHERE STARK-
WEATHER WAS CAPTURED. . . .
   WITH STARKWEATHER WAS CARIL FU-
GATE, THE 14-YEAR-OLD-GIRL WHO
FLED WITH HIM FROM LINCOLN, NEB.,
WHERE POLICE SAID HE KILLED NINE
PEOPLE. INCLUDED AMONG THE VIC-
TIMS WERE CARIL'S PARENTS.
   THE TWO TEENAGERS WERE RUN TO
EARTH IN RUGGED COUNTRY WHERE
OLD WEST GUNMEN OFTEN HOLED UP.
   "THEY WOULDN'T HAVE CAUGHT ME
IF I HADN'T STOPPED," STARKWEATHER
SAID. "IF I'D HAD A GUN, I'D HAVE
SHOT THEM."
   STARKWEATHER SAID HE SHOT HIS
NEBRASKA VICTIMS IN SELF-DEFENSE.
   "WHAT WOULD YOU DO," HE SAID, "IF
THEY TRIED TO COME AT YOU?"

—Associated Press news report, January 29, 1958

THE HARMONICA NOTES come from a long way off, a cloud of dust moving deliberately across an empty field until the particles are under your skin, vague apprehension insinuating its way out of the dim past smack into the Big Nowhere of the present. The surroundings — barren plains, dilapidated farms, deserted two-lane highways — feel claustrophobic, an immense prison without walls. Yet from the midst of this open-air, foreclosed-soul landscape, a daydreamy vision appears, rising up couched in the formal, static cadences of Once-Upon-a-Time: "I saw her standing on her front lawn just a-twirlin' her baton." The pair go "fer a ride, sir" and in the next breath, ten nameless people have died in their wake. "From the town of Lincoln, Nebraska with a sawed-off .410 on my lap / Through to the badlands of Wyoming I killed every thing in my path." Just like that, not a speck of remorse. No shock, ego, or pride. The singer-narrator's voice is preternaturally calm and steady, tender you could almost say, with the barest hint of a broken smile: a dead man looking back on these terrible events as an out-of-body experience, a bad dream come true. He could be sitting on a porch somewhere, carefully picking the simple melody out on a second-hand guitar; the instrument's acoustic, but his rocking chair is the standard prison-issue electric model.

In Bruce Springsteen's 1982 song "Nebraska," opening the sparse, quiet album of the same name, circumscribed reality and tenuous existence gradually bleed into the cornered shadows of film noir, the badlands shrouded in outlaw myth, the folklore of the dirt poor and the dust-bowled-over. It unfolds as a recurring American reverie, a movie you have watched over and over again but have never gotten tired of: boy meets girl (just a couple of star-crossed, gun-crazy kids, one or both from the wrong side of the tracks), something awful's bound to happen, violence follows as night does the day, and the couple has to flee for their lives with nothing but the shirts on their backs. As a young Henry Fonda laments to doe-eyed Sylvia Sydney in *You Only Live Once* (1937): "The bottom's dropped out of everything!" Only there's no bottom in "Nebraska" to begin with: "They declared me unfit to live said into that great void my soul be hurled." Dead or alive, jury or no jury, the singer is already there—he's beaten them to the punchline. "At least for a little while, sir," he and his baby got to play house: "me and her, we had us some fun."

There aren't telltale signs to pinpoint the time. The song has a measured stillness that's equally modern and ineffably archaic; "Nebraska" would have been no more or less curious and displacing in the 1950s or the 1930s than it was when it came out of deep in musical left field in the early 1980s. Though the elements are wholly archetypal, the details are mainly drawn straight from the historical record of the most sensational mass-murder case of the fifties, the happenstance rampage of Charlie Starkweather and Caril Ann Fugate that briefly catapulted the teens to national infamy. ("I always wanted to be a criminal," Starkweather told the Lincoln sheriff, "but not this big a one.") "Nebraska" recites the places, the number of fatalities, the caliber of the shotgun, practically the verbatim plaintive-fool words Starkweather wrote from jail ("But dad i'm not real sorry for what I did cause for the first time me and caril had more fun. . . ."), the verdict, all in that patient, true-to-life monotone. Somehow the snippets of wire service copy and court transcripts only reinforce its fablelike qualities, presented not as dead facts and figures but tattered phantoms floating across a mute landscape. They mingle with the meticulous, nearly covert allusions, echoes, and literary devices Springsteen adds: the way he politely addresses the listener as "Sir," the offhand delivery of the classic preexecution line "You make sure my pretty baby is sitting right there on my lap" (consciously or not recalling the condemned Fonda in *You Only Live Once*: "You can sit on my lap when they throw the switch") and the clipped way his last words neatly paraphrase Flannery O'Connor's story "A Good Man Is Hard to Find."

"Sir, I guess there's just a meanness in this world" is how the singer reckons his deeds and himself, invoking the self-evident with an honestly puzzled, it's-not-for-me-to-say shrug. The deferential quality Springsteen adopts has a double edge to it: partly Elvis the Good Son who dutifully reported to the army not long after Starkweather and Fugate were arrested, raised to be respectful of his elders and obey the Authorities. The other part comes from "The Misfit," as O'Connor's mournfully well-mannered escaped killer names himself in "A Good Man Is Hard to Find," who comes upon a stranded, petty, bickering family by the roadside and, together with his accomplices, kills them all. "She would of been a good woman," The Misfit pronounces brusquely over the grandmother's body, "if it had been somebody there to shoot her every minute of her life." That's the generator humming beneath "Nebraska," the live wire under Springsteen's breath: it comes from a place where faith and nihilism are close to indistinguishable, where Elvisoid yes-sir-no-ma'am piety meets the flat, hard midwestern litany of Dylan's "With God on Our Side," where The Misfit's claim "I was a gospel singer for a while" trips over Luke the Drifter, the persona Hank Williams assumed to sing homilies and parables of the Lord. Elvis the Drifter, Luke the Misfit, Camus's Stranger in the tobacco-spitting image of Hank "I'll Never Get Out of This World Alive" Williams—Starkweather country was a long way from the moral certainty of Woody Guthrie deadpanning "Mean Talking Blues" or going down that road singin' "Tom Joad," though maybe the distance traveled down this no-exit stretch of Interstate was the whole point.

Springsteen was traveling incognito here, not singing as a strict version of his subject (no "Ballad of Charlie Starkweather" here) so much as assembling a pointillist-blank composite picture from a thicket of American reference points, some obvious and plenty squirreled away from plain sight. Where Guthrie made Depression-era bank robber "Pretty Boy Floyd" out to be an Oklahoma Robin Hood ("If you'll gather round me children / A story I will tell"), the singer of "Nebraska" presents himself as an anti-Everyman, a fella who'd as soon kill decent folk as look at them. Much as Springsteen must want to understand where Charlie Starkweather came from, it sounds like he wants to escape the shadow of "Bruce Springsteen" even more—desperately looking for a way to slip out from under the burden of being the famous all-pro working-class hero, sainted musical vox populist, and full-on secular gospel paragon of rock 'n' roll virtue, which is to say a walking, preaching, boring oxymoron. That accounts for the weird air of liberation inside the serene negativity of "Nebraska": both killer and singer get a reprieve from being themselves, and both kind of sneakily like how being— playing—the Other feels. The real Charlie said he wasn't mad at anybody, he just wanted to "be someone"; here Bruce's name means nothing with capital-punishment N.

Condemned and damned, the drifter miraculously escapes his chains, those of this world and the next. Diving into the void in slow-as-molasses-motion, the man with a surfeit of future jumps into the shoes of somebody who has none at all, while the boy nobody becomes a murky tabloid legend. Switching places, bodies, the singer trades in immortality for the murderer's state of nihilistic grace. Why, it could have been a drive-in movie, featuring Jerry Lee Lewis in his first leading role as "The Killer" (a.k.a. "BABY SNATCHER," as contemporaneous headlines referred to him) and in her film debut as his milkshake-mademoiselle accomplice, his thirteen-year-old cousin and child bride Myra Gale. Moral panic!

Teen terror! Anarchy in the streets! "Those were the happiest years of our lives," Myra/Caril would muse in the voice-over. But for the prison scenes, a touch of rigor and mortality, à la Bresson directing *Big House, USA*—a man escaped, clothes exchanged, a body left behind to throw the warders off the scent, with the face and fingerprints blowtorched off.

Minimalist and eerily cinematic, "Nebraska" effectively translates the imagery of a rather more high-toned movie into folk song: *Badlands*, Terrence Malick's 1973 art-hothouse treatment of the Starkweather case, whose beautifully framed views of flat fields, tumbledown farmhouses, narrow doorways, burning dollhouses, and inert pod people turned Western panoramas into a delicately ravishing series of neon Vacancy signs seen through a telephoto microscope. (Springsteen had previously lifted the title for a grandiose song on the 1978 album *Darkness on the Edge of Town*—a show-stopping number packed to the gills with hope against hope and defiant *whoa-whoa-whoa-whoa* optimism.) Like a prematurely postmodernist John Ford film, *Badlands* parades stock characters across frontierish vistas doubling as lunar landscaping (mostly Colorado standing in for Nebraska, Montana, and the Dakotas), using the actors as sock puppet signifiers to mouth ornate contrived banalities. Springsteen ditches the movie's clinical disregard and downward-looking perspective while retaining the feel of a longshot tableaux and finely composed interior setups. "Nebraska" internalizes those lulling rhythms, the way *Badlands* orchestrates spaciousness (skies, riverbanks, horizons, farmland) as oppressiveness or at least a constant looming absence. (The absence of anything to *do*, for starters: boredom as nature, and vice versa.) Springsteen's narration is no less artistic than the faux-naif pronouncements of Sissy Spacek's blank-teller Holly or preening Martin Sheen's overcooked James Dean sausage Kit but a lot more matter-of-factly believable. Springsteen sticks closer to the facts, while every ironic-poetic embellishment Malick adds only serves to score cheap points of the fatuousness of the young killers and even their victims, whose deaths will seem less like coldblooded murder than inadvertent euthanasia—putting the poor human cattle out of their misery; that is, if they weren't too blind, deaf, and numb to recognize it as misery in the first place.

"Nebraska" deftly lifts the corn-fed picture of Holly and her twirling baton; then lights out for different territories. ("Laughing," the garage-dadaist band Pere Ubu's love-is-strange riff on the movie's Huck Finn/*Swiss Family Robinson* riverside idyll, sticks closer to the script of *Badlands*, both invoking and subverting its gum-snapping absurdism: "My baby said / If the Devil comes, we'll shoot him with a gun!") The film returns us to an instantly recognizable yesterday, that received version of America in the late 1950s, hemmed in by sterility and affectless kitsch on one side and white-trash clutter on the other, where Springsteen gets at something more inscrutable, a sense of human experience reverberating beneath the mythic and/or banal. He doesn't view "Nebraska" as a world apart, inhabited by little more than stiff-necked marionettes, monstrosities, and crash-test dummies whose heads are stuffed with true-romance and true-crime pulp: he strikes a fine balance between mundane reality and what Pauline Kael called "the glamour of delinquency," the 1950s' first inchoate wave of alienation given iconic status by Dean and Marlon Brando. In "Nebraska," those two strands of life (real and dream) intersect, commingle, fuse, as they do in photographer Robert Frank's road-trip classic *The Americans*.

Much as Flannery O'Connor's hard-nosed allegories did, Frank's storied 1958 book of black-and-white portraits (luncheonette waitresses, urban cowboys, black motorcyclists, transients, society matrons, elevator operators, gamblers, funeral attendees), roadscapes, and self-generating symbols (phantasmic flags, jukeboxes, bumper stickers, gas station signs, crosses) captured Springsteen's imagination. Whether by way of direct influence or innate affinity, *The Americans* provided a template for *Nebraska* (the album cover image was chosen for its similarity to Frank's *U.S. 285, New Mexico.*) This is especially true in how Springsteen here speaks to the idea of America as undiscovered country—vast tracts of recondite life tucked away inside of public images, conventional wisdom, official explanations. Jack Kerouac penned a metaphysical carny barker introduction to *The Americans*, extolling the way Frank "traveled on the road around practically forty-eight states in an old used car (on a Guggenheim Fellowship) and with the agility, mystery, genius, sadness and strange secrecy of a shadow photographed scenes that have never been seen before on film." But Keroauc's hype is on the mark. The plain, singular Americans Frank immortalized constituted the real Subterraneans, uncanny camera subjects belonging to a stranger and more unimagined nation than either the Eisenhower-sanctioned version or hipster-beatnik-intellectual one countenanced.

The odd stoic/empathic framework for "Nebraska"—its parched landscape and interior boundaries—can be seen in the unadorned details of Frank's photos: the shrouded body and chilly bystanders of *Car accident—U.S. 66 between Winslow and Flagstaff Arizona* (also calling to mind Springsteen's earlier "Wreck on the Highway"); the holy-ghostly *Crosses on scene of highway accident— U.S. 91, Idaho*; the stark-weathered farmhouses of *U.S. 30 between Ogalla and North Platte, Nebraska*; the dust-blown family in *Butte, Montana* straight out of Guthrie and *The Grapes of Wrath*; the plastic wreathes and bulky foot-tall white crosses on display in *Department Store—Lincoln Nebraska* with a sign reading, "Remember your loved ones 69¢." They're emblems of what endures, or what doesn't, premonitory souvenirs of a Nebraska Death Trip rolling across such plains like a shadow, casting its pall and moving on. After the dead are buried and guilty sentenced, though, that never-before-seen America of itinerant laborers, congenital outsiders, displaced personalities, and invisible lives are left as they were, absorbing those brief events as they would any natural disaster. Thus Springsteen's straightforward, impassive performance holds itself in suspension, defying its own gravity. There's that aw-shucks glint you could take a dozen ways, how he overinflates "ride" so letting the air out of "died" will sound onomatopoetic, the lip-smacking relish invested in "snaps my forehead back," the gallows mouth organ nearer to Morricone than Guthrie, the unforgiving refusal to rush either to judgment or to execution. Instead of speed, urgency, a neon moral, he gives us what *The Americans* offered, the tip-of-the-iceberg feel of people and time standing still. Waiting as the American pasttime: for a bus or a hearse, for the next man or woman through the door or last call, for the jig to be up or their ship to come in, for their steak sandwich or orange whip, for Christ to rise or the jukebox to bring forth "Smokestack Lightning."

Yet the memory of Charlie and Caril would be cast the whirlwind, dispersed almost before their separate trials concluded in 1958 (death for him, life for the by-then-fifteen-year-old Fugate, who when the verdict was read sobbed, "No! I'd rather be executed!"). Eclipsed, its place in public semiconsciousness would be taken by fresh crimes, trials, killer serials: bit and pieces of sensational Americana ranging from Perry Smith and Dick Hickok killing the Clutter family in Holcomb, Kansas (later immortalized by Truman Capote's *In Cold Blood* and the film featuring Robert Blake as Smith), Jerry Lee and Myra Gale, Chuck Berry's conviction on white-slavery charges (transporting a fourteen-year-old Indian girl from El Paso, Texas, to St. Louis for what the Mann Act designated "immoral purpose"), the stabbing death of Lana Turner's boyfriend Johnny Stompanato at the hands of her fifteen-year-old daughter Cheryl, Oswald and Ruby, Richard Speck, University of Texas Tower sniper Charles Whitman, Charlie Manson. By the time Springsteen wrote and recorded "Nebraska," *Badlands* was a faint memory, a half-forgotten movie that wouldn't really be revived until after Quentin Tarantino paid homage to it in the 1990s with his screenplays for *True Romance* and in particular *Natural Born Killers*. So Springsteen stepped into a vacuum, humming his executioner's song, shedding stock-in-trade romanticism and earnest concern like a snake-oil-skin suit. The song drew its power from his refusal to explain himself — that refusal silenced the reservoirs of tabloid noise, making the token justifications ("we had us some fun," "there's just a meanness in this world") as hollowed out as the narrator's conscience.

Nebraska the album was something else again: alternately (sometimes simultaneously) brilliant and bathetic footnotes to the title ballad, a string of morality plays, stern lessons in economic determinism, quavering parables, explanations grounded in the good salt of the Guthrie earth. Models of social conscientiousness and good intentions that spelled out everything "Nebraska" left twisting in midair, the likes of "Mansion on the Hill" posited a vast moat of inequity separating rich from poor (stuck on the outside looking in, like so many winsome Dickensian lawn urchins) as an unreal estate development owned and operated by the nascent Reagan administration. The whole scenario was a reassuringly morose throwback to the Great Depression, with the unnamed but omnipresent Reagan presiding over wrack and ruin like a Grand Imperial Wizard of Oz, part Hoover sweeper and part anti-FDR. It was a landscape of defeat, gloom, and impending catastrophe —

"Them wheat prices kept on droppin' till it was like we were gettin' robbed"; "I got debts no honest man can pay"; "Deliver me from nowhere"—but mainly presented as cut and dried, symmetrically boxed in. The dead dog along the side of the road in "Reason to Believe" had about as much chance of making a run for it as the doleful family locked inside "Used Cars," windows rolled up, their every petty humiliation affixed like a bumper sticker or a "Kick me" sign.

"Atlantic City" Greyhound-bused you right out of "Nebraska" and back to Springsteen's familiar Jersey stamping ground: night and the city, small-time dreamers, chorus hooks, mandolins under the boardwalk, irresistible Late Show melodrama ("Maybe everything that dies some day comes back"—The Eternal Rerun). There was the tragic "Highway Patrolman," a hushed dance of death between blood ties and doing the right thing, fate made synonymous with social dislocation. "Johnny 99" offered up extenuating circumstances, copping a rollicking folkabilly plea: "Your honor I do believe I would be better off dead." "Open All Night" pursued Chuck Berry's "You Can't Catch Me," though it couldn't touch his élan or souped-up language. "State Trooper" put the same Berry echoes into Springsteen's earlier "Stolen Car," headed straight into the "wee wee hours" of "Nebraska," voice and solitary electric guitar poised to fall off the edge of the world. ("Mister State Trooper, please don't stop me.") "My Father's House" was decked out in formal folk regalia, pious and biblical as a headstone: "Where our sins lie unatoned."

"You see, you see the symbolism of it. . . . It teaches a lesson, a moral lesson, it has social significance. . . ." That's the Bruce Springsteen of 1941 talking, not Woody Guthrie, not even a singer at all but the fictitious film director John Lloyd Sullivan (played by Joel McCrea as a half-baked exemplar, half naïf-savant, and half-well-intentioned bonehead) in Preston Sturges's curb-crawling "land yacht" of a motion picture *Sullivan's Travels.* You know the archetypically all-American story: fresh off a statement picture about "Capital and Labor destroy[ing] each other," hotshot director Sullivan wants to make a Capra-cum-*Grapes-of-Wrath* magnum opus, "a true canvas of the suffering of humanity" called *O Brother, Where Art Thou?* When the studio bosses impugn the strapping $4,000-a-week golden boy's experience in the area of misery and deprivation — "What do you know about hard luck?" — he resolves to embark on a sociological research expedition into the lower depths, posing as a derelict. Picking up the most glamorous bummoll in the history of Western Civilization (Veronica Lake, who makes a swell tough-sweet cynic and in hobo drag suggests a disturbingly fetching fourteen-year-old boy), they ride the rails ("You're like one of those knights of old who used to ride around looking for trouble," she laughs), rub elbows and other parts with the dispossessed, getting a lice-size dose of the plight of the poor.

Sullivan's Travels takes in screwball and slapstick comedy, mock and poetic realism, freewheeling absurdity, monochrome romanticism, satire of the Chaplinesque, and a coda of gooey rationalization so nightmarishly uplifting it all but obliterates questions of sincerity or self-parody. Like Sturges and his double Sully, Springsteen wrestled with what it meant to be a popular artist in America, with a nagging sense of obligation and unworthiness. *Nebraska* is in parts Springsteen's *O Brother, Where Art Thou?* (most literal-mindedly in the fraternal tragedy of "Highway Patrolman" but also in "Used Cars" and "Mansion on the Hill") and in other places, it's *Sullivan's Travels* with gee-tar and harmonica accompaniment: "Johnny 99" gives an antic-chaotic Sturges treatment to the grim proceedings ("Fist fight broke out in the courtroom they had to drag Johnny's girl away"), lacking only Eddie Bracken as the hero, Betty Hutton as his gal, William Demarest as Judge Mean John Brown, and a last-minute pardon. The gum-snapping, wise-cracking local color of "Open All Night" ("I met Wanda when she was employed behind the counter of the Route 60 Bob's Big Boy"), the touches of stir-craziness to "State Trooper," and the flyaway ironies of "Reason to Believe" can take their place alongside Sullivan's travails. While mass murder may have been outside Sturges's purview, the trials of Starkweather and Fugate supplied plenty of material worthy of *The Miracle at Morgan's Creek*'s octuplet-mania, including the prosecutor telling the jury: "Even fourteen-year-old girls must realize they cannot go on eight-day murder sprees."

Manny Farber (writing with W. S. Poster) pinpointed Sturges's moral versus aesthetic quandry, with well-meaning but wrong-headed admirers like René Clair

> suggesting . . . that Sturges would be considerably improved if he annihilated himself. Similarly, Sigfried Kracauer has scolded him for not being the consistent, socially-minded satirist of the rich, defender of the poor, and portrayer of the evils of modern life. . . . The more popular critics have condemned Sturges for not liking America enough; the advanced critics for liking it too much. He has also been accused of espousing a snob point of view and sentimentally favoring the common man.

This line of thought is taken up later:

> His pictures at no time evince the slightest interest on his part as to the truth or falsity of his direct representation of society. His neat, contrived plots are unimportant per se and developed chiefly to provide

him with the kind of movements and appearances
he wants, with crowds of queer, animated individuals, with juxtapositions of unusual actions and faces.
These are then organized, as items are in any art
that does not boil down to mere sociology, to evoke
feelings about society and life which cannot be reduced to doctrine or judged by flea-hopping from
the work of art to society in the manner of someone
checking a portrait against the original.

With *Nebraska*, Springsteen turns Sturges's world outside in, in-
verting the ratio of tragedy to comedy, speed and multiplicity to
stasis and abandonment (fabled car songs like "Thunder Road" and
"Born to Run" give way to born to lose and the road to nowhere),
embracing introspection with pensive ardor, working hard to do
social justice to his characters, empathizing like an unsullied-by-
commerce Sully. At the same time, "Nebraska" itself succeeds because it is far more mis- than philanthropic, establishing a locale
where he can annihilate his "consistent, socially-minded" persona
and make music irreducible to doctrine or social efficacy, where
he can be autonomous in spite of himself.

Sullivan's Travels concludes with a kneejerk epiphany that suggests "Reason to Believe" after an overdose of laughing gas. Sully
having successfully concluded his experiment, intact and thinking
himself much the wiser, decides to show his gratitude to the down-
trodden by passing out cash to the homeless. One of the winos rolls
him for his bankroll, knocks him unconscious, and steals his
clothes and identification. Sullivan awakes as an amnesiac, gets into
a scuffle with a railroad bull, and brains the goon with a fistful of
rock. Still befuddled, he's taken before a judge and without so
much as a how'd-ya-due process is sentenced to six years on a chain

gang. Meantime, the thief has been run over by a train, leaving behind nothing but a basket of remains and the director's I.D. By the time the real Sullivan comes to his senses, no one will believe his cockeyed story: the brute Captain locks him in the sweat box for reading his own obituary. ("What do you think this is, a vaudeville show?") But one Sunday the prisoners are taken to a Negro church, where the (white) convicts are led to the pews in shackles, welcomed by the proper, dignified, careworn black faces of the congregation singing "Go Down, Moses" ("Let my people go"—one of the strangest, most didactic-paradoxic displays of racial solidarity-cum-irony ever devised). Together, they watch the raucous, early-Disney cartoon antics of *Playful Pluto,* and everyone from the convicts and the congregation to the preacher, the warder, and finally even the stuck-up Sullivan himself dissolves in convulsive hilarity.

Getting his picture in the paper by confessing to Sullivan's murder, he's recognized and sprung to resume his old life. Though not to make *O Brother, Where Art Thou?* (cries a now-crestfallen studio flack: "But it's had more publicity than the Johnstown flood!"). Sullivan has seen the light and wants to make a comedy, after all, because he's learned the moral lesson that laughter is the best medicine: "Didja know it's all some people have. It's not much but it's better than nothing. . . ." What follows is a montage of delirious laughter, the toothless faces of the convicts (does that mean the movie audience being invited to join in grateful merriment is also composed of captives, prisoners who have nothing but the chains that bind them together?) fading into those of ordinary folk, one momentarily happy family of man united by the need to escape the pain of life. This rationale for escapism may be facile and unctuous, especially presented via a burst of mechanically engineered catharsis, but hysteria notwithstanding, Sturges was right about one thing: there are masses of people who truly have lives to escape from, and they don't necessarily appreciate being lectured about facing "harsh reality" by "rich people and theorists, who are usually rich people."

Mythologizing poverty and desperation—giving it an ennobling, sentimental, quasi-heroic aura—isn't far from "the caricaturing of the poor and needy." The appeal of *The Grapes of Wrath*, first as John Steinbeck's widely hailed novel of 1939 and then as John Ford's Big Statement Film of 1940, was in the way it mixed up realism, poetry, and gross hokum. Woody Guthrie based his song "Tom Joad" on the movie ("best cussed pitcher I ever seen"), but the novel feels like a massive literary elaboration of Guthrie's music, while the movie is a distillation of his great theme—namely, the displacement of Dust Bowl Okie and Arkie sharecroppers by nature and capital alike, indomitable migrant workers seeking the promised land in California but finding more exploitation and hardship. In *The Grapes of Wrath*, this breeds its own form of mystical socialism, a pantheistic blend of earth worship, Bible school Scripture, and union organizing: individuals as components of "the one big soul that belongs to everybody." As Tom Joad, an ordinary fellow driven to violence and flight by a hard, unjust country, Henry Fonda (fresh from playing *Young Mr. Lincoln* in another rousing cracker-barrel John Ford film) made a stalwart cynic turned idealist. His parting words to Ma reverberate through generations of American social romantics, from Guthrie to Sullivan to Springsteen: "I'll be all around in the dark. I'll be everywhere, wherever you can look. Wherever there's a fight so hungry people can eat, I'll be there. Wherever there's a cop beatin' up a guy, I'll be there. I'll be in the way guys yell when they're mad. I'll be in the way kids laugh when they're hungry and they know supper's ready. And when the people are eatin' the stuff they raise and livin' in the houses they build, I'll be there too."

Dogged belief runs through the story like a river: convoluted in Steinbeck, persuasively simplified in Ford and Guthrie. Springsteen picks up that thread along the riverside of "Reason to Believe," in the voice of an apostate who still has the preacher's calling— even in the face of the absurd, the great river of being runs off into the sea of souls. His old trust in testimonials like "I believe in the faith that can save me" and "Mister, I believe in a Promised Land" isn't gone, just dispersed. He tells a joke, or maybe a parable. Man's standing over a dead dog in a ditch. He pokes it with a stick, "Like if he stood there long enough that dog'd get up and run." Second man is up the road a piece, sort of bemused by the ridiculous sight, chuckling at the poor fool. He tells himself he knows better than that; he wouldn't need to poke a dog to know it wasn't going to rise again. Now a sedan pulls up, and a young fella jumps out, surveying the whole tableaux like he'd found the place he'd been looking for. He says something to the girl in the passenger seat, and then he calls to the first guy. Man looks up from the ditch, and the shotgun blast pitches him right on top of the dog. Second one still has a "kinda puzzled" smirk on his face when the next shot takes the top of his forehead clean off. That's the funny, chilly thing about "Nebraska": so devoid of insulation and affect and belief as to sound un-American, the ballad of a sub-Misfit whose life is so arbitrary and acts so capricious as to imply a tightlipped comedy spilling innocent blood on the laugh tracks.

[2004]

13

Everybody

Knows

This

Is

Nowhere

The Uneasy Ride of Rock

and the New Hollywood

Remember all the movies, Terry,
        we'd go see
Tryin' to learn how to walk like the
        heroes we thought we had to be.

—BRUCE SPRINGSTEEN,
        "Backstreets," 1975

FROM ITS BEGINNING, Martin
Scorsese's 1973 *Mean Streets* is the most
seductive union of movies and rock imaginable: a prowling, claustrophobic fever dream
where the images and music are locked in an
interpenetrating embrace, each intensifying,
elaborating, and undermining the meanings of

the other. We first see Harvey Keitel's Charlie abruptly waking from a nightmare—what looks like nightly ritual, a subconscious form of penance. But the nightmare stays with him, clinging like a caul. Going to the darkened mirror, the reflection he sees there could be his double looking back at him from the confessional or the grave: a stillborn twin. Charlie returns to the empty bed, and his head falls to the pillow in trancelike slow motion. The suspended drumbeats of a song seem to come from his pounding chest rather than the soundtrack. Time stands still, and then, as the wave of yearning that is "Be My Baby" washes over the screen, turns back on itself. The Ronettes song, produced in 1963 by Phil Spector ("a one-man millennium," as Nik Cohn tenderly described him), distilled young love into a utopia of self-fulfilling desire, where to wish for something is to make it so. As embodied by the teenage Veronica Bennett's aching soul-kiss of a voice, it's the reflection of everything Charlie's self-cancelling life is not.

As the opening titles roll, "Be My Baby" orchestrates the home movies we see projected above the neatly lettered credits, like a guilt-ridden Catholic version of Kenneth Anger's *Scorpio Rising*. Its aria of longing sucks the viewer into Charlie's penny-ante world of duty and crime: an upwardly mobile lowlife, he's an altar boy in the Mafia's hierarchy of corruption. "I'll make you so proud of me," the future Mrs. Spector sings, Ronnie's unsteady teenage voice bursting with so much passion it infuses the 8mm memories on screen with a radioactive intimacy. At the same time, we feel a suffocating undercurrent as Spector's "wall of sound" closes in, breathless grandeur taken to the breaking point, loss covertly written into the promise of total gratification. (Spector's music presents itself as an all-encompassing conspiracy against silence.) In Hal Blaine's double-edged drumming—the most fated beat anyone in rock has found—there's both tremendous exhilaration and terrible finality. It's the cadence of a lover's plea and a priest giving last rites rolled into one. Behind the tenderness of "Be My Baby" lies the inexorable pull of dread, and that is the bittersweet, doubt-haunted rhythm *Mean Streets* moves to—the steady pulse of impending chaos, the rapt trance of waiting damnation.

Mean Streets was the first movie narrative to truly integrate rock into a dramatic *sensibility*, transfiguring the blasphemous, iconographic abstractions of *Scorpio Rising* (where Anger's cheeky, experimental homoerotics simultaneously bordered on camp and porn) into a new form of heightened, pop-operatic naturalism. Scorsese reached across several eras of rock to mix the music of the Ronettes, Derek and the Dominos, the Marvelettes, the Miracles, Johnny Ace, and the Rolling Stones together to map those streets, much as Bruce Springsteen's 1973 album *The Wild, the Innocent, and the E-Street Shuffle* fused a similar range of styles with echoes of the same post-Brando bravado. The music seemed to grow out of the story, and vice versa, even if Scorsese's real inspirations for the characters and milieu came from the pre-Spector/Motown/Beatles era, the Little Italy where Dion and the Belmonts' doowop ruled supreme. He turned the manic smile of the Marvelettes' "Please Mr. Postman" inside out by scoring a wild, Keystone Thugs brawl to it in real time, as a kind of slapstick cinema verité. (Putting a lithe, high-kicking Robert De Niro on a pool table, Scorsese turned him into a hoodlum Iggy Stooge: the first punk Rockette.) The doomsday purr of "Jumpin' Jack Flash" served as a Greek chorus for a barroom Hades, while the Russian-roulette romance of the late Johnny Ace's "Pledging My Love" and the crazed jive of "Mickey's Monkey" by Smokey Robinson's Miracles foreshadowed looming disaster. But "Be My Baby" established the tone of what was to come—graffiti scrawled in the blood from Charlie's wet dream, the one he recounts to his mortified girlfriend where he ejaculates it all over the place. Charlie's a real piece of repressed work, as tortured by intimations of heaven as by those of hell.

Phil Spector had been the first rock auteur, conceiving his productions as three-minute epics. He worked in aural CinemaScope, blowing teenage home movies up into wide-screen passion plays. Early hits like "To Know Him Is to Love Him" and "Spanish Harlem," the Crystals' "Uptown," the scandalous "He Hit Me (It Felt Like a Kiss)" and "He's a Rebel" were nothing less than Spector's version of *West Side Story*. Only he stripped away the Broadway respectability, the virtuous social conscience, all the corny Hollywood bromides, and went for something wilder and more elusive: the place where fantasy dissolves all the barriers reality throws in its way. Paying homage to Spector and the fabulous Veronica (a black Lolita in bouffant hair and a miniskirt), Scorsese was also alluding to something cinema hadn't really acknowledged: the feeling that rock had replaced Hollywood as the primary source of America's most resonant, deeply felt representations of itself. *Mean Streets* used rock songs themselves as its jumping-off point, an entrance into an undiscovered country of funk. Its music defined a terrain of defiance and repression, freedom and betrayal: a secret cinema playing inside Scorsese's characters. The death dance of Keitel's Charlie and Robert De Niro's punk prankster Johnny Boy found the tragic dimension latent in Spector's pop hallucinations, in the Miracles' and the Stones' jigsaw cool, in the sign language of unattainable grace and carnal pleasures that only exacerbate the pain of eternal suffering.

Scorsese's vision was of what had been left out of American movies in the wake of rock, the upheaval Hollywood hadn't come to terms with: the new synthesis of the mythic and the quotidian ushered in, in the wake of Elvis Presley and Spector, the new style of poetic license fashioned by Bob Dylan and the Rolling Stones. The hybrid quality of *Mean Streets* drew on neorealism and film noir (on each as a version of the other) as well as rock, and it layered Godard-Bresson aftereffects in between the pop juice but ultimately had more in common with *Let It Bleed* than Elia Kazan (let alone *The Godfather*). Much as the Rolling Stones drew on blues, soul, and early rock to invent a language of pop rebellion that spoke directly to American experiences and fantasies (to America's penchant for experiencing its fantasies as revelation), Scorsese filtered new European cinema through a uniquely American perspective. Here, reinventing film in terms of rock, he was closest of all to Springsteen, who at the same time was reimagining rock in terms of Kazan, James Dean, and Marlon Brando. In Springsteen's thrilling, poignantly fetishistic cosmology, it was as if *West Side Story* had mutated into a heterosexual *Scorpio Rising*: "Backstreets" itself was a virtual answer record to Scorsese. It merged Keitel's Charlie with Steiger's *On the Waterfront* role, and Brando's Terry donned De Niro's delinquent clothes, ghosts moving through the back streets of Bob Dylan's "Like a Rolling Stone" as it might have sounded with Spector producing.

From the fifties on, Hollywood had always kept rock at arm's length even as it sought to jump on the bandwagon: it tried to cash in on the youth-cult explosion while muffling it with the wet blanket of show-business-as-usual. *The Girl Can't Help It* (1956) turned rock into baggy-pants burlesque — inspired burlesque, true, but Little Richard's monumental racial-sexual weirdness was reduced to novelty-act status, effaced by Edmund O'Brian's jowls and Jayne Mansfield's breasts. Later, youth revolt would be given the sociological-sensational treatment epitomized by Stanley Kramer's 1970 *R.P.M.* (campus "revolution" effaced by Anthony Quinn's jowls and Ann-Margret's breasts: Hollywood's idea of progress). The entertainment industry was determined to assimilate rock if it couldn't replace it, so it exploited the latest craze even as it sought to replace it or give it a wholesome Pat Boone overhaul. Thus a new genre was born, "the Elvis movie," which epitomized Hollywood's contempt for rock. Early on, with the casually insolent *Jailhouse Rock* (1957), it seemed like Presley might become the natural successor to Dean or Brando or Mitchum—that his rockabilly menace and carnality could be translated to film, and he might be able to bring the wild unseen side of America to the movies. Yet for all his swagger in *Jailhouse Rock*, Presley's line readings will suddenly go flat, his expression blanking out, the lithe body growing wooden and unsure of itself. Conviction deserts him, his sneer replaced by the obliging death mask he would wear through countless travesties to come: almost presaging the glad-handing self-sabotage of *Mean Streets'* Charlie (albeit unintentionally, as a perverse form of careerism).

There would be no *Thunder Road* for Elvis: the history of rock in Hollywood is mostly a history of travesty, or a history of what might have been. In the fifties, an icon gap had opened up in American movies. *The Wild One* and *Rebel Without a Cause* anticipated youth's new archetypes, but within a sonic vacuum. Brando's poly-Orpheus scorn and Dean's charismatic anguish seemed anomalous, harbingers strangely cut off from the upheavals they heralded. But as rock took over and elaborated their gestures, the movies lagged behind, attempting to smooth the cracks in the facade. Hollywood offered Rock Hudson and Tony Curtis—a sexless sex symbol and a proletarian pin-up, old stereotypes upholstered in rugged, durable plastic. There's no better illustration of the mentality at work here than *Rio Bravo*, which served up emasculated would-be rocker Ricky Nelson as a sop "to the kids" (he just about oozed sincerity and clean living) but made him comically subordinate to the real men in the picture. Dean Martin embodied the industry's prevailing notion of entertainment: so casual and agreeable he makes indifference signify as the height of show business mastery. (His assured Vegas-cowboy guise — the hipsterism of the unhip — is precisely what Elvis will emulate so disastrously in dozens of films.) And standing for manhood itself, none other than John Wayne — that most enduring icon of the America that wished to be purged of rock and rebellion alike.

Rio Bravo's audience is meant to identify with the likes of Martin and Wayne: they represent what teens are supposed to embrace once the young outgrow rock and become productive members of society. The story goes that Nelson endured a classic Hollywood baptism at the hands of Martin and Wayne, who threw the pretty boy into a heap of steer manure on his eighteenth birthday. This is the primal scene Elvis will be asked to symbolically reenact in one film after another, each more tedious than the one before, drowning in an excremental boredom that lent new meaning to the phrase "up shit creek." But to see what was truly absent here, and what was really at stake, imagine an alternate movie universe where instead of *G.I. Blues,* he had been cast opposite Sinatra in *The Manchurian Candidate.* Here is a film that captured the secret, encrypted side of Presleyan myth: the shellshocked, brainwashed soldier-assassin as a version of the post-army Elvis, even as the belief rock 'n' roll was a Communist plot would fit snugly into the movie's conspiratorial milieu. And surely Angela Lansbury's ruthless character suggests a deliciously malign composite of Presley's manager Colonel Tom Parker and his adored mother Gladys — totalitarian love, a military-industrial Oedipus complex. Operating in the shadow of Sinatra, this Manchurian Elvis could have given us a taste of the real one's tangled double agency, at once pawn and king, culture hero and dupe, emblem of liberation and of the all-

American craving to just follow orders. (Like an America getting ready to declare war on itself, there was no way to tell which side Elvis was really on.) From there it isn't hard to see him restored to his feral, greasy Memphis self, riding off into *A Fistful of Dollars* or playing the noble astronaut-savage in *Planet of the Apes*, finally apotheosizing his career in the seventies with the role of a washed-up lifetime — *Fat City*.

Coinciding with the emergence of rock, a quality of suffocating dislocation entered the movies: by turns borderline hysterical (Douglas Sirk) and sanctimonious (Stanley Kramer), sometimes both at once *(East of Eden)*, it gave off the hothouse air of a society on the verge of a nervous breakdown, steeped in denial and repression. Yet Kramer's terminally well-meaning 1958 *The Defiant Ones* is oblivious to the fact that its story was already being acted out to far more compelling effect by Elvis and Chuck Berry. Their odyssey across the racial barriers of American culture — this Huck-and-Jim pair bound together in the public imagination by nothing more than a shared desire to escape the shackles of their birth — was no plea for brotherhood, equality, "a better world." (Understood as the brotherhood of conformists, the equality of the assembly line, a world of drones.) "Jailhouse Rock" and Berry's "The Promised Land" drew on the divisive polarities of American life and the wish to smash through them: integration's secret promise and threat was not only to make the country finally live up to its professed ideals, but to replace a slave world with a free one. For their trouble and defiance, as a couple entirely inadvertent civil rights workers, each earned stiff sentences: Berry's to be served in a real jailhouse and Presley's in the barely metaphorical one of *Kissin' Cousins, Spinout,* and *Clambake.*

Hollywood's resistance to this wayward new strain of mass culture often took the form of vague, self-conflicted anxiety. In the 1958 *A*

Face in the Crowd, a folksinger rises to rabble-rousing prominence as a hybrid of Elvis and Joe McCarthy. The story is played straight as a grimly cautionary fable; even its pulpy undercurrent of panic is encrusted in a vertiginous respectability. Ten years later, A.I.P.'s *Wild in the Streets* will do away with all that sanctimony and turn the spectre of bubblegum fascism into acidhead comedy. There the teen-idol demagogue becomes president, imposes martial law, sends everyone over thirty to concentration camps, all as prophesied in the irresistible rise of the president's hit single up the charts: "The Shape of Things to Come." (One might as easily have substituted a garage-band version of the contemporaneous "Springtime for Hitler.") But located between these poles of self-important adult melodrama and trashy youth-exploitation fodder, *The Manchurian Candidate* treated politics as pop culture and paranoid fantasy as the shape of politics to come; it leapfrogged right over the prevailing American archetypes (Elvis, JFK) to anticipate the real and symbolic violence that will befall them (Kennedy's assassination, Elvis's disintegration). It found a knowing, implacable tone for such material, a tightrope between absurdist humor, bitter put-on, and sardonic dread—the tone Bob Dylan will make his own on his mid-sixties records. *The Manchurian Candidate* prefigured the carnivalesque undertow of Dylan's "Ballad of a Thin Man," with its sneering, pitiless refrain: "And you know something is happening / But you don't know what it is / Do you, Mr. Jones?" It offers a clue to Mr. Jones's allusive origin as well, unobtrusively tucked away inside George Axelrod's screenplay, where Axelrod sets the garden club brainwashing scene like this: "*Marco sits on the end of the line at stage right, in the Mr. Bones position (as in an old time minstrel show).*" Soon lots of people would feel like Marco, like they, too, had assumed the Mr. Bones—or Jones—position in some great, newfangled mass-media minstrel show.

*   *   *

WHILE IT'S BEEN suggested that the phenomenal rise of the Beatles in America amounted to a palliative for the first Kennedy assassination, A *Hard Day's Night* offers more than reason enough in itself. The first rock movie to display a sensibility equal to the music itself had to be British, for the Beatles and director Richard Lester were in a position to bypass the Hollywood tendency to equate pop with pap. Borrowing from the freewheeling innovations of *À bout de souffle* and *Bande à part*, A *Hard Day's Night* epitomized a playfully irreverent style (actually, its wit and quicksilver nonsense are a little ahead of the music — the Beatles' songs will never quite catch up with the jump-cutting, wisecracking bliss presented here) that captured the joy and irony of pop life while evoking their evanescence. What Lester took from Godard was offhand technique and speed, a means of expressing the rhythms of an unfolding epoch — one composed of fleeting moments, fragments of possibility that vanished almost before their existence was registered.

It was a style that was as easy to imitate as its core sensibility was elusive. Within a year, *Help!* showed Lester's mod devices had already become part of the accepted commercial lexicon; "Can't Buy Me Love" had opened the door for the marketing revolution that would culminate in MTV. It also revealed that much of what seemed so daring and original in the Beatles' personalities harked back to the knockabout, self-satirizing Hope-Crosby *Road* pictures. Only *Help!* was a more of a "Road to Nowheresville" — overdetermined, underinspired, a lot of gesticulation substituting for any sense of purpose, an exercise in sped-up ennui. In America, that road led directly to the cloned-for-TV series *The Monkees*, which from 1966 to 1968 shamelessly churned out frantic sweatshop knockoffs of the Lester/Beatle formula. But there was a weird New Hollywood twist to the Monkees' tale: they would stumble on to make the flop movie *Head*, whose chief distinction (apart from that false-advertising title) was as a stepping stone in the careers of its screenwriters, Jack Nicholson and Bob Rafelson (with Rafelson making his directorial debut there). Going from the counterculture kitsch of *Head* to the heavy-duty alienation of *Five Easy Pieces*, Nicholson and Rafelson enacted their own artwardly-mobile allegory: they raised themselves up from a chintzy little basement of hell to bigger and barer realist circles.

Belatedly inaugurating the "New Hollywood" in 1967, *Bonnie and Clyde* took just the elements of *À bout de souffle* et al. Lester had omitted from a *A Hard Day's Night*: the mixed emotions of random violence, the romance of sudden death. Set in the Depression, with charmingly dated and/or timeless bluegrass music on the soundtrack, its attitudes were nonetheless pure sixties. Its killers were depicted as instant pop stars, groovy outlaws living — and perishing — beyond the pale of law-abiding society. Their estrangement and faintly ridiculous fatalism gave off a tenderly erotic glow: the dying light of the beautiful — and impotent — damned. Presented in tragicomic pop terms, Bonnie Parker and Clyde Barrow were natural precursors of the rock-stars-as-outlaws (and as casualties-of-war) mythology that sprang up around Jim Morrison and Janis Joplin, Jimi Hendrix and Brian Jones. *Bonnie and Clyde* provoked the same alarm in the Establishment press the Rolling Stones did: "We rob banks" answered in advance Mick Jagger's mocking, "What can a poor boy do?" The movie's amorality and violence seemed like an incitement, one all the more unnerving for being so unspecified. It made antisocial behavior seem like fun and spasmodic death look like romantic fulfillment. The film conveyed a sense that a bit of fun—some laughter at the expense of social conventions, some affront to upright values—might at any second erupt into gunplay, blood in the streets, an epidemic of anarchy. The bullet-riddled past of *Bonnie and Clyde* seemed to blaze a trail into the future, as though in the mythic profiles of its stars one could already see the chalk outlines of Baader and Meinhof.

Those dumb rednecks who blow away Billy and Captain America at the end of *Easy Rider* are the descendants of the posse that finally guns down Bonnie and Clyde in Arthur Penn's film. *Easy Rider* is the counterculture's breakthrough movie: the rock soundtrack was as integral to it as the dialogue and images those songs accompanied (maybe more so). The fact that the movie (or the music) isn't much good is beside the point: everything that's desultory, crude, and obvious about *Easy Rider* merely serves to authenticate it as the genuine article. Stoned on their own innocence, its hippie-martyrs are consumed with nostalgia for paradise lost. "We blew it, man," mourns Peter Fonda's stoic Captain America shortly before he's killed—the bikers are sacrificial lambs taking gleaming custom motorcycles to the slaughter. Yet *Easy Rider*'s retrospective present appears far more remote than *Bonnie and Clyde*'s flippant Depression. Fonda, Dennis Hopper, and Jack Nicholson are served up on a hash-house platter, reefer-toking refugees from the social-injustice movies of the thirties, their persecution used sentimentally to induce audience sympathy.

"This used to be a hell of a good country," sighs Nicholson not long before *he* is beaten to death by some southern goons. (In the movie, the young are viewed with a benign, nonjudgmental gaze, but the good-old-boy yahoos are held up as examples of innate, subhuman viciousness.) *Easy Rider* deservedly made Nicholson a star, and he articulates the movie's appeal when George drawls to Billy and the Captain, "They're not scared ah you. They scared of what you represent to 'em. . . . What you represent to them is freedom." The characters in the movie are abstractions, bucolic conventions in new costumes: psychedelic zen outlaws, spaced-out cowhands (cowheads?) chasing after the ghost of the Old West / Native America, all to the anthemic tune of Steppenwolf's "Born to Be Wild."

Many years later, Albert Brooks will parody this sequence in *Lost in America*: the elephantine motor home heading "out on the highway" to the sound of Steppenwolf's as-lumbering-as-ever "heavy-metal thunder." But the true punch line comes when the leviathan is eventually pulled over by a Terminator-like motorcycle cop who wears the glint of fascism like a second badge. Told by the occupants they're trying to drop out in emulation of *Easy Rider*, that death's-head face suddenly breaks into a delighted grin. "That's my favorite movie of all time," he gushes, caught up in the brotherhood of mutual identification. Here on an empty blacktop, lost in the America of indivisible simulation, an ad executive and a cop bond on the basis of a shared chimera. Each has "based his life on *Easy Rider*": on representations of freedom that are already frozen into empty peace symbols. The incongruous pair are what the dope-dealing bikers might have become if they'd survived into middle age ("Dennis Hopper wouldn't give Peter Fonda a ticket, would he?"). It turns out the real destination of the bikers must have been the grateful funeral of *The Big Chill*—with Hopper and Fonda serving as their own pallbearers.

The music carries *Easy Rider*, gives its long travelogue shots and staged cinema verité scenes a semblance of form. When Jimi Hendrix's snaking "If 6 Was 9" appears on the soundtrack, the cruising images take on the feel of a passage through a real time and place. But more typical are the Fraternity of Man and the Electric Prunes numbers—dreary, trite relics of erstwhile hipness (in its jocular and cosmic modes, respectively). Or else the Band's "The Weight," dragged down by the albatross of lugubrious significance. But the key to the movie is the Byrds' "Wasn't Born to Follow," which director Hopper likes so much he reprises the sucker. A compendium of imitation Dylanisms and pleasantly ludicrous psychedelia, it's a marvel of blank self-righteousness. "In the end she will surely know I wasn't born to follow," bleats singer Roger McGuinn: another wee lamb lost in a big, bad country, on his holy-rolling way to a date with the dog food factory.

"Wasn't Born to Follow" was written by Gerry Goffin and Carole King, a team who had provided songs for Phil Spector as well as the Monkees. But when Spector himself turns up at the beginning of the film, wordlessly playing the dealers' dandified ferret of a buyer, it's something more than an inside joke of a cameo. For just an instant, there's a glimpse of the road not taken in *Easy Rider*. Perhaps something more along the lines of *Scorpio Rising* or Bruce Conner—moving to the rhythms of a secret society, a beat that could place the drug-dealing bikers' saga in ironic relief. Spector was an envoy from a pop world light years removed from hippie passivity (which by embracing both dope and Jesus got a double dose of mass-consumed opiates). His insistence on excess as the measure of all things doesn't connect with Peter Fonda's beatific space cowboy but rather with the majestic dimensions (and dementia) of Henry Fonda's brutalist killer in *Once Upon a Time in the West* or Jane Fonda's marvelously intrepid sex machine in *Barbarella*. European invocations of American iconography, Leone's grandiose meditation on the gunfighter myth and Vadim's homage to sci-fi cheesecake would ring bizarrely illuminating changes on their source material: Leone photographing his actors in wide-screen close-up to resemble Monument Valley rock formations come to life, while Jane Fonda's demure orgiast could have been the futuristic white sister to Spector's teen Valkyries the Crystals and Ronettes.

Writing of Creedence Clearwater Revival's 1969 *Green River*, Greil Marcus might have been describing a Leone version of *Easy Rider* by way of Mark Twain: "Stuck in the suburbs of San Francisco and dreaming of the Mississippi, John Fogerty crafted a timeless vision of America: a white boy (Fogerty) and a black man (Fogerty's heroes: Howlin' Wolf, Little Richard) sharing a raft, drifting south, finding friendship, defeat, fear, and salvation." There was everything Hooper and company missed, ignored, or trivialized—the paradoxes of race and the uneasy allure of a country where freedom and violence were chronically intertwined. "In other words," Marcus wrote of this music, "Elvis's Sun singles, without their innocence." Leone did much the same with John Ford's westerns, stripping them down to skeletal archetypes. But he draped his walking skulls in the baggage of extremity, brute force, and empty appetite, which Leone then proceeded to poeticize, giving a human face (of beauty at least) to that death wish.

In songs like "Tombstone Shadow," "Bad Moon Rising," "Effigy," "Graveyard Train," "Don't Look Now," "Sinister Purpose," "Run Through the Jungle," "Commotion," and "Who'll Stop the Rain," Creedence Clearwater Revival showed an America pinned down by its own crossfire. "Caught inside the fable," Fogerty sang, where assassination merged with folklore, good times were shot through with intimations of Judgment Day. That fable was history ("Once upon a time in America . . ." every song might easily have begun). "The true picture of the past flits by," Walter Benjamin had once declared, its images flashing out of the darkness in the cinema of time. "The tradition of the oppressed teaches us," he noted with patient irony, "that the 'state of emergency' in which we live is not the exception but the rule." Such was the storm blowing through "Who'll Stop the Rain" (a promised future "wrapped in golden chains"), the fire that spreads outward from "Effigy" to consume the countryside.

Creedence's music instinctively cast its lot with the tradition of class rather than youth conflict, the tumult of collective forces not the Messianic aura of idols. In "Who'll Stop the Rain," the messianic makes itself felt through absence, in the lack of any savior to redeem the era's state of emergency. Invoking memory as a means of grasping the times, Creedence's sound was the avatar of Bruce Springsteen's allusive, fatalist populism: using the mnemonic power of the blues and country and early rock to place the present in the context of eternal struggle, the cyclical nature of bad-moon-risings.

That context might be said to stand for all the movies that will not be made in the wake of *Easy Rider*. As the film's final helicopter shot takes its leave of Billy and Captain America, they've conveniently died for their country's sins. But on closer inspection, the imaginary cross they're hoisted upon looks suspiciously like part of the Hollywood Sign. Their celluloid martyrdom has less in common with the "Bad Moon Rising" over CCR's *Green River* than the buddy-buddy constellation in the box-office sky of 1969. Like those other phony outlaws in *Butch Cassidy and the Sundance Kid*, their fate dovetailed with *Midnight Cowboy's* down-and-out sentimentality, lending Joe Buck / Sundance / Captain America and Ratso Rizzo / Butch / Billy a wholly specious, artificially inseminated humanity. (*Midnight Cowboy's* hustlers and rustlers were a far cry indeed from the polymorphous perversity of Andy Warhol, Lou Reed, and the Velvet Underground—Russ Meyer's ludicrous rock-themed breast-fest *Beyond the Valley of the Dolls* at least recognized the camp value of its sexual histrionics.) It's easy to forget that Butch and Ratso's sagas spawned much bigger hit songs than

Easy Rider: the insidious treacle of B. J. Thomas's "Raindrops Keep Fallin' on My Head" and the dolorous folk-schlock of Fred Neil's "Everybody's Talkin'." This the prism of middle-of-the-road hegemony through which pop music was still seen by Hollywood, which viewed *Easy Rider* as a wedge into the youth market far more than a subversion of any "Establishment." It was in the truest sense a fashion statement: slap some indiscriminate rock, long hair, and love beads on that hegemony and, presto, it would become "far out," daring, radical.

Here was a surefire studio formula that would promptly bring forth disasters like *The Strawberry Statement* and *Zabriskie Point*. (Raging youth preferred *Love Story*—old-fashioned craven pathos, a respite from the new, aggressive style of alienated banality.) With the imminent deaths of Jim Morrison and Jimi Hendrix about to seal their apotheosis as Butch-and-Sundance rock demigods (good-looking corpses entering the backdoor of myth), *Zabriskie Point*'s opportunistic vision of America as Death Valley was already passé when the movie came out. MGM had imported Michelangelo Antonioni to do his ritzy *Blow-Up* number on the shallow materialism of Los Angeles and the student revolutionaries who were presumably waging war on it. *Zabriskie Point* was a glorified picture postcard from the end of civilization: Having a miserable time, it said. Wish you were here. Its big set pieces—a teen orgy in the desert that might have come straight from the pages of *Playboy* and a swank orgy of destruction that sold apocalypse the way Madison Avenue did suburban affluence—were paeans to anonymity, the finish of bourgeois individualism. But while Antonioni slapped the communal noodlings of Pink Floyd and the Grateful Dead over his images of pristine nothingness, rock had entered a new phase: the white, lumpen-teen wail of heavy metal, with groups like Black Sabbath offering a cruder, cheaper, less refined void.

The one film that really connected with *Easy Rider*'s audience was Tom Laughlin's self-financed *Billy Jack* (1971), which he directed, co-scripted, and starred in. Like Peter Fonda, Laughlin came out of biker-exploitation films: in 1967, he made the trashy, fervid *The Born Losers*, which introduced the character of the half-breed Billy Jack (he single-handedly took on a psychotic neo-Nazi motorcycle gang there). The premise of *Billy Jack* was at base *Easy Rider* if the hippies had fought back against the rednecks. Or had someone to fight back for them — Billy Jack was the champion of children, Native Americans, and women against the bigots who want to drive them out or keep them down. Laughlin's mystical, taciturn martial arts expert was the resurrection of Gary Cooper for the Age of Aquarius — a vigilante for peace and brotherhood, a real Captain America. The movie was so old-fashioned it felt brand-new to young people: Tom Mix lives!

This two-fisted moralism won out over *Zabriskie Point*'s vainglorious intellectual tourism, a mode that perfectly anticipates Jean Baudrillard's *Amérique*. "Show business kids making movies of themselves," Steely Dan sang of Hollywood's young Antonioni impersonators. "You know, they don't give a fuck about anybody else." *Countdown to Ecstasy* was what the band called the 1973 album those lines appeared on: an ecstasy of negation that nailed all that was most problematic and compromised about the lust for youth, art, and radical chic in the aftermath of *The Last Movie, Getting Straight,* and *Alex in Wonderland*. With a name lifted from William Burroughs and an attitude of malice toward all, Steely Dan drove nail upon nail into the coffin of counterculture illusions. Musical auteurs Walter Becker and Donald Fagen displayed a sensibility somewhere between Leopold & Loeb and the Coen Brothers. With the title song of *Pretzel Logic,* they anticipated *Barton Fink* by way of remaking *Jailhouse Rock:* Elvis as both a face in the crowd and the "minstrel-show" face of show-biz fascism. The insurrection of "Blue Suede Shoes" is "gone forever / Over a long time ago." Mr. Bones lives as well.

Despite this dissenting view, the shift to pop nostalgia was by then under way, epitomized by George Lucas's *American Graffiti* (1973), which looked back fondly to pre-Vietnam/Kennedy-assassination times. It used fifties hits as a locus of the quaint and innocuous (much as Elton John's insipid "Crocodile Rock" did)— the embodiment, as the title of the hugely successful TV series it helped inspire had it, of "Happy Days." In doing this, *American Graffiti* turned the moral panic over early rock and the fifties cinema of juvenile delinquency on its head: the explosive rebel without a cause was replaced with a gang of meek, ingratiating Andy Hardys. The antic demystification of Brian De Palma's 1974 *Phantom of the Paradise* bombed: it revelled in everything that was shady, underhanded, and debauched in the pop milieu. If *Phantom of the Paradise*'s score had been by someone like Randy Newman, it might have been a slapstick masterpiece. As it was, Paul Williams's hack songs were functional, though as the diabolical Swan of Death Records he was ideal: a fiendish gnome drawn from the legends of both Phil Spector and Dick Clark (the Dorian Gray–like mogul who hosted TV's *American Bandstand* for eons, seemingly in league with the devil or the FBI or both). Much of *Phantom*'s parodistic horror-movie-musical tone was recycled — and blandly defanged — in that ultimate quarter-to-midnight cult movie sensation *The Rocky Horror Picture Show* (1975). The retro-camp treatment of glitter rock and monster movie clichés there was like a Disney makeover of Warhol and the New York Dolls. Under the mascara and mock outrage, a kinky wholesomeness prevailed — a Beach Party movie in goth drag.

But at least the sublime immolation of the school gym and senior class at the end of De Palma's *Carrie* realizes one of rock's primal fantasies: the bottomless pit of teen anomie made into macabre comedy, the ultimate eroto-destructive distillation of Alice Cooper's "Eighteen" and "School's Out" (". . . *forever*," insisted the later's blithe, zero-for-conduct chorus). With *Carrie* De Palma seemed to be saying, "You want a rocky horror picture show? I'll give you one, all right." The image of a prom queen Antichrist's hand reaching out from the grave definitely has more to do with rock's place in the Western cultural unconscious than Tim Curry camping it up in drag queen hand-me-downs. There's more of the music's frisson in De Palma's jarring, tactile images than in official rock documentaries such as *Woodstock* and *Gimme Shelter*, too. Those films are souvenirs of the music—keepsakes. (In *Gimme Shelter's* case, a memento mori.) What's missing is a talismanic quality, the engine of fetish and imagination that separated the Rolling Stones from, say, Country Joe and the Fish. On screen, Carrie White's let-it-bleed catharsis conveys what most concert films elide: the invasion of the normal by the uncanny. Robert Frank's Rolling Stones tour movie *Cocksucker Blues* doesn't have that either, just the druggy, futile entropy of the road. Which is why the band had the film suppressed, less that it sullied their public image than because the staged scenes of the Stones' junkie parasite entourage confirmed it all too well. *Cocksucker Blues* has a fine eye for the rancid underside of pop life. It provides the reality behind the grease-painted gags of *Phantom of the Paradise*, the devil wallowing in the tedious details of celebrity.

The appearance of *Superfly* announced the opening of another Hollywood beachhead—the ghetto. Set against the sweetly ominous commentary of Curtis Mayfield songs like "Pusherman" and "Freddie's Dead," the movie's story of a cocaine dealer who wants to escape the life after one last big score pegs it immediately as the black *Easy Rider.* If anything, *Superfly*'s influence was even more pervasive and certainly more lasting, ushering in the low-budget blacksploitation genre (*The Mack, Slaughter, Slaughter's Big Rip-Off, Foxy Brown, Cleopatra Jones,* etc.) as well as laying the whole foundation for the gangsta-rap movement almost two decades away. What *Superfly* lacked was the conviction of its own music: it was a shaky monotone poem to the longings and blocked avenues of black life. *The Harder They Come* (1972), from Jamaica and starring the raw, charismatic reggae singer Jimmy Cliff, pointed to a far-richer vein of pop cultural cross-pollination. The movie's sound-track—merely the best one ever assembled, much of it performed by the lead himself—was overflowing with echoes of spaghetti westerns, gangster sagas, and *Jailhouse Rock.* All of which culminated in Desmond Dekker's startling "007 (Shanty Town)," which placed Kingston's self-styled outlaws in the context of James Bond's lethal Third World tourism and (even more amazingly) the Sinatra-Martin-etc. vehicle *Ocean's Eleven* (making the surreal yet inevitable connection between Jamaican Rude Boys and the Las Vegas Rat Pack).

The cocaine dealer in *Superfly* is a distant cousin of the super-stud moonshiner Robert Mitchum played in *Thunder Road* (1958). And since Mitchum then dabbled in pop music—as a Calypso singer, no less—there's even a trace of family resemblance in *The Harder They Come*: the crude, lively pseudofolkloric tone makes Mitchum's Tennessee backwoods the rockabilly antecedent of Jimmy Cliff's Trenchtown (steeped in white lightning instead of ganja). The movie also provided the title for "Thunder Road," the first song on Bruce Springsteen's *Born to Run*—an album that's drenched in movie imagery and rock allusions, recasting cinematic mythology in rock terms as intensely as *Mean Streets* recapitulated rock history in narrative terms of violence, despair, and guilt. (The scene where Johnny Boy does a crazy, taunting dance to the Miracles' "Mickey's Monkey" while Charlie watches from the getaway car is like a precis of Springsteen's first three albums, just as they in turn refract it a few dozen different ways.) When "Thunder Road" resurrects James Dean (in place of Mitchum) and Springsteen sings, "Your graduation gown lies in rags at their feet," the listener will be forgiven if she mistakes the "Mary" of the song for "Carrie." His music of the time is a call-and-response dialogue with a vast array of sources—movies old and new, the history of rock and soul musics, the American experience as seen through the warp of pop mythology. Beyond "Thunder Road," there would not only be titles taken from movies ("Badlands") but movies themselves inspired by Springsteen songs (Walter Hill's wondrous mock-operatic urban western *Streets of Fire*). There were songs that sounded like forgotten movies ("Incident on 57th Street") and ones that were basically movie remakes ("Adam Raised a Cain" as an updated but no less fraught *East of Eden*). There was "Born to Run," which encompassed seemingly every inch of cop-rebel geography under the postwar sun, and in return there would be Richard Gere's fascinating homage to Springsteen (or just about his every stage mannerism) in the American remake of *Breathless*. Maybe the most convoluted example of the whole process would be Meat Loaf's 1978 album *Bat Out of Hell*—an insanely bombastic transformation of Springsteen's style into B-movie operetta (composer-producer Jim Steinman as the Leonard Bernstein of drive-in schlock), performed by a *Rocky Horror Picture Show* cast member who had derived his bigger (and dumber)-than-life persona from Gerrit Graham's Beef in *Phantom of the Paradise*.

"I could walk like Brando right into the sun," Springsteen boasted in "It's Hard to Be a Saint in the City." But in "Backstreets" he made it stick: the song takes in *Mean Streets* the same way

Scorsese's picture played off "Be My Baby" as both touchstone and point of departure. "Backstreets" is just as ravaged, and ravishing, swallowing in addition *On the Waterfront* and "Like a Rolling Stone" — a vision of identification and betrayal forever joined, where the glimpsed freedom in Brando's walk or Dylan's tone winds up shattered, crawling from the wreckage at the end of *Mean Streets*. It's a love song to phantoms who haunt themselves: fugitives who've taken refuge in the movies, only to find there's no escaping their own lives. When Springsteen sings to "Terry," he's calling out to Terry Malloy as surely as he assumes the burden of Rod Steiger's Charlie, merging with Harvel Keitel's Charlie. It's the dream of guilt and the guilt of hijacked dreams. As Brando and Steiger in the back of a cab dissolves into childhood buddies De Niro and Keitel sharing a bed in Little Italy, "Backstreets" is caught up in how a certain kind of history is made — emotional history. It's about how myth is transmitted and then lived out, as the connecting fabric beneath everyday existence. "You don't make up for your sins in the church," Keitel mutters to us, "you do it in the streets. . . ." Those streets of fire exist only in the imagination, in the biblical chapter and verse of movies and records: "I coulda been a contender. I coulda been somebody. . . ."

We may be born to run, but what if there's nowhere to hide from the encroachment of society? That was the lament of Sam Peckinpah's *Pat Garrett and Billy the Kid,* which formulated the end of the counterculture in murderously elegiac fashion. With Kris Kristofferson's Billy representing the dying breed of rock out-laws, it offered a sepia-toned twilight of the idle idols. There's even Bob Dylan himself as the self-effacing, incoherent Alias, who seems to have wandered in from the fringes of *McCabe and Mrs. Miller* — much like Dylan's mournful acoustic score. Not a trace remained of the former "Like a Rolling Stone" wordslinger remains, unless it's to be found in the tinny echo of Kristofferson's toast to James Coburn's burned-out Garrett, "How does it feel?" "It feels," answers the old renegade-turned-lawman, "like times have changed." The movie is swamped by world weariness. "Jesus, don't you get stale around here, Bill?" Garrett asks incredulously. Billy and his commune of ragtag followers come off as narrow and hidebound as the law they reject. The poetic dementia of Peckinpah's *Bring Me the Head of Alfredo Garcia* gets far closer to the dissipation that turned the sixties' quest for existential authenticity into the cocaine self-deception of the seventies. That makes *Pat Garrett and Billy the Kid* a languid way station on the road to the Eagles' *Hotel California*, where it turns out casualties Jim Morrison and Gram Parsons had more in common with Fred C. Dobbs than Jesus H. Christ.

In the space between *Bonnie and Clyde* and *Mean Streets*, an era took shape—a rapprochement that was less between movies and rock as such than the ideal of freedom rock represented but was snuffed out almost as soon as it was born. *The Missouri Breaks* (1975) simultaneously marked its last gasp and heralded the new age of the package deal. Here we had director Arthur Penn, ultrahip writer Tom McGuane, Jack Nicholson with the full force of his post–*Easy Rider* cachet intact, even Marlon Brando to lend the whole thing the luster of immortality. But the movie's frontier parable of cattle baron imperialism versus proletarian thieves came true in its making: *The Missouri Breaks* wasn't filmed so much as brokered among all cutthroat parties involved. Nicholson wound up adrift in the morass, while Brando was acting up a storm—busy entertaining himself to keep boredom at bay, like an aging rock star on one last tour bus, trying on different masks and groupies for size. (Like an extroverted version Dylan's Alias, this performance might have served as the oblique inspiration for Dylan's own whiteface-minstrel feature *Renaldo and Clara*.) Under all that authentic-looking blood and dung, rust had set in—a preview of a future where capital never sleeps, and *Heaven's Gate* is just a mortician's kiss away.

In the dream western Neil Young had been piecing together since his days with the Buffalo Springfield, this would not be a news flash. "When the first shot hit the dock," he sang in "Powderfinger," "I saw it comin'." A chiming death-knell reverie, the song had the open, desperate feel of a lost Anthony Mann eulogy, *The Far Country* given a foretaste of *Apocalypse Now:* "Look out, mama, there's a white boat comin' up the river." The future had arrived, and everyone's number was up ("It don't look like they're here to deliver the mail" was a bit of perfect Jimmy Stewart understatement). This was circa 1975, though like "Pocahontas" (originally titled "Marlon Brando, Pocahontas, and Me"), it would be a few years till Young got around to issuing them on record. For "Pocahontas," Young even pictured himself getting chummy with Brando, chewing the fatted calf around the campfire: "We'll sit and talk of Hollywood and the good things there for hire." Out to pasture or up a creek without a paddle, he had said much the same in 1969, with his band Crazy Horse behind him, on an album that was as unforgiving as it was prophetic: "Everybody knows this is nowhere."

[1995/2004]

PART TWO

Shoot the Guitar Player

14

Let Us Now Hill White Elephants

Lester Bangs

SUI GENERIS CRITIC and painter Manny Farber stated, "I can't imagine a more perfect art form, a more perfect career than criticism." Such a declaration must sound nuts if your points of reference pattern their careerism after such fast-growing fields as termite control, postmodern interior decorating ("This edgy Radiohead end table will perfectly complement your fabulous featherette Björk recliner"), and buzzword processing (every speck of expression forced though the finer-than-thou filters of a proper Esperanto machine). On the other hand (sporting half a *Night of the Hunter* tattoo), if you think of contentiously addictive voices from the past like the now-retired Farber or the late Lester Bangs, you may recall a time when such notions were self-evident. The fearless, heady, armor-piercing vernacular of "Carbonated Dyspepsia" or "Let Us Now Praise Famous Death Dwarves," "Hard Sell Cinema," or "James Taylor Marked for Death" amounted to more than off-the-rack jobbery, gushing politesse, consumer guidance counseling. Each new piece was an adventure in thought, language, feeling, and sensibility: meeting art and life on equal terms, it was the kind of writing that opened up whole underground vistas of tough-minded possibility.

"He was a romantic in the gravest, saddest, best, and most ridiculous sense of that worn-out word." So said Nick Tosches, no lightweight as a critic himself, eulogizing his friend and comrade Lester Bangs: romantic in a punk rock / *Naked Lunch* sense of the term, the kind who thought the only love worth having was one where all parties involved saw exactly what was on the end of every fork. He was the rock critic as simultaneous true believer and loyal apostate, someone who wanted to save rock 'n' roll, Blank Generation youth, and the world at large from themselves. His rambunctiously free-associating first-person prose has spawned a host of Lesteroids over the last few decades (less recognized is the way his insistence on the intimately personal as the political helped pave the way for more assertive, irreverent female voices in rock criticism). But as with Pauline Kael, his followers have tended to latch onto the more obvious and narrow aspects of his style, centering around no-bullshit attitude and an amped-up canon embracing the guilt-free pleasures of "trash." (Brian De Palma / Iggy and the Stooges serving as the standard-bearing yardsticks of their respective aesthetics, but instead of shaking up well-bred folks from within the venerable confines of *The New Yorker*, Bangs found his calling as writer and editor for *Creem* magazine — under his aegis, a cross between *Hit*

Parader, The National Lampoon, and *The Partisan Review* if Susie Sontag had only been a glue-sniffing headbanger.)

Since his death in 1982 at age thirty-three, his notoriety and stature have gradually outgrown the strict insider status of rock cultdom: the posthumous 1987 collection *Psychotic Reactions and Carburetor Dung,* edited by Greil Marcus, has become a modern touchstone that ranks with *I Lost It at the Movies, Negative Space, Mystery Train,* and *Studies in Classic American Literature.* Think of it as "Studies in Beautifully Unreasonable Noise," for "classic" is too stately a word for its Garageland environs and outlying districts, not merely launching pads for the best pure rock criticism ever written but criticism as pure rock 'n' roll. That this hardy truism has become the bedrock cliché in the Legend of Lester — and no less accurate for it — has been helpfully nudged along by Jim DeRogatis's reverent but unflinchingly detailed keeper-of-the-flame Bangs biography *Let It Blurt* (2000) and in particular by Philip Seymour Hoffman's deeply affectionate portrayal of Bangs in Cameron Crowe's rapt valentine to early seventies rock, *Almost Famous.* The mystique of his writing and persona hasn't worn thin with the passing of time; that tightrope sense of writing without a safety net retains its capacity to move and amaze. Resolutely human scale yet larger than life, Bangs's work had a warts-über-alles, kitchen-sink candor that made every tumultuous wrestling match with the high and low mucky-mucks of rock (right along with his own tag team of highly personalized demons) into a form of screwball heroism. A Shadows-of-Knight-errant Quixote and Sancho Panza rolled into one logorrheic typewriter junkie, he tilted at white elephants, sacred cows, boredom, and rampant mediocrity with a ravenous mixture of perception and bloodshot glee.

The publication of *Mainlines, Blood Feasts and Bad Taste: A Lester Bangs Reader* finally provides the long overdue follow-up to

Psychotic Reactions. The book positions itself as a logical extension of its predecessor, but as the slightly self-conscious title indicates, there's also a wish to play to the red-meat, Wild Man aspects of the Bangs myth-cum-brand-name. (Hey, Kids! It's the Amazing New Pocket Lester! Now with Extra Nova-Expressionism & Twice the Gonzo Scrubbing Bubbles of Hunter S. Thompson!) Given its bitter ruminations on the mortality of music as well as all things human, "Death May Be Your Santa Claus" might have been a better title, one belonging to a magnificent old Mott the Hoople rant (prevailing inarguable sentiment: "You're all too fuckin' slow") that Lester took for the headline of his exclusive 1976 interview with a very late Jimi Hendrix ("Because one thing I learned while killing myself," Jimi ruminates from beyond the grave, "was that a hell of a lot of that shit was just sound and fury kicked up to disguise the fact that we were losing our emotions, or at least the ability to convey them.")

Mainlines features a good deal of corrosive material that can stand with the best of the earlier collection, along with a wider, more uneven spectrum of workaday pieces ranging from inspired to autopilot-entertaining to a few genuflecting, all-too-human duds. But even his much too solemn and dewy-eyed review of Patti Smith's *Horses* is a useful object lesson, a testament to the unavoidable occupational hazards of the profession: the awful, honest temptations of hyperbole and needful thinking, especially in barren times like the mid-1970s (or now), though many have made whole highly respected careers out of far more egregious, uninspired treacle. Compare this Joan of Art treatment to his "Jim Morrison: Bozo Dionysus a Decade Later" about the great Doors Revival: it's not that he was initially off the mark about Smith's soft parade of pent-up ambitions and influences, only that he glossed over the halfcocked, loony-tune tendencies that made Miss Smith as much the provocateur-clown-headcase second cousin to Valerie Solanis as noble heiress to Rimbaud or the Ronettes. (Of course, she was also a friend he happened to have a hopeless crush on, but even factoring that in this seems more a case of giving in to the savior fantasy: she was a better conceptual fit for him than Bruce Springsteen, the other big, street-angelic candidate for Rock Messiah circa 1975.) Taken all in all, though some of editor John Morthland's choices will doubtless be "heatedly debated," by encompassing both Bob Marley's Babylon and David Johansen's, impassioned testimonials on behalf of Black Sabbath ("Bring Your Mother to the Gas Chamber!") and the Weimar-era Comedian Harmonists (take the A train!), the undersea world of Eno and *The Marble Index* of Nico, some inspired Dylan and Beatles debunking, plus more of his running battle with spiritual godfather Lou Reed, no Bangs fan is going to feel cheated by *Mainlines.*

As the kind of incendiary book that could make a person want to become a critic, or remind one why he became a critic in the first place, it is also meant to separate the initiated from disinterested observers and intellectual dilettantes. Like *Psychotic Reactions,* and in the great cultural tradition of "Sister Ray," these *Mainlines* are dares drawn in the sand: emphatically not nice little slices of music appreciation nor Dean's List honors seminars nor funhouse slumming for squeamish gentlefolk who require a formal introduction to *Raw Power* ("I say, Jeeves, these Iggy and the Stooges characters really are dashed clever fellows." "Indeed, sir?" "Just listen to this corker: 'I am the world's forgotten boy / The one who's searchin' to destroy.'" "If you say so, sir.") Bangs practiced criticism as a hilarious form of guerrilla class warfare, the revenge of the starving underclass (as much in existential as economic terms) against the proudly oblivious Overclass, the bourgeois-boho-yoyos, the Middle-C brows furrowed in rigid anal-retentive concentration, and indeed the High ideals of Class itself, understood as a plumy nexus of ego-massaging rationalizations, humorless self-importance, affluent pretensions, good table manners, solid musicianship, starched professionalism, and an insatiable appetite for respectability at all costs.

Discomforting the comfortable and afflicting the affected was what he lived for — "you cannot kick intentional cripples awake," but gee, Officer Krupke, it sure is fun to try anyway — but there was something more at stake than just being a gadfly freelancing boils or a chaotic court-jesting nuisance. (Dear me, what'll that darn Lester say next?!) The guiding suspicion behind his work was that the language of assurance and reassurance most art is couched in was a way of insulating audiences from their own lives: by substituting overdetermined pseudo-emotions and numb freeze-dried ideas for precarious human exchange, the next thing you knew you'd wind up in a Keir Dullea pod slippery-sloping into Kubrick's remake of *The Incredibly Strange Creatures Who Stopped Living and Became Mixed-Up Zombies*, with music by Kraftwerk and "emetic narcissism" by Stevie of Bel Air (a manicure worse than the disease). Hence Bangs's writing contains more scar tissue and stealth vulnerability per square inch in than anything this side of Mo Tucker singing "Afterhours" to finish the Velvet Underground's third LP: "Ah, but people look well in the dark."

* * *

SOMEWHERE OVER THE slough of despond, *Mainlines, Blood Feasts and Bad Taste* includes his debut review for *Rolling Stone* in 1969, dismissing the MC5's *Kick Out the Jams* (he later famously reversed himself on the album, but in Bangs such diametrical opinions weren't self-canceling: they were Polaroids of the running love-hate argument with music and life that constantly went on inside his head) and the Canned Heat review that got him bounced from its yellowed pages. Fittingly, too, there's the last piece published in his lifetime, "If Oi Were a Carpenter," sizing up minuscule punk offshoots. The book starts with a few instructive chunks of wrought-up teenage angst, rites-of-passage pieces drawn from his unpublished autobiographical tome "Drug Punk: "A Quick Trip through My Adolescence" that lay out a picture of early influences, tantrums, and formative traumas. In "Two Assassinations," William Burroughs looms larger than any of the other Beats as an influence (Kerouac would show up in his more fulsome and tender paeans). Young Lester incorporates a vintage naked lunchbox slogan — "Fuck 'em all, squares on both sides, I am the only complete man in the industry" — to serve as a nineteen-year-old hipster's holy grail, but the facade is already being undercut by his own grievous sense of estrangement, isolation, and doubt. When the kid from El Cajon gets cosy with the San Diego Hell's Angels and winds up as a passive, guilt-stricken bystander to one of their come-one-come-all rapes, the horror kind of takes the bloom off the whole outlaw-rebel pose for Lester. Hipster cool held an immense attraction for him, but his determination to break through that attitude of reptilian detachment and reach for some kind of human connection, no matter what, is what would ultimately make him an indelible writer.

There's also a tour through what *Mainlines* designates as the "Pantheon" (an I. M. Pious wax museum perhaps better left to Madams Sarris and Christgau), which includes four pieces on the Rolling Stones (about two and a half too many — dutifully forcing himself to muster a response to the supremely indifferent likes of *Black and Blue*) and a couple nice exercises in ambivalence devoted to Miles Davis's queasy-listening electric period ("Kind of Grim" and "Music for the Living Dead," funk in both senses of the word). A long profile of Captain Beefheart does veer off into awestruck, witch-doctor hagiography, but a good Kierkegaard-laced review of Public Image Ltd. (belying Bangs's anti-intellectual rep) counteracts such tendencies. There's achingly fervent, can-I-get-a-drowning-witness testimony on behalf of Nico's *The Marble Index,* as well as "Deaf Mute in a Telephone Booth" on Uncle Louie entering his Scrooge McFucked decline, and an epic, positively wistful evocation of Black Sabbath. Encountering Ozzy back in 1972, when *The Osbournes* was not even a gleam in the all-seeing TV Eye, the piece is at once a completely sincere, mostly convincing attempt to find the humanist impulses secreted in "War Pigs" and "Children of the Grave" and a disarming visit with a Prince of Darkness who already is halfway to his shrewdly befuddled husband-and-father persona (right down to the wholesome sitcom wackiness when Ozzy sans Harriet attempts to avoid the breathy clutches of a chick who calls herself the Blow Job Queen).

Here you catch a glimpse of the Lester Bangs who befriended a barely teenage Cameron Crowe and offered cranky encouragement to Crowe's alter ego in *Almost Famous:* while he positioned himself as the enemy of the whole scene-making "I am a Golden God" rockstar trip, Bangs had his own streak of wayward idealism and sentimental tenderness. It was more likely to express itself in a communing singalong to "Ballerina" or "Beside You" instead of "Tiny Dancer," but so much of the rage and despair in his work came from a sense of possibilities betrayed, hope deferred or destroyed, good things turned into breathtaking travesties of themselves. (Crowe's adolescent chivalry toward beatific distressed damsels reflects an aspect of the romantic in Bangs as well.) It's not hard to imagine an alternate version of *Almost Famous* where Lester is the star, emerging from a far grungier, more stifling background, with a Jehovah's Witness mother and no prospects of an interesting, bearable life at all—his autobiography written in the albums he discovered and the books he found, which were signs not only of another world but of another self he would construct from the traces they left. Music—and writing—was his deliverance, hence the desert island album essay included in *Psychotic Reactions* about Van Morrison's *Astral Weeks*:

> It was particularly important to me because the fall of 1968 was such a terrible time. I was a physical and mental wreck, nerves shredded and ghosts and spiders looming and squatting across the mind. My social contacts had dwindled almost to none; the presence of other people made me nervous and para- noid. I spent endless days and nights sunk in an armchair in my bedroom, reading magazines, watching TV, listening to records, staring into space. I had no idea how to improve the situation, and probably wouldn't have done anything about it if I had.

The big epiphany voice-over would go something like this:

> But in the condition I was in, it assumed at the time the quality of a beacon, a light on the far shores of the murk; what's more, it was proof that there was something left to express artistically besides nihilism and destruction. (My other big record of the day was *White Light / White Heat.*) It sounded like the man who made *Astral Weeks* was in terrible pain, pain most of Van Morrison's previous albums had only suggested; but like the later albums by the Velvet Underground, there was a redemptive element in the

blackness, ultimate compassion for the suffering of others, and a swath of pure beauty and mystical awe that cut right through the heart of the work.

There was always that alternating current in him that oscillated between destructive-nihilist character traits and the deep-seated beauty-awe component, a tension that was easier and more salutary to manage in writing than a life of self-mocking, self-medicating excess. *Lester the Movie: Almost Bilious* would traverse circumscribed beginnings handing out the *Watchtower* in El Cajon, his humble start sending record reviews to *Rolling Stone* (the *Watchtower* redux), the glory days in Detroit as the conscience and soul of *Creem*, his move to New York where he submerged himself in CBGB's burgeoning lemming-demimonde (Richard Hell and the Voidoids more or less serving as his Stillwater) and freelanced for the *Village Voice*. (Though in order to survive, he wrote for anyone who'd take his byline: *Stereo Review, Musician, Rolling Stone* once again, *New Wave, New York Rocker, Music and Sound Output, Contempo Culture, Back Door Man*—publish or perish wasn't an idle threat but an imperative on several levels.) The movie would brim with obligatory romance and heartbreak up the wazoo (e.g., *Psychotic Reaction*'s love-as-absurdity classic "New Years Eve"), but Lester's most lasting lifelong relation outside of music was with masturbation, so there'd have to be one of those gauzy memory montages of the way we wanked: from early boyhood stirrings before the telephone-book-sized Sears catalog (ladies' undergarments section) on to Hef's plasticine Playmates to Runaways album covers to the pastoral nostalgia of *Celebrity Skin*. But besides sentimental journeys, you'd get action'n'adventure (remember "Jethro Tull in Vietnam"?—our correspondent goes upriver to get the skinny on a Kurtzian pied piper), rockin' intrigue (remember "Screwing the

System with Dick Clark"? — I see Michael Douglas doing a perfect cameo as Mr. American Bandstand), and even Lester's ingratiatingly mortifying attempt to become a singer himself (Andy Kaufman and the Blues Brothers had nothing on our boy).

Only the last reel would have to be rewritten: overdosing on Darvon after getting relatively straight and sober is by far the worst cliché he ever perpetrated and his one unforgivably corny stunt, going out in what he would have surely mocked as a shamelessly cheap career move. (The old die-and-become-immortal routine — the stalest joke in the book.) Maybe a *Twilight Zone* finish would be more in order: since Bangs has already entered cinema's nether realm of cultural fantasy alongside such luminaries as Sid and Nancy, Valerie and Andy, Charles Bukowski, *Naked Lunch*'s William Lee, Jim Morrison, Hunter S. Thompson, Kaufman, John Belushi, *24 Hour Party People*'s Tony Wilson and Ian Curtis, why not convene a roundtable of the living and the dead, a meeting of the minds and the mindless? Have P. S. Hoffman's Lester and Lili Taylor's Val and the Thompson twins (Bill Murray and Johnny Depp) and the rest of 'em hash out the liberties taken by film biographies, the consolations of philosophy as spelled out in the Sex Pistols' version of "No Fun," the perils and ecstasies of nostalgia, and the nigh unto insurmountable task of not turning into the very thing you despised, especially once you've been projected onto the silver screen as some kind of suitably iconic/ridiculous figure. One minute you're the Elephant Man on stampede ("I am not an animal!"), and the next you're another shiny white death mask on display in a showroom window: smile, says Miss Cynthia Plastercaster, you're on *Candid Camera!* But Lester is unfazed: he goes into bemused Rod Serling mode and addresses the camera as a battle-of-the-stars melee erupts behind him (Andy has Val in a headlock, Bukowski's holding a pillow over Morrison's big mouth) and calmly intones, "Is there a happy ending? I don't think so." Roll credits as the mandolins play and Mott the Hoople's "I Wish I Was Your Mother" serenades you out of the theater humming a pretty epitaph.

No matter how you look at it, with all the exuberance and crazed comic poetry and hot/cold running insight of *Psychotic Reactions* and now *Mainlines*, there's an aura of sadness beyond simple untimely loss (as a wisegal said to me, "Whaddayouwannaliveforever?"): the unremitting sense beneath all that beautifully overwrought manic desperation of how fragile and futile the constructs underpinning art and life really are, a rising awareness of the steep toll of all that persistent grappling with the inadmissible. No surprise then that Lester Bangs wrote some of the best obits in the business, his own dress rehearsals: for Elvis (whom he didn't much care for, and wrote all the more movingly about what that disconnection meant), Peter Laughner (a musician and writer who if he hadn't self-immolated trying to live out a fantasy camp version of alcoholic-druggie nihilist stupor might have grown up to surpass either Lou Reed or Bangs himself), "Bye, Bye, Sidney, Be Good" (for punk rock and all its slam-bam illusions, his own most of all). In addition, he invented the preventive obituary in his Lou Reed opuses and "Richard Hell: Death Means Never Having to Say You're Incomplete," bait-and-switch tracts that attempted to lure/ jolt their subjects out of downward-spiraling self-hate with a carrot of praise or a cattle prod to their numb genitalia. (His answer to the Clash's "Ya need a little dose of electrical shockers.")

And then there were those reconnaissance flights that were hard to tell from kamikaze missions, diving into a record as he does on *Mainlines'* "Your Shadow Is Scared of You: An Attempt Not to Be Frightened by Nico." Which is about trying to get past all the baggage of Pavlovian-dinnerbell art, chic dehumanization, overweening significance, cheap thrills, working instead toward a definition of art as something as personal as the most intimate, wrenching flesh-and-blood encounter. Clearing away the distractions of secondhand fashion and vicarious kicks, he then elicits a long string of Joycean dictation from an old love over the phone, a seance that ends with the woman comparing doomstruck chanteuse Nico to "Beckett's play *Breath*, she's trying to find the last breath so she can negate breath, love, anything. A soft look would killer her." Then he hunkers down with the vast hosts of the dead he hears on the album:

> She quite a rock critic, that old girlfriend of mine —
> sometimes she scares me even more than Nico. But
> then, I'm scared of everybody — I'm scared of *you.*
> My girlfriend's eloquence was one reason I loved her
> almost from first sight, but not why I had to get
> halfway around the geographical world to write a
> song that said how much I loved her. It was because
> of something obviously awry in me, perhaps healing,
> at least now confronting itself, which is one way to
> perhaps not rot. There's a ghost born every second,
> and if you let the ghosts take your guts by sheer
> force of numbers you haven't got a chance though
> probably no one has the right to judge you either.
> (Besides which, the ghosts are probably as scared of
> you as you are of them.)

Now most critics, whether good, bad, or humdrum, are usually doing their level best to suppress or deny such feelings, gloss over the awkwardness, the groping, the fear that John Cale may have said was a man's best friend, but you wouldn't ever know it from *them.* After all, that terror is weakness, which in turn is a form of need, which is just a shade removed from psychic disintegration and nervous breakdown—one slip on the stepping razor's edge there, and it's back into the bedroom armchair, counting the spiders and staring into space forever, or worse. The difference between what Bangs is doing here and what an equally personal (albeit in a more baroquely literary manner) writer Camden Joy is doing in his collection *Lost Joy* comes down to risk. Not formal risk, idiosyncratic experimentation in structure and fantasy and syntax, which Joy's work shows in rhetorical abundance after a manner that suggests Fernando Pessoa's *Book of Disquiet* remodeled as rock fan's mash notes to his own delicious sensibility. Bangs's work feels at risk in the same way the work it lauds is—in danger of coming apart at the seams, devouring its author and sucking its audience into the pit of disgust or hopelessness or fear with it. Joy's approach has a disembodied, art-project halo: as though instead of listening to "The Greatest Record Album Singer Ever" (Al Green) or "The Greatest Record Album Ever Told" (Frank Black's *Teenager of the Year*) or "The Greatest Record Album Band That Ever Was" (Creedence Clearwater Revival), you visited a gallery where they had been turned into ironic-obsessive-compulsive installations. Everything (performer, music, album jacket) becomes a pretext, each moved behind several layers of brilliant distancing devices; you marvel at the intricacy and thoroughness of every conceit, but they remain conceits, art for artifice's sake. Bangs was convinced the only worthwhile purpose of music and criticism was to break through that artifice. If it didn't implicate you, as co-conspirator or shamed silent partner, then it wasn't doing its job: it was just providing a glass-bottom service to gawk at the colorful creatures of the deep from a nice dry vantage point. The world as he saw it wasn't so much divided between the hip and the square ("Fuck 'em all") or even the haves against the have-nots so much as between those who had to live in whatever drowned world they'd been consigned to or made for themselves (if it was even possible to tell the difference) and the tourists who watched the show and then put on their warm coats and went back home.

In *Mainlines*, there's a terrific 1976 piece called "Innocents in Babylon," on the lures and traps of such tourism, going to Jamaica in search of Natty Dread while waiting for Bob Marley's Godot at the Sheraton hotel. (The Clash could have cribbed notes for "Safe European Home" from it.) There's a glimmer of utopia that looks a little like prophecy:

> All the singles have an instrumental version on the B side, so the deejays can flip them over and improvise their own spaced-out harangues over the rhythm tracks. Since Jamaican radio plays so little reggae, most of the deejays come off the streets, where until recently you could find, periodically, roots discos set up. Out of these emerged deejay-stars like Big Youth and I-Roy, and along with producers like Lee Perry and Augustus "King Tubby" Pablo they have pioneered a fascinating technological folk art called dub. An album by I-Roy can thank six different producers on the back for the use of their rhythms. Don't ask me where the publishing rights go. Don't ask anybody, in fact. And, don't ask how musicians might feel who play on one session for a flat rate, only to find it turn up on one or more other hit records. The key with dub is spontaneity, the enormous creative sculpting and grafting of whole new counterpoints on records already in existence. And this sense of the guy who plays the record as performer extends

down into the record shops, where the clerks shift
speakers, tracks, and volume levels with deft magi-
cianly fingers as part of a highly intricate dance, creating sonic riot in the store and new productions in
their minds: *I control the dials.*

But the reality beneath the pipe dream turned out to be predictably
messier: exploitation, greed, racism, violence, lunacy, enough delusion to go around for everyone involved, the writing on the wall
no one wanted to read.

The era Lester Bangs belonged to was unlike the present one in
a key respect: a lot of people hadn't learned the rules of the game
yet. All garage bands like the Count Five and the Troggs and uncounted no-hit wonders were too dumb to know any better: they
didn't have a neoprimitive paint-by-numbers instruction manual to
work from. Punk was, briefly, a smarter free-for-all: anyone could
join, and nobody had the slightest clue where it was going, oblivion
or taking over the world as equally plausible consummations devoutly and simultaneously being wished. Then people internalized
the rules or were assimilated by them—a process well under way
before Bangs's death and so that turns the later pieces in *Mainlines*
into the sound of a man tired of losing the good fight and certain
that the worst was yet on its way. The book is Lester's Last Stand
against the march of the lumbering artistic behemoths, Old Home
Week back in the human wilderness: or as the girl on the phone
once asked me in the dead of night, "What good is music if it
doesn't destroy you?"

[2003]

Bring Me the Head of Gordon Sumner

Sting—

Hasil Adkins

WELCOME ONCE AGAIN TO The All-New Bad Dream Dating Game. *Tonight's lucky bachelorette, Ms. Medea Gonne, a night school teacher and knife thrower's assistant from Redondo Beach, California, will be choosing from these three handsome, exciting guys:*

Bachelor Number One is Charlie Parker, giant of American music, reputed to have picked up the alto saxophone even before David Sanborn, a man whose life is soon to be a major motion picture directed by Clint "Birdslinger" Eastwood. Perhaps luckiest of all for Charlie, he be dead.

So we hurry on to Bachelor Number Two. He's Sting, dashing Englishman and beloved freelance rock aristocrat. His musical objets d'art are chock full of thoughtfulness, warmth, and sensitivity, or the closest facsimiles money can acquire. He affirms his profound empathy and concern for his inferiors while inviting them to vicariously partake in his privileged view of this crazy thing he likes to call life. His refreshing positivity in an age of glum naysayers reassures us that underneath whatever insignificant trappings of wealth and respectability, the ruling class are jes' folks. They have the self-same joys and sorrows as you; their best interests are yours.

Finally, we come to Bachelor Number Three: Hasil Adkins, a jabbering middle-aged loon from deep in West Virginia's chicken shack country who has been making cacophonous one-man-band rockabilly records for more than thirty years. Haze's interests include home decorating ("I'm gonna put your head on my wall"), fine dining ("commodity meat" and Mars bars), and the hell-bent pursuit of the most twisted, drooling noise ever perpetrated by man or guitar. Every step he takes, every move he makes, signals his unbounded disrespect for the smooth, covertly authoritarian blandishments of the Rock Establishment —

* * *

ON STING'S DOUBLE record . . . *Nothing Like the Sun*, one confronts once more the spectacle of the rock-star-as-conscience-of-the-free-world. As music, it is perfumed gunk; Sting's Police-era gift for cynically insinuating hooks ain't what it used to be, either. This stuff doesn't swing, doesn't rock, doesn't groove. It just circles round and round, cosmopolitan and unobtrusive, a seamless construct of secondhand ethnicity and firsthand condescension. Besides the white hole of Sting's croon, the defining voice here belongs to Branford Marsalis's soprano sax: insistently cloying, attenuated, the sound of one who is wrapped around his own finger. In essence, this is Steely Dan with all the delusions Donald Fagen used to sneer at reinstated.

What's remarkable is the level, the density, of misrepresentation Sting achieves here. He will suffer no facet of the human condition to go unreified: feelings, politics, hope, all are traduced into commodities. What remains is surrender to the way things are, to the pervasive realities of the marketplace—acceptance, submission, packaged as compassionate dissent. In the guise of moderation and conscientiousness, Sting lets it be known "human rights" are good things. Everyone should have them. They are as desirable as a high-end compact disc player on which to hear . . . *Nothing Like the Sun*, for instance. Yet they're really no different—another product, a little something to help consumers sleep easier at night, as nebulous and soothing as one of Marsalis's solos.

Hasil Adkins, the unheralded legend of "I Need Your Head," "Reagan Blues," and countless more, sounds like a forty mewl-team cross between the *Eraserhead* baby and a Clinch Mountain Jerry Lee Lewis. On his no-budget LP *The Wild Man*, the Haze mostly sings as if every pant and shudder could be his last will and testament. Tearing his cat clothes off before the great abyss, he will not be deterred from his endtime mating rites. If *The Wild Man* offers nothing as stupefyingly weird as "D.P.A. on the Moon" or "She Said" or "We Got a Date," it still sends sense scattering before it the way a Plymouth empties a sidewalk of pedestrians. Haze delivers his customary new dance, "Chicken Flop," on which he helpfully instructs: "Flop flop flop." He unleashes a shiftless instrumental rhapsody called "Do the Scalp," punctuated by the screams of mutant masseuses yet unborn, as he bloodies his fingers on the frets. Haze climbs into his "Big Red Satellite" (a car—I think) and imitates the sirens of pursuing state troopers at the top of his lungs.

Constantly, there is the search for a flailing, rutting beat that will not only approximate fucking but also subsume it: "Wild Wild Friday Night" is a song of such expansive filth as to cover all in earshot with cum-dripping anarchy.

Courtesy of the perpetually fawning L.A. *Times*, let's apply some Sting-anointment to Mr. Adkins: "It's Time to Recognize His Joyful Musicality and Sophisticated Grace." Sticks in the craw; exposed as cant, the house of marked cards collapses on itself. It's no accident of birth that at fiftysomething Hasil Adkins has more life in him than Sting ever had or will. For inertia is at the heart of the former Mr. Gordon Sumner's charade—and appeal. In the liner notes to . . . *Nothing Like the Sun*, he informs us history appears "to be nothing but a monotonous and sordid succession of robber baron scumbags devoid of any admirable human qualities." Yet the pristine monotony of the album has not a single moment that would give offense to your average captain-of-industry scumbag. Indeed, its sheen of expensive distance will fit right in with any moneyed scumbag décor. "History Will Teach Us Nothing," the bronzed white man tells us to that toe-tapping colonial beat. Sting's gilt-edged music is comfortable with this: it has dispensed with the need for anything beyond obedience to the social hierarchy rock finds itself absorbed by.

I could stand his *Sketches of Spam* cover of Hendrix's "Little Wing" and laugh off the Princely pseudo-phunk of "We'll Be Together Again." But when he turns the plight of Pinochet's victims into mood music or makes some ultradiscreet plea for tolerance (he sounds like he's talking about Martians instead of gays, though for him they might be interchangeable), that's when the gorge starts its trip to the top. That's it, Sting old man: impoverish life that much further, falsify it that extra mile. Plainly, Hasil Adkins and the prodigious noises he makes are anathema to this fuckhead idea of culture: the social significance of "Punchy Wunchy Wicky Wackey Woo" doesn't announce itself in the obsequious manner of "History Will Teach Us Nothing," but it springs from sources of euphoric craziness and freedom that are immeasurably deeper. Even when Adkins, who has mellowed a bit, serenades us with lovely country lament "She'll See Me Again," he could be a bourbon-rinsed apparition rising from Hank Williams's grave or Lou Reed's bad conscience, calling down spooky intimations of an Otherness that knows no name. Let it rock.

Not that I mean to imply here that Sting is useless. He's contemptible, but in exemplary ways. So bravo, Sting, bravo. Don't feel slighted, for as Haze reminds me, we got a date. Your head, my wall.

[1987]

16

Dueling

Cadavers

The Mekons contra

Postmodernism, or

The Cultural Logic of Late Capitalism

IN HIS ORNATE, pitiless mausoleum of a book *Postmodernism, or The Cultural Logic of Late Capitalism,* Fredric Jameson creates a prose equivalent to the fondly regarded postmodern architecture of L.A.'s fabled Bonaventure Hotel—a mound of blindly refracting glass and steel hovering serenely over a forsaken urban landscape, a monument to the universality of tourism, a Forest Lawn of the senses. By contrast, *The Curse of the Mekons* presents the music of bare-knuckle dinosaurs testifying from postmod tar pits, clinging to equally extinct stuff like history books and accordions. Theirs is a more troubled, humane vision of the age. In lieu of Jameson's impressive theoretical apologia masquerading as critique, the Mekons resuscitate a cheerfully crucified language, mouthing familiar incantations to drown their sorrows. As though a shaky hand were scribbling anachronistic threats, insults, and boasts in the white margins of *Postmodernism* (written, the creamy jacket assures us, "by one of America's foremost Marxist intellectuals"): "Magic, fear, and superstition / This is the curse of the Mekons."

Such is the cultural logic of late capitalism according to the world's greatest punk-country-and-decline-of-Western-civilization band—a logic they have tracked and resisted for as long as anyone can remember. In 1977, demystifying punk with "Never Been in a Riot"; twelve years later, demystifying the pop process itself with *The Mekons Rock 'n' Roll*: "When I was just 17," Sally Timms sang with bitter, peerless calm, "sex no longer held a mystery / I saw it as a commodity, to be bought and sold like rock and roll." The anarchosocialist party girl continued: "I saw a world where the dead are worshipped / This world belongs to them / Now they can keep it." In between, among countless releases of finished and unfinished material, the great sodden demystifications of the Reagan/Thatcher decade: *Fear and Whiskey* (1985) and *The Edge of the World* (1986). Here was a noisy, funny, distraught, finally dreamy tale—of Pythonian cowboys and tattered Arthurian knights and their misadventures in a land where culture and capital were indivisible. Here, too, was the desire to bring history back from the dead, if only for the chance to refuse its fatalistic claims anew, the wish to write a different ending to the bloody pageant of the twentieth century.

Jameson likewise sees postmodernism as the most advanced form of capitalism yet: production and consumption blissfully fused, the transnational market's siren song of itself. (His leftism is balanced by postmod relativism: call it No-Fault Marxism.) Only there's no agency of Mekonesque desire around to contest any of this — lived experience has conveniently dissolved along with the history it might seek to rejoin and instead "makes itself felt by the so-called death of the subject." *The Curse of the Mekons* answers: "How can something really be dead when it hasn't even happened?" (The line refers to the so-called death of socialism, but it will do as well for subjectivity.) *Postmodernism* throws a costly, elaborate funeral for modernity — for its hunger after poetry and negation, for utopian transformation, even for consciousness itself — but as the Mekons would holler back: "The funeral is for the wrong corpse."

Humming a few bars of "Blue Arse" under our collective breath, we join Dr. Jameson's autopsy already in progress. His voice is sonorous, dignified, densely circular; he seems to be rehearsing the eulogy with every incision:

> This autonomy of culture, this semiautonomy of lan-
> guage, is the moment of modernism, and of a realm
> of the aesthetic which redoubles the world without
> being altogether of it, thereby winning a certain neg-
> ative or critical power, but also a certain other-
> worldly futility. Yet the force of reification, which
> was responsible for this new moment, does not stop
> there either: in another stage, heightened, a kind of
> reversal of quantity into quality, reification penetrates
> the sign itself and disjoins the signifier from the sig-
> nified. Now reference and reality disappear alto-
> gether, and even meaning — the signified — is proble-
> matized. We are left with the pure and random play
> of signifiers that we call postmodernism, which no
> longer produces monumental works of the modernist

type but ceaselessly reshuffles the fragments of pre-
existent text, the building blocks of older cultural
and social production, in some new and heightened
bricolage: metabooks which cannibalize other books,
metatexts which collate bits of other texts — such is
the logic of postmodernism in general, which finds
one of its strongest and most original authentic forms
in the new art of experimental video.

Very neat — modernity eviscerated by semioticians, then the cadaver sawed up for soup bones by deconstructionists. It is like unto
a dream, the floating, oracular one Ms. Timms recounts in
"Waltz": "The graveyard scene is fine / The skull gets all the best
lines."

*   *   *

ALAS, POOR MODERNISM. . . . But not so fast. Where did that
"original, authentic" crap come from — wasn't all that swept into
the historic dustbin right along with history itself and its putative
subjects? And if discredited ideas like originality and authenticity
are to be resurrected, now that the old high culture of modernism
has been dispersed by pop, how come Jameson confines his discussion to rarefied, symbolic "experimental" video instead of real,
market-driven manifestations of the new culture — video games,
MTV, pornography? Old intellectual habits die hard: to no one's
surprise, the brave new rhetoric surrounding postmodernism mostly
talks to, and of, itself.

Hence a whole spectrum of postmodern phenomena, from fem-
inism to rap music, is pointedly omitted from Jameson's conceptual
framework. (Who can blame the guy? Women show up bleeding
all over "pure" textuality by insisting on their lived experience of

male domination; urban teens make sophisticated metamusic that directly embodies the logic of late capitalism by simultaneously deconstructing and remythologizing its sources, not to mention turning a serious profit.) *Postmodernism* is an ultraselective tome, setting up a whiz-bang paradigm, only to suppress its most suggestive, disturbing aspects: class, race, sex.

The shambolic atavism practiced by the Mekons — attempting to decode the world on the fly, trying to make meaning out of the cultural detritus they've inherited — Jameson would, I suspect, write off as one more toothless "return of the repressed." He cites the cliché constantly (like someone with a case of intellectual Tourette's syndrome), but his rote usage is shorn of Freudian violence, psychic weight. For he allows no place for the repressed to return *to*: all the former terrain of individual lives and collective struggle has been ceded to a "saturated space" of images, economic ciphers, an orderly and affectless pandemonium (as if the Home Shopping Network had armed itself and begun conducting air strikes down the block.)

"Magic, fear, and superstition" have been banished from *Postmodernism*, but they remain at large in the rites of capitalism and the longings of its discontents. I play the song "Sorcerer" on auto-repeat: in a weird, unsteady falsetto, Tom Greenhalgh calls down the spirit of Karl Marx and Walter Benjamin's mystical Angel of History, as the figure of the "bourgeois sorcerer" arises from the wreckage of the past. "Menacing, destroying / Blindly as it moves" — a harsh, robotic beat dragging modernism and p-modernism alike to the brink of a shared void — "They repress both wonder / And dread at what they've made." A bass ticks of suspended notes like a clock winding down for good. "Dark powers walk in broad daylight / Social forces driven in dreadful directions / Whole populations conjured out of the ground." Marx's theory gives in to pagan chant, or perhaps an ancient unease that finds its unnatural expression in theory: "The abyss is close to home."

"Sorcerer" is funny, haunting, and most of all alive. Hearing it, one is at once transported to the bygone Europe of *The Communist Manifesto* and William Gibson's future-is-now vision of transglobal "Cyberspace" in the novel *Neuromancer*: "A consensual hallucination experienced daily by billions of legitimate operators. . . . A graphic representation of data abstracted from the banks of every computer in the human system. Unthinkable complexity. Lines of lights ranged in the nonspace of the mind, clusters and constellations of data. Like city lights, receding . . ." The torturous formulations and reformulations of *Postmodernism* are superseded, and another space opens up. Which helps explain why Gibson functions as the structuring absence behind Jameson's "cognitive map" — the signal repression within the well-policed confines of Jameson's argument. Gibson's alluded to as the central, exemplary representative of this condition, but he's a phantom in *Postmodernism*: Jameson immerses himself in boring architecture and self-devouring theory instead of *Neuromancer's* radical plane of technology-cum-sorcery.

Postmodernism speaks of a vague, pervasive euphoria — the rush of overstimulation and narcotization — yet the most salient feature of this depoliticized new world would appear to be, in a time of frightening overcrowding, its peculiar depopulation. Jameson has appropriated the model of Gibson's Cyberspace but purged it of intruders, dissidents, grifters, wastrels: those stubbornly uneuphoric citizens of the multinational, multimedia economy like the Mekons themselves, a disorganized, unfixed starving class that finds in images of free-market abundance and democratized apathy a stunning poverty *of the imagination*. The apparatus of that poverty is what *The Curse of the Mekons* — here ranting, there falling back upon hushed speech that is nearly silence — tries to measure, elude, damn. And it is what Jameson, in this big, thoughtful, relatively well written, and doggedly obtuse book of his, seeks to make a separate peace with.

The phrase "separate peace" came into my head thinking about a jaw-dropping aside of Jameson's. He's talking about Marx's "fundamental notion of separation": the exclusion of the worker from the means of production on one level; on another, the divisions atomizing individuals from and subordinating them to the commodity. "There has not yet, I think, been a Marxism based on this particular figure," he muses royally, "although it is a cognate of other figures such as alienation, reification, and commodification. . . ." As it happens, *Postmodernism* lifts many of its most useful ideas from the Situationist Guy Debord's 1967 *Society of the Spectacle,* albeit often via Jean Baudrillard (whose watered-down gloss on Situationist rhetoric always suggests to me how Walt Disney might have gone about animating *Guernica*). Jameson generously alludes to Debord's "remarkable formulations" yet seems strangely innocent — aye, Faith and begorra, ain't repression a grand thing? — of the fact that the Situationists in general and *Society of the Spectacle* in particular rallied against separation with savage, unending disgust. Jameson offers the spectacle of the prudent American Marxist intellectual venturing into the great unknown: "the logic of separation may have become even more relevant for our own period, and for the diagnosis of postmodernism. . . ." Jameson embraces that logic of "psychic fragmentation" and "the schizophrenic present," consuming and excreting it with learned gusto. More than two decades ago, Debord ingested that present and spat it back — mocking the *hallucinatory social fact* (echoing in advance Gibson's "consensual hallucination") where human encounters were replaced by meetings with representations and simulacra. "In a society where one can no longer be recognized by others, every individual becomes unable to recognize his own reality," wrote Debord, though behind the measured tone was a howling in the wilderness. "Ideology is at home; separation has built its world."

That world appears almost magically, unbidden, in a textual juxtaposition Jameson makes early on. It looms up in the "entertaining (although bewildering) leisure-time space" of the Bonaventure Hotel, a discussion that segues into a contemplation of high-tech postmodern warfare as presented in Michael Herr's *Dispatches*. Herr rhapsodizes about how all the helicopter gunships he'd flown in came to form "a collective meta-chopper, and in my mind it was the sexiest thing going: saver-destroyer, provider-waster. . . ." It's a moment of purest sorcery: "Dark powers walk in broad daylight," the Bonaventure surveying the natives of L.A., a sexy leisure-time death dream machine high above gridlocked rice paddies. Of course, Jameson never makes such connections, the logic of separation assuring he'll remain insulated from such perversely subjective thoughts.

The image, however, like a wayward John Heartfield collage migrated to Southern California, has more raw force than all the reasonable, comfortable evasions in *Postmodernism*. I have to think it would also be right at home on *The Curse of the Mekons*. "Big Fucking Slab," the song might be called, a fitting tribute to the architecture of the now. In the meantime, here is Sally Timms again doing "Wild and Blue," her voice as full and sharp as the promise Louise Brooks made: "If I ever bore you it'll be with a knife."

"This is a simulation of a song," Jon Langford insists, welcoming us to a paradise of violence and "the industry of night"; Tom Greenhalgh dresses in punk drag to insist, "It's no joke" (though it is even if every shred of the anger's real). All of which seems to occur in the space between the unrealized possibilities of modernity and the cold comforts of the postmod. Jameson may, almost as an afterthought, float faint notions of subverting "the image society" from within: on the last page, he proposes "the need for class consciousness of a new and hitherto undreamed of kind." Except it is already being dreamt on *The Curse of the Mekons* — ideas not as inert things but as flesh and bone, the smell of sex and drink, a headful of brooding on the memories of lives we've yet to lead.

[1991]

Aftermath

Eleventh Dream Day's

El Moodio

*T*HE FIRST FEW BARS of "Makin' Like a Rug," which begins Eleventh Dream Day's fifth album *El Moodio,* make a pass at the triumphal opening of "Anarchy in the U.K." But in the split second it takes both the cheap thrill and desperate nostalgia of the gesture to register, the scene shifts to a film noir backstreet. In a dead-end room, the familiar riff recedes into the wallpaper, and drummer Janet Beveridge Bean begins to coolly speak her piece: "Frank had a plan, it was his master plan / He found Francis, said you gotta stand by your man." Deadpan pulp seaminess segues casually into shell-

shocked domesticity—doormats who kill their abusers, on the next
Geraldo . . .

But the schematic, well-enunciated sound soon enough reverts
to din, a man and a woman shouting past each other, tangled voices
slashing thin air like splintered fan blades. Then singer/guitarist
Rick Rizzo breaks loose to taunt, "You found a cheap way into me
/ But you can't buy a ticket out," his point driven home by a ham-
mering bass. The refrain sucks Bean in, as though Francis's bitter,
hapless fatalism was a leash that Frank pulled her by one moment
and beat her with the next—the scars priming Francis for her moment of truth. Waiting patiently in the hall, the table set, her piece
speaks its "fiery message" and punches the drunken bastard's ticket.
"Show me what you got," the corpse commands for the last time,
followed by a guitar solo that's as messy as an exit wound. Meanwhile, the woman standing over the body emerges as his mirror
image, her vengeance only affirming his control.

"Makin' Like a Rug," on an immediate level, simply puts the
"pig" back in Pygmalion. More unsettling is how it undercuts the
easy gratification of self-righteous violence (male monster gets what
he has coming), even as it confirms the seductiveness of force on
its own terms (lie down with reservoir dogs and get up with bloody
fleas). In the USA of "Makin' Like a Rug," anarchy has been pri-
vatized, dispersed into a network of fear, torpor, annihilation, and
complicity that feels as intimate and predestined as a junkie's next
fix.

Eleventh Dream Day takes off from everyday clichés of love and
despair, release and loss, then reaches for the passions such lip
service disarms. "Read the map and just get lost," a joyously dis-
gusted Rizzo bellows in the wet kiss-off "That's the Point": *"Just
get lost!"* With second guitarist Wink O'Bannon (replacing the departed Baird Figi—names that wouldn't be out of place in a Sal-

vation Army band / thrift store) and bassist Doug McCombs in tow, Bean and Rizzo (married although they write the majority of their songs separately) sound like they're running for their lives when they're standing still. On *El Moodio* and most of their earlier work, the group slips across all but invisible borders of the obvious, chasing meanings that have been confiscated by the Muzak of routine and appeasement. *Lived to Tell* (1991), which slips back and forth between conversational and literary modes, remains the band's defining moment: fugitives fleeing into the past, bearing stunned witness to their own slow-motion ambush, with Figi's plangent guitar approximating the "Danny Boy" machine-gun aria in *Miller's Crossing*.

You can hardly get more obvious — or more self-deprecating — than the nobody-here-but-us-chickens title *El Moodio*. "Figure It Out," goes one deceptive number, but there doesn't seem to be anything to decipher. The embroidered guitar and two-part harmonies sound thin, chalk outlines at an unspecified crime scene, perhaps tracing a real body or just a metaphor for spiritual death, either way too ephemeral to matter. On cue, a vintage English major's conceit turns up: a sidewalk Jesus with a cross on wheels.

Yet Rizzo's quizzical delivery smuggles the image out of its facile context of irony and pathos. You can hear him work through another set of implications below the surface. The Holy Roller has learned "how to roll with life's bum deals" (Rizzo trips on the last word, as though he can't remember what it meant): he's a living billboard for going with the flow. Rebounding off the entranced singer, the joke lodges in the landscape around him. Under his breath, Rizzo now is talking about a different aftermath, the flow of a cultural putsch that's swept away anything worth connecting with. But when distance as near a thing to shared experience left, people seem as unreal to themselves as they do to others. Like the homeless savior in "Figure It Out," there's no room for the isolated except as images of assent—dimmed shadows of lustrous symbols, representations of acceptance or futility.

Picking up steam as they edge through numb social fallout, Eleventh Dream Day members might be fellow travelers of the accidental terrorist in Paul Auster's novel *Leviathan:* an apolitical man who by chance winds up in a dead radical's shoes, carrying out a bombing campaign against state symbols. Auster's hero blows up small-town replicas of the Statue of Liberty. On the 1989 album *Beet* (a nice pun topped by the live concert bootleg *Borscht*), the group offered "Bomb the Mars Hotel": the hostel standing for the Grateful Dead and all those faces of what Rizzo calls "the righteous monolith," the idiom that promises liberty but produces a tedious side show instead. Interrupting this stream of empty signs, the happy squawk of signifying parrots, Eleventh Dream Day's music can feel like an oblique version of Auster's little explosions, "a disturbance somewhere deep inside the earth . . . the waves were now beginning to rise to the surface, touching every part of the ground at once."

If so, they're stealth bombers: *El Moodio* is made from a fabric of allusions and juxtapositions, some impossible to miss, some unlikely, some only in the ear of whomever might be listening. They invoke rock as a critical spirit, subjective intensity instead of objective fact, hardboiled agency instead of idiot serfdom. On "Honeyslide," the album's longest and most uncomplicated song, they do no more than play a sonic dating game, mingling the Velvet Underground's "Ocean" with the Jesus and Mary Chain's "Just Like Honey." Building the tension gradually, minute by minute, Rizzo holds that last pure note (a scream boiled down to abstract essence) for an eternity and then lets it die away. The release is immense: years of waiting seem to have gone into that moment of pleasure.

The garage rave-up "That's the Point" is distant cousin to both "Twist and Shout" and "(Sooner or Later) One of Us Must Know," but play it enough and under the brashness ("We don't have to say we're sorry"), you can make out the ghostly outline of the Brains' sardonic-pathetic "Gold Dust Kids" ("We don't care for love or money / Just drugs and magazines"). Eleventh Dream Day affirms — if "affirms" is the Mott juste — attitude won't drown out the stench of failure that clings to graying misfits who drag their humiliating, unrealized hopes behind them like so many ragged security blankets.

It's one thing to allude to the Sex Pistols or even Nabokov ("Speak, memory," Rizzo chants in the claustrophobic "Motherland"). But it's another to make them pieces of a single puzzle, revealing the Pistols' "no future" as the precise and terrifying inversion of the sunset Nabokov remembered from his youth: ". . . remote but perfect in every detail; fantastically reduced but faultlessly shaped; my marvelous tomorrow ready to be delivered to me." With tomorrow smothered and today a preview of coming repulsions, the past becomes beacon, mockery, and judge: "Motherland" unspools, and associations tumble forth. Vlad the butterfly impaler, the Pistols' solipsistic heirs Joy Division ("I Remember Nothing" — enough memory already, where's the fucking noose?), and then a real shock: Rizzo's voice picks up a thread from John Cale's archaic *Vintage Violence* tapestry "Charlemagne." The song's "tangled lines" disappear into that searing timbre, recalling the melodious ache of a Cale couplet that almost tells *El Moodio*'s whole story: "The Mardi Gras just passed this way a while ago / Making hungry people of us all."

Guitar fireworks finish off "Motherland," intensifying the hunger — the carnival has been dismantled, its posters left behind as bedding for sleeping derelicts. A song like "After This Time Is

Gone" is all that remains, the hokiest tricks in the book: chimes-of-eight-miles-high guitar, anthemic sentiment, extra mayo. A few seconds into the mantra Bean and Rizzo make of "Long after this time is gone," they step off a cliff together and take flight, into the sun or the underworld, nobody is sure which.

[1993]

18

Build

Me

an

L.A.

Woman

A COUPLE YEARS BACK, writing in *Los Angeles* magazine, Steve Erickson presented an annotated list of what he considered to be the 100 greatest records ever made in—and, in some fundamental sense, *by*—L.A. "Every city has a soundtrack, but sometimes Los Angeles seems like a soundtrack that has a city." Shrewd, imaginative, and meticulous, his Top 100 encompassed "MacArthur Park" (1968, Richard Harris, #86), "Fuck Tha Police" (1988, N.W.A., #74 with a metaphorical bullet), "Earth Angel" (1954, the Penguins, #61), "Closer" (1994, Nine Inch Nails, #48), "I Had Too Much to

Dream (Last Night)" (1966, the Electric Prunes, #38), "Laura" (1944, David Raskin, #30), "The Crystal Ship" (1967, the Doors, #20), "When You Wish Upon a Star" (1940, Jiminy Cricket [Cliff Edwards], #7), "Lonely Woman" (1959, Ornette Coleman, #3), and "A Change Is Gonna Come" (1964, Sam Cooke, #1 with a real bullet, the one that martyred the singer at a south-central motel called the Hacienda). Erickson drew a map of nomadic romanticism and urbane sprawl, utopia and its dyscontents. This was a city of sensibility so open-ended it could accommodate everyone from the Beach Boys to Captain Beefheart, country refugees (lonesome fugitive Merle Haggard, blue yodeler Jimmie Rodgers) to folk royalty (Joni Mitchell, yodeling in more exclusive canyons), the lowdown Seeds ("Unhinged lead singer Sky Saxon thought he was singing to his girlfriend . . .") to Sinatra at his most delicately existential. He cast the City of Night as one bubbling hot tub / melting pot, at least if you were on the guest list instead of the menu and remembered to bring along your personal fondue fork.

The drawback with this ecumenical evenhandedness was it tended to undermine any sense of place beyond a confirmation of the old cliché about "nineteen suburbs" — and several ghettos — "in search of a metropolis." If L.A.'s essence could be present in anything that had been recorded there, its voice and headphone mindset detected in Willie Nelson's version of "Moonlight in Vermont" or CSNY's "Ohio" or Emmylou Harris cooing "Boulder to Birmingham," then it truly was no more than a jumble of freeways populated by displaced commuters, each in a traffic-jammed auto-audio cocoon, forever imagining he or she was somewhere or someone else. (Los Angeles' definition of déjà vu might be listening to *There's a Riot Goin' On* while taking a surface-street detour and noticing outside the tinted windshield that a riot really *IS* goin' on.) Erickson's diligent assemblage, all good taste and timelessness, wasn't a soundtrack to the city so much as the soundtrack to an imaginary filmed-on-location Best Picture candidate: a heavyweight exercise in nostalgic tragedy full of important actors living up to their reputations and bright new ones making theirs, some sort of *Mystic L.A. River Confidential*. Largely missing in action was the city's "secret alphabet," as the Doors called it in "Soul Kitchen," and X dittoed on their zooming 1980 cover/answer record. There was little trace of that "succulent sound" David Baerwald enunciated so memorably on David + David's 1986 "Welcome to the Boomtown": money as hedonism, glamour as power, pleasure as growth industry, "satisfaction [oozing] from her pores." And what of rocks not turned over? Where were those creepy-crawling armies of the defeated, the underemployed day workers of the locust licking their wounds and downing Tequila shots in peekaboo dives from Hollywood to Tarzana?

"You see," Baerwald explained in the next song on *Boomtown* the album, "we'd been swallowed by the cracks." "You see" — there's a whole lost city in the nonchalant way he slips those two words into the chorus. "Fallen so far down / Like the rest of those clowns beggin' bus fare back." We're all bozos on that bus, guilty with an explanation: entropy having snuck up on each aspiring Raymond Chandler, Gene Kelly, or Natalie Wood like an incremental earthquake that took ten or fifteen years to make its damages felt. "Swallowed by the Cracks" had leaky atmosphere to burn, loss you could practically taste, a mood of suspension that could insinuate its way into your psyche like an 8-track tapeworm. This was the musical equivalent to the diffraction of light in L.A., that jarring overlap of flat, ugly, just-the-facts dullness with burnished, dreamy, imposing unreality: where unlimited possibility seems tangible even when defined by its utter absence, which is usually the case. What the song captured was the smog of memory, the air trapped in efficiency apartments dating back to the silent era. It gave a voice to the hangers-on and the almost-somebodies stuck a few rungs below the Bad and the Beautiful: a sigh of perverse nobility. That, too, was part of the myth — the purr/hiss of punctured glamour, the enduring *Sunset Boulevard* sublet allure. Unrequited hope came built into every soul kitchenette, complete with moving finger for writing pink lipstick hieroglyphs on the moldy wallpaper — in Hollywood, broken dreams were a second language. "Telling lies and singing along with the jukebox, baby." Drunks harmonizing with Eagles or Fleetwood Mac hits because those clean lines amounted to the *Architectural Digest* centerfolds of their wet, bewitchy-woman "Dreams," though the bohemia-inclined would opt for the better housekeeping mantra shared by the Doors and X: "Learn to forget."

Maybe Oingo Boingo and Berlin's "Take My Breath Away" were and always will be in heavier local jukebox rotation, but who said anything here about cinema verité? We're looking for a midnight dose of the archetypal, the poetic distillation of well-aged corn mixed with the pulp of history, mystery, and desire. A landscape of the imagination as suggestive as *Chinatown*, a *Mulholland Dr.* for the noir stereo — more than that, the spot where such mythological zones intersect with everyday life and exchange phone numbers or bodily fluids. X's "The World's a Mess; It's in My Kiss" would qualify on its title alone, but there's also that fabulous mobility ("Down we go, cradle and all") and the exhilarating devastation of Exene Cervenka, singing as the wild child of Jim Morrison and Evelyn Mulwray. (Unless once upon a time an inebriated Morrison mistook Roman Polanski for Gipetto and demanded, "Build me an L.A. Woman.") Exene merged punk chaos with hardboiled femme fatalism, lending the song even more nativist flavor than X's great Jack-Webb-on-PCP postcard "Los Angeles." At least if you read between the lines and recognized "The World's a Mess" for a civic-minded plea on behalf of the city's disabled, a heartfelt call to issue handicapped parking permits for emotional cripples. Try picturing Munch's Screamer embossed on an eye-catching blue tag—wouldn't it be the hottest antistatus symbol in town?

For my field-trip money, though, nothing evokes the city of smoke and mirrors like Dramarama's 1993 "Shadowless Heart." Ominous guitars conjuring distant firestorms, emergency sirens morphing into Odysseusian ones, a bewildered populace trying to calculate the angles of a vortex: the Hollywood hills are alive, and they have the eyes of Dr. Mabuse. Tracking in on a makeshift séance spread all across this company town, its proto–P. T. Anderson roll call includes "The ghost with your gallstones," "the chocolate eclairvoyant," "the squid in the phone booth," "the happening actress," and "the girl with the mustache who washes your blood stains." Precarious humanity gets caught in a head-on collusion between doubt ("Don't you know it's stupid to suffer for art?") and surrender ("Don't you feel so good when you're playing your part?"), with just a pinch of Nathaniel West sneak-previewing the latest apocalypse ("The coming attractions can read like a balance sheet") for luck. Everything but frogs is raining down, and they may be involved in the case, too. What makes the allegorical parade come to life is the song's reportorial cadences, its gift of understatement turning looming catastrophe into the daily weather forecast. This is the way the world doesn't end: in a city where the most ordinary occurrences may conceal bottomless fissures, the reverse is equally true.

L.A.'s image of itself hinges on the answer to the survey question, "Don't you feel the shadows in your heart?" (Follow-up poll: does the singer vary the title phrase as "You've got a shatterless heart"? And if so, is that the same thing as the Jewels's thrillingly impervious "Hearts of Stone"? Or is it but another "Heart of Gold" with no name?) About a decade prior to Dramarama's unheard query, Warren Zevon gasped in a brutally funny, Los-Anglicized version of "Werewolves of London": "I saw Jackson Browne walking slow down the avenue / You know, his heart IS PERFECT." Browne being Mr. Sensitivity to Zevon's Mr. Bad Example: the beatific face of seventies Southern California folk-pop-rock, wearing a sad, knowing smile like a halo. Not even the agitated Thomas Mann / Kafka enthusiast who rechristened himself Tonio K. was completely immune to such vicarious idealism and virtue. "I wish I was as mellow as for instance Jackson Browne," he confessed in 1978, and who in their heart of L.A. hearts didn't crave the same equanimity, enlightenment, and Mona Lisa peace of mind? "But 'Fountain of Sorrow,' my ass, motherfucker," K. continued in more of a late-for-the-Sky Saxon vein, "I hope you wind up in the ground," and who in their deepest hearts of napalm didn't share that apoplectic sentiment as well?

Stoked on the fumes of cheapjack disillusion and *Mad* mag intellectualism, Tonio sought a perfect metaphor instead of a heart and arrived at *Life in the Foodchain*. An I-shopped-with-a-zombie wallow in envy, spite, paranoia, and "H-A-T-R-E-D," the album was an erratically brilliant, fly-by-night pastiche whose songs owed as much to *The Rocky Horror Picture Show* as Bowie and Dylan. But "Life in the Foodchain" easily outdistanced "Life in the Fast Lane" and the rest of that iconic *Hotel California* cuisine by bringing dog-eat-Darwinism home to the societal supermart. (Or was it supposed to be Marx behind those wraparound greasepaint shades?) "Watching the shadows for anything moving / And hoping they don't come around," K. cultivated the manic burnout of a junior Jerry Lewis in the seventy-third hour of a telethon for Nihilist Dystrophy. Help K.'s kids learn to give up, "Because everybody's hungry and there just isn't quite enough." (Next he would make an album called *Amerika* and find Jesus. Seriously.) This was the voice of game show L.A., the land of celebrity roasts where everything "winds up on the customer's plate" as a naked luncheon special. You see, our host informs us, it's either swallow or be swallowed, deal or be dealt with. So the insult comic (I-kid-Jackson-but-really-it's-all-in-good-fun-there's-no-bigger-humanitarian-in-this-crazy-town), the producer, the grocery checker, the starlet, the waiter, the guard at the studio gate are all just doing their jobs, servicing the good life with a crooked smile, keeping the business running, the shelves stocked, the dream intact.

Whatever shape-shifting form it takes, any Los Angeles metaphor is bound to the suspicion verging on innate certainty that somewhere beyond or behind the surfaces the real movie was being made, in which theatrical releases were just movies within the greater movie, and everybody was an extra or bit player in this invisible metaproduction whether they knew it or not. Couple that with the intuition there was an entrance waiting somewhere in the city, so that all you needed to do was find the anointed place and time, and you got the Doors: "Break on through to the other side"; "Penetrate the evening that the city sleeps to hide." Starring Jim Morrison as the film student who would be lounge Lizard King, they acted out their own handheld calculated-improvised cinema absurdité piece of Los-Angeles-the-movie long before Oliver Stone's *The Doors*. Art pretenses, white man's blues, Beatnik mysticism, surf-jazz noodling, bourbon-flavored bubblegum protest anthems, topless archetypes gone wild, you name the drowning pool, and the Doors jumped into its contradictions wearing nothing but a cement inner tube. Leaving no cliché untouched, no myth un-molested, the Doors forged a city of the imagination as lesser mortals might pass bad checks, wherein the full untapped potential inherent in mockery, fraud, and travesty (intentional and otherwise) could take on a life independent of its bearers.

Forget the studio albums and authorized concert recordings. Instead, listen to the bootlegs, raw, shoddy, deglamorized feeds that sound like they were taped off a high school PA system on the cheapest reel-to-reel recorder available. Clawing through waves of reverb and distortion while fighting off audience chatter and rampant boredom, the band would routinely launch into a twenty-minute "Light My Fire," a sixteen-minute "L.A. Woman," or a never-ending "When the Music's Over" ("I hear the scream of the butterfly" — thank you, Percy Dovetonsils). Indiscriminately piling multiple types of noise (circular experimentalism, frat-party R&B, gnarly hard rock) onto music-box cha-chas and crystalline melodies alike, the Doors' genius was for bridging underground and the middle-of-the-road devices. Manzarek (organ grinder), Krieger (guitar chameleon), and Densmore (janitor-in-a-drum-kit) came off as the most way-out garage band in history, with an embryonic conception of artiness wholly in tune with Morrison's schlockmeister-of-cermonies self-presentation. Morrison adapted Dean Martin's tippling crooner act for incantory blues-pop-rock purposes, using Dino's effortless timing, slurred tomfoolery, and inside-jokiness to plumb all the great philosophical depths the counterculture brought to a head: sex, death, war, peace, religion, reptiles, "Texas Radio & the Big Beat." Hear the modestly scaled seven-minute "Soul Kitchen" from 1968 lay finger-popping waste to the era's cosmic-karmic piety, interpolating a bit of "The 23rd Psalm" followed by a heartfelt "Shake me baby all night long . . . / Pretty little girl with the red dress on / Do the pony . . ." (which may be from the Book of Samuel the Sham and the Pharoahs). Behold the "Back Door Man"–child: Mr. Mojo Rising in the new-found tradition of the Christ, Frankenstein's monster, Bob's Big Boy, and *The Nutty Professor*.

With "Touch Me" come-ons, "Love Her Madly" rhumbas, and "Try to set the night on Fii-errrahh!" mock-histrionics all going so very far beyond good and awful, the contours of a universe where all taste has been transvalued are apparent. The disquieting, maddening, innovative thing about the Doors turns out to be that the war going on inside their music wasn't a reflection of Vietnam or student unrest or Dionysian revival meetings but a clash of internalized aesthetics. It was a pitched battle between the sensibilities of hip Whiskey A-Go-Go scene-makers and their cloying, insulated, show-business-is-my-lifeblood parents. The Doors attacked from both ends of the spectrum at once, pulling art-speech and abandon "down, down, down" into TV talk-variety shamelessness while pushing ignominy in the direction of transcendence. Mingling the appalling with the astonishing until their defenses against each other collapsed, Morrison's woozy prophecy was that opposites attracted and antinomies could make like the beast with two backs, laying the synergistic groundwork for guest/host relations in a new Hollywood. The Doors opened unto a future where Tom Waits, Jim Carrey, Sammy Davis Jr.'s clone, and Artaud's ghost could all appear on the same vertically integrated talk-show panel and take their turns in the "Will It Float?" tank.

After the zip-a-dee-dada spectacle of Morrison, you might imagine nothing retains the power to embarrass. But there is still one unmentionable skeleton tucked away in L.A.'s closet, one figure who has yet to be aesthetically rehabilitated: Dory Previn, our lady of the quaintly quintessential "Mary C. Brown and the Hollywood Sign," as well as the very minor 1970 autobiographical-singalong number that went, "You were doin' it alone / You were doin' it alone / You were screaming in your car / In a twenty-mile zone." Something about her verges on fiction or fantasy, as though she were a novelist's conceit or a comedian's caricature. I'm tempted to claim she was the heroine of Joan Didion's *Play It As It Lays* (no, that exemplary sufferer was called Maria Wyeth, though DP packed enough neurasthenic baggage to pass for her long-lost sister) or the inspiration for Bowie's *Hunky Dory* (no, even as "Life on Mars?" could pass for an homage to her tinkling numbers about silver screen phoniness). Previn's career arc was straight out of a Jacqueline Susann fable: coming up through the industry ranks, she writes film songs with composer André Previn, whom she marries, and they proceed to win an Academy Award for the theme from *Valley of the Dolls* (naturally). She pops pills, has nervous breakdowns; he leaves her for a young and pregnant Mia Farrow (naturally). In recovery, Dory discovers personal expression is the best revenge by writing therapeutic songs like "Beware of Young Girls," giving herself a singer-songwriter makeover that results in albums with such titles as *On My Way to Where, Reflections in a Mud Puddle,* and *Mythical Kings and Iguanas.* (These are the kind of records Lee Grant's horny, well-heeled matron in *Shampoo* would have listened to in a sequel where she divorces her rich husband, goes into intensive therapy, and has her consciousness raised sideways.) Many phallic symbols, father fixations, and lapsed Catholic confessionals later, Previn triumphantly plays Carnegie Hall. Little Dory makes relatively good, something on the order of a middle-aged Irish female Leonard Cohen, lacking only his pinpoint delivery or feel for language, music, and irony. She compensated with unguarded neediness and soul-searching awkwardness, a schizoid Miss Liberty flashing her inhibitions, plying a gift for the obvious, the inane, and the passably sardonic: "I'm always loving someone / More than he loves me"; "I have flown / To star-stained heights / On bent and battered wings"; "Give me your has-beens / Give me your twisted / Your loners, your losers / Give me your blacklisted."

Previn's songs spoke to the dissatisfaction of Tinseltown's inner children, especially the good girls who'd been abused at the hands of those predatory iguana-boys and bad fathers: "With My Daddy in the Attic" ("That is where / My dark attraction lies"), "Scared to Be Alone" (you only miss folks when they're dead), "The New Enzyme Detergent Demise of Ali McGraw" (mad housewife's disease), "The Midget's Lament" (midget liberation), "Starlet, Starlet On the Screen Who Will Follow Norma Jean?" ("Who do you have to fuck / To get into this picture?"), "Jesus Was a Androgyne" (a she-male Jesus!), Mary C. Brown jumping from the Hollywood sign. All instant clichés shot through with painful gentility, but not without flashes of humor (especially on her Carnegie live album) or borderline insight. (She also anticipated the 1970s disaster movie craze in a series of phobic songs: "The Earthquake in Los Angeles," "The Final Flight of the Hindenberg," "The Air Crash in New Jersey.") Dory may have been a mortifying force of repressed nature (a vegetarian Medusa), but she had a dicey finger on the nervous, self-serving/loathing pulse of the place. Her songs can take you back to the moment when L.A.'s soundtrack of numbing, fastidious, Technicolorized blandness—that "Windmills of Your Mind" / "By the Time I Get to Phoenix" / "Little Green Apples" moat of complacency—was giving way, going under, the buffer zone reduced to a mud puddle. A proper lady of the chasms, Previn gesticulated politely in the direction of the Morrison Hotel: the den mother from "The End" incarnate, ordering crack-ups off the room service menu. While falling short in terms of both craft and ecstatic taste-lessness, she deserves some credit for documenting the sort of squirmy scenes and ghastly platitudes most respectable Angelenos would like to forget they'd ever embraced. (Nowadays that bathos lingers, but it has been mainstreamed, channeled, Botoxed, detoxed, and Xanaxed almost beyond recognition.)

It may help some to have been in L.A. when the big quake of 1971 hit and remember what at least one little corner of that world was like. When I was twelve years old, we were living on Vine Street in a very old, decrepit, and somewhat phantasmogorical apartment building called the Villa Elaine (it's still standing, with a rainforest-grotto courtyard where the walls actually are vine-covered). My father was an ex-stuntman and bit player with vague notions of somehow getting back in the industry at the time, while my mother had her hands full with caretaking duties. For dad rotated in and out of various psychiatric facilities owing to bouts of manic depression with the occasional paranoid delusion on the side. (That also makes me feel a touch of kinship with Previn, as though she were the gaga aunt I could have had: someone literal-minded enough to try to flush herself down a toilet would have complemented my father's flights of Blue-Velveteen grandeur nicely.) So my sense of the city derives from that submerged ambiance, where life had been swallowed by the cracks in advance, and the earthquake itself came not as a trauma but as an adventure. The world swayed, plaster fell, the pool flooded the courtyard, and life went back to what passed for normal. What did it sound like? A whole lotta studio musicians shaking their gourds, rattling their chains: like closing your eyes inside the Cinerama Dome and letting the movie's fear-mongering soundtrack wash over you. The rest of the time, the end of the sixties didn't feel quite so hyperbolic, at least from the back-row seat I had. More like a close-up yet strangely out-of-synch frame, like a print of Cassavetes's *Faces* where someone had overdubbed the sadistically catchy tunes of Herb Alpert and the Tijuana Brass to muffle the high-strung, honest-as-naugahyde soliloquies. I think Dory must have sung a song to that effect back then: "The Lonely Bull and the Psychodramatic Actress," perhaps.

I probably heard her sing it on Joey Bishop's show or Merv's, a frizzy blip on a twelve-inch black-and-white screen. Then we moved, and L.A. receded into memory, to be occasionally revisited in person or via a record or maybe the dead-end street mise-en-scène of a B-movie like *Hickey and Boggs*. It must have been ten years and a lifetime's worth of other music till Dory Previn ever crossed my mind again. Catherine O'Hara was doing Lola Heatherton, the greatest of her *SCTV* characters, the second-tier alcoholic-pillhead singer-dancer-actress par excellence. Seems Lola was starring in a very own comeback special, only Lola was a long way from back; in fact, she was a gibbering mass of personality shards, a basket case coming completely unglued. Tremors ran through her body (with some especially heavy action in the vicinity of her pouting, corpse-white lips) as she attempted to sing one straight from the heart (thumping her chest with a dagger-plunging motion for emphasis). "I wake up every night in bed / And panic thinking that I'm dead." Stunned, I realized — hallucinated? — this had to be a Dory Previn tune.

Or more convolutedly, that it was a note-perfect facsimile of the kind of "serious" Previnesque glower-ballad intent on striking a brittle chord in any aging midlevel celebrity who had ever gotten by on pushover sex appeal. Like a Rat Pack ragdoll afraid her number's up, Lola's going down and out with loaded gums blazing: "No one cares / No one dares TO / You're all just parrrr-aaaagh-sites." As an impression of bad art, a loving recreation of the immeasurably terrible captured down to the smallest nuance, this is genius — so savagely apt and still affectionate, compassionate, even devotional. The wordless milquetoast background singers, the swelling strings, it's as though the later Previn had merged with the earlier one whose *Valley of the Dolls* theme was written for Judy Garland, though Garland was unable to get through a complete take of the song and fell apart as filming began. There are layers within composite layers to this gag, reels within the real: like a time capsule containing all the most deliriously unspeakable aspects of the old regime. Twenty years further on, that frame of reference is even more deeply buried than the remnants of the old Hollywood Ranch Market. (As the friend of an L.A. friend used to say, "You had to be there and nobody was.") Gone, forgotten, but still waiting to be excavated. Waiting for the inevitable. A small but insistent Dory revival, with Jewel and Fiona and Tori and Lucinda all performing on the tribute album. Then the televised concert, where Courtney Love makes a surprise appearance singing Lola's song as a tribute to Dory or Judy or Jim or somebody: "You buy and sell my autograph / But in your eyes I hear a laugh." Just another lost angel come home to roost. Sooner or later, they all do.

[2004]

19

Do the Clam

Elvis Cinema via

Viva Las Vegas

WE SEE A HOLE in the screen where Elvis Presley is supposed to be — it might be any one of a couple dozen tawdry E-movies, torpor as genre, decades ahead of their postmodern time. But actually this is an undertaking of a more recent vintage, with an angelic Elvis figure in full drawl and gold lamé regalia materializing as a fan's Son-of-Sam superego. The King is firm yet gentle, telling the receptive fan he must do the right thing and kill his new girlfriend's pimp: "Put him down like a dog." This may seem some distance from the likes of *Clambake*, but the same devout aura of emptiness prevails; the screen overflows with vacancy. "Clarence, Ah like you," says the Elvisimulacrum. "Always have, always will."

As played by Christian Slater in *True Romance* (1993), Clarence the apostle is an ideal vessel: no one in Hollywood has more non-presence than Slater, a walking, self-congratulating repository of the ersatz. With one glance he can convey all the furious dispassion and smoldering monotony of *Tickle Me* or *Girls! Girls! Girls!* Punch-drunk on fame, he has only to set his glass jaw in an evil scowl or approximate a dangerous grin, and we are instantly transported to that back-projected sea against which Presley the fisherman (for men's souls?) once gave a heartfelt rendition of "Song of the Shrimp."

In Quentin Tarantino's hyperallusive script, poor Clarence is haunted by Elvisness, as social reality and primal fantasy: *Jailhouse Rock* is his Holy Grail of cool. ("I ain't no fag . . . ," the punk who would be King graciously allows, "but I'd fuck Elvis"—as if Albert Goldman hadn't taken care of that already.) *True Romance* is a mélange of cinematic Elvis sightings juiced up with Tarantino's reflexive appetite for cultish ephemera. Besides the bits cribbed from *Mystery Train* and *Wild at Heart* and especially *Badlands* (trading James Dean for Presley even up at the Dead Rebels Society swap meet), there are nods to martial artiste Sonny Chiba, *The Mack,* and John Woo. The whole picture operates in a realm of pop insularity that effectively approximates the self-referential nirvana of *Paradise Hawaiian Style, Spinout,* or *Fun in Acapulco.*

For the full, triumphant return of the form, though not content (anticontent is more to the point), of primo Presleyian cinema—for recapturing that world-hysterical spirit of inertia disguised as action, blatant indifference masquerading as excitement—we must thank director Tony Scott. His entire career can only be understood as a long, inexorable march back to that aesthetic of young-beautiful-and-catatonic. What are Tom Cruise, David Bowie,

Eddie Murphy, and Bruce Willis if not dutiful stand-ins for Elvis? And think how easily their vehicles could have accommodated him: early Presley takes the air corps by storm in *Top Gun Blues*, radiates androgynous passivity for *The Hunger (The Trouble with Vampires)*, returns to his rockabilly roots with *Beverly Hillbilly Cat II*, and uses his later decay to lend world-weary authenticity to *The Last Roustabout*.

Photographed with the septic chic of ad agency coprophilia, *True Romance* has the drugged look of the last days in the Graceland bunker: Elvis keeling over on the toilet, Eva Braun's name still on his quaalude-glazed lips. (Stanley Booth cites Priscilla's account of happier times at Berchtesgaden: "That night, at 3 in the morning, Elvis and I piled a huge stack of his books and magazines into a large box and dumped them into an abandoned water well behind Graceland. We poured gasoline over the pile, lit a match, and kissed the past good-bye.") Tony Scott lingers fondly over equally dim, sadistic hijinks, whether it's white-Negro pimp Gary Oldman (his whiteness hedging the racist stereotype as his dreadlocks confirm it) bloodily shot point blank in the groin and made to die a mongrel's death for our pleasure, or the protracted beating of Patricia Arquette's heart-of-gold 'ho running the cream-dreamy gamut of viciousness.

Scott choreographs these set pieces like showstopping musical numbers, as jarring and prefabricated as the badly synched, assembly-line tunes from a forgotten Presley opus: "Dead Dog Twist" and "Smash Her Face a-Go-Go," say. It may appear Scott has upped the ante of violence in these sequined moments, but what castration scene could be more graphic than watching Elvis abjectly submit to performing "Queenie Wahine's Papaya," what degradation more brutally complete than a dotty duet with Elsa Lanchester for "Yoga Is as Yoga Does"?

We've come almost full circle with *True Romance*, back to the base of Hollywood Elvisdom. But not quite. It has refined the idiom, internalized the soundtrack voice of Elvis — the voice of obeisance, a message plain as the stench on a cadaver's lips: if they can relegate me to this, if they can replace "Mystery Train" with "Do the Clam," what chance has a nobody like you got? The vestiges of chaos and possibility are put on the screen as convincing denials of what they pretend to represent. Actors, events, and scenery are made interchangeable: when every act is gratuitous, all that remains is helpless acceptance, banality as socializing force. This is eternity as defined by the King's cinema, each movie dissolving serenely into the totality, Paradise Elvis Style. It's all a happy-go-lucky blur to us now — E. as race driver–turned–scuba diver–turned–GI–turned–barnstormer–turned–beachbum–turned–daredevil–cum–singer, sameness stretching before us ad infinitum, as promised land, fountain of youth, Formica afterlife.

But in this heaven of cheapjack spectacle, movies that seemed designed to bypass even the drive-ins and go directly to trailer parks, there is something elusive. What, after all, was the allure of deracinated Elvis, that it could sustain three pictures a year for a decade? The idea of the formulaic as narcotic will take us only so far: as far as Tony Scott and Co. are capable of going. Scott's every frame is meticulously designed, ostentatiously serious — an *Architectural Digest* of sleaze and glitz, whereas the genuine Elvis aesthetic was one of infinite carelessness. The nearest analog to Presley's movies would be those of Godzilla. Too bad the celluloid giants were never brought together. Can't you picture the King — as in Kong, and clutching a tiny bleached Nancy Sinatra in his mechanical paw? Godzilla approaches, uprooting palm trees and scattering Cadillacs in his reptilian wake, only to be brought to his knees by a relentless ditty along the toetapping, mock-Calypso lines of "Limbo Lizard Akimbo."

The vapidity of the series is unmediated by delusions of grandeur and as such may contain a germ of mythic purity. It's an alternate universe governed by sheer whim, untouched by any sense of an outside world. These films are postcards from a lobotomized American psyche. Return to sender, address unknown. Yet in the apotheosis of Elvis cinema, a dream city rises out of the American Sahara of fear and sublimation: *Viva Las Vegas*, El(vis) Dorado as untouchable piece of virtual real estate. *Viva Las Vegas* (1964) is some kind of visionary artifact—not a work of art but an animated wax museum of desire and capital at their most perpetually nostalgic and all-consuming. Here are images of a semiotic urbanism, America-as-advertisement-for-itself that took over the global imagination and still rules the discourse of international marketing. All the generic defects of Elvis pictures are in place—the stilted nonacting, craven music, feeble plots, laughable dialogue, and slavish determination not to offend a living soul—but they've been given a kinesthetic, seductive sheen. Under the sign ($) of Vegas, in the convex mirrors that are Elvis Presley and Ann-Margret, every American fantasy of innocence and lust, flawless beauty and easy money, good times and charmed lives, is refracted. In *Viva Las Vegas* as nowhere quite else, neon promise is made mouthwatering, Panavision-Metrocolor flesh.

As a synthesis of the totally square (all desire reverting to latency in order to maintain the appearance of wholesomeness) and the utterly irrational (the resulting flood of displacement), *Viva Las Vegas* basks in its own drip-dry incongruity. It's an American wet dream, but a platonic one: a mating dance so close you can taste it, so remote Elvis and Ann-Margret could be Easter Island statues gazing blindly out from the ruins of a vanished race. There is a nominal story here, concerning impoverished race driver Lucky Jackson (El) and his quest to get a motor for his car, win the Las Vegas Grand Prix and the reluctant hand of sensible, down-to-earth working girl Rusty Martin (A-M). But the narrative proceeds by a mutant, scrambled logic all its own—part music video harbinger and part Las Vegas Chamber of Commerce commercial. It's a trance, but a protean one, as if Warholian Pop Art and Mailerian pop derangement exchanged vows on the consecrated ground zero of the Happy Endings Atomic Fallout Wedding Chapel and Souvenir Gift Shop.

The opening credits situate us in this dreamscape with a terse aerial tour of the Vegas Strip at night. This ultimate in elaborately tacky establishing shots plants us smack dab in the shimmering heart of artifice. The business of plugging all the major casinos transacted, the movie cuts to Elvis coolly navigating the slots and players. He selects a table, puts his money down, raises the dice over his head with an insolent grin. Cut to a Los Angeles garage, where a telegram waved by the hand of his frantic mechanic sidekick says Lucky has won the money to buy the engine he needs. Only the spoilsport garage owner insists on cash, so the sidekick dashes to a telephone: "Operator, get me Las Vegas—quick!"

. . . Meanwhile, back in Vegas, Lucky is just pulling into the Grand Prix pit towing his customized chassis. He immediately falls into conversation with the dashing Count Mancini (Cesare Danova), his affable rival. No sooner do the two slide under the Count's gleaming vehicle for an automotive tête-à-tête than in walks a pair of shapely legs. They belong to a mystery girl. She wonders if someone will take a look at her car. ("It whistles," Ann-Margret purrs; "I don't blame it," comes El's suitably robotic bum mot.) The camera inspects her instead—all that's missing from the examination are a pair of stirrups and a speculum. After a few more moments of obligatory lechery, the as-yet-unnamed sex object whirs off as abruptly as she appeared, the two drivers vowing solemnly to get their minds back on work. . . .

Cut to that night on the Strip, the guys prowling the showrooms in search of her. Now the implicit dissociation can really come bubbling up to the surface: they take a leisurely stroll through the various hotels' Duchampian assemblages of showgirl flesh. This unaccountably culminates in an impromptu, clownish "Texas" medley, staged to restore order to a drunken, rioting group of native sons. At roughly this nonjuncture, all sense of time evaporates as *Viva Las Vegas* takes on the feel of an endless lap dissolve.

Elvis spies Ann-Margret from the Count's window. He and she perform an excruciating but perversely fascinating poolside duet, "The Lady Loves Me," a number so rancid it's like watching the lovely couple sniff cleaning solvents hand in hand—the performers are high on the fumes. Losing his bankroll in said pool, Lucky goes to work as a waiter. Then the two proceed on a whirlwind date that takes them from college stage (El pausing to toss off a number for A-M's UNLV dance class) on through a pleasantly agog ballet of sightseeing. Lucky and Rusty (it's impossible to pronounce the names in tandem without an idiotic grin) go trick-riding on motorcycles, play gunfighters in a ghost town, buzz Hoover Dam in a helicopter ("One of the seven modern civil engineering wonders of this century," A-M gushes helpfully), and go waterskiing (stunt doubles and back projection giving us a taste of that Gidget / Frankie-and-Annette eternal beach party: every teenager's dream of a place in the sunlamp).

We can in good conscience skip the ensuing complications and misunderstandings—the course of true love and all that. Lucky gets his engine (courtesy of Rusty's gruff but lovable dad, played by William Demarest—you were expecting maybe Akim Tamiroff?), wins the race, and they wed happily ever after. It's all so very tidy and stupefying, but the blandness is window dressing for an innate surrealism. What else can one make of Three Stooges slapstick segueing into a pious rendition of "Santa Lucia," or Ann-Margret singing "My Rival" to a kitchen full of twinkling appliances? How about Elvis serenading her at the piano with the tender treacle of "You'll Always Be," while the Nevada backdrop has quietly been exchanged for Mars (all those A-tests, no doubt), with what appears to be a Danish flag off in the middle distance giving the shot a painterly symmetry. This passes beyond kitsch into another realm altogether, a mystic region where de Chirico and *Lost in Space* meld as one, and any second Robby the Robot might appear from the vertiginous wings.

You can rummage through all the Pop images of the sixties and not find anything more inanely suggestive than the sight of Ann-Margret in hot pants, gun-belt, and halter top, outdrawing Elvis and standing triumphantly over him as he plays dead. Planting a demure white boot in his groin, she innocently holds a smoking revolver to her lips and blows. Is it the ideal of wholesomeness that's being turned on its head, or is it deviance that is made safe as milk? When Ann-Margret later does her showstopping "Appreciation" striptease, it stands as the missing link between "Diamonds Are a Girl's Best Friend" Marilyn and "Material Girl" Madonna. More fresh-scrubbed nymphet than either of those sex bombs, her blithe mannerisms incarnate the lost connection between *Lolita* and *The Sound of Music*: a blinding white wedding of pornographic impulse and family entertainment form. (Professor Humbert, permit me to introduce Miss Dolores von Trapp.)

As *Viva Las Vegas* ascends into idyllic abstraction, it reaches a disorienting peak in the climactic race sequence: low-slung cars speed down the predawn, fully lit Strip one second and cross sunny Hoover Dam the next. Montage is arrested into suspended animation, as if to match the static, contemplative figure Elvis himself cuts throughout. The course snakes through rock formations worthy of Monument Valley, high-country pines, and Joshua tree–dotted desert, the movie intercutting frantic racing footage with mismatched reaction shots (my favorite: the repeated one of A-M aboard a helicopter, a cloned gasp at each new road mishap). Then Elvis crosses the finish line, and there's a dizzying jump cut to the wedding of Lucky and Rusty, the inevitable happy ending imposed so abruptly it undermines its own raison d'être. And before the ceremonial rice is even done pelting the beaming couple, we cut away to a reprise of Elvis performing the glitzy title song. This entire sequence sums up the arbitrary, hypnotic quality of *Viva Las Vegas*, which lends it all the woozy poetry of a city sculpted from pickled eggs and American cheese.

But the movie's consummate moment comes earlier, when Elvis sings the Ray Charles classic "What'd I Say" to a twitching, hip-shaking Ann-Margret. Less a production number than a carefully choreographed spasm, it suggests an infectious new strain of myth: a full-blown outbreak of Maileria. The "double life" Norman Mailer spoke of Americans leading then (writing in 1960 about candidate JFK as "existential hero," that is, as an Elvis for the electorate) comes into pristine focus. A black quartet is singing a pseudo–dance number called "Do the Squat" to the white crowd. They disappear from the stage as Elvis comes out of the audience, picks up a spare electric guitar, and launches into his frat-rock take on "What'd I Say." Elvis, as a whiter shade of white Negro, here straddles two rivers: the visible one of conventional appearances and Mailer's "subterranean river of untapped, ferocious, lonely, and romantic desires, that concentration of ecstasy and violence which is the dream life of the nation." He sings and Ann-Margret vibrates with near-psychotic abandon; he moans and she swoons in rapture. They come together, and the almost obscenely well-groomed dancers part like polyester waters before the pair. Holding forth from their display case, radiant merchandise blessing every surrogate lust, Elvis and Ann-Margret are the dream nation's First Couple, presiding over a republic in the guise of an orgy.

A welcome shiver of fever passes through the ontological domain of *VLV*, but it's a self-quarantining condition. The movie's appeal lies in how automatically it is able to reconcile disorder and total domestication — unifying those states with a wave of El's hand, a toss of A-M's luminous hair. But this unity is achieved at a paralyzing cost. There's a secret dread at work here, deviance as the nightmare side of the realm's coin. Systematically evaded by the postcard retrocolor of *Viva Las Vegas*, this buried unrest shows up in full festering black and white in Ann-Margret's next vehicle. With the wonderful Sacher-Masoch-goes-to-heaven title *Kitten with a Whip* (directed by Douglas Heyes), it's a tour of all the lurid possibilities *VLV* took such pains to omit.

If you're looking for projection, you've come to the right place. "You live behind walls here, man," indelicate delinquent Ann-Margret sneers at kindly benefactor-victim John Forsythe. "Where I come from, it's outer space." She's a kinky inversion of *VLV*'s Rusty, pure sociopathic jailbait — the precursor of Bikini Kill's "Alien She," invading the orderly world of a middle-aged family man and Senate candidate for the fun of destroying it. The movie stacks the deck with a paranoid-obsessiveness that rivals the most panicky Red-baiting: Forsythe's hapless suburbanite is integrity personified, set upon by a predatory slut-Goldilocks and her beatnik-hoodlum comrades. Having busted out of Juvenile Hall, the nightgown-clad lass sneaks into the bed of Forsythe's absent daughter (away visiting relatives with his wife, of course). Upon discovery, in short order she lies to, cajoles, torments, and finally blackmails the innocent hero. He's only tried to help the poor, unfortunate girl (with nary an illicit thought), but the baby-doll monster threatens to cry rape, and how would that look to the neighbors, the press, his wonderful family?

The ruthless repression of knowledge — raising multiple specters of incest only to discredit them as the calculated ploys of a bad-seed tease — is the social order of the day. Who then better to represent society to itself than the handsome, upright Forsythe, the very soul of straitjacketed middle-class respectability? Having taken over his home (violating private property—the most wanton act imaginable), A-M throws an intimate "party-party" for her youth-cult pals (one hipster-existentialist in Leopold and Loeb threads, one surf-nazi sidekick, and one zonked fluff bunny: stir well, ignite, and serve). At which point the sadistically reframed sitcom homilies (not only was Forsythe TV's beloved *Bachelor Father*, but wasn't the pet name of the *Father Knows Best* daughter "Kitten"?) descend into a hell of domestic terror, equal parts cut-rate Pinter and warmed-over Mickey Spillane.

The quest for teenage kicks spawns god only knows what forms of blasphemy, rebellion, indecency. The venereal tumors *Viva Las Vegas* sweeps under the temple of capitalism's red carpet come oozing out of suburbia's gold-plated fixtures. (*Kitten with a Whip*'s alternate title could be *They Came from Within*, though Ann-Margret's performance is *Rabid* redux.) Contrasted with the Good Elvis deferentially lip-synching "Viva Las Vegas" (the triumph of the ersatz), Ann-Margret's pussy-whipping she-devil is the insatiable surrogate for the Bad Elvis. That's the Presley of the pneumatic pelvis and the insolently curled lip, the natural-born killer *True Romance*'s clueless Clarence aspires to, the one who unleashed pagan revels and interracial Furies on an unsuspecting land. That's also the one who never made it to the screen—the longed-for, might-have-been synthesis of Dean, Brando, and "Rip It Up," whose place was taken by a wooden Dean Martin manqué, unprotestingly stumbling into a bottomless tar pit of fossilization.

It goes without saying that *Kitten with a Whip* must have its antiheroine die in the last reel to resurrect the Holy Ghost of the respectable; struck with sudden contrition, she gladly gives her life to save the good name of the Father-figure. Like the wedding that caps *Viva Las Vegas*, this death is meant to neutralize the premonitions of sixties counterculture—as if that looming explosion could be defused as easily as Elvis had allowed himself to be. In *VLV*, his beauty is blessed with the tantalizing aura of unavailability. It will curdle in later incarnations, as the infantilized postage-stamp Narcissus seems out of reach of even himself. Made into a symbol of clean living and conformity, he will be nothing but an embarrassment. Born again as an apostle of Dinoism, unlike Dean Martin he doesn't seem to get that the joke's on him, or that there's even a joke to begin with. Ann-Margret, as his mythic alter ego (ironically showing greater screen energy and presence than he cared to display), will inevitably turn up opposite Dino himself in the breathtakingly smirky 1966 *Murderer's Row*. And yet she, too, will be dragged to even lower depths of miniskirted degradation, finally being cast opposite Joe Namath, the most laughable pseudo-Elvis conceivable, for the tame-as-milk Hell's Angels wheeler *C.C. & Company* (1970), with just enough gratuitous nudity to give Russ Meyer fans palpatations.

Yet Ann-Margret's film career somehow recovered—*Carnal Knowledge* (1971) forgiving her the stain of aphrodisia by letting her wallow in victimization, always Hollywood's surefire cure for the transgressive. Which suggests Elvis might have salvaged his own if, instead of choosing *Change of Habit* (1970) for his last cinematic stand, he had sought the part of Joe Buck in *Midnight Cowboy* (1969). For wasn't that role the purest embodiment of what Hollywood thought of him, a hunk of fried Spam, a big dumb gorgeous hick cliché? Good-bye ignominy, hello Oscar—great god a'mighty, taken seriously at last! Alas, that was not to be, though *Change of Habit* was no slouch in the gritty street pathos department. There Elvis played a conscientious ghetto doctor, and Mary Tyler Moore was the nun who had to choose between Elvis and Jesus. The choice is depicted in a wonderfully literal series of shots, madly cutting back and forth between the visage of the King and that of the King of Kings—a sequence worthy of Bruce Conner and far more hallucinatory than any of the pseudo-mod effects John Schlesinger used to tart up the hokum of *Midnight Cowboy*.

Seemingly the despised, feckless Presley oeuvre deserves to have been expunged from human memory. But like the star, it has had a curious half-life after death: it retains a bland, zombiefied insistence that will not be denied. Vaseline traces smeared across the culture like butter on Wonder Bread, from the bloodletting follies of *True Romance* to the zany mix-ups of *Honeymoon in Vegas*, the long shadow of Elvis is inescapable. In the nominally real life of Michael Jackson (the miniseries-in-the-making), we see a lewd remake of the made-for-TV *Elvis and Me*: the underage Priscilla as playmate for her King of Pop guardian. (Updated with the same-sex twist and out-of-court settlement—this is the nineties, after all.) With Prince—or rather the erstwhile Prince, now referred to by that inscrutable male/female symbol whose secret Masonic pronunciation has to be "Elvis"—we encounter a figure who has turned *Harum Scarum* into a design for living. Just as Elvis portrayed a pop star–turned–Arab hostage, Prince holds himself for ransom, coyly entertaining belly-dancing protégées until his demands (world peace, his bodyguards' weight in gold, free vibrators for the masses, and a hot-tub audience with God) are met. Ever the visionary, with his self-directed and written *Graffiti Bridge* (1990) he took this cinematic tradition to a new, blissed-out level of incoherence. With its unblinking mixture of innocent salaciousness and mysticoreligious uplift, it's the ideal showbiz shotgun marriage of *Viva Las Vegas* and *Song of Bernadette*.

Yet fast-forwarding through the endless tinseled corridors of movie Elvisdom is to glimpse a work of metacinema taking shape before our eyes. Call it *Fun in Marienbad*, an American answer to all that desiccated, agonized foreign ennui. What did candy-assed aesthetes like Resnais and Robbe-Grillet know of true ennui? "Put 'em down like dogs," Elvis would have insisted; they couldn't begin to approach the numb splendor of *Easy Come, Easy Go*. Later for that sick-soul-of-Europe crap: in America, we embrace alienation not as chic decor but as leisure, a way of life. The hell with Antonioni—*Blow-Up* and *Zabriskie Point* being merely superfluous in their cultivated triteness, his hollow conception demolished by the runaway train of the Yardbirds as easily as a leatherjacketed Elvis would efface all cinematic sins with 1968's roaring Orpheus-returns TV special. The films of Elvis Presley aren't content to wallow in emptiness but turn malaise into recreation, and vice versa: when sleeping the sleep of Snow White, dreamed banality becomes sanctified reality.

Recently the entity that gave us *Viva Las Vegas* has built the brand-spanking-new MGM Grand—"hotel, casino, and theme park," its commercial modestly trumpets. Could it get any better than that? A sanitized adventure for the whole family, a cosmic Heartbreak Hotel Terminus offering an occupation regime as floor show, collaboration in lieu of the two-drink minimum, and the Resistance as lounge act (proudly presenting "Kitten and the Whips," a dozen shows nightly). "Some small humiliation before you get your reward," sang namesake Elvis Costello in "Glitter Gulch," but that was the sour grapes talking. More than a good time, this Vegas becomes a religious experience. The dispensation of Elvis-for-Everyone is turned inside out: at long last, everyone can be Elvis. At home he may have felt like a tourist, but the tourist looks right at home posing behind the cutout of a rhinestone jumpsuit. Now the lowliest of the low—you, me, even Christian Slater— can finally be King for a day.

[1994]

20

Reification
Blues

The Persistence of the Seventies

SOMETHING GRISLY HAP-
PENED to rock music in the 1970s
that it has never quite recovered from:
the sound congealed into a dense,
ponderous and soporific mass. In the
words of an all-too-popular Jethro Tull
album of the period, rock became
"Thick as a Brick." Nowhere was this
change more apparent than on FM radio.
There the playlists narrowed, rock 'n' roll
aesthetics were codified in lockstep fashion,
and the music business consolidated its
clammy grip on the public's imagination.
It was like an Iron—or rather Led, as in
Zeppelin—Curtain of uniformity had fallen
over the freedoms of the 1960s. Where playfulness, humor, chaotic weirdness, and wayward

passion once reigned supreme, now even excess and outrage came to seem stage-managed by some invisible bureaucracy of FM station consultants, management firms, technocrat producers, and record company apparatchiks.

Rock, as FM radio defined, promoted, and administered it, became less concerned with representing life than with merchandising ready-to-wear lifestyles, serving up self-mythologizing caricatures of lust, rebellion, sensitivity, and anything else bands could get away with. Somehow, though, all moods and whims of the period seemed eternally to return to Led Zeppelin's stunningly ubiquitous "Stairway to Heaven," which stood astride the era like a colossus of drug-inspired kitsch, melding the ethereal with the histrionic: Donovan inflated to King Kong size. The band's blues-based, folk-tinged metal had a monolithic bump-and-meatgrinder quality, set in crafty bas-relief by flashes of aural grandeur and medieval expertise — turning the lean, mean sound Sam Phillips produced for Elvis and Howlin' Wolf into a throbbing "When the Levee Breaks" mass. In the process, Zeppelin laid down the official borders of 1970's rock 'n' roll. From the oh-so-genteel melancholia of Jackson Browne and the Eagles to the posturing shrillness of Black Sabbath and AC/DC, just about everybody aimed squarely for the middle of the same narcissistic road (or in the case of AC/DC, the middle of the "Highway to Hell"). The heady, complicated, anything-goes openness of the Beatles, Bob Dylan, and Jimi Hendrix gave way to regimentation and gray teenage wastelands. Visionaries and weirdos were replaced by Queen-sized carny barkers and choreographed, Halloween-worthy costume parties.

We may tell ourselves that those seventies musical dinosaurs perished decades ago, thinking their remains were long since consigned to the museums of Classic Rock radio and VH1's "Behind the Music" riches-to-rags biographies. But yesterday's bombast serves as the fossil fuel in the tour buses of today's arrogant, glowering stars. The lineage of Kid Rock's redneck populism can be traced back to defiantly obnoxious forebears like Black Oak Arkansas, though his rap/boogie antics have the sterilized trashiness of stick-on biker tattoos. Other current fusions of heavy metal and hip-hop aren't necessarily so blatant about their roots, substituting a newer form of secondhand funk for the psuedo-bluesy varieties once favored by Foghat or Aerosmith. (Seen in the context of post-Zeppelin hard rock, Rage Against the Machine and Limp Bizkit play musical good cop and bad cop, respectively, offering different strokes for different angry young folks.)

On a slightly more rarefied plane, Radiohead's critically lauded *Kid A* recycles Pink Floyd's dark-side-of-the-moon solipsism to Me-Decade perfection. The album's comforting numbness folds leftover bits of trance-rock esoterica from Can and Cluster into the Floydian mix, but every spacey note and vocal tic inhabit some ahistoric twilight zone between homage and amnesia. Radiohead incarnates the feeling that the equally retrograde Wallflowers celebrated in "Hand Me Down," promising "Living proof evolution's through." Here the 1970s represents a form of reverse evolution that colonized the inner life of the pop mind. Just as the Eagles prophesied in their ultimate seventies hit record "Hotel California," we've become captives to a state of suspended animation: every performer who checks out is replaced by an identical android.

Like the fictional band Stillwater in *Almost Famous*, Radiohead and the Wallflowers are mere rock composites. But Stillwater's serviceable, uninspired hard rock was at least intended that way, encapsulating the sounds of 1973 from A (the Allman Brothers) to Z (Zeppelin's Robert "I am a golden god!" Plant). It's music rooted in a specific sense of time and place. As with so many generic seventies bands, Stillwater sounds like a bunch of stand-ins who can't live up to rock's past glories but can't quite live them down, either. It is no accident that *Almost Famous* is set in 1973, for as the director and screenwriter Cameron Crowe says, that was "the year where it felt like the last moment before rock became a little less personal, a little more global." The movie captures that paradoxical moment when mainstream rock was perched on the brink of terminal self-parody yet still retained the afterglow of enchantment.

Even as the film shows Stillwater turning itself into the quintessential image of rock-star privilege, a certain vestigial grace still hangs on beneath the growing music-business gimmickry: the residue of what came before and what might have been. To balance the star-struck enthusiasm of his young alter ego William (played by Patrick Fugit), Crowe brings the great, scabrously honest clown-poet rock critic Lester Bangs (nicely underplayed by Philip Seymour Hoffman) into the picture to serve as a reality check and as the film's subterranean-homesick conscience. "Lester Bangs is the only guy who says that it's all a dirty industry," Crowe has noted. "Yet these people — the band, the groupies, William — are all kidding themselves that they're part of a family when they're really part of an industry."

So if the Bangs character is used as the naysaying voice of doom and disaffection, it is then left to Rod Stewart's 1971 tune "Every Picture Tells a Story" to hold out a glimpse of what was about to be overwhelmed by the new order. Crowe uses the song to score the movie's most intoxicating sequence, in which the music seems to take the hero by the hand and initiate him in the ways of rock: plunging him into another world where every face, look, costume, and movement seem to conjure all the avenues and untold jokes of self-creation, one that feels like the natural culmination of every record he has ever loved. "A kaleidoscope of emotion and experience" was the critic Greil Marcus's description of the song, and it is that warmth, camaraderie, and panoramic generosity of spirit that *Almost Famous* reaches for and that triumphs over the film's pat resolutions.

Recalling Rod Stewart's swift slide from the pinnacle of "Every Picture Tells a Story" into rock's prototypical crowd-bamboozling lounge lizard is to see the death mask of the seventies taking shape. Rock's shared language of desire encompassed countless dialects from Top 40 to experimental, from surf guitar to down-home soul music, all of which were still capable of communicating with one another across cultural and racial divides. But they dissolved into so many niche markets that they came to resemble their buyers' recreational drug habits more than forms of personal expression. But even supposing, by the logic of Sadie Plant's recent book *Writing on Drugs*, that drug taking and expression were intertwined impulses, a cocktail of quaaludes and Jack Daniels did not a very mind-expanding aesthetic make.

The loosely parallel rise of disco in the 1970s didn't fully impinge on rock's stoned awareness, though, until the arrival of *Saturday Night Fever* in 1977, when the sharp-dressing ladies' man Tony Manero (played by John Travolta) made the lifestyle safe for heterosexual mid-America. To which FM rock's infamous disco-sucks record-bashing campaign was an understandably panicked, phobic reaction, given how insular rock culture had become by that point. With whitebread standard-bearers like REO Speedwagon, Styx, Rush, Kansas, and the spectacularly insufferable Journey, rock had good reason to feel nervous and insecure.

Especially when it came to black music: the heirs to Hendrix and Sly and the Family Stone were out there, all right, but were made invisible to rock audiences by FM apartheid. Bandleader George Clinton organized not merely one of the best groups of the decade but two of them at once: Funkadelic's black hard-rock band and Parliament's inscrutable, irresistible funkateers. Collectively known as P-Funk, they were a laboratory that irreverently spliced and diced the DNA of Hendrix, James Brown, Frank Zappa, and the Five Royales, in the process making the most substantial — and deliriously engaging — body of music to come out of the 1970s.

But they might as well have been on another, undiscovered black planet so far as rock's mainstream knew. (It may not be coincidental that Bruce Springsteen's stock with FM programmers rose in direct proportion to the disappearance of R&B elements from his records.) This was the same radio, after all, that ignored Bob Marley and the Wailers, preferring Eric Clapton's embarrassing cover version of "I Shot the Sheriff." (Somewhere, Pat Boone must have smiled, finally vindicated by hip taste.)

In one sense, P-Funk stood for all the countervailing tendencies of protopunk, glam, glitter, and other oddball forms that were excluded from the main discourse but whose records inspired malcontents from Cleveland to Manchester. The decade was a wasteland, but there were streams beneath it that nurtured the punk and new wave music that finally bubbled up to contest the hegemony of FM rock.

By 1976 and 1977, a tremendous frustration boiled over against the status quo, but the pressure had been building for years: far from being rootless, punk had many ancestors, avatars, and godfathers. Consider that from 1972 to 1975, the English glam band Roxy Music released five albums of a wit, breadth, and daring that put Pink Floyd then and Radiohead now to shame. During the same brief period, Brian Eno left Roxy Music and made three remarkable and, if anything, even riskier solo records of his own. At the same time, the group's moonlighting leader, Bryan Ferry, also managed to cut a couple albums of elegantly deranged cover versions, which suggested nothing so much as the imaginary soundtracks to Elvis movies as remade by Rainer Werner Fassbinder.

Roxy Music occupied a shrewdly defamiliarized zone between the Beatles and the Velvet Underground, while Ferry's unhinged suaveness had an edge of real lunatic romance that was no less winning for being so utterly gaga. This shellshocked crooner thought "*Lolita* and *Guernica*" were the latest dance crazes (let's twist again with Vlad and Pablo?), sailing through a blithe world of implied sex changes and inflatable dream girls, carrying on all the while like the manic-mannerist offspring of Cary Grant and Katherine Hepburn in a screwball medley of *Bringing Up Baby* and *Peeping Tom*. This was great popular music lacking only for wide popularity, at least in America. (Roxy Music did have a minor hit single in the United States with "Love Is the Drug" — crossing over into disco territory in a way P-Funk was never allowed to do in the rock arena.) Rock became encrusted in myth in the 1970s, and one of those myths is that of the prepunk period as a yawning musical void.

Indeed, there was more great music floating around in the mid-1970s than there is at the moment, but the frustration came out of the fact that it wasn't at the center of things any longer. Big acts found one note and held it till their lungs burst, while radical music — the aesthetic that grew out of the Velvet Underground's sensibility — became a movement unto itself: antirock, unpopular music as a genre of its own.

That split in rock music, and its aftermath, is still being played out in the culture. It could be dramatized as two variations on *Almost Famous*, each constructed around themes and material omitted or suppressed in the original. One, called *Too Famous*, would be set in the present and would star Eminem as the kid who is given the chance to indulge every nihilistic fantasy of stardom as if the music were no more than a pretext to get at the real backstage goods—the opportunity to be a cartoon Caligula in his own little kingdom of cruelty, malicious practice jokes, and ebullient self-destruction.

The other would be *Never Famous*, set in 1976, and would revolve around the Cleveland dadaist garage band formerly known as Rocket from the Tombs but by then called Pere Ubu. It would document the last show of the original incarnation of the band, as heard on a just-released, archival recording titled *The Shape of Things*. (The departing cofounder Peter Laughner, who knew something of self-destruction himself, was leaving more than the band: he would be dead inside of eighteen months.)

With the band playing such manifestos as the Stooges' "I Wanna Be Your Dog" and the Seeds' "Pushin' Too Hard," as well as such gnomic statements of their own like "Can't Believe It," "Gone Gone Gone," "Doris Day Sings Sentimental Journey," and the suicidal teenage misfit anthem to end them all, "Final Solution," nihilism is the point of departure but not the final destination. The music's dark humor—a sense of life as a cosmic joke and a boundless conspiracy—is shrouded in a corrosive, unforgiving noise. That sound is like a transmission from a vanished world of refusal and doubt, about as far from what rock had become as one could imagine. Heard today, it can make you wonder if the purpose of most of what is on the market now is simply to help you forget that anything like this music was possible in the first place or could ever be again.

[2001]

21

Moles on the Beach / Down in Flames

Ray Gun Suitcase—

The Day the Earth Met the

Rocket from the Tombs

WITH *RAY GUN SUITCASE,* the perambulatory saga of Pere Ubu has come almost full circle. Launched in 1974 as Rocket from the Tombs and shortly thereafter evolving into Ubu proper (named for Alfred Jarry's turn-of-the-century proto-dada saint / sacred monster), the Cleveland subunderground band has followed an erratic trajectory through twenty years of breakups and reformations, genius and obscurity. (More like a genius for obscurity.)

It was late 1976 when Pere Ubu released their third independent single "Street Waves," back with the hilariously morose "My Dark Ages." "I ride a street wave," shouted the A-side, while on the flip ringleader-vocal-contortionist David Thomas stammered, "I don't get around much" like Brian Wilson relocated to the far reaches of an early Roxy Music dirge. Instead of California sun and girls, there was grimy tundra and the Pirate Cove, where the band performed amid a frozen industrial zone. "Across the street," Thomas would later recall wistfully, was the weird façade of the Aeronautical Shot Peening Company and a ballast-ore dump. All of which the music absorbed as found poetry, then transformed by sonic alchemy: the disintegrating city became a "magic beach," endless winter's nights melted into days of "Heaven."

Ray Gun Suitcase washes up on the same shore, "Beach Boys" in tow: drunken sailors on the march, burning houses and plywood guitars (is that Graceland in flames?), tremors under the sand. That mole-man voice is joyously off-kilter yet fiercely serene. It quivers, dances, and leaps years: the mole is beside himself. He's traveled so far to sing these words, to make their dream his own, that he levitates right out of his hole. Performing Wilson's "Surfer Girl" is an effortless two-minute-thirteen-second lark. But it reverberates with all the recondite obsessions that have brought Thomas to this point: the rocketeer finally coming out the other side of the tombs.

In the unguardedness of the moment, there's also a connection to one who didn't make it out alive, Rocket and Ubu cofounder Peter Laughner, with whom Pere Ubu now find itself symbolically reunited, or at least sharing a record label with their late comrade. After years of floundering with bigger labels, the group signed to the small indie Tim Kerr Records, which last year released the splendid posthumous Laughner compilation *Take the Guitar Player for a Ride*. That album is full of a young man's homages—covers of Eno ("Baby's on Fire"), Richard Thompson ("Calvary Cross"), Robert Johnson ("Me and the Devil Blues"), nods to "Baudelaire" and "Sylvia Plath" (the pop-lit-myth equivalent of "Surfer Girl": "Nobody broke anything sharper than Sylvia Plath"), the ever-present shadows of Dylan and Lou Reed. Twenty-four when he died in 1977, he took to rock excess like a stone takes to water; he nullified his life to make himself the Velvet Underground's No. 1 disciple. But applied self-destruction is only the mascara around Laughner's story. The rest is in the fabled bittersweet cadences of "Amphetamine," which borrows its skeletal framework from "Heroin" and its emotional flesh from the far corners of "Visions of Johanna." It's a presciently premature epitaph for an unborn era and milieu, for the singer and anyone who might have shared his inchoate dreams of another life. "We were having a party," Laughner sings with supernal tenderness and regret, "but we weren't invited."

In a sense — in many senses — Pere Ubu's work has constantly retraced those unsatisfied desires, seeking a way to both purge and realize them. David Thomas, happy but apprehensive (happily apprehensive?), can and does seem light years removed from Laughner's inveterate negativity. But on something like "Electricity," he'll plaintively whisper, "Nobody understands / All the words we cherished for so long / Fall on deaf ears." He's put the misanthropic Rocket from the Tombs days behind him, the times when he followed their signature "Down in Flames" with a "Search and Destroy" that napalmed even Iggy's original. But here he comes now with "My Friend Is a Stooge for the Media Priests," older, perchance funnier, yet no less estranged from society: still the world's forgotten boy after all these years.

Chalk it up to "The Folly of Youth," so intensely felt it can never really be shaken. That song opens the album with a wonderful low rumble, a "Peter Gunn"–type theme bound for a beach rendez-vous with the atomic suitcase Mike Hammer's after in *Kiss Me Deadly*. When he sings, "I wanna be your ray gun," you might hear "Reagan" instead — a counter-Elvis materializing deep in the American psyche. "I want to hang around inside your brain and terminal," El Raygun clamors, driven by native insatiability, the hunger that devours itself, the A-bomb inside the Samsonite. We enter his/its city in "Electricity": biblical injunctions, guitar notes like the writing on collapsing walls, fleeing masses, shattered lives, all dismissed with a shrug. Abandoned, the city is a monument to a universe that has come unglued: "Feels like all the faded hopes that never were."

Though Thomas alone remains from the original Ubu, there's continuity in how the band translates abstract-for-its-own-sake sound into cosmology. The way meanings are put together and taken apart has always been the core of Ubu's project: to locate the mystical impulse concealed in the bosom of the modern, to find the temple tucked away inside the Aeronautical Shot Peening Company. In 1978, "Chinese Radiation" imagined a distant cultural revolution as a "big wave," the wake of sixties; "Memphis" rides the familiar backwash, surfing it through the streets as it makes culture so much warm jetsam. In the sky-high wilderness of "Montana" ("In the Year of the Ford / Nineteen Hundred and Fifty-Four"), there's upheaval, exodus, a prophet crying out over an accordion, a tale of displacement that's as old as a cave painting or a Dead Sea scroll.

Through it all, Ubu sounds as resolutely out of place as ever, *Ray Gun Suitcase* belonging no more to the punk-lite present than "30 Seconds over Tokyo" did to the Peter Frampton era. Pere Ubu's music attests to a mode of secret knowledge much as David's precursor did in *The Gospel of Thomas* a couple millennia ago. There

Jesus' twin — Jesse Garon to the King — reported among his prov-
erbs one that might be Ubu's motto: "If you bring forth what is
within you, what you bring forth will save you. If you do not bring
forth what is within you, what you do not bring forth will destroy
you."

*   *   *

HISTORY IS UNMADE at night: in 1975, Rocket from the Tombs
had all the ingredients, from the coolest name (shades of Edgar
Allan Poe fronting the Shadows of Knight or 13th Floor Elevators)
to the darkest, most desperately unforgiving sound ("All the pretty
living dead / Pretty egos to be fed"). With the Stooges and Velvets
for role-remodels, a payload of achingly funny-brutal-mortifying
songs ("Never Gonna Kill Myself Again," "Down in Flames") and
Cleveland's rust-belted heart/wasteland as ground zero, Rocket
from the Tombs were the little engine that exploded. Breaking up
without releasing so much as a single, the band molded its legend
from debris and fallout, raining down the years in the form of
rumor, fable, and ultrascarce bootlegs. But the band might have
taken that nocturnal underground-man-overboard trip a little too
far. Though the remnants regrouped as the deathless Pere Ubu
(David Thomas and the late Peter Laughner) and the feckless,
tinny Dead Boys (Gene "Cheetah Chrome" O'Connor and the late
Stiv Bators), when you mention RFTT to all but the most diehard
obscurantists, all you're likely to get is a puzzled or smirking retort:
"Don't you mean Rocket from the Crypt?"

So the twenty-seven-years-overdue *The Day the Earth Met the
Rocket from the Tombs* may finally dispel that confusion — or like
any great punk album, strew more. Culled from demos and live
performances that have circulated among fanatics on fourth-
generation tapes and the only-600-records-pressed vinyl boot *Life*

Stinks (a steal at the $20 I paid a decade ago, what with copies selling for upward of $150 on eBay last year), it's possible that *The Day the Earth* has only been pried from the Ubu Projex vaults because proliferating CD-R knockoffs of the material were flooding the market, such as it is. With as near to decent sound as home-made recordings and the band's distort-o-rama performances will allow, *The Day the Earth* is a napalmed cornucopia of lost-and-found claims to immortality: the slab-happy decomposition of "So Cold" and the yowling, thalidomide–baby flipper–punch of "What Love Is," Laughner's exquisitely self-immolating signatures "Ain't It Fun" and "Amphetamine," covers of "Search & Destroy" and "Foggy Notion" that more than hold their spleen-machine own, alongside future Dead Boys anathema-anthem "Sonic Reducer" and Ubu antistandards "30 Seconds over Tokyo," "Life Stinks," and "Final Solution."

Not all is bliss in Tombsville, though: the decision to keep the album to a single disc has meant choosing a few inferior performances with better sound. Or maybe of greater "historical interest": documenting part of Rocket's final show, where Thomas had been edged out—well, sideways—as front man, while Laughner and O'Connor took over his numbers. But there was no replacing Thomas, the spazzed-out monolith who called himself Crocus Behemoth and sounded exactly like a man rolling around a cramped stage in an XXX-large graduation gown should. Skinny-voiced Laughner was no match for the strangled, Fatty-Carbuncle misfit's hell of "Final Solution" ("Girls won't touch me 'cause I got a misdirection"), though it worked fine for his own glad-hand–death-wish material à la "Amphetamine" (with its streak of hopeless romanticism as wide and bewildered as Mott the Hoople's "I Wish I Was Your Mother" fused with "All the Young Dudes").

Also, there are small birth-of-a-punk-nation moments and sentimental dedications that have been left off, like the touching little motivational speech Laughner gave on a 1975 WMMS broadcast: It's reprinted in the sleeve notes but just isn't the same on the page as in that flushed, defiantly well-meaning delivery. (The missing link between Lester Bangs and Kurt Cobain, Laughner wore his clown-aesthete paradox of inspirational nihilism like a torn-out, still-beating heart stapled to his sleeve.)

Ex-Mirror Craig Bell's "Muckraker" is a foppish vaudeville stab at glitter-rock, worth preserving mainly for his madly affected pronunciation of "secret headquarters." (If Pee Wee Herman and Todd Haynes collaborated on *Velvet Goldmine*, this would be its theme song.) But to hear Rocket's "Seventeen" today, at once an Alice Cooperish toss-off and a hot template for the about-to-be-born Sex Pistols, is to feel the combustive spontaneity of a moment where from Cleveland to London an identical blunt-trauma impulse held sway.

The Rocket Saga stands as a story of what might have been: a mix of riotous elements (populist, dadaist, teen-revanchist) that coulda-shoulda resonated beyond the fringes of subculture. In the context of RFTT, Thomas's raw-meat bellow and Laughner's corny Dylan / Reed / Richard Thompson rock-poet tendencies have more alienated-youth-market potential than in their subsequent Pere Ubu incarnation. (In Laughner's solo work, there were even stray resemblances to Springsteen's early, street-poet-maudit tendencies.) Unless it's an aging critic's fantasy, "Amphetamine" — its bridge of sighs spanning Fairport Convention's "Meet on the Ledge" and Bob Barker's *The Price Is Right* ("You got to come on down") — might have stormed the charts as some 1970s Teen Spirit cri de coeur. (Punk's answer to "More Than a Feeling"?!) And then a strangled "Oh, god" moan leaps out from the middle of "Ain't It Fun" and brings you back to a reality where no amount of guitar heroics can soften the blow: the outline of a future that's been used up before it's even begun.

"What's become hard to imagine," David Thomas has written, "is the timeless, frozen quality of life as we lived it in 1975, in the terminal landscape of Cleveland, with our drivenness, our rage, and our dreams of breaking through." The intensity of those dreams, the rip and tear of presence and absence in this music, brings it all streaming back: here at last and gone for good.

[1995/2002]

Mouse

Trap

Replica

Anthony Braxton

ANTHONY BRAXTON'S never been cool but has always seemed mighty weird: like a three-legged duck out of water. There's the pipe-smoking, sweater-swaddled egghead persona, a nutty professor dispensing supercerebral, impenetrably systematic post–Ornette/Stockhausen compositions with all but unreproducible algebraic-schematic diagrams for titles — convoluted musical equations that softly scream for a big blackboard and a bucketful of chalk. (Try calling out their catchy abbreviations as encore requests: "Composition No. 69J [+30+108D]"!) Then there's his arsenal of peculiar, unwieldy, and flat-out obsolete reeds (Braxton's business card must say: "Have contrabass sax, will travel"). But even when he plays the conventional instrument he made his name on back with 1968's daunting two-record solo recital *For Alto*, he manages to make it sound like some archaic, stiff-gaited, *Ceci-n'est-pas-une-horn* hybrid: a C-melody saxophone outfitted with a "Dodo Bird Lives" mouthpiece. Bundle all the erudite quirks, quixotic postures, and math-freak idiosyncrasies together, and you've got a guy who might have taught music appreciation to the autistic, led the Frankfurt School's marching band, or played sopranino clarinet in Jelly Roll Messiaen's Red Hot Quartet for the End of Time.

So who is Braxton supposed to be, the Einstein of theoretical jazz physics or the Rube Goldberg of hopelessly impractical, slavishly eccentric follies? Both, actually: the opposite sides of his deadpan brainiac sensibility counterbalance each other nicely, the heavy ivory tower intellectualism humanized by an affectionate, impusive streak of try-anything amateurism. Thus the buildup of methodical tension that he manages to release into some of the most curiously playful improvisations this side of a Thelonious Monk–Pee Wee Russell conference call. Incorporating rude, bracing noises that are both funny ha-ha and funny-uncanny, his solos line up rows of crooked notes that jerk forward like a sand crab being poked with a sharp stick, stuttering eloquently through a tune's back door and/or left field. (Chord changes? Mr. Braxton has a nonexclusive relationship with any he happens to become entangled with.) From the broken-field ramble across "You Stepped Out of a Dream" that opened his groundbreaking *Five Pieces 1975* through the well-lubricated Desmond martini of "Nuages" on *8 Standards (Wesleyan) 2001*, Crazy-Legs Braxton has established a special love-bait affinity with the jazz repertoire.

He's carved out such a niche in the many-splintered tradition that a fan of diligent, irreverent revisions could bypass the thornily conceptualist composer of "ghost trance music" just about entirely and get plenty of satisfaction from Braxton's forays into the past alone. Only a humorless purist could resist the giddy hiccups of *Six Monk's [sic] Compositions (1987)* (Mal Waldron on piano and "Brilliant Corners" setting the table), the interlocking tight-formation spazzle-dazzle of *Eight (+3) Tristano Compositions 1989* (frenetic tempos, unexpected turns, beautifully mindful give-and-take), or the live/studio one-two punch of *Anthony Braxton's Charlie Parker Project 1993*: the latter made old bebop warhorses sound fresh and unpredictably volatile again, with twenty minutes worth of "An Oscar for Treadwell" getting down and dirty to signify the oneness of R&B's honk with the transcendental blurt of the avant-garde. (Play that funky shit, Brax!) And that's not even mentioning the valedictory tenderness and delicacy of his duets with Ran Blake on *A Memory of Vienna*.

Meanwhile, those craving a good, undiluted dose of Braxton's own medicine will hardly be disappointed by *Six Compositions (GTM) 2001*, four CDs' worth of field recordings from a squiggly alternate universe. The compositions are dedicated to the likes of Max Roach, Harry Partch, and Don van Vliet, which as gene pool cross-fertilizations go isn't a bad way of contextualizing his work: Roach the link to the breadth of jazz history (and with whom Braxton has had a couple definitive recorded encounters for good measure), Partch with his self-made, kitchen-sink musical language, and ever-so-idiomatic American individualism of Vliet-Beefheart. (More tangibly, those interminable tick-tock unison horn passages recall Frank Zappa's half-parodic experimental side — will the next step be an album of GTO music?) As far as the ghost-trance part goes, to the untrained ear Braxton's new music doesn't sound that much different than his atonal tone-poem efforts going back to the 1970s, though it's gotten less jazzy and, unexpectedly, less modern-sounding.

It does have a pointillistic, poltergeist-laden busyness, yet somehow harking back to embryonic times before either bop or structuralism was born. On the slithery, meandering Roach tribute, which consumes half the album, the loose-knit ten-piece ensemble's sonorities have a charmingly antiquated quality, a whiff of Threepenny Operas and Cotten Clubs hanging in the rarefied air. But the deliberate, repetitively instrumental motions have the slapstick physicality of early film comedy and primitive animation: Chaplin assembly lines running in circles, stick-figured mice giggling at the switches, knockabout gags presented in pared-down, abstract form. Everything is texture, bustle, plaintive anonymity: a decrepit, self-perpetuating lullaby for the Age of Mechanical Reproduction that keeps going and going like a bunch of nearsighted Energizer bunnies in bumptious search of the lost chord.

A few years back, Braxton put aside his horns for a little while and took up the piano, attacking jazz standards with a fearless thonk, plunk, splat. What he lacked in technique he could hardly make up in reckless enthusiasm alone, but it was fun to see someone so willing to risk a flying leap and take a pratfall with a semblance of dignity and grace. As he's settled into a comfortable middle-aged spread, it may be my imagination, but I swear Braxton's starting to resemble a blacker-and-tanner cross between Laurel and Hardy. His new stuff pales a bit beside the crackling energy of his youthful performances (cf. the Dortmund and Basel concerts Hat Art has made recently available on CD), but the slogan is the same as it's ever been: "Here's another fine mess I've gotten us into."

[2002]

23

Eyewitness

News

Wire

On the borders, there's
movement, in the hills,
there is trouble.

— "Reuters"

SKIMMING A GLOSSY MAGAZINE,
I came upon this irresistibly simple,
poignant line: "Some moments find their
place in history, and others are lost forever." That line — it's subject and author
bound for the country of amnesia, in proof
of its own proposition — somehow suggests
the whole I-feel-mysterious story of Wire.

Formed in the England of 1976, just as
punk was taking hold, Wire had the usual Brit
art credentials and a highly developed sense of

society as, in the words of their American heirs Sonic Youth, "a hole." Wire took that hole for a joke—a gaping maw of laughter and disgust. Plunging straight in, these wild boys also kept a certain distance from the tempest they sought. *Pink Flag*, their 1977 debut, was a punk classic that already intellectualized punk as structure, schema, design: a design for antiliving, seductive alienation masked as interior decoration.

The squashed urgency of Colin Newman's dole-prole irony (his voice a solid vessel oozing implication through a hairline crack) was set in relief by metageneric chords, beats, clamor. Music as Morse code, "Dot Dash" as one Wire single had it—Newman's sarcastic imperviousness, guitarist B. C. Gilbert's pointillist thrash, bassit Graham Lewis's patent murk, Robert Gotobed's rigid drumming. If the Ramones invented punk formalism, then Wire drove the form back in on itself, at exactly the pressure point in modern life where form and psyche had become indistinguishable.

One of *Pink Flag*'s oblique two-minute screeds put it more succinctly: "1.2.X.U." Decades of social engineering and media research had done their job, this cheerfully oppressive sound announced. Identity was kaput: goods and consumers, public images, and personalized nullity ruled. Society was the hole in everybody, and the whole every body was in: Plato's Cave as institutional norm. (Bring your own party favors.)

By *Chairs Missing* in 1978, Wire had moved on, passing through unregistered spaces in social and physical texts, navigators of false presence and real absence, a virus in the cultural computer. "I am the fly in the ointment," the record stated, and beyond that, there was nothingness. No hope of intervening in the mechanism, just the volatile, drowned mise-en-scène of a "French Film Blurred" and the minute pleasures of futile sabotage and paradox.

Next came surrender to the inevitable—art. 154 screamed it, albeit tastefully: the album resembled a remake-cum-deconstruction of Roxy Music's *For Your Pleasure*, draining away the lust and fun in favor of excruciating pretension. Here was the equivalent of Antonioni directing Vincent Price reciting "In Every Dream Home a Heartache," which worked on its own deadly earnest terms, but even the stray self-mockery came off as solemn, joyless. The story, now complete, unfolds of a piece with *On Returning (1977–1979)*, roughly half of each album plus a few singles (thirty-one tracks on the CD), charting the chasm between two adjacent poles: actual clandestinicity and calculated obscurantism. The band split up in 1980, moving on to hapless solo careers and unheard or unlistenable projects, even as Wire was claimed as a touchstone for hordes of disparate young bands (a legacy only made good by those, like Sonic Youth, essentially indifferent to it).

Bored and broke, Wire reformed in 1986, as though bent on unmaking their reputation one footnote at a time: the *Snakedrill* EP and *A Bell Is a Cup Until It Is Struck* have their woozy pop-psychedelic moments, while *The Ideal Copy* and *It's Beginning to and Back Again* are mainly shiny hollows, tinny voices, and dancing-robot rhythms. *Manscape* amounts to Depeche Mode for aging dilettantes, with not one instant of radicalism equal to the samples on En Vogue's frothy Top 40 melodrama "Hold On."

But I've left something out—the best Wire moment of all. That would be *Document and Eyewitness*, two vintage live records released together on Rough Trade, the first an LP of guitar feedback and irrational din from a date at the Electric Ballroom, the second a more moderate EP featuring synthesizers (though they still make ruder noises than the ones on *154*) recorded at Notre Dame Hall. The later portion of *D&E* contains a few familiar numbers like "Heartbeat" and "2 People in a Room." The rest is obscure or unknown stuff: the sinister, droll "Go Ahead"; the sinister, malev-

olent "Ally in Exile"; the sinister, hysteric "Underwater Experience." Captured is a band on the verge of art pulling back in the
nick of time, clinging to a sense of unease instead of substituting
stylish mannerisms for it.

The Electric Ballroom performance is by far the stranger of the
two. With the exception of a mad fragment of "1.2.X.U." given an
exquisitely smarmy and embittered introduction that is longer than
the excerpt heard, this is a concert of previously unrecorded material. (Included is an inchoate, even more spasmodic reading of
"Underwater Experience"—under lava is more like it.) Wire's leit-
motif here is disintegration, with no aesthetic distancing involved.
Printed on the album sleeve are stage directions that foreshadow
Madonna's blond ambitions ("Woman enters pulling two tethered
men and an inflatable jet") and fondly hark back to Hugo Ball's
greatest hits ("Zegk Hoqp" calls for "12 percussionists with newspaper headdresses," which is what it sounds like). Critic Jon Savage
has observed "Wire would differ from concert to concert," but that
doesn't begin to describe *Document and Eyewitness*: the band's
phantom repertoire sounds both meticulously worked out and entirely made up on the spur of the moment. The instrumentation
is punk, the spirit unfiltered dada—a concert of songs that never
were, with Wire playing their own secret doubles, enacting a notion
that the history they made was simply a gloss on (or cover-up of)
the real, untold story.

Perhaps, then, *Document and Eyewitness* is the covert refusal
behind the open one. What else can be made of "We Meet Under
Tables," "Eels Sang Lino" (sung with the conviction of "God Save
the Queen"), "Piano Tuner (Keep Strumming Those Guitars),"
and "5/10"? Surely these songs were created with no purpose in
mind but to have the last word on history, a word that proves to
be unpronounceable. A posthumous statistic forwarded from the

dead-letter office, the sort Wire always reveled in: "Five out of 10 / Without grounds would dismiss . . . / C'est la vie / Reba reba / Amoeba amoeba . . ."

"To avoid relegation," Wire stated in *Pink Flag*, is to win the game. But as *Document and Eyewitness* attests (a document that dispels the idea of witnessing anything clearly), relegation *is* the game. The only way out is through a field of lost moments, into the impossible.

[1990]

24

William Parker

WILLIAM PARKER'S upright
bass walks the way Forest Whitaker
does in *Ghost Dog* — a watchful,
coiled amble that appears to be moving in two or three directions at once.
You can find that touch-of-Zen implacability running through his cunningly
adroit recent trio album, *Painter's Spring*,
like a cool breeze — Parker's closely miked
instrument both leads and shadows every
downscale second of the action. But to
take the measure of his bristling sound —
the human face of the bass that has tethered the outward-bound expeditions of Cecil
Taylor and David S. Ware for years — you
have to hear the title epic from his Little
Huey Creative Orchestra's wonderfully named
double CD, *Mayor of Punkville.*

The thirty-minute piece opens with Parker's low, anatomy-of-a-murmur basslines, then drums and off-kilter horns enter the black-and-white picture: Ghost Dog goes into a bar and orders a bourbon, a jaunty Sun Ra taking requests on the bandstand, the air thick with smoke and the sweet smell of corruption. He starts getting dizzy; something's been slipped into his drink. He stumbles out the door, but the music follows him onto the street. People approach him with urgent, confidential information, but when they open their mouths, only the sounds of squalling horns come out. The next thing he remembers is waking up on the floor of a strange apartment, reaching in his pocket for the picture of the woman he's been sent to find and realizing he's wearing someone else's clothes. Suddenly, that woman is staring down at him, a tattoo of a snake covering half her expensive face. "Where am I?" he croaks. "Baby," she smiles cryptically, "you're in Punkville now."

That's one take, but there are 8 million other stories in this imaginary city — *Mayor of Punkville* is full of back alleys and trapdoors, New Orleans–style funeral resurrections ("Anthem," appropriately dedicated to the late Lester Bowie: "Very simple like a frosted window melting in the sun"), Ellingtonic Orientalia (the swaying chinoiserie of "3 Steps to Nøh Mountain"), hard-nosed wails ("I Can't Believe I Am Here": *Fight Club* as jam session), even a Ra-powered mysterioso vamp called "James Baldwin to the Rescue." Parker keeps these long, drifting flights of fancy grounded by the rough-hewn physicality of a dozen or more equally unpredictable soloists, whose riffs rain down like cloudbursts of sweat out of a clear blue sky. Trancelike concentration and random tenderness turn abstractions into loose-knit, gutbucket raves, where a weirdly ebullient current of idealism and hope hums beneath the streets of noir. In *Mayor of Punkville*'s alternate universe, cosmic jazz rises from the underground to wash away the "CEOs, gangsters, politicians, television talk show hosts. . . ." From the utopian ashes of Coltrane's *Ascension*-era war on spiritual poverty and Mister Ra's beatific, cacophonous Neighborhood, Parker posits his own oddball version of the Great Society. One where outcasts, misfits, the indigent, the indignant, and the emotionally homeless all band together to make a place they can call their own.

As a state of mind, Punkville is an open city: With Parker as mayor, he might just go and appoint Captain Beefheart (erstwhile "Sheriff of Hong Kong") police commissioner. And maybe he could make the elusive Marvin Pontiac — a.k.a. John Lurie, actor, Lounge Lizard, and host of the best avant-garde fishing show since SCTV's *The Fishin' Musician* — his reverse dogcatcher, setting the captive mutts free. "I'm a doggy," the man growls mournfully (and literally) at the beginning of the putative *Greatest Hits* of apocryphal bluesman the Legendary Marvin Pontiac. Like Parker's, this is a fantasy of eccentric mind over historical matter, perpetrated in Lurie's case by assuming the convivial persona of a deceased, superobscure singer; he's channeling the spirit of a man who never existed but should have. Marvin's funny, slippery, polyglot Afro-talking-blues owes as much to the rumpled NYC hipster-bum Lurie played in Jim Jarmusch's *Stranger Than Paradise* as it does to Nigeria or Chicago. This beat-up Pontiac runs on laughing gas and can only make left turns but cruises the passing scene like a Greenwich Village Popemobile with a pair of fuzzy dice hanging from the rearview mirror. Lurie/Pontiac speaks slowly and softly, bemused by the voices DJ'ing in his head. "Roger Maris says not to watch TV / There's too many molecules to see." He lags a little behind the juju groove, speaks in parables and come-ons ("I've got a bone for you," though the way he says it, the birds may have already picked it clean), blows a little Beefhearty harp or smuggles in a trombone, a banjo, whatever the listener isn't quite expecting.

The Legendary Marvin Pontiac and *Mayor of Punkville* come
from different directions to arrive at the same destination. Behind
the premise of Lurie's record, there's a notion of smoking out the
real Marvin Pontiacs and their forgotten 45s, bringing forth the
genielike lost souls whose unheard music might still hold a key or
two to the universe. Parker's *Punkville* plays out an equally engaging fantasy of seduction as revolution, urban legends made into
agents of urban renewal. A free society builds itself from the musical underground up: a beloved community that's stranger than
fiction and paradise alike.

*   *   *

RECIPE FOR NONGENERIC, deliciously unsweetened, naturally
surreal jazz: add wiry violin, cakewalking bass, and bubbling drums
to a country-bluesy composition called "Dust on a White Shirt,"
then churn ebulliently. The result comes off like a thirties black
string-band porch dance simultaneously pushed into we-sing-the-
body-acoustic expansiveness and stripped to bare-bones intimacy.
Down-home and out-there, folk forms and urbane abstractions, all
get folded into a surprisingly straightforward common language,
one that unobtrusively dissolves the distance between eras and
wavelengths. Bass whiz William Parker calls this unit his Violin
Trio, and their *Scrapbook* sounds like a gutbucket extension of the
central nervous system. A crisscross microcosm of plangent,
impulse-relaying grids, it's the kind of omnidirectional work that
keeps surprising you with its complicated simplicity, playful grav-
itas, and awe-inspiring lack of self-importance.

"Holiday for Flowers" has a modesty that is especially becoming:
Billy Bang's masterful violin saws out a poignant, tipsy melody, and
Parker answers with the plucked notes of a man waltzing on egg-
shells. Steadily eluding categorization, veterans Bang, Parker, and

wily drummer Hamid Drake come within shouting (or whispering) distance of jazz, classical, and folk traditions without getting bogged down in reference points and the kind of semiconscientious formalism that nowadays seems to run through everyone from Ken Vandermark to the White Stripes. "Singing Spirits" could be descended from Julius Hemphill's "The Hard Blues"—or, just as plausibly, from the Kronos Quartet's nifty arrangement of Television's "Marquee Moon." Yet the sources couldn't be more irrelevant: What counts on *Scrapbook* is the unmediated soulfulness and fierce care, not the slim residual traces of Jimmy Garrison-esque basslines, Revolutionary Ensemble dynamicism (Leroy Jenkins's nearly forgotten seventies violin-bass-drums experiment), and old-fashioned Ornette-on-fiddle interludes.

"Sunday Morning Church" covers the most ground, spanning Bang's restrained virtuosity and the unadorned Parker solo. *Scrapbook* is full of aural history—the quaver of a bottleneck slide sans guitar and dappled flecks of cotton-field dust on jukebox 78s—and personal idiosyncrasy, so while it doesn't break any big, overt new ground, it still feels like a pretty indelible little landmark. It's not pointing to some new jazz movement but perhaps indicating a newly focused tendency toward small, handcrafting gestures and skewed musical conglomerations, centered around but not confined to Parker and his associates.

Eloping with the Sun is a way more solipsistic version of the same aesthetic: Parker playing the oudlike African zintir along with longtime comrade Joe Morris on banjo and banjouke and the always dependable Drake on frame drum. "Stepdance" has a nice borderline tunefulness, but *Eloping*'s lengthy overall effect suggests ethnographic Peace Corps variants on a Captain Beefheart homily: The dust blows forward an' the dust blows back.

However, Morris's *Age of Everything* anti-power-trio manages to make opaque austerity really swing—"Way In" undulates with a hypnotic insistence that rises to *Scrapbook*'s heights. Also part of the minitrend are drummer Susie Ibarra's lovely *Radiance* (featuring the great Charles Burnham taking the bowing honors) and *Songbird Suite*—sounds that seem to float above convention with an are-you-out-of-body-experienced rapture.

But out of all these recent string-driven things, my favorite is a solo project from Derek Bailey, the éminence grise of free-improv guitar. *Ballads* is a classic counterintuitive move, putting the racket king's splayed inversions at the service of terse, sonorous, oh-so-delicately-warped caressings of staples such as "What's New" and "You Go to My Head," along with Hoagy Carmichael's "Rockin' Chair" and "Georgia on My Mind." This is sentimentality transfigured into breathtakingly direct ruminations, a wedding of melody and dissonance worthy of *Thelonious Himself* or a Django from another planet. If Bailey hooked up with Parker and Billy Bang, they could start a twenty-first-century Hot Club: unfettered beauty and crazy rhythm, a ganglionic tangle of strings wired for euphoria/melancholia.

[2000/2003]

Book

of

Exodus

Plastic People of the Universe

THE SCENE IS RIGHT out of
a dialectical fairy tale: a band that
once upon a time became a subterranean legend, an avatar of freedom
and refusal, reunites to record a live
album. The group reaches back almost
a quarter century into its repertoire to
dredge up the now-quaint signature
tune "Waiting for the Man." Only this
isn't the Velvet Underground finally paying a call on a stadium full of adoring fans
somewhere in Europa but a much more
obscure and mysterious outfit that sprang
from such fandom itself in the waning days
of 1968: the Plastic People of the Universe.

Born in the wake of the East-bloc invasion
of Czechoslovakia—Soviet tanks in the streets

on a mission of "normalization," rolling over the socialist reforms of the Prague Spring—the Plastic People were as much a secret society as a band. Keeping alive a forbidden language of disorder inspired by smuggled-in Western music (the Velvets, Captain Beefheart, Frank Zappa, the Doors), hounded by the authorities (denied instruments and venues, their clandestine concerts raided by the police, their members eventually imprisoned for "disturbing the peace"), they were a resistance movement unto themselves. In hit-and-run performances and privately circulated recordings (some of which in turn were smuggled to the West, to receive their only official release), they kept history itself alive— here was the sound of a phantasm haunting the totalitarian imagination.

On the 1992 reunion album, *Bez ohňů je underground*, "Waiting for the Man" is no more than nostalgia, a sweet, slightly wooden gesture to a different time, another world: one that gave birth to the Velvet Revolution, which abruptly overthrew the Communist regime. Those swift, surreal events in late 1989—with citizens peacefully taking to the streets to reclaim their country, almost reenacting the 1968 invasion in reverse—would thrust author Václav Havel into the country's presidency. Havel had written admiringly of the Plastic People of the Universe and contemptuously of their 1976 trial, in which band members were convicted of "extreme vulgarity with an antisocialist and antisocial impact" and of "extolling nihilism, decadence and clericalism." This trial in turn had served as a catalyst for the Charter 77 human rights group formed by Havel and other Czech intellectuals, which itself had catalyzed the Velvet Revolution. (That the Velvet Underground could be a source of revolution confirms the obvious; that gadfly-in-the-ointment Frank Zappa, who was a deeper influence on the Plastics as well as a personal favorite of Havel's, could serve as a revolutionary catalyst tells us how bizarre the politics of cultural transmission can get.)

Now another song begins, this one a version of the Fugs' "Garden Is Open," and everything scripted about the concert is driven out by the music's swirling, millenarian currents. Milan Hlavsa's voice casts a spell of allegory, as though Max von Sydow's backward-counting hypnotic-suggestion narration in *Zentropa* had been transposed into a new idiom: the Edenic promises of the 1960s instead of the Mephistophelian ones of the 1940s. All of which only sets the stage for the entrance of Jiří Kabeš's electric viola, elegiac notes turning in a circle of ritual, as underneath him the band distills the Coltrane Quartet's incantatory polyrhythms into slow-motion fireworks. Then a guitarist—either Josef Janíček or Jiří Števich—picks up the viola's melody twisting it into an emblem, the entrance to a dream. The guitarist seems to hold in his hand every utopian, absolutist wish of sixties music, but the modalities he wraps them in call up the sixteenth-century Prague where the revolutionary mystic Thomas Muntzer once preached utopian, ab-solutist sermons through an interpreter.

Returning the Plastic People to their ritualistic beginnings, this detour into the unknowable evokes how truly otherworldly their early concerts must have seemed. Wearing togas dotted with pe-culiar insignia, heavy makeup turning their faces into masks, they might as well have dropped into their occupied nation from an-other planet. Which explains the mock flying saucer they per-formed in front of, if not the sign they placed at the front of the stage, declaring "JIM MORRISON IS OUR FATHER"—another sort of extraterrestrial, perhaps, but in the translation to Czech sen-sibilities, one every bit as extreme as the beheaded heretic Muntzer.

Yet "Garden Is Open" and *Bez ohňů je underground* are really just epitaphs. For the full measure of this recondite story, or as close as you can get without having lived it, there is the Czech-import limited-edition box *Plastic People of the Universe*. This contains the four albums the group put out over their almost two decades of existence: the legendary *Egon Bondy's Happy Hearts Club Banned* (recorded 1974, released in Europe only in 1978), the dark antiopera *Passion Play* (source of the charges of "clericalism," though the liturgy most suggested here is Captain Beefheart's "Dachau Blues"; recorded 1978, released 1980), *Leading Horses* (1981/1983), and *Midnight Mouse* (1984/1987). But the box also contains four additional albums, which fill in many of the gaps in the Plastic People's saga: *Francovka* (material spanning 1974–1979), *Eliášův Oheň* (1972–1976), *Slavná Nemesis* (1979), and *Hovězí Porážka* (1983–1984).

Taken altogether, this music becomes the soundtrack for a great lost epic: an absurdist verité documentary, perverse home movies superimposed over official propaganda reels, basement tapes ransomed from a captive house. But the plot still has a familiar air. The 1970s material is rife with corrosive intelligence, while the later recordings grow ever more formal and remote — the Plastic People's sound slowly loses its resolve, its moral claim on the lives it might chance to enter. By 1984's "Kanarek," the screams are no more than a house-of-wax affectation against a tasteful scrim of chamber-rock woodwinds, violin, and viola. You hear nothing of the upheavals to come, only solemn inertia, as though orthodoxy had seeped into the band's souls.

Resignation, however, was a false ending: the Plastic People had disbanded by 1988, but their core — Hlavsa, Janicek, Kabes — assembled a new group called Pulnoc (pronounced "poolnotes," meaning "midnight"). "Kanarek" resurfaces on Pulnoc's fabulous 1991 American release *City of Hysteria*, and this time it's tough and unforgiving: the spirit of the Plastics, and of the victorious underground Second Culture they shaped, seems to have survived intact, after all. But if *City of Hysteria* is composed of sharp echoes of past struggle — "A time of memories . . . ," sings Michaela Nemcova, quietly. "A time of black holes" — strange corners of the Plastic People experience still remain out of reach. None is farther removed from rational discourse than *Francovka*'s mad eight-and-a-half-minute beatnik tribute to the deity called "Phill Esposito." From the opening, a basso introduction of the promised land ("New York, Madison Square Garden") amid noisemakers, whistles, clanging silverware, and chanting voices, the Canadian hockey player takes on new life as a cargo-cult icon. No one would call this music as such, but it's brimming with good humor and demented conviction; the baggage of East and West is melted down for precious metals, to be fashioned into nonsense charms, ecstatic symbols of disobedience.

In the essay "Stories and Totalitarianism," Havel writes of the destruction of historicity as state project:

> The fundamental pillar of our present totalitarian
> system is the existence of one central agent of all
> truth and all power, an institutionalized "rationale of
> history," which becomes, quite naturally, the sole
> agent of all social activity. Public life ceases to be an
> arena where different, more or less autonomous
> agents square off, and becomes no more than the
> manifestation of the truth and will of this single
> agent. In a world governed by this principle, there is
> no room for mystery; ownership of the complete
> truth means that everything is known ahead of time.

The Plastic People's story found its meaning in the negation of that world. In a time when most music is dedicated to the abolition of historicity and the continuation of late capitalism's narcissistic monologue of itself, the runes the group left behind remain as unconditional as ever. They constructed a dream of exemplary public life out of the conditions of their own suppression. In the face of "nihilization" (Havel's succinct term) and state-administered boredom, the band escaped into the catacombs of an unborn city. "Let the dead rise from the grave," Hlavsa sings in Pulnoc's "End of the World"; the lyric was written by Ivan Jirous, the Plastic People's most-imprisoned member. The line looks back to *Passion Play*, which began with the song "Exodus 12," and beyond that to a phrase from that biblical book: "We be all dead men."

[1994]

26

Prophecy Girls

Sleater-Kinney—Cadallaca—

Sarah Dougher—Sally Timms

STICKY LITTLE FINGERS

7IT'S TOUGH BEARING the burden of other people's dreams: Sometimes the three women of Sleater-Kinney must feel that all the expectations and desires the group has to shoulder have taken on a life of their own, independent of the music itself. When they released *The Hot Rock*, it was greeted with the same kind of ecstatic reviews as *Call the Doctor* and *Dig Me Out* ("their third perfect album in a row" and similar genuflections), automatically rubber-stamped as a masterpiece like it was unthinkable now they could make

anything less. But it didn't have the riveting velocity of those records, instead enacting an uneasy tug o' war between abstraction
and immediate gratification, with even the harshest, most unrepentant parts having a vaguely watered-down, wet-blanket quality. *The
Hot Rock* sounded like all the Great Whitegirl Band hopes that
have been pinned on Sleater-Kinney—the drama of liberation, significance, and unfettered emotion we crave because it's such an
endangered species—weighed on their voices and minds, as if they
were caught between living up to what they had come to represent
and shedding those roles for reinvented skins.

With *All Hands on the Bad One*, their latest bundle of wild gifts
and contradictions, every trace of hesitation is gone: "Go ahead
and flunk my ass," Corin Tucker dares skeptics and fanatics alike,
savoring each word with a kickboxer's taunting grin. (She can find
more tactile delight in a handful of raw syllables than most singers
discover in a whole career.) Being critical darlings (however well-
deserved ones) has always given Sleater-Kinney the air of straight-
A-student punks, the endearing kind who've always read the right
textbooks and never failed to strike the proper empower-chords. In
"Youth Decay," "All Hands on the Bad One" ("We would be no
better"), and the alternately scathing/uproarious "You're No Rock
n' Roll Fun," they wrestle with the lust for approval and break free
from it. Especially in "You're No Rock n' Roll Fun," they jump
into the backlash against their own virtuous image feet first,
bouncing different points of view off each other like blindfolded
gropers in a mosh pit. Playing hedonism against upright integrity,
they catch the ridiculous limitations of both but mainly capture
the beguiling giddiness of temptation—the inadmissible wish to get
dirty, fuck the consequences, and be what we are most afraid of.

There are still a ton of good intentions strewn across the darkly
euphoric surfaces of *All Hands on the Bad One*—songs about

eating disorders and women's exploitation, manifestos for re-claiming pop music from prefab toyboys and the engineers of social consent—but while the words can look didactic on a lyric sheet, the singing never ossifies into "messages," moral posturing, or one-way metaphors. Tucker and Carrie Brownstein own their voices so fully they can afford to lose themselves in any given moment: they sound their freest when singing about the absence of freedom, looking into the eyes of the enemy within. When they overlap each other on the glowering "#1 Must Have" or the even rougher trade of "Male Model," the cross-talk traffic between Tucker's brooding ardor and Brownstein's girly irony has a tension that slices right through the song's protest conventions, diving into a word or a line like a pair of scavengers prowling for sunken treasure. The way Brownstein ominously coos "No more" in the former or the bliss-fully obscene pronunciation Tucker gives "forked tongue" in "Youth Decay" opens up the material like a freshly undressed wound: the eternal, internalized struggle to find a home in your own flesh even as the world tirelessly works to make you feel like a perfect stranger to yourself.

But on an album whose most emblematic song, "Milkshake n' Honey" (with Corin Tucker turning herself into a sex predator/kitten combination of Serge Gainsbourg and An American Barbarella in Paris), happily rhymes "Pick up the phone" with "Meet me at the Sorbonne," desire has the first and last word. There's a sense of playful trashiness here that carries over from Tucker's side project Cadallaca, the sixty-nine-teardrop garage outfit whose new four-song EP *Out West* is as much a throwback to *Johnny Guitar* as it is to the Seeds—except on *Out West*, Sarah Dougher's organ lays siege to the saloon. With Cadallaca, the melodrama, despair, and longing are all bigger than life and cheaper than a hard-boiled paperback ("God gave up on me that day!"—not a bad send-up of PJ Harvey's spaghetti-gothic heroines, either).

No part of *All Hands on the Bad One* is quite so blatant or magnificently corny, but there's the same willingness to embrace abandon and risk looking absurd or foolish in the process. It takes as much nerve to make the hilariously pornographic noises that fade out "Milkshake n' Honey" as it does to contemplate the horror and disgust of "Was It a Lie?," where Tucker tries to comprehend the surveillance-cam voyeurism that makes the nightly news into a snuff-film factory and an anonymous woman's death into tabloid-TV fodder. The spectrum of fun and experience here is much greater than before, but the album seems no less brutally intimate for that: Sleater-Kinney have made their *Beauty and the Beat*, even if its pretty uncapped teeth still retain the bite of Liliput's "Split." Danger, glamour, sex, and dread—what sticky fingers these conspirators of pleasure have. (Particularly drummer Janet Weiss—the surehanded Charlie Watts–Maureen Tucker glue holding all this sophisticated boom-boom together.) Yet *All Hands on the Bad One* doesn't settle for the Go-Gos' demure ministrations; it means to work the whole loving fist all the way up your tight little mind.

WAKING LIFE

SARAH DOUGHER KICKS OFF her spellbinding *The Bluff* with a beautiful nightmare. In it, she's hostage to her feelings, an explosion waiting to happen: "33 bombs with 33 wicks / Strapped all over me." In spite of the angelic background harmonies, this isn't entirely what the Chords had in mind when they sang, "Life could be a dream," in 1954's mushroom-cloud reverie "Sh-Boom." The affect of "First Dream" is nearer the rising tidal wave of Max Frost and the Troopers' 1968 psych-out "The Shape of Things to Come," crossed with the shimmering night-sweat dread of Elvis Costello's 1977 "The Angels Wanna Wear My Red Shoes." Dougher dreams out loud in the voice of her unconscious, a Prophecy Girl bearing proof of her worst fears in one hand and holding out the most implacable hopes in the other.

On *The Bluff*, Dougher plays the Oracle of Delphi as Annette Funicello, or vice versa — as if a bad dream were a wish that your heart makes, and passion dissolved every distance separating Seer and doe-eyed, beach-party Mouseketeer. Desire is her great equalizer and great leveler: it puts the highest and lowest on the same footing even as it parts the ground beneath their feet. Befitting an academic who moonlights as a rock 'n' roller, Dougher's songs are finely wrought, with pop-classicist melodies even more eloquent than their extended metaphors. In "My Kingdom," the pensive lilt is as sweet and grave as the night is dark. It builds up like held breath, until Dougher lets it tumble out with a weary, "Yeah, yeah, yeah," affirming her solitude and defying it.

All the same, the proper, literate, well-behaved front these songs put up is just a cover story, meant to conceal the trashiness that lurks in Dougher's heart of hearts. She's kept that side of her selves under wraps on her solo albums until now, saving it for Cadallaca, the girl-grope side project in which she plays wicked organ and sings rubbed-raw, abjectly horny numbers like "Your One Wish" and "O Chenilla." Heard in the tawdry, riveting, thrillingly shameless live versions that surfaced online last year only to vanish into the Internet ether, Dougher sounded like the bastard child of Sappho and the Mysterians, her tongue possessed by the language of high school eros and lovesick folly.

That has carried over to *The Bluff*, sometimes between the lines, sometimes as blunt as a slap in the face ("You ask me in and then you treat me like an uninvited whore"), nowhere more obvious or more liberating than on "Must Believe." Playing wiry rhythm guitar against Jon Nikki's run-don't-walk lead, her hard voice going head-to-head with the wild backup screams of Corin Tucker, Dougher strikes a folk-punk balance that could fend off the Beau Brummels on *Nuggets* as easily as it might take over the jukebox at the only lesbian bar in Salt Lake City, where its anomalous combination of refusal and denial would be right at home.

There's an open-endedness in this music that gives it a staying power Dougher's previous albums didn't have, an expansive warmth prodded along by the great Sleater-Kinney drummer Janet Weiss on several tracks. Even partially submerged in the airy mix of "Wide Eyed" or the cluttered one of "Keep Me," Weiss gives the songs a physical intimacy, rolling her snares like a dancer's hips. Pain comes with Dougher's territory, but a hedonistic streak runs through her most forlorn laments. Her plain delight in rhyming "distances" with "difference is" or cooing a deadpan one-liner straight out of the Young Marble Giants joke book ("The system works, but not for you") bleeds into the breathtaking despair of a couplet like "Now I look over the rooftops of the houses of my new town / Hundred years to build up and seconds to fall down." In Dougher's dreams, the rain of loss never stops, but in her double-edged pronouncements, she makes heartbreak sound like the best of all possible worlds.

ARTIST OF THE YEAR

SALLY TIMMS'S DECEPTIVELY modest album *To the Land of Milk and Honey* (on Chicago's tiny Feel Good All Over label) might be the soundtrack to an allusive montage of film clips: "Round up the usual suspects," it begins, ironic images of the past displacing the impoverished present, mocking a passionless era. Her journey is composed of slow tracking shots, tight close ups, lingering fades to black. "There'll be silence from now on," she sings of a new age that lulls us with its litany of horrors—the endless sleep of shock treatment and wet dreams. Here the stolen reverie of John Cale's "Half Past France" (the vintage violence of uncounted 1940s Greene-Ambler spy thrillers reduced to nervous small talk and brutal epigrams) melts into Jackie DeShannon's "Everytime She Walks in the Room," performed as though it held the key to all the unrequited desires of the 1960s. In "King Ludwig," letter bombs travel by carrier pigeon, and the Grateful Dead play at the behest of the Czar. "It Says Here" is also a letter to—or from—another time, doubling back its own meanings like Chris Marker's video missives in *The Last Bolshevik*.

And then there is "Longing, Madness and Lust": dulcet tones against an irresistible beat, a language of unreconstructed defiance in the face of long odds. "Gotta get a gun that can shoot around corners / And a magic bullet / that can turn in the air"—shades of Brigitte Lin in *Peking Opera Blues*. As radiantly bitter as the Sandy Denny of "Genesis Hall" (Fairport Convention) or the Ulrike Meinhof of "Did She Jump or Was She Pushed?" (Baader-Meinhof Gang), Timms plunges into that abyss where life waits in exile. "A poor girl makes love, a rich man is shot," she sings with her finger on both triggers; "I will pump meaning into your dreams." You could listen to that line from here to eternity and never exhaust the audacity and resolve behind it.

[2000/2002/1995]

27

Money Jungle Music

Matthew Shipp

TAKE THE A train rumbling through Matthew Shipp's piano: repeated fistfuls of Johnny Staccato chords, gunmetal black-and-white flesh tones, Weegee-board flashbulbs jutting out at ramrod left angles, no 52nd Street exit in sight but out the window maybe a ruminative Siberian death march or two through "Summertime" or "Autumn Leaves," grand nineteenth-century storm clusters crashing into twentieth-century seawalls of silence, systematic fingers besieging sleek architecture like carpenter ants on a wood binge. Let's call this Money Jungle Music—full of static runs, urbane claustrophobia, and weird repose, issuing from an all-night lounge where the ivory distance between Erroll Garner and Cecil Taylor seem as short as the fuse on the man who keeps requesting melancholy-baby selections from the *Anatomy of a Murder* soundtrack.

Shipp's tightly wound jazz is abstract the same way any good late-Fuller / early-Godard gangster-reporter-director comes across as the distillation of uncounted tough-guy postures, profiles, gimmicks: a walking, ticking confrontation between melodrama and incredulity. Tersely didactic, his brand-spanking *Nu Bop* goes for a shock-corridor effect that condenses jazz vamping as monomaniacally as the first Ramones album stripped the British Invasion down to barest obsessive essentials. *Nu Bop*'s subway-tunnel clattershot is achieved without recourse to guitars, machine-gun horns, or a massive attack of synthesized beats 'n' loops. The electronic treatments dabbed on by Shipp's coproducer-programmer Chris Flam amount to a light impasto of computer-generated landscaping and a touch of subliminal cosmic slop, no more pronounced or obtrusive than the pianist's deep fondness for his sustain pedal. "Space Shipp" and "Rocket Shipp"—the same riff/rhythm/conception given the once-over twice—mostly arrive at their power-trio force by acoustic means: hyperpercussive keystrokes, William Parker's hard-nosed monster bass, Guillermo E. Brown's harshly syncopated, chain-gang-on-parade drum routines. Elsewhere there are short injections of Daniel Carter's sax and flute, which (except for a dream-interlude duet with Parker on "X-Ray") only pour a little localized color/anesthetic into the mix. Everything here is dedicated to getting the texture of things just so—and binding it to a clanging pulse that isn't techtronica derived so much as techtronica friendly: a sonic palette folks raised on the Chemical Brothers, Aphex Twin, and Fatboy Slim can dig without compromising Shipp's native-son audacity.

Nu Bop's intent is to reclaim a place for jazz in the hipster underground, plugging into some motherboard of Cool that would serve as the ne-plus-ultramodern equivalent of the moment circa 1947 or so when Bud Powell and *Raw Deal* film noir and the prebeatniks and postcubists were all loosely fellow travelers on the road to a darker, destabilized tomorrow. If the album nonetheless feels boxed in, that's because there is no comparably newish wave to hook up with these days — it's every artist for him- or herself, and let history bury its own friggin' dead. Once "Select Mode 1" and "Select Mode 2" rework the main theme for the third and fourth time around on a disc that clocks in under forty minutes, the shortest attention spans have had the whole repetition-compulsion drill driven home, to the point where *Nu Bop* starts to feel less like a slam-gambit of an album and more an extended single featuring multiple versions interspersed with a batch of crafty, throwaway B-side miniatures. (Even the Ramones were able to vary a one-note thesis with more subtlety.) In all fairness, Cecil and Ornette have spent the last thirty-odd years recapitulating the same adorable pet licks ad infinitum, so if Shipp wants to dance on your head with one of his own, it's hard to begrudge the guy. And maybe tossing us a brilliantly warped demolition-cum-renovation of a standard would be just too easy, old-fashioned: on this air raid, no prisoners, no interrogations.

Shipp has been David S. Ware's right-hand man in the tenor saxophonist's indomitable quartet for more than a decade, fastidiously gathering intelligence on free-jazz purism and classicism. Ware's *Corridors & Parallels*, with Shipp moving to synthesizer, laid a fair amount of *Nu Bop*'s tonal groundwork. But for all those gamelan-orchestral, atomic organ-grinder squiggles and bits, the ever combustible Ware's avant-romantic flights placed the album squarely on the doorstep of Throwback City: abounding echoes of Coltrane going agape-crazy or Gato Barbieri completely communing with the cries of sweaty wide-screen lovers. Ware's furiously rhapsodic elegy—nostalgia for a golden age that never came—has an open-ended beauty, while Shipp's futurism-is-now project goes for a microscopically calibrated functionality. His music's clean lines and rigorous designs suggest something of a good Bauhaus-keeping aesthetic: sturdy and/or delicate pieces of finely tapered furniture, indicated by past prescriptive titles like "Algebraic Boogie," "Syntax," "Inner Order," "Self-Regulated Motion," and fourteen separate layers of "Strata."

Few, however, manage to put their ideas into practice the way Shipp, as artistic director of Thirsty Ear's Blue Series, has been able to stamp the label's jazz arm with his own sensibility. The releases he's produced or shepherded there since launching the series in 2000 have carved a niche for themselves as instantly recognizable as sixties Blue Note or seventies ECM. (In fact, it amounts to a rapprochement between Afro-modern and Nordic chamber modes.) He's even collaborated on the ingenious calligraphic-geometric cover-art graphics that set apart the Blue Series—no artist photos or liner notes; a minimum of credits; a flat, handsome laser-printout look that packs all the identifying details of a highbrow bar code. In marked contrast to the old free-school approach of Aum Fidelity, where along with Shipp many of the Thirsty Ear crew (William Parker, Roy Campbell, Mat Maneri) cut their teeth, an almost military discipline predominates. The twin poles of Shipp's quartet releases, the relatively straight-ahead *Pastoral Composure* (with trumpeter Campbell) and the more abstruse *New Orbit* (Waddada Leo Smith doing valve honors), are models of shrewd, efficient introspection. But shying away from sprawling, emotive gesticulation makes Campbell's *It's Krunch Time* feel slightly attenuated, dampened—like cramming Kevin Garnett into a compact car. Craig Taborn's *Light Made Lighter* is too beholden to Shipp's schematic approach, but that seems to work fine as sweetener on the Webern-baby-burn violinist Maneri, whose *Blue Decco* sounds about as close to carefree as brooding gets. Tim Berne's *The Shell Game* departs from the formula to make its own prog-rock / art-funk gravy, consisting of drawn-out saxophonic crop circles, quaint-as-a-ring-modulator electric piano, and plate-scraping continental drift. Wild card of the bunch has got to be Spring Heel Jack's oddball collaboration *Masses:* instead of the expected dance-mix samplings culled from your favorite Thirsty Ear releases, this is a hardcore dose of atonal impressionism featuring a lineup of Squeak-King All-Stars.

Funnily enough, it's Aum Fidelity that has jumped into the remix-crossover scene with *Black Cherry* by Organic Grooves, an engaging rewiring of a William Parker / Hamid Drake bass/drum *Piercing the Veil* as ambient techno (be-blip?). But dance beats or not, it looks like Shipp's *Nu Bop* signals a new round in the great snipe hunt for that creature called fusion: still in the Thirsty Ear pipeline is a Guillermo Brown groove-thing called *Soul at the Hands of the Machine,* which strives mightily to update electrified Miles for the Rave Age. And further down the road (and off the beaten track), there is the William Parker Quartet's amazing, goofy-sublime *Raining on the Moon:* a different kind of symbiosis with singer Leena Conquest, going back to the future in search of a missing jazz link to the soul-poetry of Van Morrison. Like Laura Bush said recently about Dostoyevsky's novels: "All one summer when I was a schoolteacher in Houston, I read 'em around the swimming pool, so even though they're set in very cold Russia, they have this sort of bio-humidity about them that I remember."

[2002]

PART THREE

Waterloo Sunset Boulevard

28

Such Sweet Thunder

Pauline Kael, 1919-2001

> The greatest achievement is that you come out of the theatre, not dull and depressed the way you feel after movies that insult your intelligence, but *elated*—restored to that youthful ardor where all hopes are raised at once.
>
> —PAULINE KAEL, reviewing *Before the Revolution* in 1966

IN 1971, Pauline Kael published the long, combative essay "Raising Kane," her unbridled, impudent, and dazzling account of—and answer to—Orson Welles's most unbridled, impudent, and dazzling film. It was a

match of historic movie and groundbreaking critical sensibility—
set a shoot-from-the-hip pop sensibility to catch one—that brought
out the best in one another, like the sparring, contentious reporters
in fast-talking newspaper satires. Kael rolled up her sleeves and
plunged into the great vernacular belly of *Citizen Kane* with the
same reckless, nose-thumbing gusto that Welles found when recasting the life, myth, and times of William Randolph Hearst as
an audacious, crowd-teasing entertainment. "Raising Kane" polar-
ized as deeply as it galvanized, just as the film itself once did: she
insisted that its greatness derived not just from Welles's genius
alone but from the unique alchemy he was able to achieve with
screenwriter Herman Mankiewicz, cinematographer Gregg Toland, and the Mercury Theatre actors.

As controversial, even scandalous, as such a notion was and remains to cineastes, it merely adjusted the perspective on the director's role from autocratic-totalitarian fantasy to a slightly more
democratic—and realistic—model. She never denied Welles's
enduring greatness but suggested that a good measure of it in *Kane*
lay in drawing out—and on—the integral talents of his collabora-
tors. (Along the lines, I would venture, of Duke Ellington's best
music: with Mankiewicz in Billy Strayhorn's role, Toland in
Johnny Hodges's, and the Mercury players as the rest of the band.)
But for every person who felt "Raising Kane" cut through the tendrils of cant and bullshit that engulfed film criticism in posturing
pseudo-intellectualism and auteurist hero-worship, there were
howls of ire and indignation from those who felt Kael had smeared
the reputation of the Great Man. Though "Raising Kane" was an
obvious labor of love—not blind love but the knowing, clear-eyed
kind that wasn't dependent on self-abasing illusions—the act of
questioning the Ur-Director's all-seeing, godlike omnipotence continues to strike some (bless their resentful little heads) as a slander
that falls somewhere between critical heresy and high treason.

"A freak of art," Kael had the nerve to call the picture, but what else could you call such a triumph of pure American idiom—*fun* and irreverence mixed together with gaudy-lofty ambition—over good and bad taste alike, miraculously synthesizing and unifying smart-mouthed newsroom comedy, Expressionist atmospheres, melodramatic devices, parodic kitsch, Freudian parlor games, deliciously stylized acting, and "comic-strip tragedy." Yet Welles couldn't take that perfect bemused compliment kindly, as perhaps it came too near the truth of a former boy wonder who had by then become a monstrous joke on himself: the Elephant Man adrift in Xanadu. The vast interior spaces and looming figures of *Kane's* visual style, Kael wrote, "suited Welles; it was the visual equivalent of the Shadow's voice—a gigantic echo chamber." The voice belonged to Welles; the echo chamber encompassed both the movies and America itself, its resonances ricocheting back and forth between treasures and junk, toppled crystal balls and forgotten toys.

Pauline Kael found her own indelible voice in the same arena: *I Lost It at the Movies*, the gloriously brazen title of her first collection from 1965, insisted that movie palaces really ought to be pleasure domes. But pleasure for her took in any and every kind of experience: sensual, intellectual, emotional, or ideally, all of them at once. (She preferred movies that stimulated the full range of the senses to those that served as sensory deprivation chambers.) Extended and developed in such books as *Kiss Kiss Bang Bang* and *Reeling* (my own first encounter with her work, which was love at first sentence: "Movies— which arouse special, private, hidden feelings—have always had an erotic potential. . . ."), that seductive and defiant aesthetic inspired more people to become writers than any American criticism before or since. Her hyperresponsive, intensely personal prose electrified readers because it spoke to how most of us really absorb movies and other art, too: not as desiccated "texts" to be picked over like splayed-open med-school cadavers but living, breathing, organic forms composed of all kinds of different impulses, contradictions, cross-fertilizations, and cross-purposes. For her, the best movies, directors, and actors were often the most self-divided ones: *Weekend*, Peckinpah, Brando. Lifelessness was always public enemy number one: she felt films ought to have a pulse, along with a reason for being beyond cowing or boring the viewer into submission. The same went double for film criticism, and she wasn't shy about holding up the blind, tone-deaf, and dumb to ridicule — passing within spitting distance of an Arthur Schlesinger Jr. nuclear-anxiety "think piece" to note it contained "such glowing embers as, 'Life today is full of tragic choices' (one of them was his decision to become a film reviewer)." She loved movies and artists that embraced the full measure of mankind's "corruption and beauty and humor" — *McCabe and Mrs. Miller*, *Taxi Driver*, *The Makioka Sisters*; Renoir, Bertolucci, Godard — but had little patience with endurance-contest cinema that expected audiences to suffer for the auteur's art as if doing penance for the sins of Western civilization.

Moviegoing wasn't an act of contrition or mortification for her, which explains why Kael didn't have much use for figures like Robert Bresson: his strict, self-negating brand of Catholicism-for-atheists made as little sense to her as the notion of Jews for Jesus. She preferred comedy to misery, because comedy happens to be one of the things the movies do best and that most critics appreciate the least. There was a particular affection for those indigenous, uneven, small-scale pictures that grew out of Preston Sturges's screwy, homegrown fables: *Slither*, *Slap Shot*, *Citizen's Band*, *Used Cars*, *Melvin and Howard*, *Diner*, and even way out on the far fringes of that America, *Blue Velvet*. "I salute *M*A*S*H* for its contribution to the art of talking dirty," she once wrote, and likewise reveled in David Lynch's contribution to the dream-logic comedy of perversity. (Thus, too, her natural affinity for Pedro Almodovar, Bertrand

Blier, and of course, Buñuel—an antispiritual soul mate.) In Kael's appreciations of the films of a Jonathan Demme or the Richard Pryor concert movies, which were not deemed significant or important by conventional wisdom, she displayed a peerless feel for the textures and foibles of American life, a prodigiously sympathetic imagination for what it means to live in this oversized and cacophonously schizophrenic country, where practically everyone lives a double life as both citizen and "displaced person." She understood that Richard Pryor told us far more about what it meant to be an American than the white-on-white, Hollywood-rococo fabrications of a Douglas Sirk, or for that matter the breathtaking, vacuous, art-of-the-living-dead films of a Terrence Malick. Demme's work and Pryor's soul-baring comedy *connected* directly with people's lives in a way that too much "cinema" didn't, because they weren't alienated from or disdainful of those lives—Pryor's was a rough art (and Demme's a gentle one) born out of love and pain and compassion, not distance and scorn and incomprehension.

As Armond White wrote, her "openhearted" writing "enlivened the national discourse itself." Reviews were often openhearted surgery: ruminations on the state of things in the country, registering the zeitgeist and sometimes railing against it, going toe-to-toe with the creeping fascism of the Nixon era or the radical-chic delusions of the sixties. You can hear her think as she's writing, working out her feelings, testing her instincts against a movie's and testing the movie's content against the world's. On *Last Tango in Paris:* "it's like seeing pieces of your life, and so, of course, you can't resolve your feelings about it"—and in that review, she put every iota of herself into it, as naked and unabashed as Brando. In her headstrong way, she was able to break down the barricades separating high art and pop idioms, reaching beyond the often hermetic, specialized world of serious film criticism to engage a much broader and more diverse audience. "She didn't just make writing about the movies and the world seem possible," Manohla Dargis said in a thoughtful homage, "she made writing itself seem possible." She was that good, and that much of an original, even if like *Citizen Kane* she had influences, predecessors: Otis Ferguson, James Agee, Leslie Fiedler. (Manny Farber was perhaps not so much a source as a parallel universe: his gnomic, inscrutable Thelonious Monk chords to her endlessly wending, omniverous Charlie Parker riffs.) In the end, she wasn't just the best American movie critic; she was our best critic, period.

Her gender made that achievement all the sweeter, given the obstacles she had to overcome. Dargis again: "Kael didn't hide behind an anonymous first initial, as many women of letters once did, but neither did she factor her sex into the equation, I suspect, because being a woman critic was a challenge and sometimes an affront to the world. (It still is, to gauge by the invective that has seeped into recent remembrances, including some obituaries.)" The vicious, scurrilous sexist innuendo some of her foes continue spreading even unto death—their projected fantasy of her as some Queen Bitch Dragon Lady Master of the Universe—would make a good subject for a satiric novel about the petty jealousies and pathologies of self-styled "objective" critics who were so threatened by her they developed a collective form of castration anxiety. Her gripe with Andrew Sarris and auteurism was partly with the way any theory tends to ignore the context and ambiguities of its subject when applied exclusively, indiscriminately, instead of selectively. (She also thought there was something askew about the pride the auteurists took in directors "triumphing" over third-rate generic material while denigrating those who made something good out of smart, interesting material, as if the latter was taking an easy way out.) But it was also very much her annoyance with the silly boy's-clubby tone of the whole list-making, Pantheon-building endeavor, which always smacked of arrested adolescents trading baseball cards or collecting comic books: earnestly maintaining Otto Preminger was a better pitcher than John Huston or arguing that Robert Aldritch could beat Carol Reed in a pitched battle at the Fortress of Solitude. Top 10 lists might be a useful form of shorthand, but taking such rankings seriously reduced passion to trivia: who would really want to attempt a list rating their top ten friends or memories?

I have come this far without really dealing with the reason I find myself writing these words: Pauline Kael has died, and even if I hadn't been fortunate enough to know her and count her as a friend, I would still feel an immense and irreparable sense of loss: it is another hole in American life that will never quite be filled. I suppose I could yet take up such burning questions as whether she was "too influential" or — my favorite — "bad for world cinema." (The short answer to both would be partly yes, partly no, and mostly: "Tough shit.") Like Welles, she practiced an imperfect art and was not immune to the temptations of excess. But what counted was that she attained the same level of joy and illumination and sheer giddy nerve — at times she missed the mark or the boat (*Raging Bull* comes to mind), but even then she was vastly more enjoyable to read than most of the critics who got it "right." I may prefer Pauline's ecstatic reactions to Brian De Palma's movies to some of the movies themselves, but how can folks who slobber over practically every second-class, slapdash one-week wonder Fassbinder ever churned out complain about the incoherence or inanity of *The Fury?* What sane person hasn't sometimes prayed for the sour, hysterical cutout characters in a Fassbinder flick to explode the way De Palma's do? And what could be more poetically just than having psychodrama's glowering dark prince John Cassavetes, in the wonderfully ungrammatical mantra of SCTV critic Billy Sol Hurok, "blowed up real good."

Sometimes good trash can be more stimulating than empty,

sterile art about Big Issues like emptiness and sterility. And sometimes—more often than criticism's killjoy elite cares to admit—
high art can be just as fraudulent, evasive, and pandering toward
its own constituencies as the lowest, most shameless Hollywood
blockbuster. If Pauline Kael taught us one crucial thing, it's that
pleasure really *matters:* in the emotions evoked by the Taviani
brothers or in the Borscht-belt schtick of the Ritz Brothers, in the
screen presences of Paul Newman and Cary Grant, in the satisfaction a Pamela Reed gave whenever she turned up a supporting part
and when Rip Torn, at last, grabbed the brass ring on *The Larry
Sanders Show.* And, yes, there was Robert Altman, through all his
ups and downs, but Satyajit Ray as well (despite all the rhapsodic
things she wrote on behalf of them both, she wasn't able to make
hits of either *Thieves Like Us* or *Distant Thunder*). Her sometimes
grandiose claims and pronouncements were a way of throwing
down a gauntlet, as movies themselves are at their best: bolts of
lightning meant to shake people out of their habits and complacency, reminding them not only how rich art ought to be but life
as well. Pauline was the most vital, joyous, tough-minded person
I've ever known or writer I've read. The beautiful contradiction at
the heart of her responsiveness was that she was able, with some
of the grandeur of Melville by way of Leslie Fiedler, to say "No!
in Thunder" to pious respectability, Eurocentric aesthetics, and the
compromises of Hollywood. But in the same breath, she said Yes
to the movies' appetite for playfulness, vision, and rapture, "The
Glamour of Delinquency," that special capacity for the subversive
and the operatic, the everyday and the impossible.

[2001]

Anatomies

of

Melancholy

Chris Marker

DEFINING QUALITIES of the peripheral visionary: obliquity, modesty, thoughtfulness, humor, critical engagement, a left-handed appreciation of experience. His peripatetic, zigzag mind travels on (what else?) cat feet, sidling through crowds of refugeelike images. Melting-plot specters come from everywhere—Moscow, Tokyo, Paris, Havana, Okinawa, Cape Verde, *Vertigo*'s San Francisco, Tarkovsky's *Solaris*, cyberspace, Ouija boards. (I always keep forgetting: is *La Jetée* the archaic 1962 prequel to *12 Monkeys* or instead the science-fiction sequel to *Laura?*) These shadow couriers carry nomadic geographies with them, imprinted like tattoos:

"the map becomes the territory," inscribing the precise latitudes and longitudes of unspoken lives, hidden contradictions, telltale traces. A calm, measured voice makes itself heard above the white noise of wars, political savagery, imploded revolutions. It draws us in with the confidential, clandestine tone of a tiny ad slipped into the *Pravda* personals: lucid alertness seeks like-minded companionship, with eye toward escaping global nightmare of kamikaze ideologies, DOA utopias, domination by consumption.

Throughout a serpentine journey into—and out of—the past, Chris Marker has been the most unclassifiable of directors: a whimsical-mystical-dialectical link between Zen and Marx? A Zone-poet stalking the inner life of history? Nature documentarian tracking that most elusive of endangered species—subjectivity? Is Marker the late, semilamented twentieth century's most pitiless coroner, or its last partisan? His body of work meets us on its own heretical terms, less a series of discrete motion pictures than so many passionately sketched-out chapters—"Convolutes," to borrow Walter Benjamin's gnomic nomenclature—in a single, lifelong quest to memorialize the dream life of an epoch that vanished before his eyes. Marker's conversational, ever-evolving cinematic hybrids (newsreel/fiction, *La Jetée*'s stills-on-film, the gradual embrace of video's casual plasticity) always seem to be moving in several directions at once, full-circling back to the same eternal preoccupation—our times as they, and we, have seemingly passed into history.

One Day in the Life of Andrei Arsenevich (2002), his tender, elemental panegyric to Tarkovsky, supplies a thumbnail sketch of Marker's own aesthetic: "... Andrei was raising an imaginary house, a unique house where all the rooms open onto one another, and all lead to the same corridor...." His work could be considered the cinematic equivalent to Benjamin's sprawling, saturnine notebooks for his unfinished, literally interminable *Arcades Project* — but transposed to a world where the video arcade and Internet have replaced the nineteenth century's cathedrallike proto–shopping malls and flaneur haunts. Thus the peculiar feeling of stately yet frazzled simultaneity in *La Jetée, Sans Soleil,* and *Level Five,* that dual forward- / backward-looking quality, the anticipatory and the retrospective scrambled together in an overlapping, boundary-blurring way that feels so like what reality has become. As much painstaking editor as auteur (as if the world were a library of outtakes and lost negatives waiting to be found and restored to life), he has narrators deliver these digressive, intuitive-leaping collages of quotations and ruminations as if they were letters read aloud to absent or deceased friends (Tarkovsky, Alexander Medvedkin, you or me). Missives composed of so many types of footage that are then sent gently pinballing back into the world, in a language that's as public as a political demonstration, reclusive as a secret life, and intimate as a love song.

For instance, "Only Love Can Break Your Heart" — that quaint, scarred-for-life phrase both Neil Young and Peter Laughner built wrenching odes-to-desolation around, but Marker will substitute history as the source of doomed ardor. It's the sultry air-raid siren seducing and abandoning generations of the unwary and unrequited: as Lenin might have said, you can't make a revolution without breaking a few hearts, not to mention wills. (Stalin expedited the process: a bullet through the head was a quicker way of telegraphing the message.) *A Grin without a Cat* may be Marker's most thorough, systematic exploration of "the tricks that history plays" on us, but *The Last Bolshevik* traverses a landscape of ashes from a steeper, more closely observed angle. Instead of the downward sixties arc of intoxicated idealism and clenched-fist solidarity-in-upheaval, it follows the crushed aspirations of a generation of

Soviet dreamers, bridegrooms left waiting at the revolution's altar, or casually sacrificed upon it. Where *La Jetée* covers "the vertigo of time," it also evokes the physical space of history—its gaps and apertures, as well as an entity you can touch, taste, pursue, desire. Yet where there's desire, loss is sure to follow: the memory of a pending death already present within the moment of deepest bliss.

In the case of *A Grin without a Cat* and its companions, it isn't the death of the corporeal body Marker is so much concerned with (though he makes beautiful funeral music for Medvedkin, Tarkovsky, Che Guevara, and others) but the death of hope—that chimera of a better, more just, Cheshire-smile of a world in the offing that was to be strangled by bureaucrats, zealots, cultural conformists, media overload, spiritual exhaustion, insensate venality, apathy. His ceaseless recontextualizing and repositioning of images is a way of reading—and writing—between their lines: reediting a clip from Tarkovsky's student film of *The Killers*, its pair of overcoated baby-faced assassins become stand-ins for all the secret policemen who would serve as its century's exterminators. Cut to Andrei Arsenevich himself, making a portrait-of-the-artist-as-a-young-man walk-on in the black-and-white production. He has an incongruously jaunty tune on his lips, which Marker's narrator names with graveyard irony that transcends itself—"he whistles 'Lullabye of Birdland,' " the kind of freeze-framing moment as so often occurs in Marker, where a perfectly mundane fact/observation/punchline becomes supercharged with crosscurrents of "melancholy and dazzlement," a droll little aside-dish impregnated with tragic awareness. Here is the unmistakable euphoric-forlorn tinge of Marker's sensibility, those plucky, tactile Django-Vertov chords of thought, "things that quicken the heart" as well as rend it.

Other fleet, not-quite-random notes struck on a homemade Kino-guitar fretboard: "It was a time of bitterness and madness from which some people would never emerge." "The battle was lost in advance . . . the purpose was to fix the aftermath." "Do we ever know where history is really made?" "They opened the door and he vanished." "They want to bury the past . . . that degree of intensity." "Capsizing in a world of signs." "The malignancy of things." "Voyeurizing the voyeurs." "Morons of the world, unite." "The Marienbad game." "Pick your mask." "Style, not the author, passes judgment." "Learning to draw a certain melancholy comfort from the contemplation of the tiniest things." "One day I'll give Chris all this. . . ." "Chris, you've got it all?"

Parallels may be drawn with an indelible Marker to Godard's archly aphoristic *Histoire* lessons, as well as philosopher-cum-antifilmmaker Guy Debord's cinematic negations: lines of influence, overlap, coincidental-or-not similarities. But what *The Last Bolshevik* attains through its poignant saber wit is what is problematic in Godard and Debord—the tricky integration of the aesthetic, the historic, and the personal. Godard knee-jerks the aesthetic above other considerations, while Debord sought to dissolve cinema like clearing away so much rubbishy smoke and mirrors (even as he bathed his legend in a romantic-nihilist Harry Lime–light). Marker's self-effacement contrasts with the former's cosmic self-regard (the singular devotion to propagating his aura of significance—"Isn't that so, Mr. Godard?"), or the latter's imperious misanthropy (the would-be revolutionary with an Abel Gance–sized Napoleonic complex, whose Situationist movement boasted more excommunicated members than ones in good standing). *The Last Bolshevik* is committed to allusive density and plain speaking, to the multilayered, many-faceted, and polyphonic, the superimposed frame within the frame and the abstract picture-in-picture, letting history's witnesses have enough breathing room to say their various pieces. Marker believes in listening, in looking closely (at faces, montages, concepts), in linking generalizations to the paradoxes of the particular, and in questioning the virginal certainty behind so many assumptions of innocence. (Time and again, he shows the most effective obstacles against last century's struggles for liberation coming from within, in those authoritarian-totalitarian impulses that hitched their hunger for power to utopian visions). Debord and Godard present unified narcissistic fronts, a more didactic mode of address: the solemn voice of artistic or theoretical authority tossing its elegant pearls before swine.

Marker will end *The Last Bolshevik* with a mournful, knock-knock non sequiter of a joke: "I know what you would call these men," it says of the final remnants of Soviet cinema's long departed heroic era — "Dinosaurs." A get-out-your-hankerchiefs pause. "But you know what happened to dinosaurs" — only instead of tar pits we get a shot of a smiling little girl cradling an inflatable Godzilla in her arms — "Kids love 'em." The absurd, footloose-in-quicksand spirit of Medvedkin's *Happiness* returns here, as a strange buoyancy amid the Soviet Union's collapse: the end of the line for a long-abandoned train, the tricks history plays coming home to roost. There's no Either/Or in Marker, no split-level sacred/profane seg-regation: even in the agonized ecstasies of Tarkovsky, he uncovers a latent amusement, the existential ironies perched above the deader-than-deadpan zone between holiness and nothingness.

Animals have a special, folk-allegoric place in his heart: the real and pantomime horses out of Medvedkin, the lone wolves being hunted by helicopter in the last frames of *A Grin without a Cat*. And naturally, those cryptic cats themselves, a favorite Marker motif: the cat temple in *Sans Soleil*, the eerily dignified parade footage of medieval-costumed, papier-mâché–masked cat people that turns up in *Grin* ("The cat is never on the side of power"). Emblems of watchfulness, patience, self-possession, they are

Marker's good-luck charms, warding off the herd instincts nurtured by mushrooming cults of personality, rent-a-martyrs, information officers, televised unreality, Internet gamesmanship, and all the other pressing distractions that loom in our waking and dreaming minds like the kitschy, mocking Japanese blow-up doll of Munch's *The Scream* that flashes before us in *Level Five*.

Of course, I have one sitting in the corner of my living room too—a *Scream* someone gave me as a fond token of a shared history, though the Red Army cap she also got from a souvenir stand in Tiananmen Square keeps falling off the poor thing's head. It, too, is a dinosaur of sorts, and à la the one Marker's girl grasps like a teddy bear, if you look at it from a certain perspective, you can just about see "the black hole" of history condensed in its silent banshee mouth. (That "O" is also the spyglass-telescope shape he loves to insert in the frame: zeroing in, as it were.) "So this is the summing up," a Marker narrator would say: a cheap novelty item to show how much meaning can be emptied out of the world in a wave of indifferent mass production. Yet the same inanimate thing may also be filled with personalized meanings, made a beacon for the future, a repository of memory, or a piñata whose illusions are ripe for the bursting. Consciousness is not a theme or a trope in this work—it's the unrarefied air his films breathe, even if they sometimes must don gas masks to wade through the stench of decomposing lies.

With Marker, the same motion that weaves layers of evocation also peels them back; homing in on the beauty of images, he also interrogates them endlessly. Add one other ineffable quality to this metaphysical-materialist penumbra: the fact his films are so little circulated, so hard to track down, always something of a chance encounter. Is Marker, then, the greatest living film director (even though he doesn't make "films" exactly, or quite "direct" them in the most conventional sense of the term)? I would answer that his work, though uneven by its very exploratory, feeling-its-way-under-the-skin nature, equals the objects of his ardor: *Vertigo*, *Happiness* (repeat: always Medvedkin's), *The Mirror*. Only not in turn, but all at once, and more as well. There's a headstrong overabundance of tangents, impressions, sensations, and ideas here that goes against any smooth grain of shrink-wrapped, boxed-in, edifying perfection. This is the signature of cinema's last dissident, like a rugged Malevich cross found in an ancient Rublev painting, the future already present in the past and vice versa, the bittersweet lullaby of "negative signs of life."

In other words, the Marker touch.

[2003]

30

My Own Private Benjamin

Selected Writings,

Volume 3: 1935-1938 and

Walter Benjamin:

The Story of a Friendship

TWO ASPECTS OF Walter Benjamin face each other across a narrow, bottomless chasm: the all-too-human pursuer of meaning—redemption—and his supernatural, Doppelgangland twin. Like a man with two left hands, on one we have the solitary intuitionist, heuristic bookworm, impoverished collector (of children's books and tattoo art, among other detritus), investigator of the private, mystical dialectician, devoted correspondent, armchair flaneur, detached student of hashish and prostitution, Jewish alchemist (gnomic specialty: changing ruins into runes), and infinitely well-prepared suicide (*disappearer* might be a better term). On the other, the more imposing mythic figure of an intellectual guardian angel whose peripatetic afterlife has seen him rise from history's wreckage like a refugee from some unmade Wim Wenders film (we'll call it *Paris, Capital of Desire*).

This second, ur-Benjamin is the patron saint of lost causes and oxymoronic dreams (utopian apocalypse, illuminated distraction, Marxist unorthodoxy), providing the impetus for countless tomes (subject to such archaeological exegesis as Susan Buck-Morss's 1989 *The Dialectics of Seeing*, besides serving as the decisive inspiration for works like Marshall Berman's 1982 *All That Is Solid Melts into Air*). Benjamin's unforgettable image of "the angel of history," helplessly blown backward into the future by the "storm . . . we call progress," has even gone quasi-pop, resurrected in songs by Laurie Anderson ("The Dream Before") and the Mekons ("Sorcerer"). "Ooh," the Mekons added with a little phantasmagorical twinkle, "the abyss is close to home."

Which in a tough nutshell is the perpetual exile's lot: At home only in the void, inhabiting the space between the world as it is and what it might be, Benjamin would naturally be claimed by the tradition of the outcast and the misfit, as well as that of the prophet. And thus canonized and sanctified as a cultural symbol—the dispossessed critic as knight-exemplar of paradoxical, self-divided modernity—Walter Benjamin has suffered a similar fate to that of his spiritual cousin Franz Kafka, albeit on a somewhat more obscure academic scale. (The Benjaminesque isn't so widely recognized as a state of being or mind: it patiently awaits the transformation of the sociological into the universal.) Posthumously, he has become a convenient, all-points totem, one whose blessing and validation are sought through the offerings of a host of supplicants. In this shopworn, once-upon-a-time-in-academe form, he stands for an indivisible synthesis of blissful disenchantment and unshaken theoretical faith.

Gershom Scholem's *Walter Benjamin: The Story of a Friendship*, a memoir Scholem wrote in 1975, thirty-five years after Benjamin's death and only a few before his own, represented an attempt to reclaim Benjamin and his legacy from the early stages of the reification process. With an eloquent mix of tact, candor, reserve, and affection, the great Kabbalist scholar set out to reinstate the centrality of Jewish metaphysics to his dearest friend's life and thought. In doing so, Scholem argued the Marxist influence exerted on Benjamin by Theodor Adorno and Bertolt Brecht diverted him from his essential calling as a radical interpreter of Judaic tradition. At the same time, Scholem places Benjamin in the context of his real, unvarnished life: the milieu of German-Jewish intellectuals in the ever bleaker interregnum between the world wars, the incessant pressure of "battle fatigue on the economic front" by a thinker who was profoundly unsuitable for academic "habilitation," and a writer who was no better equipped to either the demands of the capitalist marketplace or the Communist party line.

The Story of a Friendship is a polemical yet evenhanded book: there's not a feeling of settling old scores so much as diligently, fastidiously setting the record straight to the extent the author is in a position to do so. The sense it gives of Benjamin's relationship to Adorno and Brecht is not of someone brainwashed or corrupted but, rather, of a man caught up in fraught, problematic intellectual romances—in Brecht's case, Scholem cites a "slavish-masochistic" undertone to Benjamin's hero-worshiping attitude, which is in keeping with the doomed romantic attachments he had with women. (Scholem sighs: "One of his close acquaintances told me that for her and her female friends he had not even existed as a man, that it never even occurred to them that he had that dimension as well. 'Walter was, so to speak, incorporeal.' ")

Certainly by the time covered in *Selected Writings, Volume 3, 1935–1938*, Benjamin's attraction to the terminology and assurances of historical materialism had reached its zenith: This was a system that promised not only to explain the world but also to redeem it by bringing about an absolute transparency in human relations (parallel to the transparency of God's word) and replace arbitrary, irrational power with justice. Here, then, are the desperately earnest paeans to Brecht ("The Land Where the Proletariat May Not Be Mentioned" — "Such drama . . . will emerge as a testament in bronze for posterity"), the heavy-dutiful essays like "A German Institute for Independent Research" (a positive evaluation of the Frankfurt Institute for Social Research, on whose financial support Benjamin depended at the time but that came with Marxist strings attached), and "The Work of Art in the Age of Its Reproducibility" (a longer and more convincing version of Benjamin's famous theory of film, introducing some valuable material about the role of "play").

Side by side with these efforts are more personal meditations such as Benjamin's further thoughts on Kafka, the complete *Berlin Childhood around 1900* and the ultra-quixotic, intensely moving *German Men and Women* (both published here in English for the first time), along with the remarkably expansive essay "The Storyteller" and the stunning précis "Paris, the Capital of the Nineteenth Century," his poetic outline for the massive, unfinished *Arcades Project*, that biblical-Proustian political economy (1,072 pages in its published form) that aspired to tell the full Genesis-to-Revelation story of the society of the commodity. In the spectrum of these writings, the discordance in Benjamin's thought is apparent, but what Scholem termed "self-deception" can also be seen as an inevitable by-product of his spectral brand of rational mysticism: while history awaits the Judgment Day of either the Messiah or the proletariat, Jewish gnosticism and dialectical materialism circle each other in a mating dance of the Trojan horses.

Penetration is achieved, however, in flashes, like the conclusion of 1937's "Eduard Fuchs, Collector and Historian": "Whether devoting such attention to anonymous artists and to the objects that have preserved the traces of their hands would not contribute more to the humanization of mankind than the cult of the leader—a cult which, it seems, is to be inflicted on humanity once again— is something that, like so much else that the past has vainly striven to teach us, must be decided, over and over, by the future." By this light, the quintessential Benjamin gesture of *Volume 3* is the 1936 selection of letters by a wide assortment of figures from the German Romantic era, together with his brief, meticulously sympathetic commentaries, contained in *German Men and Women*. Published under the pseudonym Detlef Holz to avoid Nazi censorship, the book was an almost preternaturally oblique excavation of what Goethe's missive therein called "the human . . . in its singularities," which is to say everything Hitler wished to destroy. It is the story primarily of friendships amidst the passages and misfortunes of time, and of ideas as the substance of friendship: their exchange becomes the fabric that connects one individual to another and binds each to their precarious, uncertain lives.

In that vein, *The Story of a Friendship* traverses a wealth of idiosyncratic allusions and details: The WB who occasionally referred to himself as "Dr. Nebbish," the anguished sufferer of "noise psychosis" and happy aficionado of Louis Lewy's *Krzadok the Human Onion and Spring-Fresh Methuselah* ("a 'detective' story without any point," Scholem tells us, "a hidden metaphysics of doubt"). Of

Hugo Ball's *A Critique of the German Intelligentsia:* "It impressed both of us with the acuity of its hatred." Other fragments that stick in the mind: "devoted absorption," "soothsaying from coffee grounds," "like a voice from another planet," "the living light and dark heart of things." These offhand remnants give *Selected Writings* a salutary context. Benjamin's universe is a compressed, aphoristic one: "The wisest thing . . . is to meet the forces of the mythical world with cunning and with high spirits," holding the splinters of a broken mirror up to Creation (or vice versa). This rearview reflection makes faraway objects seem close and near ones as remote as falling stars: "To do justice to the figure of Kafka in its purity, and in its peculiar beauty, one should never lose sight of one thing: it is the figure of a failure. . . . Perhaps one might say that once he was sure of ultimate failure, everything on the way to it succeeded for him as if in a dream."

[2003]

Blur

as

Genre

Wong Kar-wai's

Chungking Express

THE ETERNAL CITY of youth
beckons anew: romantic urban
ciphers (cops, gun moll, stewardess,
fast-food gamine) bathed in neon
reflections of themselves, style as metaphysics (sunglasses at midnight), gaiety
and sorrow entwined in a hungover
reverie. That's the mood of Wong
Kar-wai's *Chungking Express*, the 1994
Hong Kong movie–cum–international
sensation that is finally opening in America
under the banner of—who else?—Quentin
Tarantino. Wong, though, goes in for cerebral pop abstractions instead of brain-splatter
pulp. A dazzlingly adroit synthesis of art cinema

and MTV, *Chungking Express* has a deadpan cosmopolitan energy that conflates successive New Waves—Godard's and Debbie Harry's. (In Wong's most recent film *Fallen Angels* [1995], a feverish extension of this masculin/feminine mystique, currently making the festival rounds in the West, there's even a tough cookie called Blondie.) The cheerfully lost (well, maybe just misplaced) souls adrift through *Chungking Express* listen to their interior monologues as if they were soundtracks. Which they are: the movie repeats the 1966 Mamas and Papas hit "California Dreamin'" so often it becomes a sleepwalker's mantra.

Chungking Express presents life as a radiant blur. Wong's visual trademark (in collaboration with cinematographer Chris Doyle) is a look of hyperreal clarity broken with interludes of sensuous, pixilated slow motion. Unfolding in Hong Kong's overdeveloped underbelly, the cramped social space bordered by the fleabag Chungking House hotel and the bustling Midnight Express food stand, the film sketches two virtual love stories that almost but don't quite overlap. In one, a forlorn plainclothes cop (Takeshi Kaneshiro) tries to romance a mystery woman in a bar (Brigitte Lin Chin-Hsia), unaware she's a drug dealer whose confederates have double-crossed her. The second has a take-out counter girl (the endearingly gawky Faye Wong, an updated Jean Seberg by way of Amanda Plummer) stalking an impassive uniformed cop (Tony Leung Chiu-Wai), sneaking into his apartment to rearrange it like some housekeeping poltergeist. (Since he credits inanimate objects with a mind of their own, he never suspects a thing.) But plot here is merely a cursory formality, a means of ruminating on the arbitrariness of signs and relationships, the tricks desire plays on itself, the present as déjà vu.

The first policeman measures the transience of time and love by the expiration dates on pineapple cans—feeling like a discarded one himself, he calmly devours thirty cans of pineapple and then goes out drinking, reasoning that "alcohol's good for digestion." The second gives pep talks to his soap, pining for a stewardess he's lost touch with. These yearning cops are pet-shop boys peering at a shimmering aquarium Hong Kong — the local equivalents of West End girls float past, out of reach but never out of mind. Wong calls *Chungking Express* "a road movie of the heart," but it's a road that keeps turning back on itself: even as life is happening, it's experienced as memory. A convenience mart will look as lush and enchanted as an oasis, but it dissolves any sense of place in the process. The movie's appeal is partly that, like a Circle K store, it could be set anywhere: this city of sensibility might as well be Paris, Tokyo, Los Angeles, New York. In the same way, the swirl of images and sensations is so thick it tends to obscure how pleasantly familiar all Wong's pop and cinematic free associations are. Has Jean-Jacques Beineix's playful *Diva*, or even Robert Longo's ominously blissed-out video for New Order's "Bizarre Love Triangle," been forgotten so soon? Combine the two, and you have the essence of what Wong is doing in *Chungking Express*: boiling down a couple of decades worth of hip archetypes to a smooth, wonderland veneer.

It's a marvelous formula, but the solemn press buildup ("It must be blindingly obvious to anyone with eyes and ears that here is a supreme stylist of the cinema") will leave a lot of people scratching their heads when they discover that beneath its technique and elliptical form *Chungking Express* is a lighthearted comedy. (As they will, unless they mistake charm for subversive chic.) The movie treats its existential baggage nonchalantly, serving up melancholia with a smile. Yet to read Wong's press clips you'd think this was a visionary come to save Hong Kong film from itself. Wong and *Chungking Express* are being hyped as though they were the antitheses of action director John Woo and of HK's glut of what are disdainfully referred to as genre films. Never mind that quite a few of those pictures are more audacious and suggestive than Wong's work so far; what cineastes mean when they hail Wong as the greatest director to come out of Hong Kong is that he's the most Eurocentric, the most taken with the high masters of auteurism. Even so, a look at Clara Law's 1992 *Autumn Moon* shows that he's hardly the lone "serious" Hong Kong director. Moreover, Law's beautifully modulated film anticipates many of the central themes (isolation and youthful longing in a commodified world) and devices (contrapuntal voice-overs, the outsider who filters life through a video camera) of both *Chungking Express* and *Fallen Angels*. Next to Law, Wong's treatment of this material looks far less personal—he seems a swoony prankster trying out attitudes before a mirror. (This is most apparent in how the two handle sex: Wong is coyly voyeuristic; Law gives us visceral, disruptive physicality.)

The notion of Wong as a figure far beyond the crass confines of genre is misleading. Rather, and more interestingly, his movies treat "art film" as genre. He instinctively translates art tropes into pop signifiers, the inverse of the way Woo worked in his great, obsessive death-opera *Bullet in the Head*, (1990). From the start, Wong has blurred the gap between straight genre pieces (the neo-Scorsese gangland of the 1988 *As Tears Go By*) and private fixations (trauma as nostalgia in 1990's *Days of Being Wild*). *Chungking Express* strikes a lovely, sanguine balance between the poles; *Fallen Angels* goes off the deep end of self-obsession. (It's crammed with so many allusions to his past work that it's like a noisy greatest-hits medley.)

As loath as some critics are to admit it, Wong's aesthetic is a logical outgrowth of the Hong Kong reanimator mode: fusing wildly disparate styles and taking them to sublime extremes. It's much easier to wax rhapsodic over Wong's formalist panache if you've never seen the wondrously unhinged *Naked Killer*, an HK

B-movie of such elegantly deranged perversity and gleeful psycho-sexual mischief it explodes every convention it careens over. Lin's trench-coated, revolver-packing dame is fun in *Chungking Express* (the world-weary Marlene Dietrich tone when she demands "whiskey" is glorious), but the conception is anemic next to the complex, *Jules et Jim*–in–Vietnam changes that director Tsui Hark rang on these chords with Anita Mui in *A Better Tomorrow III*. Likewise, Wong's avant-garde action sequences (darting smears of frenzy and chaos, slowed down but not enough for the eye to fully register everything) in *Fallen Angels* and especially in *Ashes of Time* (1992) bowl the uninitiated over, but they're really just minor re-finements of the imagery of mainstream Hong Kong pictures like the science fiction *Wicked City* and the martial-arts fable *The Bride with White Hair*. (Wong's movies borrowed the leads from those films, too.)

Purity in movies finally breeds a puritanism of the senses, but Wong is too fond of enchanted junk-shop milieux to succumb to abstinence. What's rewarding in Wong's oeuvre, what's alive in it, is lack of artistic purity. It's no accident that *Ashes of Time*, an austere, dreamily ironic swordplay epic, is at once so anomalous and so utterly characteristic of Hong Kong film at its most satisfying: where else would someone combine Akira Kurosawa and Alain Resnais to make the equivalent of "The Seven Samurai at Mar-ienbad" (and have this constitute a genre, albeit a genre of one)? After all, the best sequence of *Chungking Express* has Leung Chiu-Wai fooling around with air hostess Valerie Chow to Dinah Wash-ington's "What a Difference a Day Makes," tenderly landing toy planes on her sweat-coated back—a scene inspired by Wong's childhood memory of a Pan Am commercial.

Chungking Express is in fact an advertisement for itself, but its characters are so good at killing time you hardly notice the film doesn't quite get around to delivering the goods it seems to promise. *Fallen Angels*, originally conceived as a third story for *Chungking Express* and now expanded into a full feature, is instead a commercial for Wong. With its showy wide-angle close-ups and punch-drunk handheld camera moves, it's more a frantic resume than a movie. And there's no way any parodist is going to top Michelle Reis's latex miniskirted, chain-smoking, strung-out-on-love routine here: clutching a cigarette even when she masturbates (a scene Wong digs so much he has her repeat it), Reis is the ultimate fantasy of supermodel self-abasement.

The one truly fresh thing in *Fallen Angels* is Kaneshiro, returning as a crazier variant of his sweet, oddball cop in *Chungking Express*. Now he's a mute ex-con who breaks into closed shops at night and benevolently accosts passersby into becoming his customers/victims. Here Wong does extend the spirit of *Chungking Express*: Kaneshiro is a present-day version of Marcel Carne's Baptiste haunting a Chungking Boulevard of Crime, in search of love and the perfect gesture. As such, Wong's alter ego isn't so far from the desert exiles of *Ashes of Time*. Perhaps he's looking for the one Lin played there, she who was nicknamed "Defeat-Seeking Loner." They were made for each other.

[1996]

Nice Gesamtkunstwerk If You Can Get It

Tsui Hark—

Ching Sui-tung

NOW THAT HONG KONG has officially been reunited with—or re-colonized by—mainland China, a great, tumultuous movie era has passed. Whatever the future holds under the new regime of corporate communism (perhaps some wistful synergy of Mao and Disney: a city of eager Mao's-keteers and a movie industry eager to match), its gloriously disreputable, shoot-from-the-id days are likely behind it. Resignation has set in over the last few years, with dread replaced by acceptance. The quicksilver audacity that made Hong Kong movies into Hollywood's oneiric second mind—as though they sprung fully formed from cinema's collective unconscious — has dissipated. That film vocabulary Ackbar Abbas speaks of as "the excavation of evocative detail," describing HK cinema's genrefied space, seems largely abandoned. In his fine, Walter Benjamin–influenced study *Hong Kong: Culture and the Politics of Disappearance*, Abbas writes of Hong Kong's sociopolitical predicament giving rise to a film aesthetic of "the incredible as real": "History now goes through strange loops and becomes difficult to represent in terms of traditional realism. If real history is becoming more incredible by the day, we will have to resort to the incredible to keep up with it." Having tried to outrun history, or at least outfox it, HK cinema finds itself about to go down in it.

With reality's other shoe (or boot) about to drop, and Hong Kong's fate so fraught with uncertainty (the perfect ghastly irony would be for the industry to start exporting tendentious, raise-the-gray-lantern art-house fare), an assessment of Hong Kong's suddenly bygone golden age is due. Whether measured from the dawn of the HK new wave in 1979 or the appearance of 1986–1987 landmarks *Peking Opera Blues*, *A Better Tomorrow*, and *A Chinese Ghost Story*, Tsui Hark and Ching Sui-tung came to define its outlandishly convoluted pop-poetic sensibilities. Producer, director, mogul, and general gadfly-about-town Tsui has been the period's most pivotal and controversial figure. Growing up in the Chinese section of Saigon but educated in Hong Kong and Texas, the eclectic Tsui has directed more than twenty features and produced another couple dozen. They run the gamut from grimly radical to cloyingly inane, brutalist to zany: take your pick of surreal fantasy, Godardian pulp art, graceful gangster romance, kung-fu allegory, broad comedy, sci-fi noir, and of course producing John Woo's signature works *A Better Tomorrow I/II* and *The Killer* — there is scarcely a genre Tsui has left unturned upside down.

Meanwhile right-hand-man Ching would direct / codirect / action-direct a slew of astonishing movies that reanimated dormant forms: the *Chinese Ghost Story* series, *Swordsman II*, and its even more daring sequel *The East Is Red*, all produced by Tsui. Bringing out the impudent best in each other, they had a uniquely symbiotic partnership. Though he worked with Tsui on the 1980 new wave kick-in-the-head *Dangerous Encounter of the First Kind* (sociopath-finding urban alienation delivered with the sucker-punch belligerence of a Lydia Lunch B-side), it was on the celebrated *Zu: Warriors from the Magic Mountain* (1983) where Ching's aerial martial arts displays paved the way for the modern HK fantasy mode. He would serve as Tsui's alter ego, as influential action director on *A Better Tomorrow II* (1987) and *The Killer* (1988) as well as *Peking Opera Blues* (1986) and Tsui's own *A Better Tomorrow III*. Ching's floating, mythic air wafts through the violence in them, but it is on the dazzling *A Chinese Ghost Story* where it fully comes into its own, though producer Tsui often winds up cited as the principal auteur. The question of who directed what on any given Tsui-associated film can be tricky business to untangle (on *Swordsman*, King Hu was credited as director though fired as shooting began, and at minimum five other directors including Tsui and Ching seem to have worked on the film), but there is a lunatic vision that is distinctly recognizable as pure Ching. Diaphanous nocturnal shots of silken veils and enchanted forests, fleeting images fusing slow motion with quick, nearly subliminal cuts, boy-meets-ghost romance soaring up into the trees and off into uncharted Busby Berserkley realms, a singing ghostbuster, a tree demon with a hundred-foot tongue, and an Orpheus-like rescue mission to hell and back are strictly par for the Ching Sui-tung course.

Though Tsui's now routinely—and understandably—identified

as HK's answer to Steven Spielberg, in practical terms his sprawling oeuvre is closer to an anarchic and/or synthetic fusion of Hawksian bravura with the contrasting pop archetypes George Lucas (glib) and Sergio Leone (imposing). A master fabulist who often sells his own work short, Tsui displays this schizophrenic quality most conspicuously in the immensely popular *Once Upon a Time in China*, a film that has so far spawned five sequels. Equal parts epic anti-imperialist tract, gleeful exploration of melodramatic violence, comic folktale, and wistful quest for spiritual unity, it encapsulates a cinema of multiple artistic personalities and irreconcilable differences. Yet when he's been able to integrate his dissonant impulses instead of smothering them under a blanket of self-imposed banality, he is as exciting as any filmmaker working. *Peking Opera Blues* offered up a new amalgam of screwball entertainment and cinematic vision: plunging a gender-inverted Hawks ensemble into slapstick Brechtian politics amid the trappings of traditional Chinese theater, with dulcet echoes of Leone-Peckinpah gunplay exploding like firecrackers off in the middle distance, it delivered wave after wave of ecstatic invention, one wondrously sustained climax on top of another.

For all his patchy virtuosity — mixing expressionist angles, ravishing tableaux, archaic wipes, shock cuts, elegant pans, and lunging, disoriented POV shots — there remains a persistent lack of core sensibility, or at least continuity, to his work. That missing "personal" touch, and the attendant haphazard quality of much of his later work, suggests another Hollywood parallel: Francis Ford Coppola. Reversing Coppola's ratio of the manic to the depressive, the hyperactive Tsui nonetheless fits David Thomson's description of the multifarious Coppola: "He tries to be everything for everyone" — along with sharing a penchant for the impractical, the grandiose, and the mechanical. Still more applicable: "No one has retained so many jubilant traits of the kid moviemaker, or has inspired darker comments" (notably for Tsui's treatment of John Woo in the wake of 1989's *The Killer*).

Narratively unrelated, both *Shanghai Blues* (1984) and *Peking Opera Blues* broke new but backward-looking ground. Each viewed the past through the prism of movie history, joining nostalgia and modernism as Coppola had in sumptuous Mafiosi operas, though in a far more allusive, punning pop style (rendering life as near-incessant montage). Directing *A Better Tomorrow III* (a 1989 project either inherited or hijacked from Woo, depending on whom you believe), Tsui took the gangster mythos to Vietnam. It's his second-greatest achievement, but he insists that "that film was out of control": it translated action-adventure excess into idyllic dreamtime, effectively occupying the no-man's-land between *Jules and Jim* and *Bullet in the Head*. (For good measure, he also produced Ringo Lam's terse, crazed 1994 martial-arts riff on *Apocalypse Now* itself, *Burning Paradise*.) *Dangerous Encounter of the First Kind* (1980) is do-it-yourself disaffection that outparanoids *The Conversation*. Then there's the autistic loveliness of the one-from-the-heart fiasco *Green Snake* (1993), as well as high-concept outings like the time-travel farce *Love in the Time of Twilight* (1995): restless, peripatetic, uneasy stabs at rapprochement between mass taste and private idiosyncrasy. The latter has a pensive, enigmatic tone that captures what American back-to-the-futurism missed: the weight of the past upon present, the sense of loss as fate. Living up to its saturnine title, this comedy of disappearance might be Tsui's spiritual autobiography: the young man whose ghost must go back in time to undo the chain of events that led to his murder is named Kong, which alludes not only to the city on the brink of its own vanishing point but the filmmaker's real forename.

While his Film Workshop succeeded (for a time), in Hong Kong he acquired a dictatorial reputation (allegedly ghost-directing or recutting a fair portion of the films that list him as producer) without ever embracing full aesthetic autonomy for himself. His ambitions and designs generally kept one eye squarely on the bottom line, reverting to the path of least resistance as easily as *The Chinese Feast* (1995) served up multiple courses of mildly pleasant stupefaction. Disastrously following Woo and Lam's path out of Hong Kong, he took his crack at directing Eurotrash action-hulk Jean-Claude Van Damme in the disjointedly mannerist, ultravapid *Double Team* (1997). Shooting the mannequin-on-steroids trio of Van Damme, Dennis Rodman, and Mickey Rourke as beefcake sculpture, taking the nonplot to the point of almost pure formalization, Tsui dropped hints of a Mapplethorpe photo session slipped into a bad, mildly outré sixties spy caper. Surely Van Damme must have expected something closer to slam-bang Tsui productions like the visually imaginative *Wicked City* (1992; a live-action remake of a popular anime feature) or the sleek Jet Li vehicle *Black Mask*. But a curious thing about Tsui: he was never particularly invested in action for action's sake, with a general ambivalence toward physical expression cropping up in his films, where violence and motion tend to be dispersed into kinetic abstraction. Energy mines space, gesture seeks pattern, flesh becomes idea: after the failure of his punk/B-flick black hole *Dangerous Encounter* (a.k.a *Don't Play With Fire*, notable for its zip-gun portrait of a hilariously sullen, "crazy bitch" sociopath), he turned 180 degrees to broad, scatterbrained slapstick and hit it big with the spoof *All the Wrong Clues . . . for the Right Solution*. (Often cited as early evidence of Tsui's "sellout," it nonetheless contains a classic tasteless gag involving a Volkswagen, a couple of nuns, an orphan who asks, "How do we get to heaven, sister?" and a very abrupt answer-collision.) From the cannibal-house gross-out comedy *We're Going to Eat You* (1983) to the unfortunately innocuous *Working Class*, there's a strain of depersonalization in his work that lends itself as easily to blatant schlock and rote dumbness as it does to lurid, intellectualized hyperbole like *Dangerous Encounter* or the beguiling Borges multiplied by *A Touch of Zen* labyrinths of *Butterfly Murders*.

His purest, most unabashed forays into conventional action movie territory have been as producer for Woo naturally (a devout aesthete caught up in the glamorous and sacramental aspects of screen violence) but also Kirk Wong's *Gunmen* (1988) as well as Johnny To and Andrew Kam's *The Big Heat* (also 1988: a good year for bloodbaths). Where *Gunmen* is a blistering, much-improved take on *The Untouchables* (the frantic reworking of De Palma's baby-carriage routine is one of the most rococo set pieces in the history of HK mayhem), *The Big Heat* remains the ne plus ultraviolence of Hong Kong cinema. With the look of a training film for coroners, it has a clinical eye for nihilistic detail that would do Cronenberg proud, turning cops and robbers into *Crash* test dummies.

But in Tsui's own *A Better Tomorrow III*, the action is voluptuously stylized: Anita Mui fires a pair of automatic rifles in such super–slow motion you can count the expended shells, and bodies seem to fall like snowflakes in a paperweight reverie. The urgency here is emotional, wildly romantic, but barely physical at all. In its contemplative sense of arrested time—the speed of life and death reduced to a painterly crawl—*BT III* anticipates Wong Kar-wai's atmospheric developments, as it carries Woo-derived tropes to the point of rapt stasis. The fall of Vietnam becomes the backdrop against which intertwined film/social/personal histories are projected, all collapsed into a tight allegorical space where the tanks of Tiananmen Square patrol the streets of Casablanca, and Mui irresistibly embodies the mythos of Bogart's Rick and Jeanne Moreau's Catherine rolled into one trenchcoated figure.

The closest Tsui has come to unrelenting, action-purist intensity is in *The Blade* (1995), in which he borrows the classic *One-Armed Swordsman* premise only to turn it into a perverse and exhaustively ferocious answer to Wong's *Ashes of Time*. Narrated in perfect mock-*Ashes* fashion by a not very bright young girl, it undermines Wong's languorous philosophizing and romantic alienation by representing life as appetite and savagery: animals and humans alike emblematically tempted into the steel jaws of waiting traps. (After Zhao Wen-zhou's character has his arm severed, it's tossed into an abyss, and he dives in after it.) But in its magisterial bleakness, *The Blade* avoids violence as release: in its universe, amputation leads to survival but not regeneration—the mutilated hero rises only to discover resurrection's a form of living death. More jarring existential horror than slice of martial artistry, the film manages to be every bit as abstract in its spasmodic hyperrealism as *Ashes of Time* is in lyric opacity. They're antithetical twins, joined at the hip: each contains what the other denies. Human feeling in *The Blade* recedes into the same opium haze of memory, which strangely enough helps us recall how *Butterfly Murders* paves the way for Wong's prismatic imponderability.

The clotted, glistening homoeroticism of *The Blade* extends Tsui's customary erotic ambiguity to the male body. Typically, he cast gender-identity elements in terms of women negotiating a man's world, most remarkably launching Brigitte Lin as a peerless icon of bisexual heroism. (This is a man who wanted Woo to make the leads of *A Better Tomorrow* female—and who can say what might have been if Woo had taken him up on that modest proposal.) *The Blade*'s violence is seen through the girl's eyes, flushed with voyeurism: there's a classic scene where she watches naked men being flogged that suggests Zhang Yimou gone mad. The brutality amounts to an elaborate system of displacement in which sexual tensions are disastrously played out in a bloody pantomime of lust and sublimation: the action concurrently sexualized, spiritualized, and ironically detached. Tsui's earlier work offers a more elusive composite of the carnal and the ethereal (in *The Blade*, the latter's interchangeable with the delusional)—an unstable mix best displayed in the riotous role-playground of *Peking Opera Blues*, the fatalistic passion of *Better Tomorrow III*, and the proto-*Blade* paroxysms that take up the last third of *Once Upon a Time in China*.

In *Once Upon a Time*, one chastity symbol (the ascetically handsome Jet Li) strives to save another (the primly Westernized Rosamund Kwan)—and indeed China itself—from a fate worse than death. Tsui seems to be reaching all the way back to the silent era for this melodramatic bric-à-brac. Yet below the spectacle of innocence, a darker fairy tale is taking shape amid the close, dungeonlike quarters: the blood smeared so brazenly on Kwan's bare shoulders, the sadomasochistic purity of Li (who might be channeling Lillian Gish as well as Douglas Fairbanks), and the captive women who push their tormentor into an open furnace. What silent age is this stuff from—the one where Artaud directed swashbucklers in lieu of descending into madness? *The Blade* sustains such extremity for its entire length while renouncing OUATC's morality-play heroics in favor of fistful-of-cruelty annihilation, it lacks the reassuring foundation that made the *Once Upon a Time in China* series a success: too arty for the popcorn crowd and too unyieldingly feral for art-house sitters.

Fusing pop and art in ways bound to dismay low-, middle-, and highbrow tastes alike, Tsui's prime work opted for a polymorphous semiotic perversity, nowhere more pointedly than in the gaga fairy tale *Green Snake*. Evoking the childish delirium of Indian musicals and picture-book Chinese mythology, it features a pair of beguilingly incestuous serpent-demons (Maggie Cheung and Joey Wong) who can assume Eve-like human form. Zao Wen-zhou's fanatical monk reaps destruction of the human world when he tries to expel them from it, making this just as feverish an allegory of sexual repression as *The Blade* under its campy, *Willy Wonka* veneer. Man's capacity to reject pleasure in the name of socialization is explored through laughable special snake-effects, indecorous shifts in tone and content (we're not so accustomed to seeing our little mermaids reach under a monk's robe and feel him up), and intermittent spells of erotic wonder always verging on accidental Pythonesque silliness. *Green Snake* makes the process of human socialization seem like a war on enchantment itself—an ancient wish to drive sex out of the world pitted against the eternal right-to-return of the repressed. These beatifically amoral creatures find earthly morality means suffering and loss, as though the capacity for emotion were merely the precondition for the puritanical need to extinguish it.

In that compulsion lies something like a parable of film morality, too: the determination to rationalize, codify, and administer experience. (Would Hollywood allow even the omnipotent Spielberg to make a *Hook* that ended with Peter and Tinkerbell incriminated and disillusioned, surrounded by a sea of corpses?) Tsui Hark's movie fabulism basks in the knowledge of places only fantasy can go and the secrets it can bring back from the domain of unreason, his most resonant work offering proof of Paul Coates's assertion: "Film alone reveals the extent to which reality yearns for another world which is not itself."

*   *   *

GIVEN HOW TSUI'S films refract upon each other, it's somehow inevitable he would have his own swashbuckling double: the innovative, daring, and nearly uncategorizable Ching Siu-tung. As much as anyone, he shaped the look and feel of Hong Kong cinema in the late 1980s through the mid-1990s (John Woo's now-trademark shootouts owed a lot to Ching's eloquent choreography and kinetic instincts). From 1990 to 1993, he would direct or co-direct the majority of Film Workshop's best productions, including *The Terracotta Warrior* (1990; costarring Gong Li and none other than director Zhang Yimou as the marvelously stone-faced, dashing hero), *Swordsman* (1990), *The Raid* (1991), *Dragon Inn* (1992; re-doing King Hu as a cross-dressing *Rio Bravo*), his masterpiece *Swordsman II* (1992), and its still more astonishing (if uneven) con-tinuation, *The East Is Red* (1993). One of the ironies of their work is that though Tsui received the accolades while Ching often went unappreciated, Ching has shown the more distinctive touch. Bathing rooms in blue light and streaming it through bullet holes, making bald sexual metaphors into rousing action sequences (trains crashing through walls, dreamers flying through the night, a bell tower taking off like a rocket or a water tower exploding like a pornographic piñata), he teases out fleeting imagery by fusing slo-mo with quick, nearly subliminal cuts. It seems to erupt out of a skewed inner world of Tinkertoy delight and vertiginous desire, making the viewer experience these images as if they were flash-backs to some unaccountable primal epiphany-trauma, in the place where Hitchcock and *Batman* intersect. (Perhaps both the cause and the effect is akin to seeing *Vertigo* when very young and having pieces of it come back later luminously entangled with childhood fears, sexual awakening, and superhero fantasies.)

Ching's comic-book sensibility links him to Tim Burton and Sam Raimi, as attested by the catwomen-galore triumph *The Heroic Trio* (1993), which he produced and codirected with Johnny To, and its sequel *Executioners* (1994; though shot back-to-back). But there he takes that sensibility much further, into areas of unrest and profane beauty, a surrealist impulse that devours the boundaries of the possible like a magician's tapeworm. His quest for exquisite incongruities can lead to something as airy as the battle scene in the Indiana Jones rip-off *The Raid*, where full-size biplane replicas are maneuvered on wires inside a soundstage so they strafe the heroes while soldiers leap from their wings and join in the attack. He assembles bewitched forests in the studio and creates playgrounds that can suggest both deep spaciousness and claustrophobic density—expanding and contracting the frame, a world opening up and closing in on the audience at the same time. Ching's extravagant excess is shaded, nuanced: wonder and the sinister go hand in hand, or hand on throat. Olivier Assayas was only underlining the obvious when he juxtaposed *The Heroic Trio* with Feuillade's *Les Vampires*: the archaic future and anarchic past collide. *The Heroic Trio*'s heroines have to exterminate the children who have been inducted into an army of darkness—a Grimm tale for an age of fanaticism and abortion.

There is a throwaway scene in *Executioners* that distills the essence of Ching Siu-tung. It's Christmas Eve in the near, post-1997 future, martial law is in effect, and weary military policemen are resting in a crowded corridor at headquarters. Suddenly an anonymous, grief-stricken woman bursts in, dragging a body past them. They order her to halt but she whirls, firing an automatic rifle and mowing down the soldiers. She kicks in the door to the captain's office and hurls the body at the officer's feet. Sobbing that the authorities murdered her husband, she kneels beside his corpse and swiftly turns the rifle on herself. The sequence is one sweeping, panoramic gesture that serves no purpose but to instill itself like a desperate cry that echoes in your brain like an aria. Another reverberating moment: "Imprison those alive as rioters," commands a corrupt officer after his men have nerve-gassed a crowded train station. "Burn the corpses."

In the first *Swordsman*, there's an instant when a wizened fighter emerges from an opponent's body the way a bird darts out of a tree—there is something so unreasonable and thrilling in the way such images distain physics and common sense. Ching is a true primitive who grew up on movie sets and seemingly knows no other world, yet he has an expansive and complex visual sense that orchestrates movement with visceral grace, images that are full of the wish to transcend themselves. First coming to prominence as martial arts director on Patrick Tam's *The Sword*, he made his directorial debut in 1982 with the fine *Duel to the Death*—a spare, quite formalist work that felt both detached and unhinged, like a stripped-down / spaced-out gloss on the King Hu aesthetic. Though he'd worked with Tsui on *Dangerous Encounter*, it was on the celebrated *Zu: Warriors from the Magic Mountain* (1983) where the collaboration took off, paving the way for the entire modern HK fantasy mode. (This also would be the first indication of the baleful influence of *Star Wars* on Tsui's thinking.) The contrast between their popular *Chinese Ghost Story* and *Once Upon a Time in China* opuses is telling: both succumb to formula and ritualized overfamiliarity, but where Tsui gravitates toward crassly genteel routines and phony-endearing characters like the aptly named "Clubfoot," Ching goes for flow almost in spite of characterization (his interest is in the particularity of the dream and not its insipid dreamers).

Generally, his instincts proved surer than his mentor's divided intellect. The *Swordsman* trilogy illustrates as much, even as it shows how well their respective approaches could mesh. The first installment is the most conventional, full of intricate comic intrigues and stop-on-a-dime plot reversals, untrusting of authority, very much the precursor of the *Dragon Inn* remake. *Swordsman II* is Ching's showcase, recasting main roles, with Jet Li at his most winning, Rosamund Kwan (in her most flamboyant performance as a bullwhip-wielding outlaw queen), and featuring Brigitte Lin in probably her most emblematic role as the transsexual Asia the Invincible. Straightaway heading into the sexually ambiguous mystic, it treats the convoluted courtship rites of Lin and Li with a lucidly bemused romanticism. (Asia can only consummate the relationship by having a beloved concubine serve as surrogate/imposter: as someone once said in a similar albeit marginally less lysergic-Shakespearean mode, "Nobody's perfect.")

Swordsman II is an ode to mutability, a world that is constantly turning itself inside out: during one clash, the ground rolls up like a carpet. The most feverishly balletic of movies, its violence moves with such uncanny swiftness it takes on the horrifying comic grandeur of a Gotterdammerung battle staged as an epic practical joke on humankind. Instead of being restored, order is scattered to the winds; power harnesses disorder for its own ruthless ends. After Asia the Invincible is destroyed, the brother he/she persecuted absorbs the same supernatural essences and becomes an even more sadistic tyrant as the cycle of cruelty rolls on. (The survivors can only run for their lives.)

This fatalism is taken even further in the story's final installment, *The East Is Red*. The title comes a famous Maoist anthem — "He shall be China's saving star" — so it is with wicked irony that the film has Lin's character come back from the dead to take revenge on authoritarian doomsday cults taking Invincible Asia's name in vain. What follows is a blasphemous fable of total destruction, dislocated sexual identity (my favorite gambit: the skin is pulled off a woman to reveal an albino ninja within), and swooning passion. It burrows into the chthonic recesses/excesses of religion, its roots in fantasy, charismatic ceremony, and erotic trance, perhaps because Ching understands as well as any filmmaker ever has that myth and the movies tap the same universal, primeval impulses.

Next to such dark flights of fancy, Tsui's *Peking Opera Blues* seems almost down to earth, yet there, too, is Brigitte Lin as a more human revolutionary, suspended in midair by Ching's invisible wires forever. The film is fast and mellifluous, while managing to linger on so many textures of life commingled with old movies: Lin's sorrow when she has to betray her corrupt father, the flush across Cherie Chung's face when a jewel box lands in her lap, Sally Yeh's shy, awkward resolve to break into the all-male opera. What the film ultimately captures is that elusive and so often falsified quality in film — hope. (Lin's heroic, melancholy intransigence suggests a pop precursor of student rebellion leader Chai Ling.)

Despite the title, *A Better Tomorrow III* is about the death of that hope, the fears of Hong Kong in the then-immediate shadow of Tiananmen Square, projected back onto the last days before Saigon's fall. Presented as a blue-tinted nightmare, it's a city administered by a roving army of gangsters, but where resistance erupts in bursts of fantastic bravado and reckless absurdism. All of which culminates in the perfect moral gesture enacted by the great Chow Yun-Fat, carrying his mortally wounded lover to her other lover's side so she can close the dead man's eyes, a sublimely operatic moment. It is as if the film passes from the reality of our suppressed lives into the history we dream of making, and back again — left in ruins, our dreams haunt us like memories of a homeland that has disappeared from the map.

Walter Benjamin observed of Kafka's *Amerika*: "No matter how one may convey it intellectually, this purity of feeling may be particularly sensitive to measurement of gestic behavior; the Nature Theater of Oklahoma in any case harks back to the Chinese theater, which is a gestic theater." In the shabby-giddy theatricality of *Love in the Time of Twilight* (with its poignant, scrambled hints of Ann Hui's *The Spooky Bunch* tucked into its margins) and Ching's witty, eye-rolling 1996 divertissement *Dr. Wai in "The Scripture with No Name"* (a comic-strip-styled greatest hits medley, with zippy nods to Walter Mitty, Indiana Jones, and of course Wong Kar-wai). They have worked to turn popular idioms and folk fables into phantasmagoric intoxicants—the alchemy Benjamin dubbed "profane illumination." But given the diminished state of the Hong Kong industry and the usual Hollywood inability to grasp anything out its slavish orbit, it may be a long wait until Tsui Hark or Ching Sui-tung again deliver their evocative once-upon-a-time details and stunning gestures with anything like their old alacrity. Hong Kong or its moneymen will not look kindly on any continuations of the post-Tianamen pre-1997 heresies *Executioners* and *A Better Tomorrow III*. More's the pity for us, for film will then have lost—or at any rate misplaced—two of its last links to a underappreciated heritage of disruptive emotionalism and anarchic delight: a music of juggled spheres that brought so many fluid artistic components together under one moving proscenium.

Postscript

THE HONG KONG that Ching Sui-tung and Tsui Hark once defined is indeed history—the industry has survived, but the singularity has migrated elsewhere. Tsui has spent the new century mired in hack work when he has been visible at all. With *Time and Tide* (2000) and the ill-fated remake *The Legend of Zu* (2001), that rapid-fire impersonality has taken over completely—they're misguided commercial enterprises given over to senseless bursts of energy, random patterns, prettified tics, and an unrelenting flashiness so insular, empty, and airless it might almost be a new mode of deconstruction. *Seven Swords* (2005) is no comeback, but manages a relatively effective (if curiously disinterested) triangulation of George Lucas Jedi-isms, *Lord of the Rings* processionals, and jumbled *Seven Samurai* lore. Except for a few dollops of gratuitous sadism, Tsui achieves little traction over the protracted two-and-a-half-hour saga: the broad handiwork of a dogged but absent-minded traffic cop.

Ching's career, after floundering for years in uninspired swill like *Naked Weapon* (a 2002 blot on the good name of Clarence Fok's trash classic *Naked Killer*), has taken an ironic turn: hired by Zhang Yimou as action choreographer on *Hero* (2002) and *House of Flying Daggers* (2004). More important, on the former he is brought together with *Ashes of Time* cinematographer Chris Doyle, with *Hero* becoming an epic distillation of the entire *wuxia pien* genre wherein Ching and Doyle get to pay homage to themselves. In the same rapt manner, Maggie Cheung's Flying Snow pays exquisitely haughty tribute to Brigitte Lin — her imperious glare spanning the elemental and the abstract, a mask of triumphant, bemused tragedy. Mobilizing massive armies of stately composition, color-coordinated acrobatics, pointed glances, sharpshooting leaf-blowers, and reverential lyricism, the Zhang-Ching-Doyle trio offers a succession of magical moments and deeply iconic faces arranged like auspicious signs. *Hero* takes an irresistibly vivid trompe l'oeil approach to the mythic, and it generates more spectacular beauty per square frame than any film to make it into the multiplexes ever has, but when the aesthetic pageantry is complete, the film feels a shade too perfect, too self-contained, too reasonable. There seems no place here for the mad, invigorating gesticulations of *The East Is Red*, which belonged to a century whose passions have passed into classicism, nostalgia, or worse.

[1997/2006]

33

Godard-Spielberg, Inc.

STEVEN SPIELBERG'S *Catch Me If You Can* adroitly recreates the swinging sixties as a cocktail of boyish guile, beehive hairdos, and well-lubricated father-son pathos. But watching Leonardo DiCaprio's baby-faced thief con a mercenary young model-turned-call-girl, a few viewers may feel a twinge of nostalgia for the intoxications of *real* 1960s cinema, the period when French director Jean-Luc Godard made history by turning entertainments like *Catch Me If You Can* inside out. In dazzling, multi-textured works like *Breathless* (1959) and *Pierrot le Fou* (1965), Godard changed the way movies looked, how they walked and talked, the forms they could take and discard, the contra-dictory ideas and feelings they could contain.

To watch the beautifully restored print of Godard's exhilarating *Contempt* (1963) is to recall how heady an experience the era's movies could be — it's a peerless amalgam of Homeric tragedy and Hollywood satire, poetic ambiguities and the comic-strip carnality of Brigitte Bardot. Somehow *Contempt* manages to feel at once more youthful and more grown up than Spielberg's retro reconstruction, which seems bent on purging the era of its discontents and reforming the New Wave, absurdist-romantic antihero who would sooner blow himself to smithereens than conform. And despite the triumph of Spielberg's methods and enthusiasms, an undaunted Godard has stubbornly continued to make intractably lyrical, flypaper-in-the-ointment pictures.

But a funny thing happened to the great director on the road to cinematic immortality: over the past couple of decades, the detached, ironic mock-classicism he employed so effectively in *Contempt* gradually eclipsed his radical ardor, and his films became cloistered still-lives, too pure for their own good.

Godard's mournfully waspish *In Praise of Love* (which received only a token U.S. theatrical release in 2002), was a facelift for his sagging reputation. A modest breakthrough in coffee-table-book cinema, the film's handsome elements included one depressive protagonist (who is both a stand-in for and a solemn self-parody of Godard himself), several other well-photographed mouthpieces posing as characters, pensive landscapes shot in imposing 35mm black-and-white and oversaturated digital-video color, and a whole shopping cart full of Philosophy for Dummies. These musings on the nature of Love, Resistance, Cultural Imperialism, and Cinema Itself serve as mood Muzak: smug, amorphous pseudoprofundities sailing over the cowed heads of the audience, even as Godard gives his beloved Parisian cityscapes the luminous *Manhattan* treatment.

And then there's the Spielberg question. Among its few traces of discernible plot, *In Praise of Love* is a rather ham-fisted attack on Hollywood's uplift-hawking Jurassic Kid and all he is presumed to represent. The film relates the fictive machinations of "Spielberg and Associates" to purchase the movie rights to the story of an aged couple who fought in the French Resistance. Spielberg's minions are depicted as the public-relations arm of an octopuslike U.S. government, which is intent on bilking little old ladies out of their pride, reducing history to glamorized mush, and *Schindler*-izing human memory until nothing is left but sentimental ashes. Pitting the two erstwhile boy-Wunderkinds against each other offers the instant intellectual gratification of an elitist-versus-middlebrow slugfest. But as the film's aura of impervious abstraction overwhelms these considerations, the notion of cinema's great revolutionary taking on its most influential counterrevolutionary promises a stronger narrative thread than the work itself can muster.

The movie divided critics right along party lines. Art-house gatekeepers hailed *In Praise of Love* as a triumph for Godard (the *Village Voice*: "... the most relaxed, rueful, and defiant happening our screens have seen in years"), while mainstreamers tended to be put off by its frosty narrative ellipses and old-time's-sake alienation effects (*The New Yorker*: "... its maker no longer seems able, or willing, to do his characters the honor of a story"). Depending on which side you come down on, this gorgeous Rorschach test either confirms what venal philistine-imperialists we "pain-in-the-ass Americans" are, or it demonstrates the folly of Godard's superficial, condescending, world-hysterical musings. There's truth to both propositions. (To paraphrase Groucho Marx, "You little bully, stop picking on that big bully!") But this conventional wisdom sidesteps the more intriguing issue of which unreconstructed movie-brat qualities Godard and Spielberg share: their quite different, but equally intense varieties of cinephilia, for example; their dinosaur-sized hunger for artistic respectability; and the problems both directors have when it comes to representing history in the context of real — as opposed to reel — life.

Two of the purest products of movie love imaginable, both men revel in technique for its own sake, in the mastery of a connect-the-shots cinematic form. A couple of autocratic romantics who do their best thinking in solely visual terms, both directors delight in parachuting two-dimensional cutout figures behind theme park lines, whether they're dropping them into the concentration-camp Never Againland of *Schindler's List* or into *Weekend's* groovy, End-of-Western-Civilization bumper cars. One of these sandbox generals earned his stripes by deploying lifelike fantasy projections as if they were so many shiny toy soldiers, the other by playing house-to-house combat with a collection of suburban-guerrilla Barbie and Ché dolls. Both Godard and Spielberg use poster-child images — the wide-eyed kids of *E.T.*, Jean Seberg's waif-fatale Patricia in *Breathless* — with heartfelt, instinctive calculation, to universalize the particulars of any given situation.

Object lessons are religiously nailed in place, with Spielberg going for the lump-in-the-throat jugular (a reverse Heimlich maneuver), while Godard delivers his sermons in the form of abstruse parables and swooning paradox. Whether they're showcasing Tom Hanks as Everyamerican or Anna Karina as Everyprostitute, giving Jean-Paul Belmondo or Liam Neeson a booster shot of Bogart's golden-hearted cynicism, turning a gnarled extraterrestrial loose in the suburbs or stranding him in *Alphaville*, there's always some terribly urgent revelation to be drummed home: war is hell, life is cruel, capitalism is unfair, youth is oh-so-beatific.

Like the personally tailored, talking-billboard advertisements in Spielberg's recent *Minority Report*, Godard knows exactly how to target the vanities of his highly specialized consumers. High-class intellectual brand names like Simone Weil or Robert Bresson are inserted into *In Praise of Love* like so much product placement. Indeed, prior to his return to crowd-pleasing form with *Catch Me If You Can*, one might argue that Spielberg has in recent years challenged his mass audience more than Godard has his own clique—putting them through two and a half hours of the creepy-cuddly, vaguely unhinged *A.I.: Artificial Intelligence* but also conjuring up the claustrophobically dystopian, thoroughly unpleasant film noir future of *Minority Report*. The septic-toned ambiance of that thriller marks Spielberg's closest encounter with the scrambled genre elements of Godard's prime work, in particular, *Alphaville*—post-Orwellian science fiction, tough-guy *policier*, black-eye comedy, the uneasy contemplation of man's place in an omniscient Big Brother society. Before pulling back from dread to enforce a happily-ever-after resolution, Spielberg came up with a conceit so blankly audacious it might even make Godard smile: Samantha Morton's close-cropped autistic seer-savant "precog" is lifted straight out of Carl Dreyer's 1928 masterwork *The Passion of Joan of Arc*, only this time St. Joan has been reprogrammed by the police as a psychic stool pigeon.

"The strangest thing is the living dead of this world are modeled on the world as it was," laments Edgar, *In Praise of Love*'s pontificating but terminally indecisive *artiste*, who can't make up his mind whether he's preparing a movie, a play, an opera, or a novel. Edgar's voice-over pronounces, "The way they think and feel comes from before," as we see a pair of silhouettes loitering in front of side-by-side marquee posters for *The Matrix* and Bresson's *Pickpocket*. But that sense of the cannibalized past is more vivid—more desperately, helplessly tangible—in *Minority Report* than it is within the purely rhetorical confines of *In Praise of Love*, where the night of the living dead seems modeled exclusively upon the gestures, devices, and stock footage of its director's illustrious past.

Although the film hangs on the surrogate-Godard's every word, Edgar comes off like a charmless, even more immature version of *Catch Me If You Can*'s teenage bluffer. Instead of bedding stewardesses, Edgar could be using the whole art scam to go after bigger game: "What I'd like is someone like Simone Weil and Hannah Arendt," he says wistfully of the type of woman he'd like to get for his "project." (Physical and spiritual nudity no doubt required.) Now Simone Weil was called "a saint of the absurd" by critic Leslie Fiedler; as a quixotic, left-wing Jewish intellectual who became a fervent, near-Catholic mystic, she would make a great film subject. But *In Praise of Love* simply appropriates her as a handy symbol of resistance and suffering, without bothering with her impossibly contrarian life and ideas. Godard mocks the way Hollywood glosses over and trivializes such figures—by casting Julia Roberts or, if they're really going for "authenticity," Juliette Binoche—but he, too, reduces complex individuals to figureheads, resorts to glib distortions and selective memory, then imposes a stylish false unity to cover the omissions.

What Godard has actually done in *In Praise of Love* is fashion a curious mirror image of *Schindler's List*, reproducing that film's banalities and evasions as well as its majestically composed solemnity, though in a more rarefied and intimidating form. *In Praise of Love* would be better titled "In Praise of Genius" (specifically, Godard's own). Its real subject is the special dispensation of great artists to create masterpieces, which in turn enshrine and sanctify memory. *Schindler* and *Praise* alike are intended as miraculous unions of art and history, virtue and virtuosity; indeed, the self-conscious way these movies position themselves as masterpieces is what undercuts the sense of humanity each director believes he is affirming. Monuments to artifice and denial, both works demand acquiescence to a director's panoramic tunnelvision and sleight-of-mind magic. A radiant black-and-white image makes an executed

Jew's blood into a perfect snow-angel composition, or converts a homeless man on a Parisian sidewalk into a hunk of prestigious statuary. The sublime becomes another way of whispering, "No questions asked."

With the best intentions, Spielberg substituted Schindler's 1,100 saved for the 6 million murdered; finding a silver lining inside the ovens was a moral imperative Hollywood had genetically imprinted on him. Godard is hardly wrong to see something insidious in such deeply wishful thinking — and to recoil from a rigid narrative logic that conditions moviegoers' imaginations and expectations, operating as a kind of internalized censorship. There are so many thoughts and memories Hollywood has placed out of bounds: so little time, so much to forget.

But Godard has grown equally enamored of his own wistful orthodoxy and pet mystifications. *In Praise of Love* sanctifies the Resistance even as it sweeps the nature and scope of French collaboration under the rug, not to mention the knee-jerk anti-Semitism that never seems far from the surface of French life. Perhaps the most lyrical, affecting passage in the entire film is the recital of some noble-sounding lines written by a man, we're told, on the eve of his execution: "As for my books and images / Let them be dispersed to the wind / Neither tenderness nor courage / Are things a court can rescind." A cryptic reference to his having been "executed at the Liberation" doesn't seem to have jogged many memories, but buried in the credits is a name that should have rung a few alarm bells: Robert Brasillach.

A writer and film historian as well as a notorious anti-Semite and Nazi sympathizer ("I've contracted a liaison with the German genius," he gushed, describing his love affair with fascism), Brasillach was sentenced to death after the war as a propagandist-collaborator. Yet from the reverential way his words are quoted —

very nearly sung—it appears as though he, too, were a heroic member of the Resistance Godard is so keen on remembering. Piddling details like who fought on which side suddenly become superfluous, when poetry takes over.

Whatever Steven Spielberg's sins against history, he never had the chutzpah to use a virulent, unrepentant Nazi's words as those of a martyred fellow poet, a secret sharer. Is Godard just playing hide-and-seek mind games with us? Is he merely being "ironic" — that escape clause he builds into every utterance and image, however moving or lovely? Or has he finally become the intelligentsia's very own gnomic E.T., floating high above history and human experience, ascending into the ether of higher life forms?

JLG, phone home!

[2003]

34

Lynch

Mob

The Straight Story and

Critical Myopia

SEVENTY-NINE-YEAR-OLD
Richard Farnsworth's performance
in David Lynch's *The Straight Story*
(1999) has a beautiful, disarming
nakedness: there doesn't seem to be
anything between the elements and his
weathered skin except the stubborn pride
the old actor projects. As seventy-three-
year-old Alvin Straight, who can barely
walk yet drives a battered lawn mower
nearly 300 miles from Iowa to Wisconsin
to visit his sick, estranged brother, Farnsworth
takes in the world and his own increasing
frailty with an aching watchfulness. Farnsworth's eyes articulate what Straight himself

can't put into words, conveying what it means to bear witness to decades of silent tragedy, shame, fear, and loss (Alvin mentions almost in passing that his late wife gave birth to "fourteen babies— seven made it"). Straight's eyesight is failing, too, but he can read the signs of encroaching mortality in the mirror. (Lynch's camera registers every sagging fold and wrinkle of Farnsworth's skin until it becomes a kind of narrative in itself.) Inching forward in a quixotic line, *The Straight Story*'s funereal procession of open expanses and Still-Life-with-Lawn-Mower close-ups hovers calmly at the edge of the abyss. And when Lynch cuts away from an aerial shot of the septuagenarian crossing the Mississippi to a view of a pitch-dark cemetery, Alvin is transformed into a hick from the Styx. Bringing oddball myth down to it's-all-true midwestern earth, this is one of the tenderest, most plangent spiritual odysseys ever filmed—a bucolic Wisconsin death trip undertaken to make peace with the life Straight can feel ebbing away, breath by halting breath.

In its regard for ordinary people and the ways it finds to honor the mysteries of everyday life—along with the film's diffuse sense of time and its synthesis of almost pure visual abstraction with un-adorned emotional intimacy—*The Straight Story* has obvious affinities with Iranian cinema's meld of realism and fable. But although the film was by and large enthusiastically if not very perceptively received by mainstream reviewers, the serious critics who have championed like-minded foreign films were less generous, even condescending or outright dismissive. Both camps tended to fixate on the dirty-David-Lynch-makes-a-G-rated-movie aspect of the production, but while unctuous middle-brows like *New York Times* critic Janet Maslin were enthralled by the film's supposed whole-someness, the highbrows were deeply suspicious. Even a largely sympathetic reviewer like the *Chicago Reader*'s Jonathan Rosen-baum called the movie "propaganda," as if Lynch's taking money

from Disney were inherently more compromising than Abbas Kiarostami working under the aegis of a totalitarian theocracy. J. Hoberman's appraisal of the film in the *Village Voice* was tacked on to
the end of his near-devotional assessment of Hou Hsiao-hsien *(The
Puppetmaster, Flowers of Shanghai)* as "the world's greatest working
narrative movie-maker," implicitly contrasting Lynch's cultural
conservatism and mid-American attitudes ("Disney material with a
vengeance," "shamelessly feel-good," plus the obligatory dismissive
Reagan reference) with Hou's homespun chickens-come-home-to-
Proust reveries ("Time ripples and folds in on itself like a brocaded
curtain"). The notion that Lynch might be Hou's peer—let alone
a more expressive, daring, boundary-crossing artist than the Taiwanese grandmaster—was simply beneath consideration. After all,
Lynch is an American, and not the good indie sick-soul-of-the-
nation-hating variety, but the worst kind of American at that: he
actually likes his own people.

A peculiar double vision exists when it comes to the way art-
house critics view foreign and American films, a myopia most lu-
dicrously apparent in John Patterson's rabid denunciation of *The
Straight Story*, which ran in the *L.A. Weekly* and concluded with
the sneer: "David Lynch meet Bill Bennett—you guys are gonna
get along just fine." Patterson's shrill, holier-than-Mao attack on
the movie, Lynch, and indeed the very humanity of folks like Alvin
Straight amounts to a cultural Red Guard action, parading the film
as a dunce-capped example of "bourgeois triumphalism." Seeing
reactionary conspiracy behind every frame, Patterson declares that
"non-whites might as well not exist" in Lynch's Iowa, which is like
faulting Kiarostami for neglecting to include Iranian Jews in, say,
Taste of Cherry. Patterson is blind to Farnsworth's nuanced performance, perceiving him only as a wizened stand-in for Reagan—
and "Gingrich, Armey, and Robertson," the whole vast right-wing,

fundamentalist plot Lynch "would like us all to choke on." Funny thing is, the hysterical tone of the piece—not one worthwhile moment is conceded to Farnsworth, Sissy Spacek's out-on-a-limb performance as Alvin's mentally challenged daughter, or anything else in the picture—resembles a Pat Buchanan tirade turned on its head. All that paranoid xenophobia has been displaced back onto the rural American masses to whom it is unfairly attributed, as if they were nothing more than a pack of pitchfork-wielding, gay-bashing, National Endowment for the Arts–defunding yokels. Yet *The Straight Story*'s headstrong old gentleman and the relentlessly single-minded protagonists of Kiarostami's films, or the equally determined little girl of Jafar Panahi's 1995, Kiarostami-scripted *White Balloon* (not to mention the upright, fiercely independent senior citizen Umberto D. of an earlier, no less allegorical brand of Neo-realism), have an innate kinship—they are gnarled branches of the same cinematic family tree.

Yet there is a widespread view among the film intelligentsia that humanity is the specialized province of the salt of the foreign earth, where indigenous cultures are typically mediated through familiar Eurocentric tropes and gestures (depoliticized avant-Godardisms, Bresson-oil rubdowns, the many moods of Antonioni). For these rigidly positioned film missionaries, places like Iowa are what they fly over on their pilgrimages to Lourdes-like film festivals—where true believers seek healing epiphanies, artistic "miracles," the blessings of directorial saints. The corollary to this critical fundamentalism is a self-flagellating notion of Americans as Hanna-Barbaric "Other," a derisive cartoon wrapped in a cliché wrapped in a tourniquet. Harry Dean Stanton's great, grubby credo in *Repo Man*— "Ordinary fuckin' people, I hate 'em"—has been taken up selectively by the pious gatekeepers, who are content to imagine the rest of the world as the repository of every virtue we soulless Americans have forsaken. (Thus the enthusiasm for neat-freak smorgasbords of schematic formalism and shrewdly compartmentalized affect à la *Safe, Kids,* and Solondz's dismal *Happiness:* one-note arias in the key of smug.)

Stanton, as it happens, turns up at the end of *The Straight Story,* as Alvin's dilapidated brother — a lean-to shack on legs — and there's something immensely satisfying about the pairing of Farnsworth and the eternally ornery ex–repo man. Together, these two aged character actors embody a range of American experience that encompasses the iconic and the breathtakingly quotidian, and in turn the incongruous serendipity of their reconciliation speaks to just how much of that far-flung experience David Lynch's films have laid claim to. From *Eraserhead* in 1977 to *Straight Story,* no living filmmaker has gone further into the unresolved recesses of America's dream life or fashioned so indelible a universe from such spectral matter. Yet in spite of that — or maybe because of it — he is close to a joke among film purists, an eccentric poor relation to those lofty saints who have raised movies up from their embarrassing popular origins and made them fit for monkish contemplation.

Film theologians like Kent Jones lament the absence in this country of "a genuine, shared sense of national poetics," the kind "that exists now in France, Taiwan, and Iran." Of course what these movie mullahs have in mind by that is a renunciation of the idiosyncratic, visionary, irreverent strain of American culture (which produced Melville, Ellington, Pollock, and Dylan) in favor of dour burnt offerings purged of America's wicked temptations. When a real work of loopy American poetry like *The Straight Story* comes along, giving faces and voices to people no less worthy than their brethren in Iran, the cineastes are oblivious to the national poetics right in front of them. Greil Marcus saw what most critics missed in *The Straight Story*, the sense of ungainly folk communicating in their own made-up sign languages. As he wrote in *Salon*, "They make gestures that are in some profound and casual way absolutely self-legitimating: gestures that say that those who wave their hands, stutter or proffer strange talismans have as much a right to speak, to tell the story, as anyone else." To lose sight of that, of what it means to see America in the fullness of its desires and contradictions, the promises it has broken and the promises it has kept, is to give up on the chance of ever really understanding the country you live in. The critic becomes nothing more than a belligerent tourist, insulated, ignorant, and resentful, wishing he or she were anywhere but here.

[2000]

35

Flattering
the
Audience

American Splendor

BURSTING WITH vending-
machine freshness, the HBO Films
production of *American Splendor* is
the latest caustic, art-flavored slice-of-
life to come down the homogenization
chute. This shrewd, scruffy-charming
distillation of Harvey Pekar's autobiographical comic books is another example
of the convergence between indie-auteur
hipness and cable-ready conventionality,
their mutual appetite for buzz and prestige
eating away from opposite ends toward a
boxed-in aesthetic. Ingeniously diminishing
audience expectations, this movie turns
splenetic candor and frustration into an anger-
management program for cranky outsiders.

A situation-alienation comedy, it's an outwardly verbatim movie hybrid in which Paul Giamatti's raspy, stoop-shouldered approximation of Harvey (a portrait of the artist as a declawed crab) is played off against interview/voice-over inserts of the real, more or less mellowed Pekar. *American Splendor* transforms him from a defiantly working-class observer of everyday pain-in-the-ass reality into a curmudgeonly comic-literary lion: Bert Lahr gone Underground Man, endearing even when he's sputtering about "fucking yuppie scum." (His embittered, albeit nonviolent, Travis Bickle-ishness—as if the taxi driver had quit and become a seething file clerk who found a way to let off steam by turning his diaries into comix—is essentially downplayed for laughs.) Writer-directors Shari Springer Berman and Robert Pulcini affectionately string together favorite incidents, anecdotes, jokes, and caricatures from nearly thirty years of Pekar's work, fitting them into a snug narrative arc along a stopwatch-timed conveyor belt. Plot points include: becoming a writer, whirligig marriage to Joyce Brabner (Hope Davis doing a wonderfully astringent anti–Annie Hall routine but no less beguiling for it), our cult hero's combative appearances on *David Letterman*, overcoming cancer, and finally finding hard-won domestic contentment (cue Harvey, happy at last, watching Joyce and their adopted daughter ice skate to John Coltrane's easiest-listening track).

Among other key Pekar elements that have been filtered out or soft-pedaled in the processing are the perpetual grip of daily-grind boredom and "everyday horror"; its antidote, his jazz-record collecting fanaticism (his passion for music never comes into focus); and especially his proud "From off the streets of Cleveland" credo. (Given the indifference to urban site-specifics they display here, the filmmakers might as well have shot *American Splendor* in Toronto.) Streamlining a mordantly depressive world of humdrum clutter, toil, and mess into a brisk, pleasantly droll 105 minutes, *American Splendor* locates Pekar squarely along the Woody Allen / Wally Shawn / Larry David / Charlie Kaufman continuum of cute desperation and facetious misanthropy. The overall effect is of a weirdly decaffeinated form of halfway–art-house refreshment: a fat-free, modestly self-congratulating, "My Favorite Things"–sweetened smoothie of a film.

American Splendor may lack the impressively hollow guile and headily involuted, windmills-of-your-mind structure of *Adaptation*, but Giamatti does his level best to match Nic "Sweaty" Cage tic for bug-eyed tic. Never threatening the audience's knowing sense of intellectual well-being, it's the kind of work that methodically translates self-doubt and self-loathing into a big I-scratch-your-ego-you-scratch-mine contest: the actor gets congratulated for his daring willingness to embrace his inner outcast, whose ingratiating mortification in turn strokes the audience's resolute complacency. But Giamatti's a wily, distressed cartoon ferret who lacks Cage's mannered firepower as the twins Kaufman; he just can't summon the heavy-artillery bombardment of manic anxiety, smothering physical discomfort, and obtuse boorishness. *American Splendor* aims for a mildly stylized, comic-book cutout realism, using Giamatti as a live-action illustration, a figure without any real vehemence or bite. Like Cage's mock Charlie Kaufman worrying he's a fraud, the more Giamatti's Pekar twitches and rails against phonies and *Revenge of the Nerds* and Letterman, the more we're meant to think there's some kind of genius under all that balding, furious insecurity. At the same time, the movie distances itself from anything that might constitute depth or emotional penetration, any tangled issues that might impede the forward progress of the story.

American Splendor is aiming for something less tricked-out and fancy than the cool metacinematic irony of movies like *Adaptation* and *Being John Malkovich* or the specimen-jar condescension that passes for satire in such pull-my-string puppet-masterpieces as *American Psycho* (mannequin theater of cruelty), *Happiness* (Norman Bates's Taxidermy Playhouse), *Election* (run, wind-up toy, run), *The Good Girl* (Wal-Mart Barbie ventriloquist act), and two thirds of the Coen Brothers' oeuvre (laboratory mousetrap mazes for talking mice). To its credit, *American Splendor* doesn't look down on the usual trite American stereotypes with a gaze of derisive superiority, though its notion of jes' folks is skewed toward benign eccentrics like Toby the Nerd and the elderly black interlocutor Mr. Boats. Pekar inveighs against media travesties of ordinary life and their cardboard mockery of anyone who doesn't fit the social norm, but the movie's good intentions don't translate his anger into tangible resistance so much as a canny reformulation of TV standbys: the Everyman grouch (a Ralph Kramden for our time), his zany co-workers, his fractious marriage, thrown-in kid, the follies of minor celebrity, "My Big Fat Cancer Scare."

Of course, "It's not TV. It's HBO." Pekar and the gang could slip straight into the cable monolith's Sunday night lineup, perhaps as a lead-in to Larry David's Son-of-*Seinfeld* squirmfest *Curb Your Enthusiasm*. This wouldn't be the first time a film with artistic pretensions served as a de facto HBO pilot. Dishing up an elegantly appointed widescreen platter of lame family-dysfunction gags, greased-handjob tragedy, and morbid wish-fulfillment, *American Beauty* laid the tonal groundwork for the network's popular *Six Feet Under*. Created and produced by the same writer (Alan Ball), *SFU* has literalized *Beauty*'s fabulous home-sweet-mausoleum compositions by setting the show in a mortuary, utilizing the same tree-lined, watered-down dreamscape of sex and death but populating it with a largely different set of personable stock figures (though

Lauren Ambrose's sullen, unsure teen is pretty close to the resentful daughter Thora Birch played in the movie). What's surprising isn't that *American Beauty* has been retooled as a wistfully neurotic soap opera (one where family members periodically chat with their cackling dead father) but that its suburban japes and programmatic epiphanies were never recognized as glorified television in the first place — a fancy compendium of interior-decorated banalities packaged as trenchant social commentary and poetic revelation. The need to compress a full season's worth of twists and "shocking developments" into a two-hour framework partially accounts for the shrill way Kevin Spacey's Mid-Life Crisis dad ("And in a way I'm dead already") and Annette Bening's Real Estate Robot mom ("I watched you very closely. You didn't screw up once.") telegraph every punch line, not to mention in-your-face hokum like Chris Cooper's closet-case ex-Marine and Mena Suvari's foul-mouthed Lolita of Sunnybrook Farm. Given the room to unfold episodically, *Six Feet Under* at least manages such bundles of calculated affect with slightly less overkill (or sometimes: a different, quirkier form of overkill), allowing the interlocking relationships to breathe a little.

But sleek absurdity and secondhand angst have become trendy platitudes, oozing and ahhing significance from every pore: with *Adaptation*, Kaufman and Spike Jonze in effect split the difference between the surreal-metaphysical garden trimmings of *American Beauty / Six Feet Under* and *Curb Your Enthusiasm*'s fictionalized celebrity abjection. (Kaufman's stabs at intellectual slapstick also recall a lot of Donald Barthelme's prematurely postmodernist *New Yorker* stories, wherein Joyce and Kafka meet *Attack of the Puppet People*.) Throwing up an artful silk screen of faux-intimate detachment, Jonze/Kaufman ingenuously deploy Meryl Streep and Chris Cooper to simulate real feeling even as the film denies its possibility, all in the service of some boogie-woogie variations on a minor *Malkovich* theme: "Truth is for suckers, Johnny Boy." *Adaptation*'s an ode to the powers of rationalization: a narcissistic eyeful celebrating its own limitations, it gives us Kaufman's remote-control brain surfing between the Discovery Channel, Comedy Central, the History Channel, and Lifetime.

His real alter ego isn't slobbish *True West* refugee Donald, it's polyester TV's Chuck Barris, come-hither protagonist of Kaufman's pseudo-irreverent screenplay for *Confessions of a Dangerous Mind*. Game-show honcho by day, self-professed CIA assassin by night (so who really killed JFK: Regis Philbin?), this was a man whose fuck-hate relationship with the passive viewing masses led him to launch *The Dating Game*, *The Newlywed Game*, and *The Gong Show*. Here was a genuinely prophetic sensibility: the man who invented what would become reality TV. Barris sought a common denominator so low everyone could feel superior to it—the missing link between ridicule and identification, where the viewing public could hoot at the embarrassment and scorn heaped upon those eager unfortunates even as they themselves awaited their own turn as contestants. And yet Barris-Kaufman might well insist, taking a page from *Malkovich*'s ultra-manipulative Maxine, that he, too, loves them all, "in my way." Take him for an exemplary figure: the domineering puppeteer making his herky-jerk people jump through ludicrous hoops, all for the chance to win fifteen minutes inside John Malkovich or a weekend getaway in the fabulous Everglades.

The trick is to apply a rich, lustrous coat of irony to the subject matter, so viewers won't feel like they're wasting their time with a dumb biopic about a second-rate TV personality or some half-assed Mr. Showbiz parody. In short, adapting to a devolutionary cultural marketplace by catering to lowered aspirations: fashioning an audience-stroking form of entertainment with pretensions to hipness, an intellectualized game of Trivial Pursuit. Tapping into the cerebral audience's vanity the same way classy mainstream fare taps into virtuous, socially conscious themes, Jonze/Kaufman's notion that people are really puppets is a good way of immunizing the audience against the idea that they, too, might be vulnerable to chain-yanking, button-pushing manipulations. So an inverse Other has to be constructed—a boorish Them composed of the white-trashed drooling class and sterilized suburbanites (the great unwashed and a free-floating *Gong Show* of spasmodic losers, deserving victims, and walking clichés).

A vacuum-packed movie like *About Schimdt* uses a narrow, limited perspective to funnel every telltale detail toward the big, meretriciously orchestrated cathartic payoff. Which goes off like teary, spectacular Fourth of July fireworks, for such is the power of positive repression. But director Alexander Payne deterministically herds each monochromatic character into his or her respective pen, dividing life up into two kinds of desperation (quiet or noisy, introverted or abrasively extrovert). It might be argued that the world is full of such constricted personalities with their nonexistant horizons, but if we're going to throw around favorable comparisons to Preston Sturges, should the shelves really be so overstocked with predictable, one-sided human knickknacks? In this survey of parched mid-American splendor, why is it that there's only room for one Jack-in-the-box emotional surprise? Do approving critics see their own lives in this circumscribed way, or do they see such tacky, wall-to-wall waterbed emptiness as a fate they alone have escaped: there but for the grace of good taste go I?

Regardless, the Masterpiece Factory rolls along undaunted, churning out its own set of reverential pieties, aspiring to a movie so blissfully self-conscious it reviews itself. *Far from Heaven* attained just such a humorlessly cloned critical mass, existing to certify the discernment of its audience, a Good Housekeeping thesis that re-ifies the matronly snobbery it supposedly critiques. By the same token, Home Box Office continues to work from the other middle-brow end of the prestige spectrum, with absorption rather than adaptation being its corporate/aesthetic forte. Besides Sundance Grand Jury Prize winner *American Splendor*, it's got big-gun Cannes winner *Elephant* waiting in the wings: from Harvey Pekar to *The Sopranos*, Columbine to *Sex and the City*, they're aiming to sew up all the upscale demographics in sight. One of their coy signature moves is to run *The Sopranos* and *Six Feet Under* in letterbox format, while continuing to pan and scan the feature films they show. A subtly nose-thumbing way of indicating that cinema as we knew it is dead and that the future belongs to "program-ming"?

Looking at *Sopranos* / *Sex* / *Six Feet Under* / *Curb Your Enthu-siasm* as varied pinpoint models of this mode of address, you can see the specific social nerves they strike with clockwork precision: amusingly bad Hollywood manners, single white female troubles, relationship crises du jour, married upper-management men full of pent-up rage and unresolved "issues." All have enough ingenuity to offset their set-piece shallowness: *Enthusiasm*'s casual borderline nihilism, for instance. *The Sopranos* initially took off from a smart premise—an American gangland *I, Claudius*, in which the cas-trating effects of disordered matriarch Livia on her long-suffering son are treated with a witty dose of Freudian psychotherapy. But petrification/gentrification was the price of success: the show's cre-ators have locked in on audience expectations, serving up the same slow-burn, long-suffering expressions again and again, garnished with the occasional decapitation or Russian stripper. So much for "cutting edginess."

The slightly less overwrought *Six Feet Under* has a ponderously embalmed, imitation-of-modern-life glaze that goes nicely with its funeral home setting—the Sirk-some qualities aren't stylistic but located in the repressed-hysteric content, where the glue of lightweight realism is always ready to dissolve or erupt into a death reverie or masochistic paroxysm or sex fantasy/nightmare (the line between dream sequence and waking reality always seems precarious at best). An exercise in micromanaged irrationality, *Six Feet Under* has a bifurcated quality that's endearing as well as infuriating: a smug self-awareness that masks vast tracts of unconscious motives, illusions, and evasions. It's a perpetual-emotion engine gone tastefully berserk, like a DVD of *American Beauty* set on "shuffle" (characters pop out of or disappear into thin air like poltergeists in the machine).

Ideally, Donald Kaufman's funeral would have been held at Fisher & Sons Mortuary; you can just picture Peter Krause's Nate Fisher inscribing "I want to know what it feels like to care about something passionately" on the tombstone, at no extra charge. That's the dilemma of so much post-whatever art, trying to maintain its poised disengagement and yet still pining for some kind of connection: if only it could be snorted like powdered ghost orchid or bought with a monthly Save-the-Children check. The promise an *American Splendor* holds out is one of instant authenticity, vouchsafed by the actual people themselves. As the movie wraps up, they all appear at an office retirement party for Harvey. There, in just a few quick shots, the sense of a richer, funkier-textured, more unrehearsed life suddenly comes into play: exactly what Terry Zwigoff caught in his documentary about Pekar's friend and collaborator R. Crumb. *American Splendor* lacks both the tenacity of *Crumb* and the nerve of *Ghost World*, the film Zwigoff made from Daniel Clowes's comic book, in which he remained true to the source material even as he rethought and deepened it. In Zwigoff's movie, clue by clue, the hilariously scornful heroine comes to see that life is just as strange, contradictory, and infinitely mysterious as blues singer Skip James's ancient, otherworldly "Devil Got My Woman." The main difference between little Enid and the rest of the current neo-absurdist clowns: she learns what it is to care about something that passionately, and she discovers, beneath all the desperately shallow American appearances, what an inscrutable, oblivion-haunted world this really is.

[2003]

36

Lars von Trier × 3

Savant-

Idiot,

or

Pull

the

Last

Train

to

Dogville

WETLANDS

THERE'S SOMETHING ABOUT
Lars von Trier's prodigiously assured
films that elicits indignation, as though
their labyrinthine descents into the undermind of movie history were affronts to
the sanctity of cinema itself. It's one thing
to invoke Carol Reed or even St. Orson,
but *Zentropa*, von Trier's third feature, insists upon a third auteur: Harry Lime, black
market muse, at your service. Indeed, von
Trier's work regards the audience much as
Lime does his hapless chum (fish bait by any
other name) Holly Martins—with bemused,

affectionate disdain. Expectations are rakishly toyed with, idealism ridiculed, perversity converted into a sort of caustic grandeur. In von Trier, illusions travel by sleeping car, destined for a rendezvous with the bottom of a moonlit river. Like the man said when asked what brought him to Alphaville: "I came for the waters." Which are everywhere here, from *Zentropa*'s black-and-white Danube turned mass grave to the virtually submerged police archives of *The Element of Crime*. The ornate Vienna sewers Lime fled into respected no borders; in von Trier's films, Lime's sewers stretch beneath the whole of postwar Europa. The offal of history backs up in its drains, a deluge-in-waiting oozing out of the walls and over the floorboards, pouring from the filthy sky. All the while the decrepit bureaucracies of Europa-Disney try in vain to quarantine the past, to recycle yesterday's shit as tomorrow's Perrier.

These conditions breed such stuff as fever dreams are made of — rot, infection, madness, all the luminous metaphysical baggage aboard the Twentieth Century Ltd. as it carries its passengers back to the threshold of the Dark Ages. A virus incubates, metastasizes: the germ of *Zentropa* (1991) is already alive and gnawing away in *The Element of Crime* (1984), sure as *Epidemic* (1987) contains the cells that will mutate into von Trier's medical-supernatural TV miniseries *The Kingdom* (1994). The same sanguinely deranged motifs recur, strewn like the chesspiece talismans the murderer leaves behind in *The Element of Crime*: gnomic clues that mock the very idea of solutions. (In the chaotic department store of Europa, it is one big fire sale of the vanities, all solutions stamped FINAL.)

The detective brought back from exile in *Crime* pursues the child killer by becoming him. A fanatical pathologist in *The Kingdom* winds up having the cancerous liver he wants to study transplanted into his own receptive body. With von Trier, a terrible intimacy is always present in the exchanges between the law and crime, medical science and infection, innocence and atrocity. In *Epidemic*'s film-within-a-film, the doctor who travels into the plague zone only spreads the condition. *Zentropa*'s American pacifist travels "through the German night" of 1945 to help rebuild the country but instead is duped into becoming a Nazi saboteur. Such deadly Samaritans aren't so much unwitting as half-witting: they adhere devoutly to the code of movie heroism just as Holly Martins meant to live up to the chivalrous pulp Westerns he churned out. Jean-Marc Barr's Herr Kessler is the lone rider of Santa Fe as one-man Peace Corps, trying to "build a better world" from Hitler's ruins through goodwill gestures, as helpful as the Disorderly Orderly in a burn ward. His purity of heart keeps him oblivious to the ironic machinations of both the Allies and the Nazi partisans, each side recognizing the strategic value of his naïveté. Kessler's ideals fog up his glasses so that he can't see straight: he imagines himself bitten by the love bug when in fact he's contracted a fatal case of (Harry) Lime disease.

The symptoms are a trance state of malaise, dizziness brought on by being in way over one's head, a sense of being drawn into some infinitely beguiling spell of corruption. "You will now listen to my voice," beckons *Zentropa*'s Nietzschean mesmerist, guiding us down into the abyss of the West. "The dead are happier dead," Lime reassures us with a smile, as we follow the caressing voice (Max von Sydow's) still deeper into a secret kingdom of the negative. "Europe has become an obsession to you," says the hypnotist at the beginning of *The Element of Crime*, hypnotic suggestion being von Trier's other fixation. It's both his metaphor and his prescription for moviegoing experience, where somnambulist and detective merge, as though the dying lips that pronounced "Rosebud" had ushered us into a dream history we could neither escape nor be part of. *Zentropa*'s spellbound Kessler (whether he is our surrogate or we are his is anything but clear) is taken through a grand maze of celluloid, a torrent of projection and conditioning that washes over him until it slowly dawns on the transfixed sleeper that he is not dreaming but drowning. "You want to wake up, to free yourself of the image of Europa," intones von Sydow, sardonically echoing detective Fisher's plea at the conclusion of *Crime*. The urbanely sepulchral von Sydow is the nearest living approximation of the Welles who introduced *The Trial* with Kafka's Parable of the Law—like a sinister magician pulling an accused rabbit out of his hat. "But it is not possible," shrugs the narrator, dismissing all but the prospect of endless sleep. The dead are happier because they can relax and enjoy the show; they already know how it turns out.

For von Trier, hypnosis is a device that renders present and future alike as past-life experience: death comes dressed in a fortune teller's costume. Von Trier doesn't give us characters so much as refugees from a catastrophic Tarot deck (Fool, Authority, Werewolf Fatale). In turn, these walking omens serve as heralds of eternal return, whether of fascism, plague, or plain old Original Sin. It's remarkable how single-mindedly the director milks the hypnotism gambit. Both *Crime* and *Zentropa* are framed by the sound of memory-salvaging prompters, scavengers of the repressed. In *Epidemic*, the doomed idealist of the film-within-the-film (played by von Trier) is even called Dr. Mesmer, while at the movie's climax its would-be filmmakers have an unfortunate girl hypnotized to enter their doomsday scenario. She will witness firsthand the ravages of the disease, but they can't bring her out of the trance: her shrieks presage by mere seconds the onset of the epidemic among the imaginary movie's creators themselves. (Dredged out of the psyche, medievalism isn't content with a percentage of the gross: it claims the right of final cut.) With *The Kingdom*, hypnosis recedes into the background (as a novel form of surgical anesthesia), replaced by its disreputable sibling the séance. Spiritualism divines the hidden guilt of rationalist orthodoxy, its protoplasmic fingers tugging at the sleeve of bureaucratic reality until everything begins to come undone.

Banished superstitions and dead gods return in toxic forms: the continuum of animal sacrifice and ritual murder in *Crime*, the Aryan tribalism of the Werewolves of *Zentropa*, the invasive past— history as virus—of *Epidemic* and *The Kingdom*. Beneath the edifice of the Marshall Plan and the Common Market lies a landscape closer to *The Golden Bough*, riddled with strange sects, evil spirits, crosses painted on doors. In von Trier, this is the living legacy of fascism—"The Burning of Human Beings in the Fires" having gone underground, or more precisely underwater, out of sight but not out of mind.

Like some millennarian synthesis of Mesmer and Caesar, Martin Luther and Henry Ford, Hitler rationalized the occult. His aborted kingdom put the pogrom on the assembly line, giving it the imprimatur of commerce and social hygiene. Defeated, Nazism dispersed the occult into the bowels of Europe, smuggled from zone to zone aboard trains full of displaced persons. Young Kessler, apprentice conductor, is escorted back through unknown carriages (including a boxcar full of emaciated Jews, as though the line's concentration camp timetables were still in effect) to help effect "a proper burial" for the industrialist Max Hartmann. The funeral procession resembles a nostalgic night rally, until the American military police scatter the faithful back to their catacombs.

But suppose the ceremony was all a ruse, that the coffin unloaded after Kessler pulled the emergency brake contained not Hartmann's body but some crooked hospital functionary from another zone who had outlived his usefulness. The true destination of Hartmann's remains then is to be Occupied Vienna, where the romance of lost causes can be converted into the hard currency of "international enterprise" (as the deceased described his beloved Zentropa railway—the postwar dream of capital without borders).

There waits a jaunty American, fresh from a funeral of his own, to broker the whole deal. Max Hartmann's final resting place will be fellow businessman Lime's waiting grave, on the theory that one good turn deserves another. Playing the stalemated powers against each other, Citizen Lime sees through the Cold War's ideological sham. "Nobody thinks in terms of human beings," he grins. "They speak of the people and the proletariat—I talk about the suckers and the mugs." Still, this is posturing, public relations sleight-of-hand. "Go into the future," commands the voice on the soundtrack: it is already here, on this train, in this divided city, taking shape in the chasm between Kessler's lifeless form as the sewers bear it out to sea and the resurrected Lime peering out from the shadows of history. Not only are von Trier's films a relentless series of variations on a theme (Wagner played on a zither sounds a lot like "Moritat"); their sense of cinematic correspondences add up to a recondite master narrative. The project called the Free World is to be constructed on the ruins of the old, the corrupt, the abominable one. "You will be there" at the sound of the narrator's voice; go forward and backward in time when the hour strikes midnight; be there when I say, "Cuckoo clock."

"This dump of yours isn't Alphaville, it's Zeroville," said an exasperated Lemmy Caution; in *The Element of Crime* he is called Fisher. For in *Crime* von Trier elaborates the interstices of such modern legends. He locates Fisher (Michael Elphick) at the intersection of *Alphaville* and *The Trial*, in the wasteland where Akim Tamiroff once commuted between their respective (and complementary) dystopias. Hardboiled Fisher is Advocate, Examining

Magistrate, and Executioner rolled into one: he is Lemmy C. whose mission is to become his own Josef K. Here, though, the polarities have been reversed, so that instead of crime sans punishment in the film's Year Zeroville there is crime without boundaries. In other words, totalitarian order has been superseded by a theology of annihilation. "Where did you get your training," mutters Fisher at an overzealous coroner, "Auschwitz?" His bullhorn-toting superior Kramer certainly could have cut his teeth there, gloating, "I've got the world by the balls." Fisher diligently applies the system of his mentor, Professor Osborne; it spells doom for them both. "How're your theories now, Fish?" taunts Kramer at picture's end. Osborne hangs himself (or else is framed and hanged by Chief of Police Kramer, who hates loose ends as much as gruff old Hank Quinlan); the mystery is stamped SOLVED, and the guilty Fisher is condemned to go free. The last decent man in Europe finds his method is at one with the irrationalism it opposes — as Fisher drags back the terrified child he is ostensibly protecting, a monstrous aura of paternity envelops him as her twitching limbs grow still. The atmosphere of burnished fatalism in *The Element of Crime*'s sepia-toned noir composition is a bit too polished, too facile. (It's an apocalyptic elegy.) But the same could be said of *Blade Runner*, which it resembles after a deromanticized fashion. And certainly *Alphaville* and *The Trial* are both facile, if in different ways. Godard's city of tomorrow is cursory, austere — a fluorescent abstraction of a beehive populated by cardboard drones. Von Trier goes overboard on everything but sterility; his flaws are closer to Welles in that he imparts a playful sense of dread. With *The Trial* Welles couldn't help jazzing up Kafka until the crazy-quilt array of protonarcs, arbitrary bureaus, and pallid, jittery suspects suggests William Burroughs as much as the sainted Franz. (As Lime's Vienna is the precursor of Dr. Benway's Interzone, this is somehow fitting.) Of course Tony Perkins was miscast, yet who could begrudge Welles the wondrous, impudent joke of revealing the pride of Amerika, Norman Bates, as poor, tormented K.? *Crime* operates on a similar principle of poetic effrontery. Shot in English, but with a disembodied sound à la *The Trial* giving its voices the same quality of forlorn cries in a deserted building, it's a tone poem to crumbling Europe.

Von Trier's intertextuality turns cultural artifacts into alien runes. If in *Crime* he's too free with the mysterioso suggestiveness (pouring chaos atop ritual), it's still a beautifully assembled debut feature. Its callowness is leavened by the stirrings of a cosmic gallows humor — the sense, out of Kafka, of the universe as a vast, inscrutable joke at the expense of humanity. When his *Crime* cameo is dubbed "Schmuck of Ages," he also shows a peculiar, latent affinity with another Kafka offshoot, namely Woody Allen. "Traitor, renegade, creep, quisling" goes the litany of insults heaped on his goggle-eyed Dr. Mesmer in *Epidemic*, which plays like a crackpot gloss on *Stardust Memories*. (Call it "The 8½th Seal.") The scene in which von Trier's longtime co-scenarist Niels Vorsel recounts how he posed as a teenager to become the pen pal of American schoolgirls, then laughingly reads aloud their silly, earnest letters, is unflinchingly discomfiting, a true squirmfest — a portrait of the artist as a sublimated serial killer. Where Allen is done in by his lust for respectability, his reverence for European high muckymuck, von Trier has no such compunctions: the war finished off the comforting belief that tragedy ennobles. *Epidemic* charts the progress of artists who "based their work on the suffering of others" — their sense of immunity dissolves as the symptoms suddenly materialize at the dinner they give for their producer. (As they keel over — one guest stabbing a fresh boil with a fork for good measure the dissatisfied producer gets his wish: instead of talking heads, a bloodbath.) In its black-and-white mixture of pseudodo-cumentary 16mm and pseudo-high-flown 35mm, *Epidemic* feels more like a first movie than *Crime*. It eats away at the premises of the "art film" — who could watch something like *Suture* with a straight face after seeing this? — while attempting to reestablish a beachhead for film art, even if it's as art against itself. One thing von Trier isn't, for all the severity of his images, is an ascetic. He's got a crypto-pop streak that comes out most blatantly in the odd, catchy theme songs he coauthors, like the disco anthem that concludes *Epidemic*: "The end is near / The plague is here / Bring out your dead. . . ."

With *The Kingdom* he opts for a still more eschatological refrain: "O death where is thy sting?" This post–*Twin Peaks* miniseries elaborates "The Hospital" section of *Epidemic* on a baroque institutional scale. Yet it's a laborious setup (even the jokes are ponderous; this is von Trier's most Danish work) for a payoff that never arrives, at least until all hell begins to break loose at the end of Part Four. There a dead ghoul is reborn in a gynecological version of Nicholson's "Heeeeeere's Johnny" entrance, but that's the only truly startling moment. *The Kingdom* is too familiar in terms of both von Trier and TV/movie conventions (as if *St. Elsewhere* were infiltrated by the restless souls of *Poltergeist*); he gives himself over to those conventions a little too wholeheartedly. Besides, the idea of the hospital as microcosm of society and society as incubator of infection (the fascist organism) is underdeveloped here, almost taken for granted. It seems quaint in the wake of *The X-Files*, which as a symptom rather than a diagnosis goes deeper into political economy of the occult. In *X-Files*, paranoia takes on an evangelical hue: evil residing out there among inhuman Others (the figure of the vampiric Jew revamped according to the UFO gospel) and covered up by a secret society working within the government.

That milieu of occult history and the romance of conspiracy is the heart of *Zentropa*; it abducts you into the movie past and strands you in an upside-down world. You are alone, at the mercy of forces you don't understand. All the signposts of heroism and truth are present but twisted into strange totems: the cross has been bent into a swastika. You are being given an examination, a test, but cannot concentrate. The questions, the protocols, are gibberish. Your thoughts turn to Katharina Hartmann, your Kate: her glamour and virtue got to you, but your white goddess was a terrorist. These things happen. You were sucked into a black market of child assassins, sympathizing priests, sweet Kate orchestrating the death of her father. Your head is going to explode. At last you snap; you will only be pushed so far. For any proper movie hero, the time comes to take a stand. Destry rides again — so you detonate the bomb, extinguishing all those wretched dots. I'm afraid that was a bad idea, old man. Where did it get you but in the same boat with them? Wait. You hear a tune in your head, "Take the A Train." Tap your foot. Imagine it is half a century later, and all of this history has been buried along with you. Above, a sleek Zentropa trans-Europe express is running right on time. In the first First Class sleeping compartment, movies are available. Today you could watch an American feature. An Aryan secret agent / family man (Herr Schwarzenegger) saves the Fatherland and families from a filthy Arab plot. For a moment, your head would spin, you could not remember who won the war (maybe the villain is an Arab because all the Jews were exterminated, after all). The cinema's *True Lies* suck you in and leave you no escape: its images are everywhere, especially inside you. Relax. Let them wash over you. No need to worry anymore — the werewolves are hibernating. Sleep. It's just entertainment, old man. And besides, we're all carriers.

CANNES GAMES

THREE YEARS BACK, under the aegis of a radical (and largely spurious) Danish filmmaking collective calling itself Dogma 95, Lars von Trier and Thomas Vinterberg issued a directorial manifesto in the daft form of a "Vow of Chastity." (Later, Kristian Levring and Søren Kragh-Jacobsen signed on, effectively doubling Dogma's membership.) Set forth in ten severe back-to-naturalism commandments, coupled with additional proclamations like, "I swear as a director to refrain from personal taste!," the vows' monastic regimen is first put to the test in a pair of movies, both of which premiered in 1998 at Cannes: Vinterberg's *Dogma 1: The Celebration* and von Trier's *Dogma 2: The Idiots*. Each displays a thoughtfully ambivalent misanthropy and miserly economy of means, though neither is remotely chaste in attitude. *The Celebration*, digs up the skeletons in a wealthy family's closet with all the tact of a tabloid show (welcome to "Denmark's Ghastliest Home Videos"). An acute eye prying for sacred monsters and festering wounds, Vinterberg's lens refracts blood ties as sadomasochism. Meanwhile, *The Idiots* plunges into more scattered, uncharted terrain—the antisocial space occupied by a band of troublemakers who impersonate the retarded. A fragile, damaged woman gets sucked into their ragtag commune, and her life is either saved or destroyed (perhaps both) as a result.

A profile of von Trier aired on TV recently, and in it he talked about Dogma 95's curious manifesto (that document, it should be noted, marks the fourth different aesthetic declaration von Trier has authored or instigated since 1981). Scarcely able to keep a straight face, he wore the agreeable smile of a well-medicated mental patient—or else the cat who had swallowed the canard. At forty-two, riding the crest of his art-house success with *Breaking the Waves* and known for a headstrong verve recalling Orson Welles at his most prodigious, von Trier acts more like a refugee from *The Idiots* than an internationally renowned director. Chuckling about directing the film in the nude and maintaining that every day the entire cast cried, he appeared to be sending up the whole moviemaking process from conception to postproduction promo interview. In his own (Andy) Kaufman-esque fashion, our lovable Lars is being helpfully candid, explaining the rules even while conspiring to mock them.

Von Trier insists that the Vow of Chastity's flesh-scourging injunctions (all shooting is to be done on location without additional props or sets, using a handheld camera, live sound, etc.) are more or less arbitrary; the important thing is to set self-imposed limitations as a way to stimulate the imagination by forcing it to work around obstacles. "The Dogma rules are very much made for me," von Trier confesses, and they are intended to make the director "give away control." Thus the manifesto doubles as a control freak's twelve-step (minus two) program. First describing the commandments, as "Some orders to myself, like in hypnotism, 'Don't use artificial light,'" von Trier paused a beat before dropping the other shoe. "But then again, if you can't control it all, what's the point?"

What indeed. From the dystopian noir of *Element of Crime* (1984, aptly) to the stunning metacinema of 1991's *Zentropa* (Hitchcockian devices mordantly wed to *Our Hitler*–like evocations of the romance-trance of movies and fascism), von Trier's work masterfully explored the possibilities of artifice. His earlier films largely rejected a Danish identity for a polyglot, polysemous one, while spoilsport critics carped about their rootless cosmopolitanism. *Breaking the Waves* featured a dour Scandinavian sensibility gone pop, its demented ventriloquism owing as much to Edgar Bergen as Ingmar Bergman: here, the director seemed a perversely affectionate puppet master and God an inventively cruel auteur. In view of von Trier's past vanities and excesses, one can see how he might feel the need to atone, to make a clean break lest he wind up a nut-job self-caricature like the megalomaniacal director in *The Stunt Man* (Richard Rush's cryptoparodistic sleight-of-hand film [1978/1980], which might be the unacknowledged source of von Trier's delusion-and-reality brinkmanship).

"The director must not be credited," the tenth Dogma commandment enjoins, which is too bad for Thomas Vinterberg, since *The Celebration* looks more like a von Trier film than *The Idiots*. Meant to "force the truth out of . . . characters and settings," the strict Dogma framework proved weirdly liberating for Vinterberg: "There was a great lightness of feeling [during the shoot]. We could romp to our heart's content." That's apparent in the film, shot like a series of guerrilla home movies so painfully intimate that material winds up framed with blank, surveillance-cam detachment. Peppered with gothic family secrets, *Godfather* allusions, and an Ophelia ghost for good measure, Vinterberg's film has the poised, nervous energy of early Godard and Fassbinder but with a different kind of stylization altogether: one whose revisionist tendencies cross-pollinate the found antiart of reality TV with the awkwardness–cum "bad taste" of daytime soap operas and the cramped, prowling mise-en-scène of shot-on-video pornography.

Vinterberg (with only one previous film to his credit) absorbed more than just von Trier's freewheeling camera moves and staccato, helter-skelter edits; he has also adopted his mentor's unstable, omnisatirical point of view, which abstains from telling the audience how to react to what he shows them. *The Celebration* uses that impish, ambiguous quality to sinister comic effect, tossing preconceived reactions back in our faces. Vinterberg's seamless ensemble never strikes a false note; no one is seen acting but simply caught behaving as impulsively (or guardedly) as the moment dictates. *The Idiots* takes the Vow of Chastity's notion of "the instant as more important than the whole" to even starker, more disconcerting extremes. With its unadorned, public-TV-documentary look and deliberately murky psychology, *The Idiots* successfully effaces — or at least defaces — von Trier's trademark tics. The troupe of scareartists who give the film its name may be seen as surrogates for the posing-as-inconspicuous auteur who created them. "Spazzing" it up, eliciting hypocritical reactions, hustling guilty donations, and generally fucking with the heads of anyone who pays them heed, they might be teen-acting a loopy, mummer's version of *Breaking the Waves*. (For its American release, black boxes have been superimposed on the frequent frontal nudity and odd bits of explicit sex, needlessly upping the absurdity quotient.) But *The Idiots'* encounter-group antics haven't got the same safety net of redeeming aesthetic significance to fall back on. With their blurry role-playing and displacing reversals of perspective (are they pretending to be what they're not or what they fear they might really be?), von Trier's scraggly bunch of sadist-idealists are like slacker descendants of the Baader-Meinhof gang: emotional terrorists, yet oddly affecting ones. At last the real Dogma 95 program emerges as catharsis interruptus — a leap into an ice-water void that proffers its own shock-to-the-system release.

TOP DOG

ON A MAP OF the cultural unconscious, you'd find Lars von Trier's *Dogville* a "Lottery" stone's throw from *Our Town*, about two miles as the crow flies from *The Shining*'s Overlook Hotel,

20,000 leagues under Kafka's *Amerika,* and the furthest conceivable distance from Middle Earth. Follow the yellowed-myth *Road to Perdition* beyond "The Petrified Forest," then take the last exit to Elm Street: Welcome to Dogville, Colo., population 22, not to be confused with Mudville (though there is no joy here, either), a place so godforsaken it makes the town Clint Eastwood painted red and renamed Hell in *High Plains Drifter* look like the Garden of Eden.

Since its 2003 premiere at Cannes, the Danish filmmaker's seventh feature has been wildly praised and just as bitterly scorned for its austere, malevolent vision of America as a broken dreamland of violence, cruelty, and spiritual impoverishment (a glimpse of how the world may imagine us). Set in the Rocky Mountains during the Great Depression, *Dogville* unfolds on a nearly bare soundstage, the town reduced to a blueprint outline populated by a Sears mail-order assortment of hypocrites and brutish caricatures. On the lam from her gangster father, Nicole Kidman's pitiable Grace stumbles into this den of sleeping dogs, only to see the townspeople's veneer of civility and community fall away, revealing their true predatory natures. Viewed from an overhead camera's lofty perspective, *Dogville*'s ant-farm layout resembles a schematic for predestination — everything in its assigned place and everyone playing their designated Dispassion Play roles, as Grace first becomes the happy indentured servant and later the town's shackled scapegoat and sex slave.

While *Dogville* may not look much like a conventional film, this is nonetheless familiar territory: the land of the godlike director, the all-powerful Creator perched high above the action, pulling plot strings, yanking the actors' (and audiences') leashes with disciplinarian relish. Von Trier employs the techniques of art to achieve something closer to a behavior-modification experiment: this might as well be Pavlov's *Dogville.* By putting an internation-

ally pedigreed pack of actors (including Lauren Bacall, Ben Gaz-
zara, and Stellan Skarsgard) through obedience-school paces, von
Trier revels in the *Clockwork Orange* possibilities of applied dehumanization.

The hyperbolic responses of critics to the director/researcher's
clinical bells and whistles have an equally reflexive quality, whether
they come out of the picture salivating "masterpiece" or frothing
"anti-Americanism is a small matter when a movie is anti-human"
(as Charles Taylor did on Salon.com). But the most fascinating
(and alarming) thing about *Dogville* is how it simulates all the
trappings of a cinematic breakthrough: designed to generate the
maximum moral and aesthetic polarization with a minimum of
intrusive depth, it seems to herald a new age where con artistry
triumphs over art. Under layers of ironic cliché, glib appropriation,
and press-on nihilism, there lies a remorselessly efficient calculation to match that of any beady-eyed Hollywood kingpin.

Indeed, the most striking thing about von Trier is the way he
plays the role of the great director as if his whole career were a
shameless fictional conceit, from the phony "von" surname (to
evoke von Sternberg and von Stroheim) to his carefully cultivated
eccentricities (the agoraphobia that keeps him from visiting
America) to his creation of the half-tongue-in-cheek Dogma 95
manifesto, with its renunciation of sets and lighting and anything
else that might smack of "production." Von Trier has cast himself
as a gadfly and cultural subversive, but what he is supposed to be
subverting grows more opaque with each new gesture. And his
latest, most grandiose intellectual quagmire suggests he may have
pushed his autocratic auteurist shtick to its limit. Ploys and prov-
ocations need to be about something more than generating contro-
versy; ultimately, a genuine auteur needs to make movies of substance, not just brilliant publicity stunts.

Von Trier's rise to international prominence has followed a crooked route. After breaking through in 1991 with *Zentropa* (that fiendishly sharp riff on postwar thrillers of the *Notorious–Third Man* school), he solidified his cult following with the archly effective haunted-hospital TV miniseries *The Kingdom* (1994) and *The Kingdom II* (1997), as well as the Dogma demonstration film *The Idiots* (1998). But lately his main preoccupation has been to synthesize a new strain of exalted female victimhood out of Christian hagiography and the movie-melodrama past. The perversely religious *Breaking the Waves* (1996) bolstered von Trier's reputation as a pseudo-visionary—with its dimly sweet *Song of Bernadette* heroine talking to herself in the voice of God, undergoing sexual mortification and death on her way to a crackpot sainthood that was nearer to Señor Wences than Carl Dreyer. The 2000 capital-punishment musical *Dancer in the Dark*, starring the unbearable Björk as a factory worker going blind and trying to save her son from the same affliction, elaborated this fondness for putting feminine doormats through the self-sacrificial wringer.

Dogville is the apotheosis of these tendencies, with the pummeled Kidman attaining her state-of-Grace via overdoses of passive suffering and abuse endurance that goes thorn to bloody thorn with *The Passion of the Christ*. Her humiliations are as much a nasty running joke as moral edification: rape as object lesson, with moralism and prurience going hand in hand down the brimstone path. The would-be subverter of film cant builds sanctimony back up faster than he can tear it down: *New York Press* critic Armond White says, "Von Trier is antagonistic toward the cinema's traditions," but it may be more a matter of an unresolved (and unresolvable) lust-hate attitude toward the medium. With von Trier, it's as if the moral (or amoral) universes of Hitchcock, Kubrick, Bergman, and Dreyer had imploded, together with the worlds of kitsch and horror and soap opera, and suddenly the boundaries between Dreyer's *Day of Wrath* and George Romero's *Night of the Living Dead* have ceased to be meaningful.

In this sense, von Trier is like a Scandinavian Quentin Tarantino: replacing reality with convoluted frames of reference, endlessly regurgitating favorite film tropes, taking twisted pleasure in lumping together the spiritual and the debased as if he were trying to bridge the chasm between faith and porn. The difference is that Tarantino's art-cartoonishness is rooted in a genuine ardor (if only for the movies, which for him supplant life), whereas von Trier's revanchist fantasies are geared more toward fucking with the audience than anything else.

By the film's conclusion, when Grace is reunited with her father and turns the tables on her victimizers with a cold-as-Eastwood vengeance, she seems ready to change places with the Bride of *Kill Bill*. (Or ride off into the divine retribution sunset of *High Plains Drifter*, a joke Q.T. would surely appreciate.) Not content with mere cinematic connections, J. Hoberman's enthralled review of the movie in *The Village Voice* highlighted its alleged literary heritage, citing D. H. Lawrence on *The Scarlet Letter* in his *Studies in Classic American Literature*. But where Lawrence detected the hellish, fabulist undertow in Hawthorne and those other bleak voices of destruction he compared to "the weirdness of old Carthage," he thought the difference between American art-speech and that of the prissy European moderns was that the latter had to labor harder at extremity.

Indeed, "the pitch of extreme consciousness" Lawrence spoke of coming naturally to Americans is out of von Trier's emotional range. With its bottom-of-the-crackerbarrel English (Ma Ginger: "Don't give me any of your lip, Tom Edison Jr."), *Dogville* is more a Cliffs Notes version of Am-Lit and Film 101. When James Caan's

Big Man rolls into town for the denouement, the movie becomes a pixilated version of Jonathan Edwards's classic sermon "Sinners in the Hands of an Angry Godfather."

What does give Kidman's Grace her creepy frisson is not some residue of Hester Prynne but the idea of subjecting a blond movie goddess to gross indignities, much as Hitchcock pecked away at Tippi Hedren in *The Birds* or Norman Mailer portrayed Marilyn Monroe as a figure of disheveled porno-pathos. "This town is rotten from the inside out," Grace is warned shortly after she arrives. Rejecting its savior, it must be punished accordingly. Everything in *Dogville* is as illustratively arrayed for the viewer as Mel Gibson's holy gorefest, but it's more painterly and abstractly refined. When Kidman is spread out in the back of an apple truck and raped, the beautifully layered scene could be a Cézanne still life superimposed on a crucifixion scene overlaid on a Monroe calendar pinup.

But von Trier isn't through toying with us yet. After Grace initiates a pogromesque, kill-everyone final sequence (all lovely red tones and deft editing), the end credits run over a photo montage showing several decades of white poverty and black squalor, set to the fake R&B of David Bowie's 1975 disco-casualty anthem "Young Americans." The harsh juxtaposition of the movie's rotten make-believe poor and the real poor rekindles the suspicion that, deep down, von Trier has no more feeling for the underclasses than a kid with a magnifying glass has for the ants he sets on fire. (In fact, this music video sequence could be shown as Aryan propaganda: a demonstration of mongrel America's racial inferiority.)

Dogville is corrosive in a way that allows the viewer to feel safe, untouched—it implicates the Others, the Ugly Americans, certainly not the kind of people who go see Lars von Trier movies. Real suffering tacked on to high artifice assumes a gloating quality: as if these filthy hordes were merely a stick to poke America in the eye. Instead of Bowie, I couldn't help then recall "Lead Me On," a soulful, dignified 1961 song by R&B singer Bobby "Blue" Bland that packs more awareness and profound emotion into three minutes than there is in all three hours of *Dogville*: "You know how it feels, you understand / What it is to be a stranger, in this unfriendly land."

While von Trier passes off clueless malice as trenchant exposé, one wonders what unconscious terrain his next film will wind up exposing. *Manderlay*, the second part in a projected *Dogville* trilogy, is currently in production. It will feature Ron Howard's daughter Bryce taking over the role of Grace, fleeing to a town in the South where slavery is, anachronistically enough, still practiced. You almost laugh in spite of yourself at the huckster's indefatigable hubris: Frantz Fanon goes to "Uncle Tom's Cabin in the Sky"! Perhaps von Trier will at last succeed in offending—indeed mortifying—his progressive, enlightened constituency. Or perhaps this trilogy is just a stepping stone to bigger things: a Dogville theme park, where one can ride the animatronic Grace and free the animatronic slaves. Maybe there's some of the American Spirit in Lars, after all.

[1995/1998/2004]

37

Buffy the Vampire Slayer

and **Studies in Classic**

American Literature

WHY BLOOD?" Good question,
Xander — Buffy the Vampire Slayer's
semihapless friend, factotum, and stand-
up fall guy is wondering why it happens
to be the currency of yet another typically
cruel rite of underworldly passage ("Why
couldn't it be, like, a lymph ritual?"), to say
nothing of demonic exchange and appetite.
" 'Cause it's always got to be blood," answers
quasi-reformed, chip-in-head, Slayer-loving
vamp Spike. "Blood is life, lackbrain. . . . It's
what keeps you going. Makes you warm.
Makes you hard. Makes you other than dead.
'Course it's her blood."

Sounds like our peroxide-haired, other-than-dead boy's been reading a tubercular spot of D. H. Lawrence down in his dusty bachelor crypt. And such extracurricular inspiration would scarcely raise a Buffy Summers eyebrow—by this time, the girl's already suffered and abetted his twisted romanticism at close range, with so much more yet to come. Underneath that leather-jacketed pose of sneering Billy Idolatry, walking phallic symbol Spike's got the whole destructive-eros mojo down hot *and* cold: as the eternal voice of bittersweet unreason, sexualized aggression, and the sacred profane, he might as well have "Love that burns and consumes" tattooed on his pale chest. In Lawrence's magnificent, rictus-grinning, virtue-slaying *Studies in Classic American Literature* (final version, 1923), he wrote only half incongruously, "The essential function of art is moral," by which he meant a darkening, prophetic something not so unlike *Buffy*'s tapeworm diet of essences and black humors, extremity and antinomy. "But a passionate, implicit morality, not didactic. A morality which changes the blood, rather than the mind. Changes the blood first. The mind follows later, in the wake."

It's easy to see *Buffy* in Lawrencian terms, even as its females-on-top end-of-the-worldview relentlessly inverts his dour male chauvinism and turns his apocalyptic apoplexy on its purple head. (Amusingly, too, her generic California hometown is chronically awash in fugitives from Old England and Ireland, stowaways from the eighteenth or nineteenth centuries, slouching toward Sunnydale to be reborn in Mall-America.) It was virtually predestinated that the finest single episode of this absurd, self-divided, utterly mad American classic—as if for Lawrence there could be any other kind—would be titled "The Body." That is where this novelistic TV series' acute, DHL-ish "spirit of place" is absolutely rooted, in the flesh of an undiscovered country, in the physical's knock-down, drag-out, love/hate affair with the soul, life instinct and death wish commingling as tidal pools in the supposedly metaphoric Hell-mouth's tooth-and-maw war zone. And yet a remarkable stillness and lyric desolation so often pervade the show—the most potent, naked image of our heroine has her painstakingly sopping up her own vomit after finding her mother sprawled dead on the couch at home. Another beautifully rhymed shot in creator Joss Whedon's script evokes the emotional vacuum of death as follows: "the outline of a figure, but not the figure itself. Negative space."

Which comprises Buffy's sense of her, you know, personal space as well. Speaking in jokey, stammering, polyglottal tongues, *Buffy the Vampire Slayer*'s New World–confronts–ye–Old Gods self-consciousness always comes down at base to Body Language: shy, infinitely touching Willow painting sapphic verses on her lover Tara's back, Spike thrusting into love's void and sinking like a millstone, Giles wearing his English reserve as a coat of armor against his own pagan nature. And above and below the lot of them, there is Buffy, the good American cheerleader turned blessed-cursed Un-redeemer, nailed to the cross that divides her single-minded Puritan duty from her instincts, desires, and vulnerability, so poignantly estranged from her own body when she isn't using it as a weapon, wearing a forget-me-not crucifix around her neck like an absent-minded symbol of the stake life has driven through her heart of hearts.

Bearing this in mind (wake-wise, what precisely is the relation between jetsam and jism anyway?), a book called *Buffy the Vampire Slayer and Philosophy: Fear and Trembling in Sunnydale* might seem to hold a measure of promise. I mean, here's the opportunity for that big Buffy versus Nietzsche face-off of our dreams, perhaps a reckoning with the avant-Kierkegaard implications of B.'s sacrificial "leap of faith" and subsequent hellish resurrection (young Søren gets *Carrie* for a prom date?), or maybe a point-by-point elaboration of Dark Willow's insightful neo-nihilist Critique of Pure Buffy: "You really need to have every square inch of your ass kicked." But sadly no, lest we for even one moment forget: There is NO fear or trembling in contemporary philosophic discourse, and zero joy is a given. Though in fairness, this relatively benign slip of a tome is less post- than resolutely semimodern, a textbookish but not too jargon-overdosed attempt to introduce your average unwary college freshman to fundamental questions of ethics, epistemology, and morality by dressing them up in safe, familiar pop-cult drag. Unfortunately, by watering down *Buffy* even more than Nietzsche, *Fear and Trembling in Sunnydale* casts a fuddy-dud pall that even the best essays here (Thomas Hibbs on the show as feminist noir, Melissa M. Milavec and Sharon M. Kaye on Buffy and "Aristotle's Love Paradox") never really manage—or attempt—to escape.

Mostly, there's a stolid, anemic didacticism that fails to do justice to *Buffy* or, for that matter, the bloody mess that is existence itself. Content rather to professionally disinfect both with a swab of Kant, a Lysol cloud of Plato, and some "gender construction of femininity" air dampener, the book provides little to dispute the show's account of the education system as a well-orchestrated conspiracy against knowledge and understanding. Just enough hardcore zombie prattle is on hand—in one case, exposing B. as ringleader of a fascist death squad persecuting what she would insensitively refer to as "undead Americans"—to remind us of theory's life-draining, brain-sucking potential. (With characters like Principal Snyder, Professor Walsh, and the Prof's deconstructionist-Frankenstein protégé Adam representing the pedagogic nether realms, the Slayer's institution-assaulting response appears unequivocal: ACADEMIA MUST BE DESTROYED.) If you really crave an informed, comprehensive, and impassioned commentary on the show, 2002's *Reading the Vampire Slayer* (edited by Roz Kaveney) is a far better bet—actual moments of real thought, real feeling, even real writing.

Or you could pick up a copy of Cambridge's brand-new complete edition of Lawrence's eighty-year-old *Studies in Classic American Literature*, including all the distinctive variants and utterly alternate versions of his groundbreaking essays on what then were regarded as mere "children's books." All the old, weird, uncanny figures, places, and beasts come home to roost: the Deerslayer, the House of Usher, Moby-Dick. All the simple, homespun, Christian lessons: incest, blasphemy, and the open-road real-estate mantra of negation, negation, negation. "There are terrible spirits, ghosts, in the air of America." Scarlet-letter fever, devil children, cleansing floggings— a death-haunted new world rising from the corpse of Europe, out of so many heady native contradictions and competing myths. Land of subterfuge, scourging, amputation, displacement: "And displacements hurt." (I can hear Buffy saying the exact same thing.) It's all there, the innate "pitch of extreme consciousness" and the ravening daemons of the American unconscious, the Gods of materialism and rootless freedom pulling this way and that, the flight to and from oneself, the doomed wish to escape human nature.

The backward-looking moral universe Lawrence conjures up in his *Studies* prophesies the one Buffy and her friends and enemies inhabit as sure as their words and deeds echo with his diabolic obsessions and laughter. The Poe-reeking, thrill-killing Drusilla's childlike singsong of the "under-consciousness" purrs with such innocent malice: "We're going to destroy the world. Want to come?" Yes, please, Lawrence answers, with a cherry on top: He reinvents American Lit in his own image and himself in its shadows, recreating his voice as this amazing vernacular ventriloquist act—a case of two-way possession. (Tracing the evolution of

that condition through the different stages of these essays is a
journey in itself, though that doesn't excuse the book's coach-
airline-ticket price.) The final result is a biblical proto-hipster poet-
crank tone: treating Whitman as a pop figure ("And Walt's great
poems are really huge fat tomb-plants, great rank grave-yard
growths") before there was pop, bedrock cool remorselessly crossing
over the borders of emotion into the bowels of the "life-mystery."
Here is Lawrence on the Puritan-Calvinist legacy: "It is absolutely
necessary to realise once and for all that every enthusiasm, every
passion, has a dual motion: first a motion of liberation, of setting
free; and secondly a motion of vindictive repression of the living
impulse, the utter subjection of the living, spontaneous being to
the fixed, mechanical, ultimately insane *will*."

Which describes the struggle at the core of *Buffy the Vampire
Slayer* lo these past seven years. But writing about Whitman, he
put his finger on another indispensable quality: "Sympathy," that
empathic fellow-feeling so crucial to the denizens of the Buffyverse,
the interconnectivity that transcends salvation. (B. learns firsthand
saviorism isn't what it's cracked up to be.) So we have this little
show about a girl and her plain, ordinary friends, coming face-to-
face with the unthinkable, with their own daemon selves. To each,
Lawrence says, his or her own Holy Ghost (with every Kaspar the
Holy Ghost for his/herself, and God against all). Thus a would-be
"regular kid" stands before her dying, "cradle-robbing, creature-of-
the-night boyfriend" and delivers the classic American ultimatum
that would leave Lawrence speechless with blushing pride or
maybe puritanical shock: "Drink me."

[2003]

38

Wrecked

in

El

Dorado

Angel

LET US GO THEN, you and I, when the city's spread out like an anesthetized starlet — Los Angeles in the form of a comic-book relief map, cul-de-sac popsicle stand or plaster-surgery Angelyne billboard. Scaled down to modestly evocative, letterboxed-in TV dimensions, a utilitarian assortment of low-budget genres and garbled mythologies cruise deserted 3:00 a.m. streets or hole up in haunted apartments. They clash by night with the angels of their better natures in cheap abandoned hotels and travel by day through spacious, immaculate sewers.

Think of this as Philip Marlowe's old town overrun by gothic refugees — furtive echoes of

Cast a Deadly Spell and *Ride the Pink Horse* bouncing off the balconies of a deserted Firesign Theatre, where Ross MacDonald is either Kenneth Anger's nom de plume or demon half brother. Lucifer's rising, doomsters are painting the company town red, Stevie Nicks's "Sisters of the Moon" are convening over blue cocktails in Bel Air, and Roky Erickson's "Two-Headed Dog" is howling in the Hollywood hills, all unbeknownst to a plumy-accented supporting character called Wesley Wyndam-Price who is ardently scanning the very latest in ancient prophecies. He might be auditioning to play the know-it-all butler for a "Nick Danger, Third Eye" repertory company: "Here's something . . . a razor-toothed, six-eyed harbinger of death. No, wait, that's due to arise in 2003 in Reseda."

In short, a land of No Respect: a satiric tinderbox ripe to go up or down in a rain of fire and one-liners, an overdue apocalypse in the wings just itching for its day of reckoning to arrive. The city's just a kiss of death away from a storm that will bury the warm California sun for good. Knee-deep in unemployed New Age gods and prosthetic monsters, all jockeying for their end-time close-ups, the place is awash in mulitasking demonoids, satanic babes, eager-cleaver sacrificial cults, vampiric pyramid schemes, creature-of-the-night karioke bars (pernicious fallout from the *Star Wars* cantina scene), mind-clouding messiahs, and zombie cops who walk "The Thin Dead Line." Of the entire teeming back lot of 'em, the most sinister, malignly entertaining bunch comprise the Armageddon-fomenting associates of Wolfram & Hart, crack attorneys from — or at least working on expensive retainer for — hell itself. It's hard to beat a literally self-cannibalizing version of *L.A. Law*, an ethos securely rooted in the knowledge that Ally McBeal was advance woman for the Antichrist, and David E. Kelley deserves his own personal ring in (Joe) Dante's Inferno.

And in the opposite corner, taking the equivocal side of light in the eternal struggle with the forces of the other thing, a surprise contestant: the undead-but-tanned, trenchcoated, mood-swinging Angel. For five seasons (1999–2004), titular hero of TV's second-most-engaging killer serial, he would be summed up once and forever by Wolfram & Hart's stylishly hateful minion Lilah with a dismissive shrug: "Vampire. Cursed by gypsies, who restored his soul. Destined to atone for centuries of evil. Wacky sidekicks, yada, yada." (*Angel* was big on atonement: partially tongue-in-cheek servings of arduous, slippery moral development and forever deferred redemption.) Spun off *Buffy the Vampire Slayer*, where he spent three years as her on-again/off-again good-bad heart-of-gold-then-heart-of-darkness-and-back boyfriend-adversary, Angel moved to L.A. to follow that crazy Mannix-to-Rockford private-eye dream. The Angel Investigations motto: "We help the helpless." (That's what it says on the business cards, though it could also read: "We defeat the feetless.")

This pensive muscleboy couldn't help but come on as the reluctant Zorroesque champion of the trodden down—the word "champion" being the most overworked term in the *Angel* lexicon. But star David Boreanaz did yeoman work to redeem the concept of a buff, hunky knight errant who stepped straight out of *Don Quixote's Baywatch*. Beefcake with a well-aged sense of humor, he sent up his brooding, hero-too-sensitive-for-this-world persona without treating it as merely a Conan the late-night Barbarian joke. The show's punch line being that its stock figures were drawn with real feeling, resourcefulness and unexpected nuance: the sidekick ensemble inhabited their readymade personas so well that their development of tragic dimensions snuck up on you, as fresh calamities, scars, and irrevocable acts kept pushing them to new extremes, testing their limits as if aiming to break an internal sound barrier.

Beyond rote action and horror gimmicks treated like standard chord changes to run interlocking Blue Note riffs around, *Angel's* familiar conventions lulled the viewer into contentment with close-knit, bantering byplay. (Things like Charisma Carpenter's bitch-ditz-sweetie Cordelia grousing about too much boiled-down information: "I got loads of gist.") But the series could as readily shift gears and reach for fervid *Out of the Past* emotional grandeur: "God doesn't want you," murderous old lover Darla spat/purred at Angel, "but I still do." The show's braintrust liked to indulge a taste for Tournier sobriquets wedded to Sirk-ish extravagance, but administered in Visine teardropper doses. More intensely pulp fed and genre bound than *Buffy*, it struck unbalanced grace notes worthy of, if not lifted outright from, just about every square acre of phantasmagorical real estate between *The Thing from Another World* and *Donnie Darko.*

The episode titled "Shells," *Angel's* most primal foray into Marvel Comics existentialism, closed with a Mad-Worldly pan/montage across Angel's crew, each in his or her own individually shattered compartment of life, with the lesser darkness of loss/betrayal and the greater one of ashen death encroaching while the pretty, countrified melody of "A Place Called Home" bound the passing images together. Home as wasteland, office cubicle, alcoholic stupor, prehistoric sarcophagous, or dispossessed shard of memory lost in the ether of transience. All in a day's tired work at the edge of the end of the world—flickers of pierced selves coming undone inside their armor, suspended out of time, preparing for the descent that awaits them.

It's only been off the air a year, but *Angel* already seems to belong to another era—as if the show ever really had much purchase on a cutthroat industry devoted to supersized superheroes, ambiguity-free fantasies, "ripped from the headlines" crockplots, heavy-breathing hype jobs, and the infinitely unmalleable forms of pantywaste pseudo-hipness. The series worked up an ultrashadowy milieu—compositionally, probably the deepest pockets of shadow and pitch black ever broadcast on commercial TV—worthy of the crisply economical, suggestive forties mood pieces of producer Val Lewton and the fleet knockabout likes of Don Siegel's early chase-romance *The Big Steal*. What *Angel* lacked in high-voltage star presence it compensated for in illogical chemistry, vivid recurring characters, and a keen eye for bit-playing, moxie-infused bit gargoyles who kept the regulars on their toes. Key on-and-off figures like Stephanie Romanoff's brutally tactless Lilah, Christian Kane's bitter, squinty nihilist litigator Lindsey, Keith Szarabajka's "low, scary voiced" vampire hunter Holtz, Jack Conley's impatient time-shifter Sahjhan, Juliet Landau's daft vamp Drusilla, and Julie Benz's rapturously miserable one Darla all breathed the air of B-picture dreams. Benz left no vibrantly unhappy femme fatale stone unturned in the sex, mayhem, loathing, and sad-eyed mischief department: a one-woman wrecking crew who scattered corpses like petals in her wake.

Initially populated with *Buffy* characters who had outlived their usefulness (Cordy, Alexis Denisof's Wesley) or approximations of indispensable ones (substituting for geek-goddess Willow Rosenberg in socially awkward left field, they fashioned twangy polymath wall-flower Winifred "Fred" Burkle), a not displeasing air of the second team and also-ran clung to *Angel*. Stuck with schlocky leftovers its parent had outgrown, it added some ethnic diversification (a sincere black stud called Gunn, a deeply closeted green lounge demon called Lorne—Lorne, green, a *TV Guide*–dog joke, get it?). In no time, though, they were branching off into oddly recombinant corners: a breathrough McCarthy Era–as–*Twilight Zone* fable, a couple of long and convoluted apocalypse-related pregnancies, a

through-the-looking-glass side trip, one crowded *Das Boot*–with–
Nosferatu mission given an ironic Captain America twist ("Why
We Fight"), a spooky-silly-sexy night at the ballet, a puppet show
(think evil *Sesame Street*), the vaguely Hernandez Brothers–tinged
saga of legendary Mexican wrestlers Los Hermanos Numeros. Exposition usually jostled with baroquely digressive pieces of say-
what? subbackstory: "The devil had a robot?" "El Diablo Robotico."
A long, gratifyingly deranged plot arc involved the L.A. ascension
of a savior with serious *Invasion of the Body Snatchers* tendencies,
taking over the media and turning SoCal into a harmonious, wor-
shipful "Wouldn't It Be Nice"–blaring utopia where BMW drivers
courteously stopped for pedestrians and glassy-eyed zombiehood
prevailed.

Team Angel eventually rallied and beat back the threat of shiny-
happy peace on earth. Jasmine the Messiah was slain, and as reward
for committing Deicide (restoring global disorder in the process —
you can't kill a god without a few unintended side effects), the
Senior Partners of Wolfram & Hart hand over the keys to the law
firm to them. This set up the sporadic last season, where Angel's
plucky crew become embedded in the belly of the enemy and,
after some water-treading longueurs, came to an impressively bleak
shitload of grief. The old gang is pretty much wiped out by the
time the bloodied survivors assemble to make their last rain-
drenched stand in "the alley just north of Hyperion." By then it
was apparent their real motto all along was: the ad hoc family of
outsiders that slays together goes down in a blaze of stoic camaraderie together.

Backtracking a few seasons and through the salvage of many a
creaky premise, their resuscitation of the old "evil-hand" dodge was
especially enjoyable. Wolfram & Hart rewarded Lindsey with a new
right hand (Angel having divested him of the old one during an

earlier altercation). Wouldn't you know the transplant was from a murderer, so the hand not only restores his folk-rolk guitar playing but starts automatically writing "Kill, kill, kill" on the legal pads. If you ask for water and life gives you gasoline, you better learn how to make Molotov cocktails. So he mockingly hijacks the meeting where they're announcing his promotion, mau-maus the suits about not being able to get a grip on himself anymore ("I just can't control my evil hand"), impishly firing a few pistol shots into the walls as well as the security guard. "Stop, evil hand, stop it," he grins, as his finger-wriggling, hair-mussing, colleague-goosing, room-terrorizing American Psycho riff culminates in declining the promotion. "Me, I'm unreliable. I've got these evil hand issues"—and here we pause to savor the burnished throwaway sarcasm invested in that phrase, honoring the compulsion to insult everything that is sacrosanct to the arbiters of Cultural Importance—"and I'm bored with this crap." What I cherish about that scene is not only its keen synthesis of hilarity and unhedged disgust but also how for its five-minute duration, a small-time fringe actor seizes the moment with the taunting, powerhouse giddiness of early Widmark or Cagney. He earns his hand and deserves to take a bow, which he all but does upon exiting.

Another *Angel* trait: meshing the past with the present, particularly for much of the second and third seasons where modern-day plot strands were interwoven with flashbacks from centuries or decades earlier, creating a chain-reaction mosaic of events that reverberated across time. As in most any good film noir, memories and guilt were made flesh: the past always coming back to bite those who seek to escape it. Angel perpetually had the bad old days of senseless violence and sensual cruelty nipping at his heels, tugging at his trenchcoattails, pulling him back into the vortex. And where Angel went, the Group followed: Cordelia wracked by head-splitting visions and finally consumed by their source, upright Wesley banished as a Judas and fucking Lilah while keeping another woman chained in his closet, sweet Fred gutted and her ravaged body used to host yet another destroyer god. (But Amy Acker was smashing in those last episodes, transformed into the leathered-up Emma Peel / Dark Willow creature Illyria, enveloped in a shipwrecked aura of crazed, glowering pathos.)

We're in a ruined temple inside of or next door to (parallel-universe-wise) L.A., a CGI-enhanced warehouse space decorated in the locust-plague vein of the Sisters of Mercy's goth-Egyptian "Temple of Love" (the *Slight Case of Overbombing* version, with Ofra Haza's wordless Coptic-priestess benedictions juxtaposed against Andrew Eldritch's heavy-mettle croon). Fred's dead, replaced by Illyria, who falls to her knees in woe: "My world is gone." Wes looks down at her: "Now you know how I feel." Reverse angle to her mute, stricken face — millennia of desolation captured in a single clean shot. Like *Buffy*, the series could be counted on to deliver excellent death throes: pregnant Darla staking herself (performing a self-administered, supernatural C-section), Lindsey (screaming to Lorne in disbelief: "You kill me? A flunky?"), Fred in Wesley's arms, Wesley imagining he's in hers ("Would you like me to lie to you now?" "Yes, thank you, yes").

In the end they always retreated into the narrow tunnel between self-aware comedy and romantic melodrama, the confines of a small but roomy and well-half-lit hotel, a strict diet of distilled appetite, a patch of asphalt jungle corresponding to the dimensions of that alley north of Hyperion. Instead of moving upward and outward into the diffuse, they dug in. Lots of diligent spade work went into plowing through Halloween detritus and hardboiled glop toward the center of whatever mysteries these recycled, ground-down characters might contain. Eventually they come face-to-face with a great abyss that runs all the way through the earth. "There's a hole in the world," one says to Angel. "Feels like we ought to have known." That's old news to most of us. But the show's dogged rear-guard maneuvers got their power from an always bemused but never condescending determination to drag us back to the way we felt when both that world and that hole seemed like revelations.

[2005]

39

Whatever You Desire: Movieland and Pornotopia

From *The Big Sleep*

to Max Hardcore

Nouvelle Vague Hookers

*T*HE GIRL—first name Carmen, age twenty-going-on-twelve—beckons to us, a thumb-sucking premonition of an X-rated universe in the offing: Lolita as Rollergirl. "She tried to sit on my lap while I was standing up," shamus Philip Marlowe informs her unsurprised father. This Marlowe's less a private eye than a professional voyeur, a wisecracking tour guide and audience surrogate, navigating a cheerfully sordid terrain where maniacal nymphets pose for blackmailing pornographers calling themselves "rare book" dealers. He will appear in every scene; we will watch the story unfold, or rather disintegrate, through his well-traveled peepers as he traverses this fantasy Los Angeles where sexual availability is inescapable. From librarian types who let their hair down at the slightest provocation to randy, semibutch taxi drivers, the succession of easy lays rivals a Little Oral Annie loop collection.

"I assume they have all the usual vices," says General Sternwood of Carmen and big sister Vivian, "besides those they've invented for themselves." *The Big Sleep* immerses us in a Los Angeles of exquisite dirty laundry—is there another movie so serenely bemused by the nocturnal business as usual of confidential L.A., so cavalier about indecency and "sinuendo"? Bogart's Marlowe slips easily into this well-lubricated virtual reality while acting out every moviegoer's fantasy of the observer who can join in the action at will.

Marlowe's surveillance of "insolent and provocative" behavior has nothing to do with the solution to any particular crime. Instead, his work becomes an investigation of deviance-by-proxy, conducted at the expense of coherent narrative. Hence the picture's wholesale replacement of tedious exposition with a string of double entendres, dissolving the story line into a series of hard-boiled non sequiturs as promiscuous as its characters. Viewing the unreleased 1944 cut beside the familiar 1946 version, we discern a form of reverse censorship. What wound up being suppressed was conventional plotting and morality, replaced with a wonderfully illicit catalog of smut-peddling shutterbugs, sexually aggressive women playing pussycat-and-mouse with violent men, and petulant sex toys who bite the hand that doesn't feel them up.

It's Martha Vickers's debauched Carmen, whose hobby is posing for then-unspeakable pictures, who offers us a glimpse into the Hollywood of salacious legend. Her glassy eyes are crystal balls revealing a city where life imitates stag films and art fantasizes about the machinations of pornography, where *L.A. Confidential*'s high-class porno-and-call-girl operation—Fleur de Lis, with its motto, "Whatever You Desire"—blends into the landscape of *Boogie Nights*. This is the intersection of Hollywood and Vice, where prostitutes are surgically altered to resemble movie stars and movie stars are mistaken for whores, a place where a Shirley Temple lookalike might grow up to become the real-life teenage stripper Candy Barr, immortalized in the 1951 bachelor-party classic *Smart Alec* humping a middle-aged sleazeball in a motel room on the road to Hollywood.

Poised midway between Veronica Lake and Miss Barr, a femme as infantile as she is fatale, Carmen's anesthetized gurgle anticipates a little too well the proto-porn stardom of Marilyn Monroe: the dazed ingenue also prefigures darker little figurines like *Kiss Me Deadly*'s Lily, *Breathless*' Patricia. Put those fragments together, and you get Kim Novak as her own body double in Hitchcock's most touching ode to fetish and scopophilia. In dutiful course, Jimmy Stewart would go on to play Carmen's father in an unwatchable 1978 *Big Sleep* remake, but *Vertigo* had already brought the pair together by way of an incestuous folie à deux (or is it trois?). Shameful desire and acquiescent role-playing groped their way back to the future of fetish as cinema and cinema as fetish: Carmen had developed into a full-blown archetype, passed from movie to movie just as Vickers's character bounced from man to man.

Carmen assumes her most distilled and ambivalent form as the buried animus inside Godard's parade of inflatable prostitute-dialecticians. Over and over, the archetype again finds herself on the business end of a phallic lens, made up as the perpetual mystery woman-child at the behest of a director who behaves like a cross between post-Marxist private dick and invalid father. She's interrogated by the camera with a sadistic lyricism—an entranced dismay. Where Eddie Constantine's weather-beaten PI in *Alphaville* combines Marlowe and General Sternwood, on another level Uncle Jean's own exquisite surrogate eye belongs to Raoul Coutard, the cameraman assuming Stewart's role and gaze, tracking successive yet eerily similar objects of romantic surveillance. As *The Big Sleep* was a preview of the nouvelle vague, the erotic anomie of *Weekend*'s pornographic opening monologue heralds the "end of cinema" as pronounced by the brazen hardcore of *New Wave Hookers* in 1985. In that trance of eager debasement where pimps turn nice girls into docile prosties by plying them with lame new wave pop music, the final dissolution of narrative is inscribed with the language of MTV, presided over by the impish countenance of sixteen-year-old Traci Lords. Those unseen photos of Carmen had finally turned into moving pictures transporting Brigitte Bardot's pout and Anna Karina's opacity into the commodified future Godard prophesied, a seven-day weekend of money shots and orgiastic pileups. In the twenty-first century's sex-arcade utopia, fucking is spectator sport, a form of window shopping—capital made video flesh.

Debbie Does Stella Dallas

"MEANWHILE, BACK IN THE STATES": Paul Thomas Anderson's *Boogie Nights* succeeds in providing a complete inversion—and repudiation—of *The Big Sleep*'s breezy antinarrative stratagems. Instead of chaotic perversity lurking beneath society's respectable façades, Anderson gives us a sex industry where outward sleaze masks a secret lust for normality and convention. *Boogie Nights* shares with its characters a yearning for the incestual-family trappings of post-Victorian hypocrisy. Despite many mildly outré bits and an enjoyable amount of aimless whiz-bang technique, Anderson surrounds his plucky Gump of a hero with a narrow range of similarly one-note wonders. His nostalgia for the seventies—as a golden age spanning *Nashville*'s hip condescension and *The Jade Pussycat*'s skinflick kitsch—isn't enough to make his stock characters more than a set of Heartbreak Hotel pinups.

Timid antipuritan pretensions aside, *Boogie Nights*' satire turns out to be way more old-fashioned than Howard Hawks's. Piling on the white powder and blue eye shadow, Anderson arranges all that disguised wages-of-sin crap into "expensive hunks of well-regulated area" (to use Manny Farber's "White Elephant Art vs. Termite Art" phrase): instead of the shit hitting the fan, it's been molded into shiny baubles, eye-catching knickknacks, and souvenir-concession set pieces. (Codpieces?) Next to the treatment of not-unrelated themes in R. W. Fassbinder's sardonic 1971 *Beware of a Holy Whore* (where corruption and moviemaking are synonymous), Anderson's rose-colored semidisillusionment might as well be a San Fernando Valley *Best Years of Our Lives.* Here we have this wonderfully mordant setting, the porno world as logical extension of that fantasy factory/brothel L.A., and yet Anderson elects to populate it almost exclusively with naifs, saps, and dupes.

To picture the Hanna Schygulla of Fassbinder's heyday as Amber Waves—all hip-hugger indolence, Cheshire Cat smiles, and iron will under the broken-blossom makeup—is to see something of what Anderson has pointedly expunged: the X-rated industry's revolving-door parade of the young and the damaged suggests nothing if not a never-ending Fassbinder casting call, one driven by as much cunning and guile as the neurotic Hollywood star system it emulates and parodies. But the caricatures of *Boogie Nights* don't have an iota of street smarts. The director's gilt-edged ambitions toward masterpiece-making subsume everything else, cleverly dispersed into a milieu where they can be presented with a modicum of faux irony, allowing the pseudo-hip and the square to reach the rapprochement with Hollywood's golden-age verities that porno thankfully never achieved. *Boogie Nights* laments the symbiosis that was not to be, even casting the dignified Veronica Hart—the late seventies skin-flick answer to Irene Dunne—as its stern judge. (What Anderson is really mourning here are all those lost opportunities to lift up the genre, those classics that might have been, like *Streep Throat* and *Gashville.*)

But even if you accept Anderson's presumptive formula for High Porn—the seamless integration of story, character, and sex—the actual efforts along those lines were quite different from the ones presented in *Boogie Nights.* The real-life equivalent to Burt Reynolds's Jack Horner would have to be the relatively ambitious Anthony Spinelli, who made a slew of potboilers like the 1980 *Talk Dirty to Me.* Spinelli's penchant was for gutter psychology and a worm's-eye-view of sexual conquest. *Talk Dirty's* shoestring mélange of soap opera and buddy picture lifted its central relationship of John Leslie's fast-talking stud Jack to slow-witted sidekick Lenny (Richard Pacheco) from *Of Mice and Men.* Embracing trash clichés with gusto, the picture's attitudes are retro-lurid: the serial seducer who promises to release the animal trapped within outwardly respectable dames (prim doctor, man-starved real-estate saleswoman, neglected hausfrau). Jack bets Lenny he can seduce the restive beauty they spy on a beach in three days. So much for plot. Predictably enough, the sex scenes are more persuasive than the line readings, but despite the picture's antediluvian sexual politics and technical shortcomings, it manages a few B-movie charms: Jessie St. James's pleasantly melancholy air as the object of pursuit and the adroit ratpack-bastard persona of Leslie, breaking down her defenses with his knowledge of old (read: romantic) movies. Doing an impersonation of Jimmy Stewart in *Carbine Williams*, he uncovers a shared passion for . . . Hope and Crosby.

Such byplay is engaging for the way it goes against the grain of expectation — our assumptions of what a porn film is supposed to be like and how its one-track-minded characters are meant to behave. By the same token, the good-natured appeal of Chris Cassidy overcomes the lady-doctor-cliché she hardly bothers to play, her sybaritic grin rebuking *Boogie Nights'* reductive coke/airhead typologies. And Juliet Anderson's "older woman" routine is so cannily polished it belongs in the Smithsonian — or, like Cassidy, on the wise-gal fringes of just about any Hawks picture. Hapless as *Talk Dirty's* stabs at seriousness are, the sex scenes hint at something that sober, artful movies seldom own up to. Leslie's romantic predator demonstrates how, in the hands of an accomplished prick, lust will beat intellect, discriminating taste, and meaningful emotion almost every time. It's fitting Jack uses movie nostalgia as a seduction device. He takes sexual advantage of the thwarted desires and bland illusions Hollywood has always catered to.

Made as video was starting to take off and films like itself were on their cost-ineffective way out, *Talk Dirty to Me* embodies porno nostalgia for good old-fashioned movieland virtues in a manner oddly akin to *Boogie Nights'* nostalgia for seventies American cinema. A eulogy in the argot of obscene phone calls, Spinell's will toward redeeming artistic value is equally misguided, but perhaps more instructive than P. T. Anderson's: what's memorable about *Talk Dirty* are the stray images and unguarded bits of absurd intimacy, the convergence of the nakedly real and the patently burlesque, along with whatever wayward, playful spontaneity slips through the cracks of its hastily assembled pastiche: the voracious track of Juliet Anderson's tongue across Leslie's chest; Cassidy's breast lactating in midfuck, making secreted history—the elusive female cumshot at long last.

"Were these actors, hoping for careers, or derelicts resolved to treat the idea of a movie with contempt?" asked David Thomson about the male and female leads in *Detour*, a movie whose budget and sleaze-en-scène anticipates feature-length porn by a quarter century. Say all you want about the felicities of Edgar G. Ulmer's style, the impact of that film owes more to the desperately prurient grubbiness of its performers. It's easy to imagine *Detour* incorporating the grainy footage of *Smart Alec*, the anything-for-a-buck stag film entering the tawdry nightmare without missing a beat. Pornography is the domain of such hitchhikers, from Carmen Sternwood to Traci Lords: submissives on the make, rough-trade on the lam, a hard-bitten sisterhood of (Ann or Becky) Savages.

BLASÉ-MOI

SINCE THE ADVENT OF feature-length hardcore films with *Behind the Green Door* (1971) and *Deep Throat* (1972)—which, coupled with the 1973 release of *Last Tango in Paris*, gave rise to a short-lived moment of "porno chic"—critical tendencies have been to read porn in terms of its failure to live up to Hollywood formulas, production values, and overall sanctimony. But from the mid-Reagan era onward, in the privacy of uncounted VCRs, porn has evolved into a closed-circuit subculture even as it has entered the mainstream through a host of unseemly forms. Somewhere in the crawl space between Brian De Palma's drill 'er thriller *Body Double* (1984) and its instant shot-on-video echo *Holly Does Hollywood* (1985), a cheaper, tapeworm form of sexual athleticism began to obliterate the residual niceties of character and plot. Torchbearing

Miss Libertines with names like Ginger/Amber/Porsche Lynn and Christy Canyon (the perfect comic-strip nom du porn, and physique to match) led the acrobatic procession away from narrative-as-such and blazed a trail into the nether-netherland dreamed by David Cronenberg's prophetically warped *Videodrome* (1982).

There Debbie Harry's therapist / talk-show host is a closet super-masochist who craves discipline and punishment. She wonders aloud "how you get to be a contestant" on that televised torturefest the way stymied housewives fantasize about being on *Wheel of Fortune*. The emergence of a multibillion-dollar video porn industry is indicative of that blissfully blank, repetition compulsion logic: *Videodrome* imagined as paradise. Porn performers behave like sexual contestants reaching for the brass ring of quasi-fame and fortune while the audience gains entree into a subterranean theme park whose motif is forbidden fruit, a suntanned, surgically enhanced tour of unsafe sex, exotic practices, and formerly unnatural acts. It's promiscuity by proxy, a brand of couch-potato deviance where women are both objects and male surrogates, plunging into polymorphous, freak-show realms into which straight masculinity remains too fearful to venture without a kneeling nursemaid to reassure it. Yet the neatest irony of video porn is how readily "transgression," stripped of all self-important buzzword splendor, turns right back into show-business-as-usual. It's as if Warhol's abandoned Factory had been taken over by trailer-park runaways and middle-class squatters, with all these industrious piece-workers on Pornoland's assembly line churning out whistle-while-we-suck product with the alacrity of Disney sex-serfs. A tricked-out Snow White may be paraded as a streetwalker, but through it all she maintains the ingenuous, smiling composure of ex-Mouseketeer Britney Spears, who in turn radiates the same wholesome sexual professionalism as porn's Shayla La Veaux.

The all-American glee with which video starlet Alisha Klass (who cameos nicely as a stripper in Wayne Wang's DV film *The Center of the World* and is the featured attraction of the movie's Web site) throws herself into her shuddering, dervishlike conniptions can be a wonder to behold. Her Good Bad Girl attitude seems more second nature than acting—maybe it has to do with growing up a world where XXX-product is just another facet of the entertainment industry and where the difference between casually performing outlandish acts and "being yourself" is moot. Klass emerged from the newest, biggest sector in the adult-vid economy, the bare-bones, low-rent "Gonzo" tapes that anticipated both the Reality-TV and Dogme movements. In lieu of Dogme's ascetic "vow of chastity," gonzo porn has taken a vow of poverty—or Poverty Row, at any rate. Meaning motel location shoots, live sound, handheld cameras, no music or special effects. Not to mention the approximation of sex in real time: with video's claustrophobic scale, so intensely particularized, alienation and pleasure can assume the intimacy of doppelgangers. Like the anything-for-my-fifteen-minutes participants on *Survivor*, gonzo's wild girls are the soi-disant cousins of Warhol's speedfreak-narcissists. But this underground feels closer in spirit to gamy sixties garage rock than the Velvets. The random bursts of sexual energy and aggression in this underground tunnel their way up from the depths of a proudly desperate, slovenly amateurism, with a trashy ambition that's not only blind but tone deaf and dumb as well.

At its most unfettered, joyously infantile fare like Ben Dover's *British Housewife Fantasies* (a sexual mockumentary highlighted by a supercalisthenic Julie Andrews type who takes the better part of an hour to decimate three suitably grateful blokes) or *Seymour Butts Meets the Tushy Girls* (which introduced "squirting" specialist Klass through a similarly casual, day-in-the-lifestyle format) assure us all

the world's a sexual slumber/Tupperware party. Irreverence coupled with the absence of retakes imposes a degree of spontaneity
on fantasy machinations (when the men ejaculate, nowadays female recipients are as likely to break out in giggles as oooh and
ahhh). Whereas the mechanical giddiness of *There's Something
About Mary*—with its cum-adorned heroine and displacement ga-
lore—translates the onanistic/gross-out preoccupations of porn into
slapsticky, screwhead romantic comedy, the deadpan postnarratives
of these tapes have abandoned all recourse to such throwback or-
thodoxies. Instead, they have arrived at their own equivalent to
Total Cinema: call it Total Porn, a practice that blithely eliminates
all distinction between "reality" and pornography. Now the man
with the video camera even participates in the orgy action. Roll
over, Dziga Vertov, and tell Peeping Tom the news: your Kino-Eye
has been eclipsed by their Video-Dicks.

ARTCORE JOLLIES

WHEREAS PORN IS LESS and less beholden to any conventions
but its own, commerce and art have inexorably moved in the direction of quasi-hardcore: from gross-out teen comedies to "artcore"
films like *Baise-moi* (featuring female porn talent both behind and
in front of the camera), Catherine Breillat's hopelessly ponderous
Romance, and Lars von Trier's *The Idiots* (his Zentropa Productions
has even opened a hardcore subsidiary, promising to make high-
end adult products). In *Romance* especially, the exploration of flesh
and its mortification is constrained by a lingering artistic decorum,
a dour illustrated biology/psychology lesson that seems every inch
as preprogrammed as any robot-sexpot ecstasy. Breillat recruited the
prodigiously endowed Rocco Siffredi for stud service in *Romance*

but cast him against type as a sensitive hunk instead of a ruthless erotomaniac. Yet as a performer, director, and self-described "madman," the romantic sadist Siffredi has taken heterosexual video into the underbelly opened up by the bathhouse-era gay porn of people like Fred Halsted. It's a place inaccessible to art, theory, or virtue — half dungeon and half bed-and-breakfast retreat, where pure unreason is converted into recreational activity.

As such, the series of videos he's made with the proper but willingly debauched accomplice-submissive Kelly Stafford reveals more about the allure of sexual danger and self-abnegation than Breillat's trite philosophizing or all of *Quills'* politely diagrammatic cure-is-worse-than-the-disease ironies. The death-wish-as-sex-game pièce de résistance of their latest encounter, the improbably titled *Rocco's Way to Love* (2001), is genuinely unnerving because the line between sadomasochistic play-acting and virulent acting-out is all but erased: there's no safety net of rationality or artistic mediation between this Sade and his ardent victim. Sex isn't a metaphor or a representation here — it can't explain or justify itself but makes itself felt entirely "in the flesh" that Siffredi goes to such lengths to rub in the viewer's nose. (Even this pales beside his encounter with Careena Collins in *Kink* — a true meeting of the limit-pushing minds.)

By flaunting the queasy stuff the movies airbrush away — not merely engorged organs and bodily fluids but the problematic relationship of desire and capital, the grind of work and the grind of pleasure — every hardcore production asserts that prostitution isn't the world's oldest profession but, as per Godard, the world's only one. Thus in *The Private Diary of Tori Welles* (1997), the abortive comeback bid of a porn legend who had retired nearly a decade before, there are protracted random images — faces and orifices merged — as potent, irrational, and even touching as anything Cassavetes could hope for. But it's merely by chance, not as a form of art but a found artifact documenting the neurotic camaraderie of social outcasts. Despite some token posturing, it gets a lot closer to the facts of life (and sex) in extremis than *Leaving Las Vegas:* a grainy, home-movie hodgepodge of the genuinely raw and the obviously contrived affords a glimpse into the real underside of Las Vegas and the San Fernando Valley.

Traversing scary sadomasochism and funny, drunken erotic revelry, an awful lot of Welles's *Diary* comes through between the improvised lines: manic-depressive ambivalence, pragmatism tangled up in thinly veiled despair, the fine line between put-on and breakdown. An even halfway adept filmmaker would interpret and shape such footage, formalize and comment upon it. The video is fascinating precisely because of the lack of any aesthetic buffer between the viewer and the forlorn bravado of Welles's behavior.

Of course, such videos are few and far between the literally hundreds of titles released per month; customarily striving for a Spam-flavored insipidity that would gladden the heart of any Hollywood studio exec. Besides the dismal ripoffs of mainstream hits so beloved for their smirky titles *(Pulp Friction, The Sperminator)*, there's also the dubious porn equivalent of the art film — typically a blatant midnight-movie amalgam of underground comix, indigestible Fellini leftovers, and too-hot-for-MTV self-parody. Probably the best-known example is Rinse Dream's glibly postapocalyptic *Cafe Flesh* (1982), though the director's earlier *Nightdreams* (1981) is the superior pop-expressionist burlesque. Greg Dark, as the directing half of the infamous Dark Bros., further refined (or debased) the mocking style he pioneered with *New Wave Hookers* and proved himself the Ken Russell of porn with *The Devil in Miss Jones III and IV.*

In recent years, young muckslinger Rob Black has updated the formula with bitter, brutalist smut like *Miscreants* (1997), adding schlock-corridor flourishes inspired by Tarantino, Oliver Stone, the Beastie Boys, and Howard Stern—a mélange of clockwork outrages, crack-pipe nightmares, and the cartoonish hubris you would expect of a mogul whose idea of synergy is to branch out and start his own pro-wrestling league. He pushes the envelope of sexual nausea while still producing occasional forays into ineptly artsy twaddle such as Thomas Zupko's *In the Days of Whore* (2000), a Catholic-schoolboy barf-fest replete with grunting Vikings, horny lepers, and a maiden being raped every twenty minutes.

With the boys-will-be-pigs culture of pornophiles like Eminem and Kid Rock in ascendancy, art's decidedly beside the point nowadays. The American porn industry as yet has no impetus or inclination to produce a crossover equivalent to Virginie Despentes and Coralie Trinh-Thi's *Baise-moi* (2000), whose offhand trashing of road, action, and porno movie fealties inverts the mainstream's typical violence-to-sex ratio (the fucking is real, but the bloodshed's transparently faked). But there is one work of authentic pop art in porn's past, purportedly directed by one Veronika Rocket (according to cyber sexpert Susie Bright, a pseudonym for "two people named Michael Constant and Rubin Masters"). Made in 1983, *Smoker* was metaporn in precisely the way Godard's *Made in USA* is metacinema. A kandy-kolored S&M noir complete with sexual terrorists, hilariously hard-boiled philosophical musings, and a coolly objective spatialization of voyeuristic impulses, *Smoker* offered up John Leslie's dissociated Mister Sunglasses persona as the ultimate reduction of the Marlowe-Bond-Lemmy Caution hero to a mask of male cluelessness. ("I've been called a misogynist," the secret agent's sang froid voice-over informs us, "but only by women.") *Smoker* pulled the camera back from porn's customary "monster shot" by placing an impotent, narcissistic masturbator in the foreground and putting the sex action in the background: a strategy guaranteed to make guys squirm as much as graphic penetration close-ups unsettle many women. Although the version currently available on video has been trimmed of fifteen to twenty minutes of Strangelovian discipline-and-punish material, rendering its already inscrutable gestures nearly incoherent, it stands as a premeditated violation of its alleged genre, an insurgent joke on moribund film typologies.

BLUE MOVIE, BLACK HEART

TODAY THE MORIBUND is more dead-alive than ever. Porn may no longer feel compelled to imitate anachronistic Hollywood models (even if companies like Vivid still court mainstream acceptability with token plots, characters, and "production values"), but the movie industry finds itself in the position of competing with the senseless, circular gratifications of hardcore. One response has been the move toward Total Spectacle: hundred-million-dollar action films now offer up the same dependable reliance on money shots, an equal or greater number of buff action figures, and porn's former ratio of fig-leaf plot to wham-bam-thank-you-ma'am. Another has been to perfect a terrifying equivalent that exchanges rough sexual pleasures for comely representations of death and dismemberment. Instead of copulation, a host of psychothrillers offer peekaboo mutilation and sexual retribution—high-toned snuff films.

When Paul Schrader's *Hardcore* came out in 1979, it was a turning point, an anti–*Taxi Driver* that all but inaugurated a Cinema of Self-Censorship, retreating behind the limits of the R rating and leaving sex to the industry Schrader couldn't face head-on. It was the first and most blatant of numerous Schrader films to invoke and then repress the pornographic unconscious: think only of the deeply closeted *American Gigolo,* the mumbo jumble of *Cat People,* and the great nullified opportunity of *Patty Hearst,* where in real life a band of young fanatics had collapsed Godard's *La Chinoise* into *Behind the Green Door,* with Patty as their Marilyn Chambers. *Hardcore* canceled out the possibilities of a terrific, volatile theme, the confrontation between Calvinism's patriarchal superego and the mortifying id of Sodom-wood. It needed to be as unflinching about the mysteries of the profane as Bresson was about the sacred; it needed Travis Bickle's archetypical X-rated moviegoer drowning in his own secreted rage and longing.

Twenty years later, *8mm* loosely and scurrilously retraced *Hardcore*'s steps, but now the rules of a new Production Code were firmly entrenched under the selectively censorious eye of Blockbuster Video. It continues to insist that sex be fleeting and perhaps "steamy" but never as graphic, elaborate, or enjoyable as violence. *8mm* comes from the same turd processor that gave us *Seven,* that solemn parade of coroner's centerfolds and peepshow disembowelments, where one by one the enemies of decency (Prostitute, Pervert, etc.) got their just deserts. *8mm* is even more transparently a set of lip-smacking loops: craven domesticity for the Bible Belt, enemas and payback for the Jerry Springer crowd, well-paid actors humiliated before our eyes (Catherine Keener's simpering zombie-wife is the stuff of purest Republican fantasy).

Silence of the Lambs is the genre's template, and father-confessor / molester Hannibal Lecter is its best proselytizer, Sade in Freud's clothing. Renegade authority figure Hannibal the Cannibal legitimizes cruelty and torture as gourmet entertainment. "People will say we're in love," Lecter coos to his little Starling, but he's actually addressing the audience. The seducer promises to give them what they really want, bring them face-to-face with their nastiest impulses and most deliciously shameful fancies, but then absolves them of their complicity. In *Silence* and the rest of its far-flung progeny, the world is seen as a more interesting—and certainly entertaining—place because serial killers and sex fiends populate it. Slice and dice becomes another mode of slap and tickle—Jack the Ripper's Way to Love.

Unacknowledged sexual phobias are the currency of modern "thrillers," where AIDS and moral panic secretly prey on the mind. In *Seven*, Brad Pitt mutters, "Sadistic fucker," encapsulating David Fincher's aesthetic there as much as the killer's. The director sounded too much like a porno king for his own good when gushing about the film's modus operandi: "It's . . . 'come down this alley with us, there's something we want to show you.' And then they lead the audience down and then they just go, 'Take your pants down, we're going to rape you.' I like that." Only *Seven* isn't a Rob Black video but a putatively serious, upscale film rendering voyeuristic cruelty as almost abstract mise-en-scène. Fincher's psychosexual Inferno—all suppurating flesh and antiseptic surfaces—is a charnel funhouse catering to the status-conscious viewer, its cheap thrills bound in imitation Book of Corinthians leather. In this manner, Kevin Spacey's cherubic, scum-cleansing Everymaniac reconciles impulses from opposite ends of the ideological spectrum. A self-righteous puritan who stages his sermonettes-in-blood as transgressive performance art, he is the love-hate child of Jesse Helms and Karen Finley. With a serrated dildo as his sword of vengeance, "John Doe" hits on a formula to satisfy the needs of body-piercing ritualists and the Moral Majority alike.

In *Videodrome*, David Cronenberg predicted that this blurring of identities would saturate the emerging video epoch, spawning a Sadeian "new flesh" of shock images, hallucinatory myths, and schizophrenic appetites: a mutant body politic. *Seven* and *8mm* domesticate that process, turning *Videodrome* into simply another outpost of Blockbuster. While *Crash* might have been expected to illuminate this pathology, the problem with Cronenberg's vision of shell-shocked sex/death cultism is that it's been totally outstripped by current multimedia reality. The film winds up being tamely anachronistic, as though set in a pre-*Videodrome* world.

Crash also lacks any sense of male aggression (except the passive kind), an emetic dose of *Videodrome*'s Max Renn (James Woods) and his gutterball hunger for the cutting edge of violation. Or rather the pathological energies of his real-life porno alter ego who has translated *Videodrome*'s torture-chamber aesthetic into one of porn's most successful franchises. Best known as "Max Hardcore," this enterprising capitalist also goes by the far more cinematically resonant pseudonym of "Max Steiner"—the composer of *The Big Sleep*'s score, reincarnated as a James Ellroy version of that film's dirty-picture-taker. Staging sexual encounters as traffic accidents, producer-director-star Max induces a parade of would-be Carmen Sternwoods to submit to a demolition derby of humiliation, abuse, and malignancy. "Absolutely brilliant," Cronenberg's Max would say of Steiner's one-man cottage industry. "There's almost no production costs." Just the jaded satyr-auteur, his more or less willing victim du jour, and a two-man camera/sound crew to document the grueling commencement exercises of the Roman Polanski Finishing School.

Combining Hunter S. Thompson's cadaverous looks with a fear-and-loathing quotient straight out of Larry Flynt's meat grinder, Steiner's performances obliterate the line between meticulous calculation and barely contained psychosis. Featuring three interchangeable twenty- to thirty-minute vignettes per tape, Steiner's formula shrewdly encapsulates movieland's politics of sex, power,

and money. His videos are paeans to the lecher's holiest of unho-
lies, the casting couch, that backdoor altar on which a cattle call
of aspiring starlets/models/dancers ("Are you sure Marilyn Monroe
got started this way?" one typically asks) will be auditioned/sacri-
ficed. Bridging the gap between *Videodrome* and the Fleur de Lis,
Steiner offers an unnerving glimpse into the precious relationship
between defilement and celebrity. Shades of would-be "contestant"
Nicki Brand in *Videodrome*, "Max TV" offers an address where
potential recruits can apply to join the New Flesh.

If Steiner has yet to find his perfect Martha Vickers / Lolita, in
Max 15: Street Legal (1997) a Jayne Mansfield lookalike (Dakota)
undergoes near-surgical procedures that end on an image straight
out of some ghastly synthesis of *Dead Ringers* and *Crash*: spread-
eagled on Max's couch, with a speculum in every orifice including
her mouth, transformed into the perfect receptacle. I can't help but
recall Marilyn Chambers in Cronenberg's *Rabid*, left for human
refuse in a dumpster: the projection of male anxieties onto women
has never been more graphically embodied than in Steiner's overdetermined irrationality, yet his choke-on-my-big-shtick cruelty is
closer to the charming sacred-monster turns by Spacey or Sir Anthony. Max even caps the Dakota episode with a truly sick hooray-
for-Hollywood touch: picking up a handy guitar and serenading the
gargling starlet with "Happy Trails."

To sleep the Big Sleep, perchance to dream: "Until we meet
again." We find Robert Blake's white-noise apparition materializing
in David Lynch's *Lost Highway*, a video dybbuk with the power to
rewind the future or fast-forward the past. He's a porno-geist
haunting the movie's world, and ours, a walking Betacam spying,
recording, and replaying scenes from a recurring nightmare / wet
dream—the Peeping Tom as all-seeing, all-distorting Private Eye.
A far cry from Bogart's Marlowe, except for that one vicious mo-

ment when Marlowe executes the unarmed Eddie Mars, a preview of Robert Loggia's Mr. Eddy being forced to view his own murder on (what else?) a Watchman TV. Mr. Eddy is also shown a black-and-white stag film, a bit of black-magic exotica that looks like one of Carmen Sternwood's lost 8mm wonders. The twin sisters, or rather personae, Patricia Arquette so uncannily embodies merge there finally, dissolving the boundary between fantasy and trauma, pleasure principle and paranoia. Two forms of sexual distance smear together like the ending and beginning of a perpetual loop: the unknowable remoteness harbored within human intimacy and the kiss-me-deadly nirvana promised by that sex-bomb mask. At long last Carmen speaks, as if for the first time, whispering the secret of her infinite prowess and infinite contempt in the ear of her red-faced audience: "You'll never have me."

[2001]

Gold Diggers of 1935

Pennies from Heaven

and London Calling

LITTLE KNOWN in America, Dennis Potter's 1978 BBC miniseries *Pennies from Heaven* is one of the most thrilling, confounding pieces of pop culture to appear in the last quarter century. In its own surreally realistic way, it's a classic of imaginative dislocation that ranks with *Blue Velvet*, the third season of *Buffy the Vampire Slayer*, and the best English punk records of 1976–1979. Unseen since it was first broadcast here in 1980, it has recently become available on DVD and has lost none of its capacity to dissolve expectations, to disconcert and astonish. Worming its way into the bad graces of yesteryear, *Pennies* doesn't treat the past with embalmer's kid gloves but instead gives it a lived-in, pug-ugly mug: it's the eager, sweaty, manic-depressive face of Bob Hoskins's Arthur Parker, a "common as muck" traveling sheet-music salesman with his head in the clouds and both feet firmly planted in the bleak-house Britain of 1935.

It doesn't take long to realize this isn't your average period piece: the art deco title cards give way to a drab bedroom, but the jaunty lark of "Down Sunnyside Lane" plays on as the camera pans in on Hoskins's Arthur in the dark. "Someday" is the first word out of his mouth, and there's a beat before he forlornly finishes the line — "if luck is kind," the words of the song that has just faded from the soundtrack. "Someday," he repeats with clenched vehemence, and then the alarm clock rings. Instantly the hamster-cage limits of a life are sketched, the deadly treadmill routine and sexual rebuffs by his mousy, commonsensical wife Joan (Gemma Craven), who treats him like an overgrown child when she isn't overcome with revulsion at his physical overtures.

We think we know where we are (boxed-in television naturalism) and what's coming next ("little people" drama-turgidity), then Hoskins opens his mouth and a sweet, melancholy female voice comes pouring out. He's transformed, a man possessed — lip-synching "The Clouds Will Soon Roll By" and swaying with dapper, song-and-dance-man agility.

In *Pennies from Heaven*, at pivotal moments pop songs bubble up into the character's throats and minds: a wife's murderous fantasy set to "You Rascal You," a homeless man acting out the title song with unnervingly intense dignity, Arthur endlessly daydreaming to the tune of "Roll Along, Prairie Moon." Potter perfected this technique — gimmick, even — later on in *The Singing Detective* (1986), which is more cinematically fluid and narratively complex but doesn't quite match the startling mix of intimacy and displacement he first stumbled upon in *Pennies*. It could easily turn hokey or quaint, but amid touchingly crude attempts to simulate a filmlike palette on videotape, the cast throw themselves into their performances with such an emphatic (and empathetic) once-in-a-lifetime gusto that all residue of nostalgia is obliterated.

The effect isn't merely ironic — juxtaposing the era's putatively innocent songs with sordid realities, casting shadows on Sunnyside Lane. It's a vagrant, spasmodic irruption of dormant passions from inside a landscape of repression, sprinkled with autobiographical details from Potter's childhood in Wales' idyllic Forest of Dean as well as almost Gnostic religious-carnal undertones. Arthur longs for a heaven where sexual transgression and spiritual transcendence are the same thing, a world without end "where the songs come true."

In *Pennies*, the walls between standardized genres (movie musical, realist drama, film noir) start to crumble, as over the course of six episodes and nearly eight hours Potter's emotional absolutism dissolves the barriers of convention: thrown together, the cockeyed optimism of musicals and the inexorable fatalism of noir fiction reveal a common ground of unmet desire. Both the noir and the musical reject the social limits expressed in and enforced by naturalistic drama, a mode Potter mastered even as he sought to subvert it and escape its kitchen-sinking confines. Following his dreams, Arthur's efforts to live out the songs in his head sets in motion a down-and-outward spiral: he destroys his marriage, puts the spinster schoolteacher Eileen (the phenomenal Cheryl Campbell) he carelessly impregnates on the path to prostitution, and winds up pursued by police for a rape-murder he didn't commit — except perhaps in his imagination.

Eventually, Arthur will again meet up with Eileen, and they'll reunite, now vandalizing the failing record shop he's started with his wife's money, a defiantly futile act of desecration. On the run, she'll calmly turns tricks, and he'll bitterly mope, as if they'd taken a wrong turn at, oh, *Gold Diggers of 1935* and fallen clear through the looking glass into the bad-woman/weak-man vortex of the 1950 cine-pulp landmark *Gun Crazy*, whose heroine utters the flat, definitive sex-and-violence equation: "I want action."

Banished from Eden and forced to hide out in a ramshackle barn, Arthur and Eileen are discovered having sex by a ranting, Jew-hating farmer. Eileen assures the crazed old coot it's all right if he watches (and humors him by saying they are Jews), then afterwards gently takes the shotgun and blasts him to kingdom come. A mortified Arthur asks her why. "Because I felt like it."

"The world," Potter once remarked, "is full of the murmur of human beings trying to reshape reality." Potter heard that murmur in the simple, overwhelming directness of Arthur Tracy's 1937 recording of "Pennies from Heaven," which begins, "A long time ago, a million years B.C." Tracy's bare-bones reading turned the song into a Depression hymn: "The best things in life were absolutely free," a mournfully hopeful marriage of pity and wonder. He tells us, "It was planned that they would vanish now and then," so "you must pay before you get them back again." Storms are the toll we have to pay for the promise of happiness on earth — in the song, every cloud has a silver (well, copper) lining, poverty is a secret form of wealth, and drowning allows us to truly appreciate life's sweetness.

Madness, perhaps, but like any good prophet, Tracy (who billed himself as "the Street Singer") made it sound like the soul of reason. In his miniseries, Potter puts the song in the mouth of the Accordion Man (Kenneth Colley), a wraithlike allegorical figure who is Arthur's nightmare double. (He commits the murder Arthur will be convicted of, but he is also a sort of holy fool.) Mimed by the Accordion Man, the song carves out an upside-down space where any shabby, stuttering busker could turn out to be an epileptic Jesus Christ in disguise.

When MGM remade *Pennies* in 1981 as a feature film — from Potter's screenplay, directed by safe Hollywood bet Herbert Ross — the story was transplanted to Chicago and Steve Martin cast as Arthur, but they were smart enough to keep Tracy's version of the song. Vernel Bagneris, as the Accordion Man, managed an even more piercing, haunted intensity, lip-synching the words "You must pay" as if hellhounds were nipping at his worn-out heels.

The movie's schizo Edward Hopper / Busby Berkeley viewpoint has other attractions: Martin suggests a darker underside to the lovable coward and miscreant that Bob Hope played in so many films, while Christopher Walken's show-stopping "Let's Misbehave" dance routine and Jessica Harper's eerie turn-of-the-screw "It's a Sin to Tell a Lie" equal anything in the original. But on the whole, the stylized and reglamorized Hollywood version has a tendency to play the pathos and comedy a little too broadly and generally nudge the material in the belated direction of a downbeat but still up-tempo *Singin' in the Rain.*

Then and now, however, Potter's original *Pennies* had less in common with nostalgic backward-glancing entertainments than with the British punk explosion that was cresting in 1978. Coincidentally (or serendipitously), punk also sought a world where the songs came true. A common-as-muck person opened his or her lips and in lieu of "Love Is the Sweetest Thing" came "Anarchy in the UK" or "Oh Bondage Up Yours!" or "Complete Control" — to sing them was to make it so, at least for the three-minute duration of the performance.

In the wake of the Sex Pistols, the unpredictable dislocations of punk occupied a universe parallel to the one Arthur Parker wandered through like a singing defective. It wasn't that *Pennies* projected contemporary attitudes backwards onto another era but that it uncovered the latent extremity in the popular culture of the past, the riddle of human nature in all its nihilistic/idealistic contradictions.

The strongest link between Potter's contradictions and punk's can be heard on the Clash's 1979 double album *London Calling*, itself recently reissued in a deluxe twenty-fifth anniversary edition. The most cinematic of rock albums, a guttersnipe extravaganza that absorbs a dozen kinds of music as it moves in and out of the past, *London Calling* is even more audacious than Potter's work. Underneath the bravado and rallying cries, there are shady character studies, broken souls and comedians, the not-so-young and the feckless.

Arthur Parker might not recognize the sounds (except for the Fats Waller–Louis Armstrong ramble of "Jimmy Jazz") or the references (Montgomery Clift and *The Night of the Hunter* were a little after his time), but he'd know the sentiments: the giddily melodramatic fate of "The Card Cheat," the lunatic tenacity of "Rudie Can't Fail," the broken but unbowed humor of "The Right Profile." (Eileen would jump right into "Brand New Cadillac," and Joanie would quite naturally get "Lost in the Supermarket.")

Love and hate, "Death or Glory" — such was the double-edged sword of Arthur's dreams. At last, the promised land of "Revolution Rock" beckons, a new world rising out of the reggae mists. Instead of a revolutionary hero, however, singer Joe Strummer could pass for either Arthur or his Accordion Man doppelganger, babbling inside his reverie ("Any song you want, playing requests now on the bandstand"), drunk on life yet shaking with fear. "This must be the way out," he shouts, looking over his shoulder, far from convinced. "Everything's gonna be all right," he croons. Someday.

[2004]

Apocrypha Now!

An Imaginary Discography of

Thomas Pynchon's Paranoids

NO LONGER CERTAIN *what I had been looking for, this is what I found: Immanent circuitries and interstices folding back on their own mute gravity, the Word inscribed in texts designed to be lost or dissolved in music that ostensibly never existed, desires reconstituted out of ideograms that had been purged of them, all roads leading to—or perhaps from—a place where everything stood for something else.*

This is the terminus of a story that began in America around 1965 and would end in a different America a short while ago. Its origins are in those of a group that formed in

California called themselves the Paranoids. Like a lot of bands of the time, they seemed to come out of nowhere, though in due course they would return there more completely than most. They left few outward marks on history. But their absence is all the more suggestive: omission itself as a codex.

The Paranoids made a handful of records, none now in print. The authorities confiscated the rest. There were bootlegged out-takes, particularly during a flurry of interest in the late 1970s, but these are likewise no longer in circulation. The band seldom gigged, and they received scant attention in the press. A hundred times more was written about them in staccato FBI/CIA teletypes, but in truth that wasn't very much, either.

It was said the Paranoids pseudonymously backed Captain Beef-heart on *Mirror Man*, though the veracity of this is doubtful. Thus the only record attributed to them still in print is an album on which the members are present in neither name nor person, only in rumor. (They probably did a few sessions with Beefheart in late '65 or '66, but these went unreleased, and no one knows what became of them. The forty-five-minute-long cover of his "Tarot-plane" the group recorded in 1968 would, however, come to be widely bootlegged and established the cornerstone of the band's spectral legacy.)

Started in 1964 as a drilled, uniformed band complete with mo-hair suits, fake British accents, Rickenbacker guitars, groovy shades, and tight three-minute songs, the Paranoids rapidly mutated along with the times and soon came to resemble a sect. Only a sect that was too enigmatic and insular to attract disciples, so the Paranoids became a cell: unseen observers of the era unfolding around them, collecting incriminating data, certain the worst was coming on every front but never bothering to raise their voices and warn any-one.

That would be later, though, after the one breach in the anti-immortality—a career that as such was nothing but breach—and their sole properly sanctioned entry into the annals of art. One night in 1965, in a Redondo Beach dive called the Pipeline, author Thomas Pynchon happened to catch a rare Paranoids set. He was impressed enough with the band's music (or at least with its name, which he found almost too perfect) to go backstage and meet the quartet. He discovered that they went by first names only, and assumed ones at that: Miles (after Davis) on lead vocals, guitar, and musette; Dean (after Moriarty or Acheson) on vocals, guitar, violin, and theremin; Serge (after Chaloff) on vocals, bass guitar, and bass saxophone; and Leonard (after no one identifiable) on vocals and drums.

They gave the author a test pressing of their first, about-to-flop single "She's About a Tumor" (poppy British Invasion cum Sam the Sham R&B, with already dated Merseybeat harmonies set on edge by a possibly accidental feedback loop), backed with the instrumental "Tristano" (a tribute to the blind jazz pianist that nonetheless sounded closer to Druidic surf music). Pynchon never saw or heard of the Paranoids after that. But he liked the idea of the band enough to incorporate it into a short novel he had nearly completed that was to be called *The Crying of Lot 49*. The name had just the right youth-cult ambiance for a geek chorus hovering on the periphery of the novel's real action.

Life imitated art dismantling life: upon publication, Pynchon's book left a far deeper impression on the Paranoids than the group did on him. It became their grail, the dark and exacting shape of, as Pynchon wrote, "another world's intrusion into this one." The four lads began detecting signs of such a world everywhere, signs they tried to absorb into their music. Late in 1966, they were given a weekend's worth of studio time by Rubicon Records, the label that signed them during one of those sprees where anyone who even looked like a musician could get a deal. Recording for forty-eight straight hours with no producer and a space-case engineer named Buzz Balm, the band resolved to throw whatever they could think of against the studio wall in hope something would stick. When the amphetamines wore off and the smoke cleared, they had an album in the can. Twelve songs in all, titled "One," "Two," "Three," and so on. The Paranoids wanted to call it WASTE. The record company called it "unreleasable."

Maybe it was the strangled, scarcely intelligible voices that seemed to be calling out from some crawl space in the unthinkable. Or the two fuzztone guitars, one pitched in the chasm between Link Wray and Charles Ives, the other playing what may have been Hasidic variations on Dick Dale. It might have been the groaning bass sax playing elephantine riffs out of Bulgarian Dixieland, or the drummer going apeshit on the skins in 9/8 or 13/4 time. The staggering mania of the Paranoids attack was offset to a degree by the chilling serenity behind it: a mysterious doomsday composure that sprouted in remote nooks of the sixties like wild mushrooms. But Rubicon Records had no idea what to make of it or how to market it, only the certainty that there was no way this shit would sell and there was no way anything this crude could be mistaken for art.

Which ought to have been the end of the Paranoids' story, with the boys scattering to return to college or find gainful employment in entertainment conglomerate mailrooms or fast-food engineering think tanks. (Didn't someone have to develop sturdier burgers and thicker shakes?) However, it happens the tapes of WASTE fell into the bejeweled hands of maverick record producer and aspiring catatonic Desmond Norman (hands that would later consign the reel-to-reel spools, at the band's request, to a gin-soaked pyre of negated posterity). Upon first hearing the music, Norman had cried for joy: at last the man had heard something even his jaded ears could not believe.

*   *   *

IT IS FAIR to say that Desmond Norman — expatriate Englishman, rogue self-promoter, echo-chamber visionary — was the most successful failure rock 'n' roll ever produced. Projects he masterminded sank brilliantly without a trace; every artist he got his hands on fell into obscurity and ruin. Arriving in Hollywood in 1959 with an impossible sound in his head that fused Elvis and Wagner, doowop and *Paradise Lost*, he set about seeking his fortune. All who met him were instantaneously convinced this enormous, laser-eyed man had true vision, even as J'Accuse Productions churned out single after single that went absolutely nowhere, as Desdaemonic Records choked on red ink, as Norman Conquest Publishing left a battalion of accountants sifting through its cooked books in search of laundered mob money and kickbacks from ghost songwriters. Norman grew rich as he bankrupted one willing backer after another, but he also grew dissatisfied. As wonders of amuck overdubbing like Eulia Blue's "Baby's Comin' Back (Or Else)" (1962), the Sacred Profanes' "(Good God) Where Is the Ship of Love?" (1963), the Cosmic Rays' "Quarter to Saturnine" (1965), and the Jamaican foray of Judge Dread's "Ska Face" b/w "Occam's Stepping Razor" (1966) failed to find an audience, Norman became increasingly unbalanced. First he thought Phil Spector was intercepting his mail. Then he became convinced the Beatles were tapping his phone (he swore he heard the wiretaps being played backward on "Being for the Benefit of Mr. Kite" and "A Day in the Life"). Eventually, Norman even believed that the leader of the

Beach Boys had a radio telescope at the Mount Wilson Observatory pointed at his bedroom to steal his dreams before he could have them himself.

It was roughly this Des Norman the Paranoids encountered. Having lost his mind but not his powers of persuasion, Norman convinced the record company he could salvage *WASTE*, though he had no such intention. Actually, as he informed the enthusiastic Paranoids, he wanted to produce an entirely new album for them, farther than far-out, a record that would shake heaven and earth. Not a collection of songs but a fucking self-contained universe, a totality writ in bloody noise and arcane rituals. Yeah, said the Paranoids collectively, sheer genius. So through the waning months of 1967, the group toiled. The one called Miles wrote songs at a furious rate; Dean and Serge added a few burnt offerings of their own; Leonard based one or two on the chords to "I Can't Explain." They worked nonstop in the dank confines of Gold Calf Studios on Sunset, though it might as well have been a missile silo for all they knew of the fall after the Summer of Love. Countless songs were recorded, scraped, and rerecorded; strings, horns, and percussion would be overdubbed and discarded; words and even the keys to some songs changed almost daily. By November, Norman was mixing down the final twenty-four numbers on a jerry-rigged soundboard, searching for a density that went beyond mono, elemental, and bottomless, a big bang going back to Genesis (the book, not the fledgling band).

So it came to pass on New Year's Day 1968 that newly formed Rubicon subsidiary Coptic Records rush-released the Paranoids' gatefold two-record set *Gospel of Thomas* (its astoundingly detailed—and uncredited—sleeve art suggesting a cross between Bosch and Goya, as though reflecting a struggle between religious and political interpretations of a nameless inquisition). The songs were given roman numerals for titles, from "I" to "XXIV." The records themselves were unbanded. The first words on the album, emerging from a twisted rush of liquid Methedrine guitar, were "Not all true things are disclosed to all men." The last ones, chanted over strangely tuned organ chords, were "Blessed are the solitary, for they will find the kingdom." In between was an impenetrably cryptic picture of counterexistence—not the easy blandishments of sub-to-counterculture but an arresting image of what Pynchon had called "the separate, silent, unsuspected world."

Gospel of Thomas caught a sense of total paradox. Ancient and futuristic, ascetic and licentious, it embodied contradiction and the critique of contradiction. Anticipating "Sympathy for the Devil" and Godard's *One Plus One,* exposing the limitations built into the point of view of each, the records made no concession toward any constructive or productive purpose. *Gospel of Thomas* had at its center a contemplativeness that was inexplicable and beyond dispute: it seemed like a handwritten message smuggled from the country of last days.

Only 5,000 copies of the album were pressed, but that amount proved too optimistic. At best, a third of them were sold—you couldn't, as the saying goes, give them away. (Even review copies were returned.) As the full extent of the commercial debacle became clear, and the $200,000 production tab quickly became legend, Des Norman's luck ran out. He had crossed the thin line from genius to pariah; his mansion in the Hollywood hills became a leper colony for one from which he never ventured again. The Paranoids were stunned by the depth of indifference that greeted their magnum opus. Broke, with no bookings or prospects, they were able to land but a single gig, as the opening act for the Turtles in Lodi. The band made it all the way through "II" when they were driven from the stage by beer bottles and flying chairs; they destroyed their equipment returning the audience's fire. Final tally for the "Valentine's Day Massacre," as it would be called: seventeen hospitalized, fifty-three arrested, $64,000 in damage, 107 lawsuits. The short, peculiar career of the Paranoids had seemingly found the ignominious conclusion it had always sought.

* * *

THE GOVERNMENT OF the United States, however—or at least a certain baffling faction hidden deep within its infrastructure— had other ideas. With the election of Richard Nixon, a tiny CIA offshoot unit devoted to "cultural intelligence" was suddenly promoted from analytical duties to operational status. In 1968, MASSCULTINTELNET, as the outfit was officially designated, was given a green light to put some of the notions it had developed about media counterinsurgency into practice.

MASS (as the operation acronym was affectionately abbreviated) had been formed in response to what a senior company analyst dubbed the "crisis of authority" in America. With an eclectic mix of conspirators and conspiracy theorists staffing the unit, it was a place where the ghostwriters of the Warren Report and the obsessives postulating what the report was really covering up could bounce ideas off each other. Developing strategies for the containment of unsettling currents in popular culture, MASS was provisionally overseen by G. Gordon Liddy: the group was intended to serve as a resource and testing ground for psychotechnologies on the cutting edge of spookdom. Its first and most successful undertaking was the White Album Project, which evolved from Liddy overhearing a snatch of the song "Helter Skelter" in the background of a Weathermen phone tap. A directive was issued shortly thereafter that led the unit to ferret out a subject named Manson— small-time grifter, would-be singer-songwriter, hippie communard, and borderline schizophrenic. Interned at a secret holding area and fed a diet of customized hallucinogens while being programmed with messianic theology, their discovery was then turned loose to recruit a cadre of strung-out acolytes. A star, as Liddy later remarked, was born.

The idea behind the Manson Family was to saturate the media with lurid images of unspeakable acts, all carried out by druggy, demonic representatives of pseudo-insurrectionary youth. A citizenry thus gripped by terror would be ripe for any law-and-order solutions it might be asked to accede to. (The Symbionese Liberation Army was a later, more shrewdly political bid to achieve the same MASS media hysteria.) Paranoids members already had FBI and CIA files on them, begun merely on account of their name and the Pynchon association, then expanded after the Lodi incident. Not anyone's idea of a threat to the Republic — yet — though the official reasoning was: you never can tell. Likely this is how they came to the attention of Col. Cal Aquinas, head of covert ops for MASS, who happened to be looking for a band to sponsor. His plan for them was to be the Manson program's logical continuation — Darwin's Monkees became their interagency code name.

The Paranoids would be persuaded to record the most crazed piece of filth and disorder they could be goaded into devising. Not only would the authorities then orchestrate the inevitable backlash (under the aegis of the preexisting Operation Tom Thumb's Blues), but they would also use the record to flush out hardcore dissidents and potential antisocial activists, putting buyers under surveillance. Thus was Project Revelation born: a deep-cover enterprise to test how far the immanent structuring of experience could go. The band was given a huge cash advance through an agency front label to regroup and return to the studio to cut what they believed would be their last, best chance at immortality, or at least some small recognition that the Paranoids were more than a figment of a cerebral author's infernal imagination. But as the months dragged on, they were only able to finish one song; everything else the band attempted seemed redundant. Released late in 1970, the almost-nine-minute single (so long it was released on a 7-inch 33-rpm record—with a blank B-side) wasn't what Aquinas or anyone else anticipated. "Plastic Curtain" surpassed their expectations of relentlessly unprecedented obscenity ("Fuck the world" was the chorus), an assault of corkscrew invective implicating Tricia and Julie Nixon in a Masonic sex ring overseen by Henry Kissinger, John and Martha Mitchell, as well as archpervert J. Edgar Hoover. Pornographic content aside, the metaphor of "Plastic Curtain" was straightforward enough: an Americanization of the Iron Curtain, materialism, apathy, and instant gratification as its own totalitarian reward. But something other than a bargain-basement metaphor was apparent here: an aural passion play that took place on a completely different level, shifting constantly between minimalist dirge time to guitar-and-drum churn to abstract shapes cast like shadows in rec-room basements or on cell walls. The sound was itself a negation so encompassing and scrupulous it welcomed all manifestations of fantasy and denial as proof they would finally turn on themselves and devour each other, leaving behind nothing but the charred remains of their own repression.

There was just one snag, though. No amount of ads bought in the underground press could convince people to buy it; no wads of clandestine government payola could get radio station managers or DJs to play it. Word of mouth was that "Plastic Curtain" was a bad trip, a major bummer, a heavy downer: the grapevine had spoken. Once more, the band was left with little choice but to break up all over again. They vowed nothing would lure them into making another sound, individually or collectively; the Paranoids were through with music. And thus Project Revelation regretfully had to be abandoned; its partisans were reassigned to MASSCUL-TINTELNET's situation comedy division, where they would conduct fresh reconnaissance missions and new info-wars.

"Plastic Curtain" and the Paranoids were not even a memory by Election Day 1972, when Richard Nixon's was reelected, his sovereignty sealed by the fatal shots Manson follower Squeaky Fromme fired into Vice President Spiro T. Agnew's torso outside a voting booth in Bethesda, Maryland. In the weeks, months, and years that followed, life in America was a blur. In the ensuing panic, as every manner of irrationality and voodoo offering was accepted as public policy, the country acted out the implications of "Plastic Curtain" and *Gospel of Thomas* en masse. Nixon's declaration of a state of emergency and subsequent suspension of the Constitution were only the most obvious manifestations of this. Disinformation permeated every existence. To create the appearance of order, troublemakers were put in detention facilities, as prime-time show trials of radicals and rock stars garnered high ratings. These proceedings demonstrated how grave the threat to the nation had been and would be again if citizens were not vigilant. (Strangely, only confessed Manson sympathizers the Beach Boys were executed for their part in the web of countercultural conspiracy these trials disclosed.) Forgetting became the central business of the media and the central tenet of citizenship.

By 1978, as President-for-Life Nixon finished bringing the Vietnamese Occupation home, subterranean communications networks sprung up across the land: pirate radio stations, guerrilla TV transmitters mounted on flatbed trucks, secret mail drops the authorities could never quite pin down. In these new and evolving matrixes, tapes of "Plastic Curtain" and *Gospel of Thomas* along with outtakes like "Tarotplane" began to appear, sporclike and un accounted for. They made their way into hit-and-run broadcasts; they circulated as contraband. The Paranoids had vanished into new aliases and public silence, but the group's debris became a language of its own, a language dozens of regional bands carried on as they performed makeshift concerts in basements and deserted fields and illegal clubs, all using the Paranoids' name.

I heard a few of those tapes in college and later saw a couple of the bands who performed under that name in places like Skull Valley. Then I came upon a used copy of *Gospel of Thomas* and was hooked. I had to find out where it, they, the whole splintered mystique, came from—if there were any answers left. After Nixon's sudden death in 1981, followed by the gradual restoration of the Constitution and the easing of travel restrictions, I began to re-search the Paranoid's music in depth. People were willing to talk again, though much of the relevant information I obtained was in response to small personal ads placed in cabalistic publications that were sent out anonymously through the still-flourishing covert postal system.

This past summer I was finally able to arrange a meeting in Portland with one of the original members. The one who had called himself Miles didn't have much to say about the music, the belated recognition (such as it was), the changes the country had submitted to, or what he thought of the forces behind them. The music had been enough, once. Now, for him, nothing was. He had no feelings of vindication and wanted none. The Paranoids were in the past, he said; they had really always been there. Time to move on—to something, but he had no idea what.

Before I left, he said he had one thing he wanted me to hear. It was a tape of "the band's swan song," as he put it, though it was only his stately electric guitar and a hoarse voice giving a rambling speech. The voice was Richard Nixon's. Miles had somehow obtained the audio to the farewell address Nixon had videotaped but that never was broadcast and had overdubbed impassive guitar feedback. Nixon began, "My fellow Americans, not all true things are disclosed to all men." He concluded half an hour later by stammering, "Blessed are the solitary, for they will find the kingdom." Then there was a pause, and the guitar dub dropped out. The next sound was the discharge of the president's pistol into his temple, followed by static.

[1990]

SOURCES

Abbas, Ackbar. *Hong Kong: Culture and the Politics of Disappearance* (Minneapolis: University of Minnesota Press, 1997).

Adaptation (Columbia, 2002), directed by Spike Jonze.

Adkins, Hasil. *The Wild Man* (Norton, 1987). "Reagan Blues," "D.P.A. on the Moon," and "Chicken Twist" are compiled on *He Said* (Big Beat, 1985). "I Need Your Head," "No More Hot Dogs," and "Chicken Walk" are on *Out to Hunch* (Norton, 1986). "She Said" and "We Got a Date" appear on both.

Albany, A. J. *Low Down: Junk, Jazz, and Other Fairy Tales from Childhood* (New York: Bloomsbury, 2003).

Almost Famous (Columbia/Dreamworks, 2000), directed by Cameron Crowe. Available in a lovingly protracted DVD version, *Untitled: The Bootleg Cut* (Dreamworks, 2001).

American Splendor (HBO, 2003), directed by Shari Springer Berman and Robert Pulcini.

Angel (WB Network/20th Century Fox, 1999–2004), created by Joss Whedon and David Greenwalt.

Apocalypse Now (Paramount, 1979) and *Apocalypse Now Redux* (2001), directed by Francis Ford Coppola.

Ashes of Time (Jet Tone, 1994), directed by Wong Kar-wai.

Badlands (Warner Brothers, 1973), directed by Terrence Malick.

Bailey, Derek. *Ballads* (Tzadik, 2002). "Laura": Chris Marker travels back in time to meet Django Reinhardt, but finds Anton Webern's body instead.

Bangs, Lester. *Psychotic Reactions and Carburetor Dung* (New York: Knopf, 1987); *Main Lines, Blood Feats, and Bad Taste* (New York: Anchor, 2003). His single "Let It Blurt" (Spy, 1979; love that Jehovah's Witness sleeve) lived up to its title, but on the album *Jook Savages on the Brazos* (Live Wire, 1981), he's no Roky Erickson.

Beaver, Ninette, with B. K. Ripley and Patrick Trese. *Caril* (Philadelphia: J. B. Lippincott, 1974).

Benjamin, Walter. *Illuminations* (New York: Harcourt Brace Jovanovich, 1968; New York: Schocken, 1969); *Selected Writings, Volume 3, 1935–1938* (Cambridge, MA: Harvard University Press, 2003).

Berry, Chuck. "You Can't Catch Me" (Chess, 1955). Roll over, Walt Whitman.

A Better Tomorrow III (Golden Princess/Film Workshop, 1989), directed by Tsui Hark.

The Big Sleep (Warner Brothers, 1946), directed by Howard Hawks. An unbreakable spell cast over everybody from Godard to the Only Ones.

The Blade (Film Workshop, 1995), directed by Tsui Hark.

Boogie Nights (New Line, 1997), directed by Paul Thomas Anderson.

Booth, Stanley. *Rythm Oil* (London: Jonathan Cape, 1991).

The Brains. *The Brains* (Mercury, 1980). Smart guys who vanished into the fog of cultural indifference, remembered if at all for originating "Money Changes Everything," but "Gold Dust Kids" deserves an afterlife too.

Branded to Kill (Nikkatsu, 1967), directed by Seijun Suzuki.

Braxton, Anthony. Ten (plus three) beautifully inscrutable selections: *For Alto* (Delmark, 1968); *Five Pieces 1975* (Arista); *Creative Or-*

chestra Music, 1976 (Arista); *Six Monk's Compositions (1987)* (Black Saint); *Eight (+3) Tristano Compositions 1989* (hatArt, 1990); *Quartet (Dortmund) 1976* (hatArt, 1991; reissued hat-OLOGY, 2001); *Knitting Factory (Piano/Quartet) 1994, Vol. 1* (Leo); *Anthony Braxton's Charlie Parker Project 1993* (hatArt, 1995); with Ran Blake: *A Memory of Vienna* (hatOLOGY, recorded 1988, issued 1997); *Quintet (Basel) 1977* (hatOLOGY, 2000); *8 Standards (Wesleyan) 2001* (Barking Hoop, 2002; this group is heard to fuller, more elastic effect on *23 Standards (Quartet) 2003*, Leo, 2004); *Six Compositions (GTM) 2001* (Rastascan, 2002).

The Bride with White Hair (Mandarin Films, 1993), directed by Ronnie Yu.

Bring Me the Head of Alfredo Garcia (MGM, 1974), directed by Sam Peckinpah.

Buck-Morss, Susan. *The Dialectics of Seeing* (Cambridge, MA: The MIT Press, 1989).

Buffy the Vampire Slayer, created by Joss Whedon (WB and UPN Networks, 20th Century Fox, 1997–2003).

Cadallaca. *Out West* (Kill Rock Stars, 2000) and *Live in Seattle 7-23-99* (bootleg download, no label).

Cale, John. "Charlemagne," from *Vintage Violence* (Columbia, 1970). Sam Peckinpah's Welsh blood brother. See also *Fear* (Island, 1973), with the very apropos "Gun" and "Fear Is a Man's Best Friend."

Catch Me If You Can (Dreamworks, 2002), directed by Steven Spielberg, but stolen by Jennifer Garner.

The Celebration (October Films, 1998), directed by Thomas Vinterberg.

A Chinese Ghost Story (Cinema City/Film Workshop, 1987), directed by Ching Sui-tung (though Tsui Hark may have directed some of the expository scenes).

Chungking Express (Miramax, 1994), directed by Wong Kar-wai.

The Clash. *London Calling* (CBS, 1979), as directed by Joe Strummer and Mick Jones, produced by the bad and beautiful Guy Stevens, starring Montgomery Clift, Robert Mitchum, Stagger Lee,

Fredrico Garcia-Lorca, the extras from "Waterloo Sunset," Dr. Alimantado in his Sunday "chicken-skin suit," and Mr. Phil Spector as "The Card Cheat."

Coates, Paul. *The Story of the Lost Reflection* (London: Verso, 1985).

Cohn, Nik. "Phil Spector." In *The Rolling Stone Illustrated History of Rock & Roll*, edited by Jim Miller (New York: Rolling Stone Press, 1976). One of the great pieces of music journalism—or hardboiled fiction, as the case may be.

Coppola, Eleanor. *Notes* (New York: Simon & Schuster, 1979; revised edition, New York: Limelight, 1991).

Creedence Clearwater Revival. Ruling the American charts from 1968 to 1973, the great hits of this patently obsessive, intensely anomalous Top 40 band—the "perpetual motion" of "Up Around the Bend," "Who'll Stop the Rain," the gloriously bitter "Fortunate Son," the napalm hoodoo of "Run Through the Jungle," "Bad Moon Rising," "Commotion," the idyllic funk of "Green River," and the timeless misery of "Lodi"—can be found on *Chronicles, Vol. 1* (Fantasy, 1976); *Vol. 2* (Fantasy, 1986) gathers up "Born on the Bayou," the tough-as-nails country of "Don't Look Now," and lesser-known fables like "Tombstone Shadow," the weary "Wrote a Song for Everyone," and the wondrous "It Came Out of the Sky" ("Ronnie the Popular said it was a communist plot!"). "Graveyard Train" and the anxious "Bootleg" appear on *Bayou Country* (Fantasy, January 1969); "Sinister Purpose" is found on *Green River* (Fantasy, August 1969). The chilling "Effigy" closed *Willy and the Poor Boys* (Fantasy, November 1969) like a coffin lid.

Dargis, Manohla. "No Mercy" [interview with David Fincher], *L.A. Weekly*, October 13–19, 1995; "Pauline Kael," *L.A. Weekly*, September 14–20, 2001.

David + David. "Swallowed by the Cracks" and "Welcome to the Boomtown," from *Boomtown* (A&M, 1986).

Debord, Guy. *Society of the Spectacle.* Anonymous English translation of *La société du spectacle* [Paris: Buchet-Chastel, 1967] (Detroit: Black & Red, 1977). His 1973 film adaptation of the book pales somewhat in comparison, but for my reassessment of Debord's extremist cinematic oeuvre, see "The Devil's Envoy," *Film Comment*, May–June 2006.

Detour (PRC, 1945), directed by Edgar G. Ulmer.

Dirty Harry (Warner Brothers, 1971), directed by Don Siegel. Also the inspiration for the Jamaican toaster Big Youth's "Screaming Target" (Trojan, 1973), a work of stoned, immaculate genius.

Dogville (Lion's Gate, 2004), directed by Lars von Trier.

The Doors. *Boot Yr Butt* (Bright Midnight/Rhino, recorded 1967–1970, released 2003). The real, live, unvarnished sound of the sixties, and You Are There—no overdubs, no retakes, no second thoughts, no turning back.

Dougher, Sarah. *The Bluff* (Mr. Lady, 2001).

Dragon Inn (Seasonal Film/Film Workshop, 1992), directed by Raymond Lee and Ching Siu-tung (uncredited).

Dramarama. "Shadowless Heart," from *HiFi SciFi* (Chameleon, 1993). Peter Laughner's ghost goes west and moves into Man Ray's old Vine Street apartment in Hollywood.

Dream Lovers (Rin/Tak Bo, 1986), directed by Tony Au.

The East Is Red (Golden Princess/Film Workshop, 1993), directed by Ching Siu-tung.

Easy Rider (Columbia, 1969), directed by Dennis Hopper.

L'Eau froide (Pan-Europeenne, 1994), directed by Olivier Assayas.

The Element of Crime (Kaerne Film, 1984), directed by Lars von Trier.

Eleventh Dream Day. *Lived to Tell* (Atlantic, 1991) and *El Moodio* (Atlantic, 1993).

Eno. "The Fat Lady of Limbourg," from *Taking Tiger Mountain (By Strategy)* (Island/E.G., 1974)—Harry Lime's daughter; Pere Ubu's aunt.

Epidemic (Elemental Films, 1987), directed by Lars von Trier.

Erickson, Steve. "L.A.'s Top 100," *Los Angeles Magazine*, November 2001. His novel *Our Ecstatic Days* (New York: Simon & Schuster, 2005) is itself a great song of secret, submerged L.A: P. J. Harvey taking a "Moonlight Drive"—or swim—through the city's penetralia, overhearing "Mohammed's Radio" on a private frequency.

Essential Logic. *Essential Logic* (Virgin EP, 1978); *Beat Rhythm News*

(Rough Trade, 1979); *Fanfare in the Garden* (Kill Rock Stars, 2003).

Executioners (Paka Hill, directed by Ching Sui-tung and Johnny To).

Farber, Manny. *Negative Space* (New York: Praeger, 1971; expanded edition, New York: Da Capo Press, 1998).

Ferry, Bryan. *These Foolish Things* (Atlantic, 1973). A hard rain a-go-go.

Fiedler, Leslie A. *No! in Thunder* (Boston: Beacon Press, 1960); *Love and Death in the American Novel* (New York: Stein and Day, 1960; revised edition, 1966).

Fighting Elegy (Nikkatsu, 1966), directed by Seijun Suzuki.

Forrest Gump (Paramount, 1994), directed by Robert Zemeckis.

Forty Guns (20th Century Fox, 1957), directed by Sam Fuller.

Frank, Robert. *The Americans,* with an introduction by Jack Kerouac (New York: Grove Press, 1959).

Funkadelic. *One Nation Under a Groove* (Warner Brothers, 1978).

The Furies (Paramount, 1950), directed by Anthony Mann.

Gate of Flesh (Nikkatsu, 1964), directed by Seijun Suzuki.

Ghost World (MGM/United Artists, 2000), directed by Terry Zwigoff.

Gibson, William. *Neuromancer* (New York: Ace, 1984).

Gloeckner, Phoebe. *A Child's Life and Other Stories,* revised edition, introduction by R. Crumb (Berkeley, CA: Frog, Ltd., 2000); *The Diary of a Teenage Girl* (Berkeley, CA: Frog, Ltd., 2002).

The Grapes of Wrath (20th Century Fox, 1940), directed by John Ford.

Green Snake (Seasonal Films/Film Workshop, 1993), directed by Tsui Hark.

A Grin Without a Cat (First Run, 1977), directed by Chris Marker.

Guns N' Roses. *Use Your Illusion I* and *II* (Geffen, 1991).

Guthrie, Woody. "Tom Joad Parts 1 & 2," from *Dust Bowl Ballads* (RCA Victor, 1940).

Haden, Charlie. *Liberation Music Orchestra* (Impulse, 1969).

A Hard Day's Night (United Artists, 1964), directed by Richard Lester.

Hearts of Darkness: A Filmmaker's Apocalypse (American Zoetrope, 1991), directed by Fax Bahr and George Hickenlooper, but the key footage was shot by Eleanor Coppola on location, up river.

Help! (United Artists, 1965), directed by Richard Lester—a blown opportunity, but others dove into the vacuum. John Boorman's

Catch Us If You Can (Warner Brothers, 1965) engulfed the semi-hapless Dave Clark Five with mod ennui and "Meat for Go!" billboards, fashioning a more telling pop moment—bubblegum Buñuel. Donald Camell and Nicholas Roeg's gangster-popstar *Performance* (Warner Brothers, 1970) crossed Boorman's wild weekend with his art brut *Point Blank*: genius and travesty intertwined in a full blown, split level personality crisis, an orgy of dislocation where you couldn't tell Borges from the Borgias without a scorecard. Yet swinging the sixties full circle, Yo La Tengo's "Tom Courtenay" (from *Electr-o-Pura*, Matador, 1995) brought it all back home to a shimmering mirage of the Beatles and Eleanor Bron—if *Help!* did nothing but partially inspire this song, it was more than worth it.

Hero (Miramax, 2004, though released internationally 2002), directed by Zhang Yimou.

The Heroic Trio (Paka Hill, 1992), directed by Ching Sui-tung and Johnny To.

Ibarra, Susie. *Radiance* (Hopscotch, 1999); *Songbird Suite* (Tzadik, 2002).

The Idiots (October Films, 1998), directed by Lars von Trier.

In Praise of Love (New Yorker, 2001), directed by Jean-Luc Godard.

In the Line of Fire (Columbia, 1993), directed by Wolfgang Petersen.

Irma Vep (Zeitgeist, 1996), directed by Olivier Assayas

Jameson, Fredric. *Postmodernism, or, the Cultural Logic of Late Capitalism* (Durham, NC: Duke University Press, 1991). Albatross.

La Jetée (Argos, 1962), directed by Chris Marker.

Joy, Camden. *Lost Joy* (Seattle: TNI Books, 2002).

K., Tonio. *Life in the Foodchain* (Epic, 1978): the City of Angels in full crystal-meth cathedral splendor—listen for Joan of Arc's visitation in "Funky Western Civilization."

Kael, Pauline. *I Lost It at the Movies* (Boston: Atlantic–Little, Brown, 1965); "Raising Kane," from *The Citizen Kane Book* (Boston: Atlantic–Little, Brown, 1971); also included in the career-encompassing *For Keeps* (New York: Dutton, 1994).

Kaplan, Alice. *The Collaborator: The Trial and Execution of Robert Brasillach* (Chicago: University of Chicago Press, 2000).

Kill Bill (Vols. 1 & 2) (Miramax, 2003, 2004), directed by Quentin Tarantino.

Kitten with a Whip (Universal, 1964), directed by Douglas Heyes.

L.A. Confidential (Warner Brothers, 1997), directed by Curtis Hanson.

The Last Bolshevik (Arte, 1993), directed by Chris Marker. Available in a double-DVD set from Arte Video as *Le Tombeau d' Alexandre*: the DVD lets you choose between the English or French narration, while the other DVD features Medvedkin's *Happiness (Le Bonheur)* (Slon, 1934). What more could you ask for?

Laughner, Peter. *Take the Guitar Player for a Ride* (Tim Kerr, 1994).

Lawrence, D. H. *Studies in Classic American Literature* (Cambridge: Cambridge University Press, complete edition, 2002; originally published in 1923).

Level 5 (Argos, 1997), directed by Chris Marker.

Lost Highway (October Films, 1997), directed by David Lynch. A classic of American psychogeography.

Lost in America (Warner Brothers, 1985), directed by Albert Brooks.

Love in the Time of Twilight (Film Workshop, 1995), directed by Tsui Hark.

Magazine. "Shot by Both Sides" (Virgin, 1978). The original seven-inch version.

The Manchurian Candidate (United Artists, 1962), directed by John Frankenheimer.

Marcus, Greil. "Journey Up the River: An Interview with Francis Coppola." *Rolling Stone*, November 1, 1979; "Treasure Island" in *Stranded* (New York: Knopf, 1979); "The Cowboy Philosopher," *Artforum*, March 1986 [citation from the Lettrist International's *Potlatch #8*, August 10, 1954].

Mean Streets (Warner Brothers, 1973), directed by Martin Scorsese.

The Mekons. *The Curse of the Mekons* (Blast First, 1991). "Club Mekon" is from *The Mekons Rock N'Roll* (A&M, 1989). "King Arthur" graces *The Edge of the World* (Sin, 1986): the void as Camelot.

Metallica. *Metallica* (Elektra, 1991).

Morris, Joe. *Age of Everything* (Riti, 2002).

Morrison, Patt. "Dostoevsky, Twain and the First Lady," *Los Angeles Times,* February 13, 2002.

Mott the Hoople. "I Wish I Was Your Mother" is from *Mott* (Columbia, 1973). "Death May Be Your Santa Claus" is from *Brain Capers* (Atlantic, 1972). My best friend totaled his car on the freeway listening to an 8-track tape of *Brain Capers;* he swore he heard Ian Hunter screaming his ex-wife's name on "The Journey."

Naked Killer (Golden Harvest, 1992), directed by Clarence Fok. Hong Kong cinema at its bullet-in-the-groin maddest: take the unhinged audacity of Sam Fuller's *Naked Kiss* opening and then extend it with all the indefatigable, flat-field energy of Godard wolf-whistling a Looney Tunes medley.

Natural Born Killers (Warner Brothers, 1994), directed by Oliver Stone.

New Wave Hookers (VCA, 1985), directed by Gregory Dark.

Nirvana. *Nevermind* (DGC, 1991). "Smells Like Teen Spirit" video directed by Samuel Bayer.

O'Connor, Flannery. "A Good Man Is Hard to Find," from *A Good Man Is Hard to Find* (New York: Harcourt, Brace & Company, 1955).

Once Upon a Time in China (Golden Harvest/Film Workshop, 1991), directed by Tsui Hark.

Once Upon a Time in the West (Paramount, 1969), directed by Sergio Leone.

One Day in the Life of Andrei Arsenevich (First Run, 2000), directed by Chris Marker.

Parker, William. *Painter's Spring* (Thirsty Ear, 2000); with the Little Huey Creative Orchestra, *Mayor of Punkville* (Aum Fidelity, 2000); *Raining on the Moon* (Thirsty Ear, 2002); *Scrapbook* (Thirsty Ear, 2003).

Pat Garrett and Billy the Kid (MGM, 1973), directed by Sam Peckinpah.

Patterson, John. "Golly!" *L.A. Weekly,* October 15–21, 1999.

Peking Opera Blues (Cinema City/Film Workshop, 1986), directed by Tsui Hark.

Pennies from Heaven (BBC miniseries, 1978), written by Dennis Potter.

Pennies from Heaven (MGM, 1981), directed by Herbert Ross.

Pere Ubu. "Heart of Darkness" (Hearthan, 1975); "Final Solution" (Hearthan, 1976); "Heaven" (Hearpin, 1977; later on the *Datapanik in the Year Zero* EP, Radar, 1978, and *Terminal Tower: An Archival Collection*, Twin/Tone, 1985, which included all the early singles); *The Modern Dance* (Blank, 1978); *Cloudland* (Fontana, 1989); *Ray-Gun Suitcase* (Tim Kerr, 1995); *The Shape of Things* (Hearthan, recorded 1976, released 2000).

Phantom of the Paradise (20th Century Fox, 1974), directed by Brian De Palma.

Pistol Opera (Shochiku, 2001), directed by Seijun Suzuki.

The Pixies. "Where Is My Mind?" is from *Surfer Rosa* (Rough Trade/ 4AD, 1988); "Gouge Away" comes from *Doolittle* (Elektra/4AD, 1989).

Plastic People of the Universe. See their chapter for individual titles and dates; all are on Globus International.

Pontiac, Marvin. *Greatest Hits* (Strange and Beautiful, 2000).

Power, Cat. "Maybe Not" and "Names," from *You Are Free* (Matador, 2003).

Powers, Ann. "No Future," *Village Voice*, April 19, 1994.

Previn, Dory. *Live at Carnegie Hall* (Liberty, 1973).

The Private Diary of Tori Welles (Sunshine, 1997), directed by Paul Norman. There has to be more than enough alternate/unused footage for an Arkadin-type three-disc set of this, especially of the omitted Mr. Marcus S&M material.

Pulnoc. *City of Hysteria* (Arista, 1991).

Pynchon, Thomas. *The Crying of Lot 49* (Philadelphia: J. B. Lippincott, 1966; New York: Bantam, 1967).

Radiohead. *Kid A* (EMI, 2000). Canned estrangement's always good for a chuckle—here we have a plush sensory deprivation chamber with a wet bar, a 48-inch Liquid Crystal TV, and the Pink Floyd dub of *The Wizard of Oz* spinning in the high-definition DVD player.

Red Dust (Golden Harvest/Tomson, 1990), directed by Yim Ho.

Rocket from the Tombs. *Life Stinks* (Jack Sprat lp, recorded 1975, released 1990); *The Day the Earth Met the Rocket from the Tombs* (Smog Veil, recorded 1975, released 2002).

The Ronettes. "Be My Baby" (Philles, 1963).

Roxy Music. Pop Art that didn't hedge either side of a bent equation: "Re-Make/Re-Model" (*Roxy Music*, Island/Reprise, 1972) packed more Dadaist glee and riotous alienation-innovation into five minutes than those Radiohead boys have managed in a whole career. "Do the Strand," "Editions of You," and the sublime hilarity of "In Every Dream Home a Heartache" (*For Your Pleasure*, Island/Reprise, 1973) are cultural landmarks of the highest twisted order.

Sans Soleil (Argos, 1983), directed by Chris Marker

Schindler's List (Universal, 1993), directed by Steven Spielberg.

Scholem, Gershom. *Walter Benjamin: The Story of a Friendship* (New York: New York Review, 2003).

Seven Swords (Film Workshop, 2005), directed by Tsui Hark.

Shipp, Matthew. *Symbol Systems* (No More, 1997); *The Multiplication Table* (hatOLOGY, 1998); *Strata* (hatOLOGY, 1998); *Pastoral Composure* (Thirsty Ear, 2000) *New Orbit* (Thirsty Ear, 2001); *Expansion, Power, Release* (hatOLOGY) 2001); *Nu Bop* (Thirsty Ear, 2002).

The Sisters of Mercy. "Temple of Love" from *A Slight Case of Overbombing* (Elektra, 1993). There were layers within layers to the pastiches these sinister-funny Goths made. Taken as a convoluted piece, their shapely, fevered "greatest hits" (well, they must have been hits *somewhere*) sounded like Iggy and the Doors mating with the Addams Family.

Sleater-Kinney. *All Hands on the Bad One* (Kill Rock Stars, 2000).

Smart Alec (1950), director unknown. Located in the underground channels between Bruce Conner's *Marilyn Times Five* and the Zapruder film, its twilight zone mystique was only enhanced by Candy Barr's later association with the man responsible for a different kind of money shot: Jack Ruby.

Smoker (VCA, 1983), directed by Veronika Rocket. Double-bill it with *Naked Killer*.

Sonic Youth. *Experimental Jet Set, Trash and No Star* (DGC, 1994).

South, James B., editor. *Buffy the Vampire Slayer and Philosophy Fear and Trembling in Sunnydale* (Peru, IL: Open Court, 2003).

Springsteen, Bruce. *Nebraska* (Columbia, 1982). "Badlands" and "The Promised Land" are from *Darkness on the Edge of Town* (Columbia, 1978); "Thunder Road," "Backstreets," and the fuel-injected title dream machine are from *Born to Run* (Columbia, 1975). "It's Hard to Be a Saint in the City" is from *Greetings From Asbury Park, New Jersey* (Columbia, 1973).

Steely Dan. Pop noir, with a pinch of Burroughs, a touch of evil, and a bottomless supply of catchy innuendo. "Show Biz Kids," from the fearsomely assured *Countdown to Ecstasy* (ABC, 1973), has lost nothing of its surgical precision and buried mystery; "Pretzel Logic," from the album of the same name (ABC, 1973), is both a satire of a Napoleonic-Elvis complex and a pitiless send-up of the Band's "King Harvest (Has Surely Come)." The musical miniatures of *Katy Lied* (ABC, 1974) can hold their malevolently empathetic own with anything disgorged by the seventies' vaunted cinema of disillusion.

Stewart, Rod. "Every Picture Tells a Story," Mercury, 1971. Talking drums.

Sting. . . . *Nothing Like the Sun* (A&M, 1987).

Story of a Prostitute (Nikkatsu, 1965), directed by Seijun Suzuki.

The Straight Story (Disney, 1999), directed by David Lynch.

Sullivan's Travels (Paramount, 1941), directed by Preston Sturges.

Swordsman II (Golden Princess/Film Workshop, directed by Ching Sui-tung).

Talk Dirty to Me (Four River, 1980), directed by Anthony Spinelli.

Taxi Driver (Columbia, 1975), directed by Martin Scorsese.

The Third Man (SRO, 1949), directed by Carol Reed.

Thomson, David. *A Biographical Dictionary of Film*, third edition (New York: Knopf, 1994).

Timms, Sally. *To the Land of Milk and Honey* (Feel Good All Over, 1995).

Tokyo Drifter (Nikkatsu, 1966), directed by Seijun Suzuki.

True Romance (Warner Brothers, 1993), directed by Tony Scott.

Videodrome (Universal, 1983), directed by David Cronenberg, and *Viva Las Vegas* (MGM, 1964) directed by George Sidney: inter-locking twin pleasure domes for secret sharers Debbie Harry and Ann-Margret if not James Woods and a TV-blasting Elvis.

Ware, David S. *Corridors & Parallels* (Aum Fidelity, 2001); nice, but the real story is on *Live in the World* (Aum Fidelity, 2005), an incredibly sustained blast of thorny, luminous, soul-cleansing spiritual intensity.

Weekend (New Yorker, 1967), directed by Jean-Luc Godard. Highway 61 revisited.

Weil, Simone. *The Simone Weil Reader*, edited by George A. Panichas (New York: David McKay Company, 1977).

Wire. *Pink Flag* (Harvest, 1977); *Chairs Missing* (Harvest, 1978); *154* (Warner Brothers, 1979); *Document and Eyewitness* (Rough Trade, 1981); *On Returning (1977–1979)* (Restless, 1989).

X. *Los Angeles* (Slash, 1980). Including "The World's a Mess; It's in My Kiss," "Soul Kitchen," and the eternally unnerving title rant.

X-Ray Spex. "Oh Bondage Up Yours!" (Virgin, 1977, though I first heard the song on the trend-hopping 1978 Dutch mish-mash *Geef Voor New Wave*, where it instantly turned the likes of Tom Petty into "How Much Is That Doggie in the Window?")

Young, Neil. *Everybody Knows This Is Nowhere* (Reprise, 1969): wiry, human-scale soundtrack to the great unmade counterculture Western. "Pocahontas" and the uncannily cinematic "Powder-finger" first officially surfaced on *Rust Never Sleeps* (Reprise, 1978).

Youth of the Beast (Nikkatsu, 1962), directed by Seijun Suzuki.

Zabriskie Point (MGM, 1970), directed by Michelangelo Antonioni.

Zentropa (Miramax, 1991), directed by Lars von Trier.

Zevon, Warren. Music for the closing credits: "I Was in the House When the House Burned Down" is from *Life'll Kill Ya* (Artemis, 2001). "Ain't That Pretty at All" is from *The Envoy* (Elektra, 1982). "Splendid Isolation" is best heard on the anthology *I'll Sleep When I'm Dead* (Elektra, 1996), along with the strikingly apt "Suzie Lightning" and a few dozen others of note. The live "Mohammed's Radio" is included there, but deserves to be heard in the context of his idiomatic testament *Stand in the Fire* (Elektra, 1981). That the album's "Jeanie Needs a Shooter" virtually recapitulates *The Furies* without the happy ending is mere icing on the cake: with its excitable boys and femme fatales, Hollywood werewolves and Bo Diddley wanted posters, it suggested a bar-band equivalent to Leslie Fiedler's Love-and-Death trip: "a kind of gothic novel (complete with touches of black humor) whose subject is the American experience."

ACKNOWLEDGMENTS

Through the years, I've been lucky enough to work with numerous editors who threw lifelines as well as assignments my way. Kit Rachlis of the *Boston Phoenix* was the first and best: there and later at the *Village Voice* and L.A. *Weekly*, he gave me crucial guidance and encouragement when I must have seemed like Kaspar Hauser with a portable typewriter. Milo Miles also made the *Phoenix* music section a fine, fine place to learn my craft. At the *Village Voice*, Doug Simmons, Eric Weisbard, and the ever-congenial Chuck Eddy always gave me enough rope. I fondly salute my *L.A. Weekly* comrades of yore—Steve Erickson (later at his journal *Black Clock*), Judith Lewis, the great RJ Smith, Sue Cummings, and the delightfully allusive Arion Berger. Lane Relyea, who ran the defunct-but-not-forgotten *Artpaper*, was up for anything, the stranger the better—we had some serious fun there. Then at *Artforum*, I was fortunate to work with the estimable David Frankel, and later with Don McMahon, along with Andrew Hultkrans at *Bookforum*.

This book wouldn't begin to exist without the acuity, patience, and thoughtfulness of Gavin Smith at *Film Comment*: he has made it possible for me to do my best work and write in good company while doing it. While I gave my colleague Kent Jones a rough time in print, I also learned a lot from him — perhaps sharing a certain propensity for "flying into the propeller blades of issues." At both the *Village Voice* and *The Believer*, Ed Park has had an impeccable knack for helping a writer rise on stepping-stones of his dead self to higher things. Andrew Leland at *The Believer* has also been a stalwart presence. At the *Boston Globe*, Alex Star and Jenny Schuessler were a pleasure to write for, as were Liz Helfgott and Jason Altman at the Criterion Collection.

Lindsay Waters, my editor at Harvard University Press, believed in my work from the outset with an inspiring tenacity, making this collection happen when I reached an impasse with my original, interminable project. His friendship and persistence have sustained me through hard times. Phoebe Kosman was a helpful liaison as I navigated the weird and winding road to publication.

Charley Taylor has been a bosom buddy, sharer of spleen, and all-around sounding board; I'm also lucky to know Stephanie Zacharek, even a little. Our beloved friend Pauline Kael is missed in too many ways to count, but for her peals of incisive laughter most of all. Terri Sutton's intelligence, imagination, and lionhearted spirit have nurtured me for the length and breadth of this book — my heroine. Sue Tarjan and I go back even further: one dark 2:00 a.m. of the soul, she uttered the best line in this book, and while those days are gone forever, she remains an irreplaceable friend and an indelible song I'll never get out of my head.

I first wrote to Greil Marcus a quarter century ago, drawn to his work and sensibility by an unformed desire to make sense of—and war on—the world. That affinity evolved into a dialogue that in turn became a lasting friendship. This book is very much a part of that conversation as it spilled out of countless exchanges that followed: if it charts my learning curve over that time, as well as many doors opened for me along the way, there's no one I've learned more from, or owe more to. I remember my late *Boston Phoenix* colleague Mark Moses with the deepest affection, for he was never far from my mind when these dispatches were written—missives to an absent friend.

Finally, my loving and indefatigable mother Anneliese took me on my first record-buying sprees, as well as to movies ranging from Peckinpah double features to *A Clockwork Orange* and *Sleeper*. She has simply been my salvation, and it is my fondest hope that this book is worthy of her faith in me.

CREDITS

The author gratefully acknowledges the following sources where these essays and reviews first appeared (original dates—and titles, where significantly different—are in parentheses):

Copyright © *Artforum*: "Metal-liad" (April 1992); "Blood Poet" (published as "Secret Vices," Summer 1992); "Book of Exodus" (March 1994); "Blur as Genre" (March 1996); "Vamp" (as "Heroic Brio," May 1997); mid-section of "Savant-Idiot . . ." (as "Cannes Men," November 1998); "Screaming Target" (as "Four Play," April 1999); and "Lynch Mob" (January 2000). Reprinted by permission.

Artpaper: "Chinese Radiation" (September 1989); "Apocrypha Now!" (January 1990); and "Eyewitness News" (September 1990).

The Believer: "Fairy Tales from Strangers" (published as "The Flannel-Swaddled Insomniac," August 2003); "Let Us Now Kill White Elephants" (September 2003); and "Build Me an L.A. Woman" (June 2004). Reprinted by permission.

Black Clock: "Wrecked in El Dorado" (published as "This Corrosion," Fall–Winter 2005). Reprinted by permission of Cal-Arts.

Boston Globe: "JLG/SS" (published as "Catch Me If You Can," January 12, 2003); the conclusion of "Savant-Idiot . . ." (as "Top Dog," April 18, 2004); and "Gold Diggers of 1935" (as "Where Songs Come True," October 17, 2004). Reprinted by permission.

City Pages: "Artist of the Year: Sally Timms" (December 27, 1995).

The Criterion Collection: "Screaming Target" (liner notes to *Youth of the Beast,* DVD, 2004). Reprinted by permission.

Film Comment: "Sympathy for the Devils" (published as "Sympathy for the Devil," November–December 1993); "Do the Clam" (as "Elvis Dorado," September–October 1994); "American Maniacs" (November–December 1994); first section of "Savant-Idiot . . ." (as "Wetlands," November–December 1995); "Venus, Armed" (September–October 1996); "Nice Gesamtkunstwerk If You Can Get It" (as "Once Upon a Time in Hong Kong," July–August 1997); "Jungle Boogie" (May–June 2001); "Whatever You Desire: Movieland and Pornotopia" (as "Whatever You Desire: Notes on Movieland and Pornotopia," July–August 2001); "Such Sweet Thunder" (November–December 2001); "Anatomies of Melancholy" (as "Remembrance of Revolutions Past," May–June 2003); "Flattering the Audience" (as "Instant Authenticity," July–August 2003); and "Meet *The Furies*" (as "Extreme Prejudice," November–December 2005). Reprinted by kind permission of the Film Society of Lincoln Center.

L.A. Weekly: "Dueling Cadavers" (August 9–15, 1991); "Aftermath" (April 30–May 6, 1993); "Smells Like . . ." (May 20–26, 1994); and "Moles on the Beach" (October 13–19, 1995). Reprinted by permission.

The New York Times: "Reification Blues" (published as " '70s Rock: The Bad Vibes Continue," January 14, 2001). Copyright © 2001, by The New York Times. Reprinted by permission.

The Village Voice: "Bring Me the Head of Gordon Sumner" (November 11–17, 1987); "Prophecy Girls" (including "Sticky Little Fingers," May 3–9, 2000, and "Waking Life of a Prophecy Girl," February 5, 2002); "Imaginary Cities" (published as "The Imaginary City," October 11–17, 2000, and "Holiday for Strings," October 10, 2003); "Money Jungle Music" (March 20–26, 2002); "Down in Flames" (as "Born in Flames," May 8–14, 2002); "Mouse Trap Replica" (October 23–29, 2002); "My Own Private Benjamin" (as "All About the Benjamins," March 3, 2003); and "American Daemons" (in *Voice Literary Supplement*, May 2003). Reprinted by permission.

W. W. Norton: "Nebraska," published in *The Rose and the Briar*, edited by Sean Wilentz and Greil Marcus, 2004. Reprinted by permission.

Wespennest and the University of Amsterdam Press: "Everybody Knows This Is Nowhere," first published in Wespennest's *The Last Great American Picture Show*, edited by Alexander Horwath, 1995; a shorter revised version was published in *Film Comment* as "Scorpio Descending" (March–April 1997); the final version is from the University of Amsterdam Press's English-language edition of *The Last Great American Picture Show*, edited by Thomas Elsaesser, Alexander Horwath, and Noel King, 2004.

*   *   *

Grateful acknowledgment is also made for permission to quote from the following:

"Albert," "Collecting Dust," "The Order Form," "Popcorn Boy," "Quality Crayon Wax O.K.," "Shabby Abbott," "Wake Up," and "World Friction," by Lora Logic. Copyright © 1979. "Under the Great City," by Lora Logic. Copyright © 1997. Published by Bug Music. Reprinted by permission.

"King Arthur," Copyright © 1986. "Club Mekon," Copyright © 1989. "The Curse," "Funeral," "Waltz," "Sorcerer," and "100% Song," Copyright © 1991. All by the Mekons. Published by Low Noise Music. Reprinted by permission.

INDEX